Library of Congress Cataloging-in-Publication Data for the original edition.

Published through Canam Books Ltd., Canada

Ladouceur, Debby, JM
Handbook for Youth: Thriving Through Chaos /Debby JM Ladouceur
ISBN   978-1-7753385-0-5 (paperback)
1. Health. 2. Holistic Healing. 3. Self Help. 4. Education

ISBN 978-1-7753385-0-5

1st edition – April 2018

Printed in Canada

Acknowledgement

I gratefully acknowledge the editorial contributions of Claris Cowan. I gratefully acknowledge the inspiring painting on the cover by Saeda Rose (Age 15) of Dunster, BC. I am extremely grateful to David Salayka for his unrelenting editing and formatting, and his reshaping of my version of talking and writing into text that is more readable. I thank Logan for the chapter photos which are a small sample from a huge collection captured during our family travels and explorations in Canada's wilderness.

I am also extremely grateful to our sons who have inspired me and taught me the brilliance, creativity, kindness, and resilience of Youth today. So many other young people have confided and communicated their world views and personal challenges to me, and with them all in mind I dedicate my book to this generation and seven generations yet to come.

The miraculous and healing power of Nature continues to be my inspiration each day.

About the Author

Debby has lived in the Canadian Rocky Mountains for the past 30 years, where her and her husband raised their two sons and numerous dogs. Throughout that time many trips made into wilderness & wild places in Western Canada have reinforced in her family, the interconnectedness of us all to Nature.

With her skills as an Iridologist, Herbalist, Reflexologist, & Nutritional & Health counsellor, she has reached out to a great number of people of all ages assisting them in finding their personal recipe for wellness on all levels.

Her greatest interest has always been Youth and searching for solutions and greater understanding to assist Youth in navigating the shifting landscape of life in today's chaotic world. She believes it is time for all people to speak the truth and endeavour to find solutions for many of the problems humanity faces today.

CONTENTS

Introduction

I have been an activist for the good of my family, my wilderness, my community and human health for most of my adult life. Writing this book is my activism for Youth, identifying the truth for Youth about the world you inherit and offer options and choices you can make to assure your own happiness and prosperity.

What you will gain from reading this book, is information that will assist you in making choices to better your life and your community. There is no doubt in my mind that the primary reason you may not be living the life you want or deserve is because of a severe lack of information and fact. In this world of media saturation, the truth about creativity in thought and action, responsible stewardship and your ability to be healthy and happy, are buried beneath trivia and distraction.

Reading this book will enable you to gain enough information, and encourage you to continually seek more of the truth to assist you in building a better you and an extraordinary life.

Of the 7.5 billion people on the planet, 3.7 billion are under the age of 29. Almost 50% of the entire world's population is Youth. 1.8 billion are between ages 15 and 29, leaving 1.9 billion children under the age of 15. This gives me great hope considering the limitless potential for positive change in the world. Only 8.5% of the world population is 65 and over, and they generally are responsible for the majority of laws and governments that control your life. Imagine the potential for the future if the majority of Youth cared deeply for themselves and for their future.

In spite of an overpopulated planet and unstable social and political state around the globe it is critical to remember the best work you can do for the world is to take care of yourself. The truth is that you have no control over the population, other than the number of children you choose to have or not have; however you can control the safety and health of your own future wherever you find yourself. Opportunities for yourself and those around you improve greatly when you take positive action in your own personal life.

Evolution, adaptability and success are well served when each generation is wiser, more liberated and more courageous than the previous generation. I believe it is also true that the families from all generations before you truly want you to be more fulfilled than they were.

The *Shifting Baseline Syndrome* is a concept formulated by Daniel Pauly in 1995, in *Trends in Ecology and Evolution*. The phrase describes an incremental lowering of social, environmental and health standards that results in each new generation lacking knowledge of the historical natural condition of the environment and their society. This means that each generation defines what is 'natural' or 'normal' according to current conditions and their personal experiences. The result is that, with each new generation our standards are lowered almost imperceptibly, and over time healthy living becomes redefined by industrialization, fast food, technology and dysfunctional politics.

This syndrome results in a continuous lowering of standards of nature from generation to generation. *Shifting baselines affect the quality-of-life decisions you make daily*. Shifting baselines are the chronic, slow changes around you such as the disappearance of species in nature, or the increased drive time from work to home, or the denatured food that you consume every day. Because there is no longer a reference point for nature before human disturbance, each generation redefines nature and accepts degraded natural ecosystems to be the norm. This can be applied to the state of your neighborhood from one generation to another, rising crime rates and garbage in the city and all over the planet. Disrespectful attitudes on the street, corrupt politicians, higher cost of living and unaffordable housing costs all become the new normal, and people forget or don't have any idea what has changed or been lost.

Here is one example to define Shifting Baseline Syndrome. "The number of salmon in the Pacific Northwest's Columbia River today is twice what it was in the 1930s. That sounds great -- if the 1930s are your baseline. But salmon in the Columbia River in the 1930s were only 10% of what they were in the 1800s. The 1930s numbers reflect a baseline that had already shifted." (1)

Without the knowledge from previous generations, it's easy for each new generation to accept baselines that have shifted and accept tainted food and empty oceans. One example of what we so easily accept is the near total decimation of coral reefs around the world. Presently Hawaii is debating banning sun screen because the chemicals in sunscreen is killing coral reefs which are essential to the health of the planet and our future. We must consider the shifting baselines in our own lives, identifying how and where we have lowered our personal standards to the point that we accept things that once would have been unacceptable. Scientists estimate that 150-200 species of plant, insect, bird, and mammals become extinct every 24 hours. This is nearly 1,000 times the 'natural' rate and biologists say is greater than anything the world has experienced since the vanishing of the dinosaurs nearly 65 million years ago. Humans have become so desensitized that they don't recognize themselves as a species at risk. Because of a shifted baseline these losses have become accepted as normal. If you do not measure the current conditions in your life, you will have no data to prevent the baseline from shifting again to a newer normal which further limits your possibilities for success.

Another stark example of Shifting Baseline Syndrome is global racism. Colonization and white supremacy can't be ignored and have imposed enormous harm and conflict around the world. How do you find your own way without first dismantling views that have been imposed on your heart and mind from a global misinterpretation of a word or phrase from a Bible/Qur'an/spiritual book that gave dominion to mankind over all, or dominion over one race or another. Is there such a thing as pre-racism? No matter what religious book you or your family or your church follow, any words that do harm were not spoken or written by any benevolent God or Creator (whoever or whatever you perceive that might be) of the universe. Whether you are a creationist, atheist or evolutionist the same do not harm principle applies in all the choices we make. *You must see the truth of the past*, question it at least, discard the flaws and find your own way.

For 1000 years many countries colonized, pillaged and enslaved aboriginals in the name of one religious book or another. Out of a global population of 7.5 billion there remains somewhere between 200 – 300 million aboriginals left worldwide. Ninety percent of the indigenous people of the Americas were wiped out during 500 years of European colonization. There remain a mere 4% of present populations that are indigenous, the original inhabitants of those lands. Defining culture and people has been conflicting and insulting around the world. 'Indigenous' is the expansive classification of communities that claim a historical continuity and cultural affinity with societies native to their original territories. 'First Nations' is a term used to describe Aboriginal peoples of Canada who are ethnically neither Métis nor Inuit which replaced the title Indian in the 1970's and 80s. The term "Indian" refers to the legal identity of a First Nations person who is registered under the Indian Act. Of course the reality of The Indian Act itself in 1887 was a result of colonialization, violence and theft. In 1888, the Prime Minister of Canada, John A. Macdonald said, "The great aim of our legislation has been to do away with the tribal system and assimilate the Indian people in all respects with the other inhabitants of the Dominion as speedily as they are fit to change." This is an example of taking away the rights and life of cultures around the world that differed from white men.

Each of us must reconcile this history within ourselves and be part of a solution for humanity's survival. You can argue that this is not our collective global history and you would be wrong. You can also blame it all on your ancestors and, because you personally didn't participate it's not your problem; you would still be wrong. If you are not part of the solution, you are part of the problem. Institutionalized racism is a disease of the mind and the heart. Human greed is the fundamental cause of colonization, excessive resource extraction and cultural genocide wherever it has occurred. Taking control of resources around the world whether it is forests, precious gems, water, people or land lends equal partnership to racism and dominion.

It is an **absolute game changer** in your life when you value right action in all your choices, decisions, and intentions. **It's a game changer no matter your belief system when you decide that your behavior matters!!** Once you decide that change is inevitable you get to direct the energy of change. **Conflict acting on intelligence creates imagination.** Faced with conflict animals are forced to make a decision, and determine where the next threat will come from. Wits arise in answer to danger, to pain, to tragedy. People undamaged by greed cannot imagine how other people would willingly destroy the common good for personal gain. Build yourself an ark...whether it's a farm, or a community, a relationship, or a business that is a new model. Instead of pessimism or non-compliance or avoidance, imagine your own life better and make it happen.

The precept of shifting baselines has answered my long time search for the **'glitch' in humanity.** I will remind you throughout this book that you are a culmination of the generations before you, both on a cellular level and on a psychological level. **I have always believed that with correct knowledge a person of good conscience would take correct action.** Because our human history has proved this wrong century after century I am left wondering why people choose wrong action when the majority knows full well what the right action in most situations would be. We are not accountable for the actions and thinking of previous generations, though we may be responsible for cleaning up their mess. However, we are accountable for our own choices and actions. Considering there are 7.6 billion people on the planet, who all share the same need for food, shelter and comfort, why is it that violence, famine, and poverty continue to be the state of the majority alive today?

A simple example of generational habits that limit your future is the fact that entire families have voted for the same political party for 200 years. If people really analyzed the platforms, intentions, integrity, and past records of success or failure, you can bet people would vote differently than the habit of generations before them.

Hence the question, **where does your moral compass point**? Science has proven that people begin to believe a lie the more often they hear it. Politicians and their spin propaganda, advertising and promotion of all the products you buy successfully convince you to not think for yourself. The state of global affairs, perhaps even in your own backyard, has become so unstable that we become uncomfortable with the reality that we face. In 1949 George Orwell said "While hiding our heads in the sand with perhaps shame, or immobility or fear or greed or sheer ignorance we begin to believe the lie and forget how to correct our path and be good people, good neighbors and good global citizens. What level of complicit accountability do we have when we willingly participate and perhaps even worse become bystanders to a lie? What kind of lie can achieve this?"

Your moral compass is your internalized set of values and objectives that guide you with regard to ethical behavior and decision-making. Like the directional needle on a compass, you are guided by your ability to distinguish between right and wrong. *Morals* are like a code of conduct that has been established and agreed upon by the majority of a society. *Values* refer to the ideologies that specific individuals and communities consider important. *Beliefs* are convictions that are held as true by an individual or group, and these inform a person's world view and will influence your causes and values. For centuries, differing cultural and religious beliefs, not generally based on facts, have been cause for conflicts and war around the globe.

Therefore it is absolutely critical for you to fine-tune your own moral compass. This gives you a sense of integrity, self-worth and self-confidence. When this comes from your internal feelings of justice, compassion and honesty, you will have the fortitude to not be swayed by the broken moral compass of the world around you. Of course it helps if you are surrounded by a loving and compassionate circle of family, friends and coworkers, and then your moral compass is pointing you in the right direction.

People who have a healthy functioning moral compass are more grounded, focused, content with life and productive. They minimize harm to this world and maximize their contributions and give back as much as they take and more.

Writing a book for and to Youth in a time when all things are digital, with hardly a book to be found might seem ludicrous. Neuroscience, in fact, has revealed that humans use different parts of the brain when reading from a piece of paper than from a screen. Reading on paper instead of an electronic screen is better for memory retention and focus. The more you read on screens, the more your mind shifts towards "non-linear" reading, and they call it a 'bi-literate' brain suggesting we skim the screen and/or have our eyes dart around a web page. When you immerse yourself in a book; the brain moves into long established linear reading, called deep reading mode. After all, books have been around for a few thousand years and even your generation can recall story books of your childhood.

Putting the pieces together in *your life tapestry* takes time, contemplation, and a little or a lot of help from select friends and mentors from all ages to answer the big questions in your life. Only when you decipher the truth where you live in the world can you build a life that works for you, fix a life that might be destroying you, and most important of all, find value in yourself and believe you can have the life you want and deserve.

9

Chapter 1

A Call to Action

Consider the state of affairs in the world today. We have put blind trust in, or in many cases given over all authority to governments, educational and medical institutions, banks and churches for centuries. Perhaps it would all have been worth it if war, famine, climate change, disease, unemployment, vast inequity, and poverty, were not the prevalent state of life today for most. With blind trust people have become bystanders while 1% of the world's population holds 99% of the wealth of the planet, and hunger and stress weave through the rest of humanity in varying degrees. How can you in good conscience not consider the cause and effect of all this incredible inequity and imbalance in the world in which you live? You can and must choose to think for yourself in all matters that concern you and your family and your community's future.

Each individual, of which there are over seven billion on the planet, has a unique memory and point of view based on experience. The simple concept of solving problems by harmonizing and communicating different points of view has been lost in families, communities and governments. Many views yield the truth and the masterful *art of communicating and listening* are very likely the two most valuable aspects of democracy, of achieving success in any task great or small. When one person asserts his or her version of history, he finds himself alone without any other views to correct or balance his own, with no voices of hope or curiosity to relieve his isolation. Communication and listening are the primary ways that help humans with varying views to align with each other for society's success. It was American author and presidential speechwriter, James Humes who first coined the phrase, "the art of communication is the language of leadership". *Every time you open your mouth you influence your situation for better or worse.* It is important to understand the difference between one-way and two-way communication and the best way to stay on track and be heard *is to listen more than you talk.* Communication is only effective when your message is delivered and received. By communicating what is important to you, you inspire trust and loyalty and initiate change in your life, your community and your country.

I have no intention or desire to convince you of my point of view. I want you to do the research yourself for every question you might ask in your world. *My goal in writing this book is to assist you in realizing what is working in your life and what is not working for you.* I want to show you how to see through the chaos and confusion of the social, political, environmental and medical present-day realities that have partly shape who you are and quite likely limit what you can accomplish. *With respect and honesty you must question all that you have been taught, what you read, what you eat and then assess the options you think you have in this life.*

In no way do I judge your circumstance, nor challenge the responsibility entrusted to those who have cared for you during your life. Most caregivers do the best they can with what they know based on what has happened to them amidst the chaos and conflict that infiltrates most people's lives. *Learn to be grateful* for what you have been given, what you have been taught, and learn from your experience. Then turn it all into success for yourself in your own life. I have no interest in convincing you that my way of thinking is correct for you. I want to talk to you about *youthful rebellion*, *finding purpose*, how to *see through the chaos* all around you, give you some insights into your parent's generation to help you move forward, discuss with you the *comparison between the industrial revolution and your technological revolution* and their implications. Begin to think for yourself, and make choices that make your life better. There is so much to be grateful for no matter how severe your circumstance and so much to look forward to, no matter what the system in charge tells you. We live in a world of limitless information yet most have not considered what wisdom truly is. Psychologists generally agree that *wisdom involves an integration of knowledge, experience, and a deep understanding that brings awareness that plays out over time*, reminding us of a sense of balance.

Wise people generally share optimism that life's problems can be solved, and experience a certain amount of calm in facing difficult decisions. *What are your guiding principles?* Many elders solve all problems and challenges from the simple standpoint that 'life is to be honored'. (1)

Adapt or die is natures' motto - you get to choose; adapt or stay the same as your parents, adapt or repeat the calamities of the past or adapt and rise to greater heights and realize your full potential. With that in mind you can always choose to accept the status quo which is how corporations, governments and institutions want you to remain so that they can be in control. One of the greatest limitations you can put on your life is to be blindly obedient to authority. It's a forfeiture of your identity. *It takes a great deal more thought to reject the status quo than it does to accept it.* Keep in mind that making a choice to reject the status quo can be done with respect and determination. This is especially true when you understand that our society is founded on obedience to its laws, taught to the vast majority of our population through 13+ years of public schooling. Keep in mind much good can be said of laws that protect you and your neighbor, much good can be said of your education; however, like so many institutions today they are imploding on themselves from financial indebtedness and outdated traditions and thinking. These institutions I refer to are filled with many dedicated, loyal and brilliant teachers and employees; however, if the institutions they work for are archaic and burdened with conflict then a great deal of that brilliance becomes lost in delivery. Don't underestimate the powerful control and influence of the 1% who own the corporations and control 99% of the worlds' wealth.

If we truly taught people how to succeed, corporations might wonder who would work in their factories. This is not in any way a slight against workers or industrialists. No matter how good or bad your parents were, they did the best they could with what they had and what they knew in 'their' circumstance. *Do not limit yourself with anger, blame, and most importantly, don't use your parents as an excuse for your lack of success or happiness.*

Nelson Mandela said, "Our deepest fear is not that we are inadequate. Our deepest fear is that we are powerful beyond measure. It is our light not our darkness that frightens us. Your playing small doesn't serve the world. There's nothing enlightened about shrinking so that other people won't feel insecure around you." Keep in mind this hero to the world wrote this while spending 27 years in an African prison for telling the truth.

Do not believe in anything simply because you have heard it, read it in religious books or been taught it by your teachers and elders or read it on social media. *Some traditions handed down for many generations may not apply in this time in your life*. After thorough observation and analysis, if you find that what you have heard, been taught, read or observed agrees with reason and is *conducive to the good and benefit of one and all*, then accept it and live up to it. **'Do no harm'** is a measuring stick for what is right action and should most definitely be a foundation for any spiritual or political action.

Some of you simply need shelter, safety and nourishment, some of you want to climb a mountain, many of you don't know what you want, some of you want to know what to do with the education you have struggled to pay for and achieve. There are so many possibilities. Each and every one of you deserves good health, happiness, security, love, and a bright future. You can all have that. **You get to build your life if that is what you really want, no matter what situation you find yourself in right now.**

Don't compromise your own intelligence by asking other people to do it for you. Remember that people can only do for you what they have done for themselves. So be observant of those you seek advice from and how they live their lives. Of course advice, experience and knowledge from others is extremely useful to you, as long as you know how to listen and don't turn others advice into your mistakes. Dare to make up your own mind about puzzling matters with your own research. Unlearn what won't work, and if there are things you believe that you should no longer believe, let them go. From personal experience I can tell you that procrastination is the thief of time. Get your life in shape, one step at a time or in leaps and bounds. Procrastination can be replaced by good habits if you take small steps toward change. You simply must begin.

Why else are you here except to live a good life? The human brain is the new frontier in medicine today. Choose to develop your brilliant brain and have the most rewarding life possible. Realize that your life is about change and progress; don't settle for less. Have an open mind.

Too often humans complicate solutions and get lost on a convoluted path towards wisdom and open mindedness. Seek out the simplest solutions first. The concept of "hygge" (which is pronounced hoo-gah) is a restorative state of mind practiced for centuries in Denmark (by way of Norway). It may be translated as coziness or contentment and finding warmth and intimacy in everyday things. Denmark has topped the latest UN World Happiness Report as the second happiest country on earth, and boasts a lifestyle filled with a feeling of contentment. It is as simple as creating relaxed opportunities to visit with family or friends, being kind to yourself and each other and basically just chill. Some simple ways to bring hygge into your home is to create comfort spaces for you to have friends over or to sit alone and enjoy peace of mind. Getting outdoors in nature and walking can be the fastest way to find inner calm to plan your next step.

Neither be a victim nor a perpetrator of someone else's pain. Above all else don't be a bystander. Science has shown us that what we focus on expands. What you resist persists. So pay attention and deal with the small and large details of your life. Whatever you might resist, decide to deal with it, fix it, choose it, release it, move on, or ask for help. Choose your habits in thoughts and action wisely.

Nurture an understanding of what rebellion really means. A mistake repeated over centuries has been the rejection and disregard for youthful rebellion. Socrates was a Greek philosopher who lived 2000 years ago and is considered the father of western philosophy. Socrates wrote; "Our youth now love luxury, they have bad manners, contempt for authority; they show disrespect for elders, and love to chatter in place of exercise. Children are now tyrants, not the servants of their households. They no longer rise when elders enter the room. They contradict their parents, chatter before company, gobble up their food and tyrannize their teachers." This is similar to the Hollywood version of teen rebellion today and this disregard for youth has been prevalent for more than two thousand years.

Generally rebellion on any level is about change, resistance to what preceded you, and of course, it always comes with consequences and risk. In the extreme, rebellion can replace evil and unless a solid plan is in place it comes without a warranty. From the moment you become aware of a need for change, and commence an intervention, you become a part of the story. You are no longer the bystander but a participant whose choices and actions will either help or make things worse. Nothing grants you immunity from responsibility for your own actions. So if you are to revolt, rebel, avenge, or mitigate, your duty is not only to the course you set but to what you leave in your wake. One of the problems with being so certain of what you don't like is that it can start to define you unless you have a plan. Be careful not to get lost in dethroning authority in your life, replacing it with your own authority only to lose yourself with this thought: "Nobody is going to order me around, not even me!" *If change is necessary, build a new model that makes the existing model obsolete.*

It is paramount to have a solid understanding of how you fit in your society and how your society fits your vision. A recent sociological analysis of emerging adults (the age range was 18-23 years) discussed the loss of a moral compass which limits their choices in a moral perspective. Based on hundreds of detailed interviews, the book 'Lost in Transition' explores the moral side of emerging adulthood. The primary finding was that emerging adults in America follow a loose, poorly defined moral individualism. *The emerging adults' reflections on right and wrong generally "reflected weak thinking and provided a fragile basis upon which to build robust moral positions".* The authors found this group does not rely on any moral traditions or philosophical ethics to make decisions. Finally, the authors discovered that "the vast majority of emerging adults could not engage in a discussion about real moral dilemmas, and either could not think of any dilemma they had recently faced or misunderstood what a moral dilemma is".(2)

Generally moral values are the standards of good and evil or right and wrong which govern an individual's behavior and choices. Though morals can vary from person to person and culture to culture, many are universal. Most often morals are a result of basic human emotions making sense of gut instincts. You could consider cultivating five top virtues in your life from a long list of possibilities. Kindness, integrity, self-control, generosity, compassion, courage, fairness and equality are just a few to consider. Rebellion is best served with these moral foundations. In the times we are living in, simply telling the truth can be considered an act of rebellion.

A Call to Action (CTA) is used in business as part of a marketing strategy to get your targeted mark to respond through action by buying your product. In a presentation or pitch to sell a product it is generally a statement designed to get an immediate response from the person reading or hearing your promotion. The same phrase 'A Call to Action' has been used throughout history during clashes between different belief systems, the development of new governments, and the changing roles of men and women. Each of us may be confronted by internal and external conflict and a person easily can feel a divided sense of self torn between different identities. We all have or had parents and moving into adulthood may present the need to reconcile the past, present and future. In order to be a whole person there exists in all of us a call to action to incorporate change, choices and potentially rebellious decisions to build a better future for ourselves and our communities. Too easily a person can become numb to their life yet when they take action feel a kind of awakening which points to a better choice and a better life. Consider a sales pitch for your own life, a call to action to remind yourself of your vision of a new future. A call to action comes from a place of self-awareness which allows for conscious choices rather than simple reactions to the environment in which you live. *It is the ability to choose that must be fostered for your best life.*

Your greatest power is to know you are both the question and the answer. You must seek to understand the conditions in your life that are rewarding and those that hold you back. Don't let fear immobilize you, and do what is in your best interest to change your circumstance. Keep in mind what is truly in your best interest is always in the best interest for those around you, whether they are willing to admit this or not. There is enormous satisfaction in taking a positive step in the direction you want your life to go in.

Chapter 2

Who do you think you are?

Give your true self a voice. You are a unique byproduct of many generations. There is only one you amidst 7.5 billion people. Choose to be open-minded as you get to know your own life from a different perspective.

"During times of universal deceit, telling the truth becomes a revolutionary act." — attributed to George Orwell, British author, 1903-1950.

When searching for the truth on any subject there comes a precise point when the answer you seek rises above your ability to understand. *The challenge is to move up as well as forward.* The brilliance of realizing this precise point is that you are about to learn something new; you are about to elevate your level of knowledge and understanding to greater heights and a deeper understanding of what you seek. It has been said by many wise people that you cannot solve a problem from the level the problem exists. When people don't recognize this precise point because they are only looking at it from previously-understood assumptions, an opportunity is lost. I call this the EASY ROAD because they are seeking the answers from the point of view of what they think they already know. *Their comfortable assumptions prevent opportunities for authentic change.* The high road on the other hand, is the complex, brilliant, determined and intelligent road to true success that allows the development of new ideas, perhaps a higher truth based on deeper and less obvious facts.

You are part of nature. In the last hundred years we have detached ourselves from nature and have forgotten how to live in balance with it. This is partly due to the industrial and technological revolution. As mentioned above we have advanced tremendously in new directions for mankind. The consequence of living out of balance with the earth that sustains us falls on a point or line between distraction and extinction. In our quest to gain scientific knowledge through rationalization of the mind, we forgot the wisdom of our ancestors. Hence, common sense has gone by the wayside. With so much chatter, noise and distraction in this dense reality we have forgotten our purpose. More importantly many have forgotten how completely interconnected we are with all life on earth.

Richard Louv wrote of Nature Deficit Disorder in 'Last Child in the Woods: Saving Our Children from Nature-Deficit Disorder' in 2005. More than 10 years ago children and adults spent more time in the electronic world than in the natural world. It's easy to assume that divide is even greater today with the explosion of technology and digital gadgets. If you lose your connection with nature, what could that possibly mean for the very planet that provides you with all you need to live? As of 2009, 93% of teens and 77% of adults were online, according to a Pew Internet Project Report. (1)

Kids age 8 to 18 spend an average of 7.5 hours a day, 7 days a week, plugged into computers; TV, video games, music, cells phones, etc. reported a Kaiser Family Foundation Study. An internet security company investigation found that more very young children can play a computer game and open a web browser than swim or ride a bike. Meanwhile there has been a steady decline in visits to U.S. national parks, and a drop in hiking, camping, fishing and hunting. Symptoms of Nature Deficit Disorder include reduced awareness and a diminished ability to find meaning in life for people of all ages.

With 74% of the world's population in developed countries now living in cities, opportunities to spend time in nature need to expand into restoring or creating natural habitats in cities and neighborhoods, on rooftops and in backyards. The idea that nature is 'out there' has to change for urban youth to reconnect with nature.

E.O. Wilson, the renowned biologist, believes that we are hard wired with an innate affinity for nature, a hypothesis he calls biophilia. But research shows that if children do not have the opportunity to explore and develop that biophilia during their early years, biophobia, an aversion to nature, may take its place. Biophobia can range from a fear of being in nature, to contempt for what is not man-made and managed, to an attitude that nature is nothing more than a disposable resource. This may be at the root of resource extraction and environmental devastation at the hands of industry and globalization.

Most of our greatest scientific minds over the past 200 years have stated in their senior years that Love is the fabric that holds all life together. We all have an idea of what love is or could be, and most times it is underestimated as an essential ingredient in life, business or a country's success. The love a parent has for a new baby is undeniable. If you can imagine turning that love inwards, towards yourself, common sense would tell you the more you love yourself the greater capacity and ability you have to love others. *Love of self is the real key to success and a healthy life.* Refer to Chapters 16, 18 and 19 for more information on love.

We must be free to be who we are without fear, though society doesn't want you to realize that. We have been bound to false ideologies, material rewards, misconceptions, and held ransom to rules and laws laid down to safeguard a few. Freedom has been lost for so many. Learning from history isn't working in our world: politics, science and religion continue to repeat the mistakes of the past. But y*ou are a free person*. Individually we must learn from our personal history. We must stop expecting change in our lives while we repeat the same behaviors that created the problem. *When you begin to look at a situation differently, the situation changes.*

Simple is good. Learn to simplify and understand the power in simplicity. Too often you overthink and complicate the situation you face, getting distracted by all the influences around you and end up disempowered to solve the problem. Don't worry, you can still be elaborate and outrageous, however, even these choices evolve from a simple action or first step.

Make sense of your personal heritage and represent yourself well. Determining your own life and character can start with knowing the history of your race. Culture today is often a distorted accumulation of conflict/religion/climate change and politics. *Make an effort to understand the patriarchy* and its centuries of history that has resulted in persistent lingering imbalances. Educate yourself on gender equality and the fact that no matter what you think you know humanity is miles away from equality on any level. Understand the difference between religion and spirituality.

These big concepts along with your personal set of circumstances are the sum of the influences that become your life. The influence of your parents, teachers, siblings, peers, politicians and religious leaders can be taken on as beliefs and defenses to bury your true self. However, it is critical to know what you are being protected against; perhaps your personal leaders don't want you to realize your true purpose, your role in your world, the reality of truth and change. Along with this can come anger, addictions, blame, insecurity and all are forms of fear. *It is time to peel away the layers of influence and become self-sufficient and master of your own destiny within your own personal life picture.*

Analyze your expectations in your life with the awareness that your actions are the key to manifesting them. Be grateful for what you have. The responsibility for determining the truth sits squarely on your own shoulders. You must not believe something because you heard it on some media platform or because the majority of people think it's true. You must base your life and choices on what you can observe and verify with your own experience, and with your own research. Ultimately, this makes you an authority unto yourself. You become a liberated individual who is responsible for directing your own life based on the care with which you have determined fact from fiction, and right from wrong.

It is a fact that the thoughts, habits, actions, words, behaviors and intentions you have today shape your future. Be brave enough to tell yourself the truth in all of these areas of your life and sort out what you want. *What does the best year of your life look like?*

Pay attention to your moral compass. The simple and eloquent purpose of a compass is to point you in the right direction, adding a moral sense of right from wrong. This suggests it could be simple to choose right action in most life situations. What we might call democracy today accentuates tolerance. Yet, in too many instances we have come to tolerate things which no society wanting to remain healthy can or should tolerate.

Einstein's definition of insanity was to do something over and over and expect a different result. *Change is good, re-evaluation is essential to get the best results.* I also understand apathy, which for youth may be a kind of syndrome based on a severe lack of correct information. However, if the boat is sinking, should one remain apathetic?

If you are having fun some of the time, doing okay at 'stuff' mostly, and think your present life is all you are meant to have then keep on that path if you so choose. Do your best, find joy where you can. If you blessed yourself with a grateful and joyful attitude and your life is fulfilling, then Congratulations, you have figured out your formula.

If you intend to have an exceptional life and have all kinds of goals and dreams of adventure, success, happiness and love then stay the course. The most important thing to remember is that Youth goes by fast, and before you know it you may be 30. If you find yourself 30 or older, reengage in your life dreams; it is never too late to start the journey. Most people alive today have been manipulated and managed by culture, religion, governments, technology, and social media of all types and may have lost sight of their true selves.

When was the last time you felt curiosity and were guided through your day by common sense thoughts? What does common sense mean to you? *The definition of common sense is "sound and prudent judgement based on a simple perception of the situation or facts", otherwise known as normal native intelligence.* The world around us is ever evolving. All species of plants and animals adapt or die, yet most humans are not even paying attention. Humans are de-evolving. We have moved so far from being part of the miracle of life on a spectacular and vibrant planet that we stay stuck in epidemics of depression, varying degrees of addictions, distractions and complaining, and prevent the very thing we are here to be. The list of ways to describe purpose is endless - happy, prosperous, having fun, in-service, kind, tolerant, inclusive, and brilliant. What words describe your purpose?

Isaac Newton's 3rd law of Physics states that *for every action there is an equal and opposite reaction*. It only makes sense that a person pay attention to choices, decisions and actions they take. Your life today is a summation of the choices you have made and of course, to some extent the choices others have made for you. Part of the equation is also choices you have not made. Keep in mind that missed opportunities can often be revisited. Each choice you make leads to another, for better or worse. What may seem like a small decision may lead to a cascade of other decisions that either serve you well or distract you, or cause you harm.

What defines you? There is no greater awareness than knowing who you really are. It is foolish to allow yourself to be manipulated by media/society/trends and foolish to believe without question what you read without your own personal research and opinion. Take an interest in propaganda; it has shaped the world as you know it for centuries. (Terry O'Reilly "Age of Influence" CBC Radio) Advertising is the business of influencing consumers.

What do you actually remember? Science has proven that memory is malleable. Each time we re-member or re-tell a story from our past the brain records it differently, and then the next time you tell that 'same' story you are working from an updated version and so on. Studies have proven that with implanted memories (stories told enough times) 70% of adults in the study were convinced that they had actually committed a crime, when they hadn't. Many conflicts can arise when people argue about memories of events. If you are fully present, in the now and paying attention you will have better recall later. (2) (3) Science also tells us that negative events are remembered in a more accurate way than positive events. When there is a negative emotion attached to the experience the emotional circuitry in the brain gets turned on and enhances the processing in the memory network to help you more effectively learn from the experience. Whereas with positive experiences the brain doesn't focus on one aspect, such as the gun, the abuse or the fear in the negative event, and so positive experiences become generalized and details are more difficult to recall later. (4)

You see, all of us have degrees of resistance to the very truth that could save us. Many people believe suffering is necessary, or that life is hard. I do not believe either of those statements. Life is full of challenges, the very nature of finding one's way in a chaotic and confusing world leads to many challenges and choices. Too many minds are closed by beliefs that are irrelevant or just plain wrong in this time. *Individually, collectively, historically and culturally, we are programmed to forget our potential.*

If the face you always show the world is a construct of what the world expects of you, then someday you may lose sight of the real you, the individual and creative person that defines you as unique from everyone else. When you spend too much time concentrating on everyone else's perceptions and expectations of you, or who everyone else wants you to be, you eventually forget who you actually are. So don't fear the judgments of others; you know in your heart who you are and what's true for you. If you don't know who you are, dig deep and ask for help to find out. You don't have to be perfect to impress and inspire people. Let them be impressed and inspired by how you succeed in your own life.

You cannot find the solution to a problem at the level the problem exists. So rise to be at the level of the solution. Re-examine all you have been told, find your own way. Free thinkers have always seemed crazy to those who don't take the time to research. Never apologize for evolving past other people's comfort zones.

In knowing your true self you will begin to understand what you most desire. It is never too late to know your place in the natural world, your purpose, your dreams, how to forgive, how to love, how to be free, how to simplify and most importantly how to trust and be truly you.

Deepak Chopra suggests our future success will be based on survival of the wisest not survival of the fittest. *Wisdom is about how we use our knowledge.* Its essence is discernment; discernment of right from wrong, helpful from harmful or truth from delusion. At present, humanity has vast amounts of knowledge, but still very little wisdom. Why wait to acquire wisdom in later years. The discernment between right and wrong is an intrinsic part of being human. The challenge is that the quiet voice within is often obscured by our over thinking minds.

"People who really want to make a difference in the world, usually do, in one way or another. They hold the unshakeable conviction that people are extremely important. Every life matters. They are willing to feed one stomach, educate one mind and treat one wound. They get very excited over

21

one smile. They aren't determined to revolutionize the world all at once; they are satisfied with small changes. Over time though, the small changes add up. Sometimes they even transform cities and nations and yes even the world." Quote by Beth Clarke, author of 'Kisses from Katie: A Story of Relentless Love and Redemption.'

Anna Lappe said "Every time you spend money you are casting a vote for the kind of world you want." It may be correct that Youth are morally adrift. However, it is obvious that way too many adults are as well. It makes sense in the world today that Youth do not have a clear sense of how to ground their identities and actions to fit the world in which they live. If high moral standards were your benchmark for choosing where to spend money, where to travel, where to recreate and most importantly who you spend time with, a great deal of good would align in your life.

Gaining wisdom can also be defined by the progression from data to information to knowledge. Data are the raw facts that carry information and meaning. We attain knowledge by using those facts to understand the world and ourselves. Of course this can be used for the benefit of all or be used to manipulate others to meet your needs. Wisdom manifests when you use knowledge to determine right from wrong, which would lead to benefits for yourself and others. We have been told by elders for centuries that wisdom is at the heart of your being but can be obscured by over-thinking minds. The most important thing to remember is your innate wisdom will serve you well in all situations if you learn to listen.

If someone asks you *'Who do you think you are?'* know that you are worthy and good enough to stand up for yourself and what you believe in. Remember the most influential and powerful thoughts you have that shape your life are the thoughts you have about yourself. Make them count, value yourself and your wellbeing, and you will find your way. You are the main character and the author of your own life story; upgrade your thoughts of yourself and opportunities will present themselves as you need them.

Chapter 3

Health & Performance

Your body's ability to heal far exceeds what you have been led to believe.
You are here to live a vital, energized and productive life. Whatever symptoms you may have that prevent you from feeling energized and enthusiastic about your life can be resolved. The majority of youth today suffer from a disrupted endocrine system which means the brain is not getting correct input and feedback to instruct your body, mind and heart to function properly. All of your glands are the receptors to information passed on to the brain. Today there are endless plastic, chemical and toxic influences in the food, water and air that you eat, drink and breathe. These toxins mimic your hormones and block your natural hormone receptors to your essential glands and throw the system out of balance. The longer this goes on the more severe the symptoms and setbacks. There are very few people of any age that are not affected by these toxins today.

It is an interesting phenomenon of human behavior that, while knowing a particular activity will improve your life (like eating well, exercising, being kind, etc.); there exists simultaneously a default behavior of procrastination which prevents potential positive results. However, the more we care about ourselves the easier it is to do what is necessary. Good health equals happiness on all levels. Too many people of all ages give their reflection in a mirror, a piece of glass, the power to dictate their happiness. When the relationship you have with yourself suffers from neglect over time, you will see only your flaws. *When you care deeply about yourself you will see your potential in the mirror*. Always reflect back a smile to yourself, knowing you are doing the best you can.

The link between emotional health and physical health has only recently begun to be discussed in conventional medicine. Our version of who we want to be and who we actually are can be miles apart. Chapter 12 'Emotions' will further elaborate this connection. Let's look at skin problems that can and do occur for young teens and young adults. Puberty and hormone changes have been blamed for decades as the cause of acne and skin problems. In truth most people never get to separate themselves from the toxins in the foods they eat every day. There are so many factors that affect the skin. Your skin is the largest eliminatory organ you have and therefore when the liver is overworked and the lymphatic system can't keep up with congestion and detoxing, the skin becomes the organ of choice for eliminating toxins. Your innate body intelligence maintains homeostasis and internal health. But it doesn't account for the emotional impact of acne or other skin problems. The health of your skin has become, for many, the defining factor in fitting in, finding friends, and being happy. The state of your skin influences choices you make every day. It is a fact that the condition of your skin is a result of the health of your internal body and the food you eat and the water you drink.

To complicate matters more, the effect of skin problems on self-esteem is so enormous that it can define whether you are happy or not. It not only defines whether you socialize or interact with others, it can define the actual direction your life is taking, because self-doubt and self-criticism create a stress loop that locks the problems in. Stress causes a chemical response in your body that makes skin more sensitive and reactive and also makes it harder for skin problems to heal. Stress causes your body to make hormones like cortisol, which tells glands in your skin to make more oil, which is more prone to acne and other skin problems. Skin problems can become a disability that prevents your health and performance from ever reaching their full potential. Many young people have become so emotionally invested in the state of their skin that they fail to see that for the most part no one else realizes they even have this problem, or if it exists people that care about you aren't concerned about it. Like any disability, perceived or real, the only correct action is to live your life as if it didn't exist. Once you hydrate and nourish your body with real food and a good attitude your skin will improve and you will have all the tools in place to manage stress. Patience is essential with these changes. In the case of skin (perceived or real) you must go out and take those surfing lessons, buy a bike and join a club, go dancing. Whatever you want to do you must do. I can guarantee that 99% of the people you meet will not notice your issue and if you are positive and enthused about your own life the majority of people you meet will be as well. *Attitude is everything,* your body hears the message when you care and accept yourself and hormones balance and your skin improves. It is your biology; the body heals with the right building blocks of self-care in all areas.

"*Let medicine be your food, let food be your medicine*." is a well-known quote from Aristotle, the Father of Medicine from 432 BC. You might be more familiar with the term 'You are what you eat'. It is as simple as that for most of us. Just as you would only put good gas or diesel in your vehicle to avoid expensive repairs, so also put good food in your body to avoid expensive health problems in the future. Whether you want to believe it or not, your government, schools, and your medical establishments have approved a diet of grocery store and fast food that is so deficient in nutrition that the more you eat, the sicker, more lethargic and less creative you become. It's a fact; take the time and do the research yourself. Those corporations have gone to great lengths and much propaganda to brainwash you into eating fillers, chemicals and non-foods that rob you of energy and health.

Deep fried fast foods are a favorite for many. A study released in late 2015 found that when oils containing Omega-6 fats (all of the unsaturated oil used in fast food and frying), are heated at a normal cooking temperature (of 180°C), they create significant quantities of aldehydes. Aldehyde damage is implicated in allergenic hypersensitivity diseases, respiratory allergies, and liver disease. Each time the oil was re-used in commercial kitchens the concentration increased massively. Studies showed that by the fifth day of oil re-use it had 5 times the concentration of these chemicals than it had on the first. (1)

All fast food restaurants use similar cheese, beef, sauce ingredients that are all bought from the same source, just rearranged for a different presentation and taste. Because you choose what you put in your body, you decide if fast food is okay once in a while or if fast food is your regular fare. If the latter, please reconsider how these food choices negatively affect your health and performance. Remember it's what you don't know that might kill you. Even worse is what you think you know to be true that isn't true, can cause you harm. The life of the animal that you happen to consume in a burger is also extremely relevant in your food choices. Choosing to be a meat eater is part of your genetic make-up; however the integrity and health of the animal you are eating matters. If you are choosing vegetarianism educate

25

yourself on the best way to get the nutrition you need for good health. With more public awareness that fast food may not be the best choice there is a new advertising trend to convince you that fast food is now fan food and good for you. It is important to know the ingredients, and how fast or fan foods are prepared. There is a big difference between eating these foods once in a while as compared to three or more times a week.

Did you know that there were 58 trillion chickens slaughtered in 2011 alone, all requiring cheap labor, cheap feed, cheap energy and cheap water to deliver your mcnuggets and various fast food chicken meals? With 7.5 billion people in the world that worked out to 77,330 chickens annually per man, woman and child. Poultry is expected to become the world's most consumed meat by 2020. The poultry industry has been linked to a growing number of animal rights' violations and in the U.S. where chickens and turkeys are not afforded the same legal protections against abusive treatment in slaughterhouses that cattle and swine are supposed to have. There is much debate over the ethics of eating meat in today's society. You have to decide for yourself, keeping in mind the difference between consuming meat from an animal that was raised and slaughtered ethically versus the unethical feedlots, cages and barns where animals are raised in unhealthy environments.

The Big Mac is the signature McDonald's hamburger and is well known globally. Any time you have a fast food meal, toxins and chemical additives from the food get stored in your body's cells and this can set you up for cravings that will cause you to eat unhealthy, unnatural foods again and again. The list of Big Mac ingredients contains a minimum of 91 ingredients consisting of sugars, fats, salts, chemicals, dairy, wheat gluten, soy, and lots of GMOs (genetically modified organisms). Some of these chemicals include artificial food colors, MSGs (Monosodium glutamate) and dyes that can put people at high risk for autism and cancer (yellow #5 and #6 and red #40). In addition, if your meal includes French fries (additional 18 ingredients) and a soft drink your meal now includes potentially 109 ingredients!

The challenge to the consumer is that you think you are eating *a 100% all beef patty*; however that actually means that what small amount of actual beef is in that patty is 100%, not 100% of the patty is beef. Tricky to understand actually, but there are fillers (soy and corn) that make up the beef patty that are not beef. What the animal has consumed in the industrial feed lot also becomes the meat you eat. Factory farm animals are fed GMO corn, soy, and cottonseeds, and in some documented cases animal feces laden with dangerous bacteria, toxic wastes which include pesticides, fats laden with PCBs, mycotoxins, rendered animal parts (diseased animals that died and body parts that are not used for meat products), metals and antibiotics. These toxins are stored in the muscle which is then cut up and distributed as "100%

pure beef patties". It is time for a revolution in animal husbandry and care that service fast food restaurants. (2)

The bright *yellow American cheese* breaks down into 17 ingredients : Milk and cream(containing bovine growth hormones and pesticides), water, cheese culture, sodium citrate, and chemicals for enhancing the flavors (MSGs from glutamate), eliciting the salivary response (lactic acids) to get the brain excited about the flavor and texture, GMOs, and phytoestrogens from soy lecithin.

The big mac sauce ingredients are soybean oil, pickle relish (diced pickles, high fructose corn syrup, sugar, vinegar, corn syrup, salt, calcium chloride, xanthan gum, potassium sorbate (preservative), spice extracts, polysorbate 80, distilled vinegar, water, egg yolks, high fructose corn syrup, onion powder, mustard seed, salt, spices, propylene glycol alginate, sodium benzoate (preservative), mustard bran, sugar, garlic powder, vegetable protein (hydrolyzed corn, soy and wheat), caramel color, extracts of paprika, soy lecithin, turmeric (for color), and calcium disodium EDTA (to protect flavor). (3)

Don't forget the high amounts of salt that has been bleached, demineralized, iodized, and filled with anti-caking agents like aluminum silicate so it pours easily. The salt also contains sugar, added to stabilize the iodine. It is dried under extreme pressure which changes the molecular structure making it toxic to the human body. This causes high blood pressure and it actually leeches important minerals from the body.

That may all sound bad enough however there is value in completing the picture and pointing out the hydrolyzed vegetable protein from corn, soy, and wheat. Hydrolyzing is a process to break down the proteins into amino acids by boiling them in hydrochloric acid and alkalizing them in caustic soda (aka sodium hydroxide or lye). The FDA (Federal Drug Administration) approves this process. I'm sure most people would say they do not want to eat anything with lye residue in it. Lye is sodium hydroxide, a chemical compound that has the ability to dissolve natural matter with ease. It is highly corrosive and used mostly in industrial settings to clean machinery, pulping wood, and dissolving some types of metal. A famous food application is the New York Bagel, boiled in diluted lye. The unseen part in the hydrolyzation process of vegetable protein is the glutamate that is produced in high concentrations from the hydrolyzing process. Glutamates mean MSG which means "excitotoxins," substances that your brain can't resist and so it leads to food addiction and brain cell death from overstimulation.

Let's not forget the bun which is made up of enriched bleached flour (wheat flour, malted barley flour, niacin, reduced iron, thiamin mononitrate, riboflavin, folic acid), water, high fructose corn syrup, yeast, soybean oil, salt, wheat gluten, sesame seeds, leavening (calcium sulfate, ammonium sulfate), and may contain one or more dough conditioners (sodium stearoyl lactylate, DATEM, ascorbic acid, azodicarbonamide, mono and diglycerides, monocalcium phosphate, enzymes, calcium peroxide), and calcium propionate (preservative).

Lastly the fries made from potatoes, vegetable oil (canola oil, soybean oil, hydrogenated soybean oil), natural beef flavor (made from hydrolyzed wheat and hydrolyzed milk derivatives), citric acid (preservative), dextrose, sodium acid pyrophosphate (to maintain color), and salt. These of course are prepared in vegetable oil (canola oil, corn oil, soybean oil, hydrogenated soybean oil) with tertiary butylhydroquinone (TBHQ) and citric acid to preserve freshness of the oil and dimethylpolysiloxane to reduce oil splatter when cooking.

McDonald's for example switched from frying in beef fat to canola oil in 2004 after incessant pressure from the Heart Foundation. And KFC followed suit in 2012. Seed oils are now the primary source of fat in almost all food on the supermarket shelf, at the local snack bar and served in every restaurant. Seed oils can turn into trans fats when cooked with high heat. (4)

The troubling truth is these Big Mac ingredients and other similar fast "foods" are extremely addictive and cheap and convenient. Needless to say the factory farming of chickens, pigs and beef are also suspect for toxins and trauma. Fast Food places are now shifting advertising to regain your trust by dropping the fast food label and turning it into "fan" food. Relying on gullible people pays off for them. As long as a salad costs four times that of a big mac things won't change anytime soon. Do your best to weigh healthy foods in your favor as compared to indulging in foods that cost your energy instead of give you energy.

The single most important action you can take for your health and your family's health is to cook from scratch. Get into the kitchen, mix up some healthy range fed ground beef, a couple of eggs, bread crumbs or oats, garlic, and onion and fry your own burger in butter. That's only 6 ingredients. Stock your shelves with sensible and healthy condiments and build a loaded bacon burger of your own. If you can, choose organic products, even though there are slippery slopes in labelling with the 'fad' of organics and industry. The flavor can't be beat and the food value will contribute to your health rather than cost you your health. Cooking is so much fun and so very satisfying. Cook with friends, cook with family, lovers or partners, or just cook for yourself and see big changes in your life.

The real job of taste buds is not to make you happy or unhappy. The job of taste buds is about survival. Originally your taste buds job was to distinguish safe food from poison. This is referred to as the omnivore's paradox. Any time our Stone Age ancestors tried a new food, there was a chance it might kill them, and they were reluctant to sway from the familiar trusted foods. Eventually though if they didn't try new foods they would have starved. Therefore, the adaptive response to survival depends on your taste buds having intrinsic preferences for the tastes that are most reliably safe, sweet in particular, and the equally strong tendency to favor the familiar.

People are often reluctant to try foreign foods at first, yet with effort some foods become important comfort foods. *Beer, coffee and wine are good examples.* These are generally not favorite tastes at first, but become acquired tastes, after repeated efforts. Habits of foods can be beneficial or harmful. We have a strong and innate predisposition to love foods rich in sugar, salt, starch and fat. These taste preferences seem to permeate all cultures. When sugar spread around the world in the 16th century where sweet was relatively rare and sugar immediately became a food of comfort. Sugar, unhealthy fat and salt have a powerful ability to create addiction. In excess these foods put you on the fast track to getting fat, and over time, high blood pressure, diabetes, and inflammatory disorders such as MS, Alzheimer's, atherosclerosis, arthritis, osteoporosis, Parkinson's, fibromyalgia, and more. Over the next few years sugar will continue to be linked to an overall inflammatory response that creates many of the diseases we fear today.

I could fill volumes with current data on what is in the food you eat that should concern you. Once again it's the marketplace, as naïve and uninformed consumers enjoy engineered food that is making you sick, if not with an immediate Big Mac hangover, most definitely negative symptoms accumulated over time. Did you fall for the million dollar advertising scheme that changed your mind about fast food, convincing you that 'It's not fast food it's fan food?' I don't judge you whatsoever for your choices, but I also do not apologize for bursting your bubble of loving' those fast foods. You get to choose for yourself and your family.

If you take into account the cost of food, the quality of food, the fast food (that isn't food), and the misguided additives and chemicals and fertilizers and pesticides in food, we are no longer eating life supporting, health supporting, performance supporting food. *And of course don't overlook the fact that your governments condone and allow this unhealthy food to be sold to millions of people who are not in a position to stray from the conveyor belt of modern grocery stores and cheap fast food eating.*

In addition to healthy calories and carbohydrates we need healthy fats to maintain proper cellular function. During WWII governments in the 1940s passed a law that each person use margarine as a portion of their fat allotment per week. *Margarines* are made from poly-unsaturated vegetable oil (e.g. corn, rapeseed, safflower, sunflower, grape seed): hydrogenated oils that stay liquid when refrigerated, are unstable at room temperature, prone to oxidation and rancidity, and when cooked and deep-fried become toxic to human health by turning into trans fatty acids. The industrial process of hydrogenation involves pesticides, solvents and metals which remain in the final product (Puligundla et al, 2012). Hydrogenated oils are used to make margarine, french fries, donuts, popcorn, commercially baked goods, potato chips, snack foods, sauces, crackers, mayo and salad dressings. Most vegetable oils come from genetically engineered plants (GMO, genetically modified organisms). This industrialization of food creates changes in molecular shape which challenges highly specific (shape-dependent, as a key to a lock) enzymes that break down fats. There is plenty of research, from 1997 to the present demonstrating that trans fats negatively influence cholesterol levels and can activate a systemic inflammatory response. They cause or exacerbate cancer, atherosclerosis, heart disease, auto-immune disease, tendon and bone degeneration, type 2 diabetes, endothelial dysfunction, problems with fertility and growth, osteoporosis, allergic sensitization in 2 year olds, eczema, and more. They are also present in mother's milk, if the mother repeatedly consumes these foods. (5)

Choosing healthy fats is essential to human health; sources from healthy fish (much harder to find these days), avocadoes (best source), nuts, organic eggs, chia and flax seeds, organic olive oil, and coconut oil all contribute to systemic health and brain performance.

Our bodies must use the building blocks we feed them. The consumption of trans-fats provides no apparent benefit, but considerable potential for harm. They pose an unprecedented challenge to our bodies from their multi-generational evolution, while foods rich in trans-fats remain abundant in our food supply. Denmark enacted legislation in 2003, virtually eliminating industrially produced trans-fats. (6)

Whoever builds his home next to an active volcano cannot complain of feeling threatened. Well, I can tell you that much of the food in grocery stores and fast food restaurants, the food that the majority of people are addicted to and the water you likely drink are the active volcanoes in your life.

Sugar is an addictive drug. A highly cited study in the journal Neuroscience & Bio behavioral Reviews found that sugar meets the criteria for a substance of abuse and may be addictive to those who binge on it. It does this by affecting the chemistry of the limbic system, the part of the brain that's associated with emotional control. The study found that "intermittent access to sugar can lead to behavioral and neurochemical changes that resemble the effects of a substance of abuse." Once you start reading labels on foods you buy, you will note that sugar is in everything processed; meat, dairy, processed foods and drinks. You may not consume it in direct sugar form but I can guarantee that you are likely eating too much sugar. As described in a later chapter, 7 days in your life with no sugar will change your entire view of health and energy levels. The biggest challenge is for parents changing their sugar addicted children's' diets and watch as the children go through all the withdrawal symptoms of addicts. They may resist, fight, rage, cry and not sleep for days as they go through withdrawal from sugar.

Become a fringe shopper and make best choices for your own health and performance. Choose organic butter over margarine every time or do without. Incorporate organic coconut oil into baking, cooking and frying if you prefer a vegetarian option. Support your conscientious local farms, local growers and farmers markets, read labels and choose sources that respect the animals that become the food you eat.

Here is the challenge for youth. We are not educated on the basics of health and food in the 21st century. Food today is simply not the same as the food of a generation ago. Along with the Industrial Food Revolution in the 1940's and the post war boom came the introduction of white fluffy bread to replace the solid, whole grain breads that were nutritious. High sugar instant cake mixes took the place of Mom's homemade birthday cake and breastfeeding was replaced by free milk formula provided to hospitals by pharmaceutical companies. Breastfeeding has finally become fashionable again, though what the mom eats is what the baby drinks and the quality of that breastmilk is critical to the intelligence and health of that baby.

For some, the presence of inflammation is an immediate response to a poor diet and for many it may not occur for years before you feel the effects or a health problem occurs. How long it has been smoldering depends on your constitution and inattention to a healthy lifestyle. Inflammation results from an acidic internal environment and is at the root of the earliest stage of all diseases. One in 12 women and one in 24 men are dealing with full blown autoimmune mediated inflammation. Of course the number of people undiagnosed and tolerating pain and discomfort is much higher.

Our society is in a crisis of overmedicating and looking for a miracle cure in drug form as a solution to disease instead of determining the cause and starting first with nourishing the body and eliminating toxins. Another multi-billion dollar industry that needs better regulation is the *Vitamin supplement industry* that has been found to be full of chemicals, additives, based on supplementing deficiencies that are always better corrected through diet. However who is qualified to regulate this considering the lack of evidence-based science today? The fact is, there are definite benefits to specific supplementation for specific issues. However, with profits at the core of this thriving business, research, science and successful results are not always applied. Vitamin C is essential to human health, but humans do not

31

produce their own Vitamin C. They must therefore, ingest it through diet. Intravenous Vitamin C is a respected therapy for cancer today partly based on the research of Linus Pauling who won a Nobel Prize for his Vitamin C therapy and cancer research in 1931. While Vitamin C is depleted in conventional foods yet vital to health and performance, most Vitamin C supplements sold in the N. America market is derived from GMO corn produced in China and is too often contaminated with heavy metals and toxins, the root cause of so many diseases today. There are healthy source vitamins but you have to seek them out and read labels and know dosages that work best for your situation. The first step is to eat whole and healthy foods, organic if possible, for at least a month to determine if there are any residual symptoms that need to be specifically. One month of excellent nutrition may not solve all your problems (but it might), however, I would say for the majority of you it will dramatically change your health and performance for the better.

Dr. Philip Maffetone published "Serious Dangers of Synthetic and Unnatural Vitamins" and demonstrated that "the vitamins that you think are derived from fruits and vegetables are extremely suspect." It is a mine field of conflicting data to sort out your personal recipe in regard to medications and supplements and healthy food. Even Dr. Maffetone states that an orange hits the recommended daily intake for vitamin C. However, non-organic oranges do not have the same nutrient content as organic oranges and the recommended daily intake of vitamins (RDA) is extremely low for these times. A healthy person living in a city today experiences so much subliminal stress from noise, air pollution, and people stress that 1000mg Vitamin C a day is essential for good health. RDA (Recommended Daily Allowance) from the government is 75 mg of Vitamin C daily. If you are eating a lot of organic fruits and vegetables, then you are definitely on the right track toward good health, as colorful a diet as possible is the best direction to take. Unless you feel vitalized, energized and healthy on a daily basis, you are deficient in one nutrient or another. If you feel as though you need a supplement make time for research and consult with people who know. I am in support of herbalists and naturopathic doctors and homeopaths and the revival of these traditional healing modalities. It is of grave concern that the cost of that road to recovery is prohibitive for most average people.

Your body is designed to heal itself, based on the proper building blocks. A simple example is a cut on your hand. You can watch over time the body fight the good fight against bacteria, the wound bleeds to cleanse, may get red and inflamed and then slowly build a scab. *I believe parents and society at large have not educated youth on their own body functions and health.* If you have not been given the tools and allowed to make good choices for your best overall performance you must seek that knowledge yourself. Now is when you lay the foundation for your later years. It is a lot more difficult to fix a problem at 40 or 50 or 60 (that has been developing for decades in the body) than it is to change a behavior in your teens or 20's, or even your 30's. It is never too late to correct an imbalance.

Much research now teaches that the fate of the individual cells in your body is not solely based on genetics. The *science of epigenetics* challenges the conventional view of genetics, proving that the environment determines which traits a gene will express. Your inner body environment (based on your attitude, environment, food intake and other choices) controls the fate of your cells. They're all genetically identical, yet the cells are always adjusting themselves to a changing environment. This is what you have control over. In 1999 a new science called epigenetics became public, epi means above and therefore epigenetic control means control above genetics. Science has proven there is no gene that causes cancer and only about 1% of human diseases actually have a genetic cause. *Ninety-nine percent of human illness is environmental, lifestyle and consciousness controlled.* (7)

Environment actually selects and modifies the genes. You can alter every one of your genes and create one or two thousand variations of proteins from the same gene blueprint just by how you respond to the environment. When you change how you respond to the environment, you change the genetic read out. *Remember that the ideal cellular environment is based on good nutrition, hydration, exercise, sleep and the absence of stress.*

Cancer is rampant in North America for young and old alike and the generally accepted belief is that we have no control over it. Cancer has existed since life began on this planet and its expression manifests based on the resiliency and strength of each of your individual immune systems and system functions. It must be considered that the prevalence of cancer today can be attributed to deteriorating and weakened immune systems and extensive bombardment of toxins. Billions of dollars is funneled into genetic research, and virtually nothing is spent on determining the extent to which our food and environment triggers disease.

Food and biotechnology trade groups – Monsanto (creator of pesticides and chemicals) being the most prominent – use front groups to divert you from the truth. They have recently formed a coalition called 'Alliance to Feed the Future'. This alliance, coordinated by the International Food Information Council (IFIC), was created to "balance the public dialogue" on modern agriculture and large-scale food production and technology. These front groups are specifically created to mislead you about products, protect industry profits, and influence regulatory agencies. This multi-billion dollar collusion would not be necessary for a food or product that is inherently safe with great intrinsic value, but it must be done for inferior and/or dangerous products that cannot stand up to closer scrutiny by truly independent sources.

Of course these 50 front groups have more seats at the Codex (International Food Standards) meetings, which gives chemical companies and major food manufacturers control over decisions made. (8) The decisions made at Codex affect food regulations around the world. This is sadly also the case in medical science, where the majority of research is funded by the very companies and industries that stand to gain from a particular result, and which has undermined the core of evidenced-based medicine.

Mark Twain once said "It ain't what you know that gets you into trouble. It's what you know for sure that just ain't so!" This is a brilliant comment to consider. Too many people think they know, have assumptions and believe what they are told but never take the time to research the truth for themselves.

Common-place items in your medicine cabinet that are dangerous to your health and performance are birth control pills, condoms and any type of women's hygiene products. Above and beyond birth control items are the prescription drugs, over the counter painkillers, etc. that are also in your medicine cabinet are discussed further along in this chapter. The Birth Control Pill has been proven to be a contributor to depression in a recent study from the University of Copenhagen in Denmark as a result of a nationwide study involving more than one million women. A high percentage of the participants had been put on anti-depressant medications by their doctors within months of starting the birth control pill. It's been found that birth control pills side effects can include cystic acne, anxiety or moodiness, breast tenderness, weight gain, or for some infertility when trying to get pregnant after stopping the pill. Many young women, including 10-12 year olds, are now taking birth control pills to regulate or temporarily stop their menstrual cycles or reduce symptoms associated with PMS and/or hormonal imbalances (such as acne, heavy bleeding during menstruation or painful cramps).

In 2012 the estimate worldwide was 100 million women using the pill. The total number of women exposed to any type of "synthetic hormonal contraception" is even higher, since most figures don't account for women using the "morning-after pill" — a type of high-dose hormonal birth control available in the United States without a prescription since 2000. I am sure you all know they are made with synthetic chemical hormones that mimic the effects of estrogen and progestin, two powerful hormones in your body that play a critical role in brain receptor development, thyroid health, preserves bone mass, supports libido, and a multitude of other tasks. Birth control pills, patches and shots promote continuously raised estrogen levels in a woman's body. According to the Food and Drug Administration, it's been found that the effects of continuously raised estrogen levels in the female body due to taking birth control pills may include: potential increased risk of breast cancer, potential increased risk of blood clotting, heart attack and stroke, highest risk of blood clots for very overweight women, headaches or migraines, gallbladder or liver problems, including benign tumors, increased blood pressure, weight gain, mood changes, and with some women experiencing symptoms of depression or anxiety, nausea, cramping, irregular bleeding or spotting between periods and breast tenderness. (9)

The pill also does not protect against sexually transmitted infections, including HIV. Therefore if not using another form of protection/contraceptive method, it's possible to get any type of sexually transmitted disease your partner might have. It's also obvious that the toll 'the pill' can take on any relationship is high; the emotional ups and downs, and the old PMS jokes that have been made for years, remind us that emotional stability in a relationship can be extremely stressed simply because of the birth control method of choice.

Evidence on cave drawings of the early use of condoms goes back 15,000 years. More recently around the 15th century condoms were made from lamb intestines, animal horn or tortoise shell in Asia. In 1855 the first condom was made of rubber. Condoms today can have up to 11 unsexy ingredients; benzocaine (a local anesthetic), casein (made from dairy, so if you are allergic you'd want to know this), dry-dusting powder (chemical to prevent sticking and roll it out easily), glycerin (can aggravate yeast infections), l-Arginine (an amino acid that converts into nitric oxide that improves blood flow by opening blood vessels), latex (a latex allergy is common and you most definitely want to find non-latex condoms), lidocaine (has a stronger numbing effect than benzocaine, absorbing deeper into the tissue), nitrosamines (a byproduct of latex production, (the World Health Organization has recommended this not be in condoms as they are related to nitrates in smoked meats and considered carcinogenic), Nonoynol-9 (is a lubricant to prevent sexually transmitted diseases and to kill sperm), parabens (chemical preservatives to prevent bacteria growth which accumulate over time and can cause cell damage and cancer) and silicone (a lubricant). Because the FDA (Federal Drug Administration) does not have regulations, many of these ingredients need to be on the label. Do you know that condoms have an expiry date? **Today there are choices, such as Sustain Natural which is a company that produces 100% organic condoms and personal hygiene products.**

In addition to the above, the vaginal wall is the most absorbent and sensitive tissue on a woman's body and so the potential damage from the chemicals on the condom is not to be underestimated. And then there are the

35

accumulated effects of repeated use. There is a great deal of research regarding health concerns and condoms going back to mid-1970.

Last of the delicate items would be women's hygiene products. Chemicals from tampons are absorbed by the vaginal mucosa, and from there are able to pass almost directly into the bloodstream. Exposure to phthalates, a class of suspected endocrine disrupters linked to developmental issues like lower IQs and higher rates of asthma is common throughout hygiene products.

Another group of chemicals are dioxins, which are byproducts of the bleaching process involved in the manufacture of tampons. The World Health Organization calls dioxins "highly toxic" and categorizes them as a "known human carcinogen." Women's risks for toxic shock syndrome (TSS) have been linked to tampons however no label is required by FDA. A women's advocacy group fighting to eliminate toxic chemicals from consumer products and the environment has published a new report highlighting the dangers associated with many feminine hygiene and personal care products. Entitled "Chem Fatale," the paper by Women's Voices for the Earth (WVE) addresses the many toxic chemicals still being used in feminine products like tampons and deodorants, which expose women to a host of chemicals linked to endocrine disruption, reproductive problems and cancer. The report specifically targets the consumer giant Procter & Gamble (P&G), which manufactures Tampax and Always, two of the most popular feminine care product brands in North America.

Consider the environmental impact of disposable feminine hygiene products. An average woman will use over 16,000 tampons or pads (up to 300 pounds) in the course of her lifetime, sometimes more. Most of these products end up in landfills and water treatment facilities. These throw away items contain chemicals and ingredients that make them able to absorb 10x their weight in liquid, but the effect of these chemicals have not been comprehensively studied for their toxic effect on the environment. (10)

If you choose to use tampons, buy organic tampons. There are other options as well such as the menstrual cup, cloth reusable pads, and menstrual sea sponges. There are many women who switched to natural menstrual products and their menstrual cramping disappeared. This is another reminder that women tolerate such discomfort and pain until the knowledge that alternatives provide healthier options, which overall can prevent toxic buildup in the body which can lead to bigger problems than just menstrual cramps.

Any time you see 'fragrance' on a label it could be a mixture of ingredients that can include any of over 3,000 different chemicals. According to a master list of fragrance chemicals made available by the International Fragrance Association, fragrances can include chemicals which are carcinogens, irritants, allergens, and potential endocrine disruptors. Pesticides in feminine hygiene products have been identified across the board with most brands of feminine products. The American Public Health Association and the American College of Obstetricians and Gynecologists are recommending a switch to safer, cleaner alternatives such as unscented, chlorine-free, unbleached tampons and pads.

There are many toxins in our homes that greatly impact our health and performance. Fabric softeners contain a grim list of known toxins which can enter your body through the skin and by inhalation, causing a wide range of health problems, particularly for young children. The list is long with chloroform, A-Termineol, Benzyl Alcohol, Benzyl Acetate, Ethanol, Pentane, Camphor, Linalool, Phthalates and others, all extremely toxic to human health. Manufacturers are well aware that the products contain toxic chemicals. The packaging on many brands includes a warning that the product should not be used on children's sleepwear. Since some of the same brands also have large images of children and toys, however, consumers may miss the small print message. Whenever you are inhaling that laundry smell you are inhaling toxic VOC's (Volatile Organic Compounds), and no matter how many times you wash that article it will always smell like perfume. Fabric softener is the #1 indoor air polluter. It is the most toxic product produced for daily household use and has been found to be associated with numerous illnesses and chronic conditions. (11)

The unanswered question that continually has me wondering is how or why would any product consumed by humans, put on their clothing and skin and freely injected into the air the family breathes have unnecessary toxins put there in the first place. There is a willful suspension of logic and common sense that has contaminated so many of our food products and fabrics and household tools with proven poisons. It just makes no sense. You can be sure that the smell of the clothes from the fabric softener is as addictive as sugar. A simple but outrageous example of how industry and marketing affect your health and most people pay no attention to it. According to the Environmental Protection Agency, air freshener contains four basic ingredients: formaldehyde, petroleum distillates, aerosol propellants, and p-dichlorobenzene. Formaldehyde can cause a long list of health problems. The history of the car freshener, the familiar little tree you hang on the rear view mirror goes back to 1952, in Watertown, N.Y. Canadian-born Julius Samann, a chemist who missed the smell of Canada's evergreen trees extracted the oils from the pine tree and saturated cardboard in the shape of a tree and patented it. Why would manufacturers add formaldehyde and other toxic chemicals to an already successful and healthy solution to smelly cars?

Modern medicine has developed miraculous solutions for so many human health problems. It does poorly, however, at solutions for curing chronic illness. We have become obsessed with finding a cure without trying to learn the cause and more importantly focus on prevention. The default use of prescription drugs to solve a problem that has never been assessed for severe nutrient deficiencies or other underlying deficits is extremely flawed. The excessive use of prescription drugs to solve problems that may be solved by food, exercise, hydration and sleep is irresponsible. A 2012 study published in the Annals of Family Medicine found that the "prescribing cascade" exists because doctors have to prescribe more medications to control the effects of the first prescription. And, just like the fast food industry direct marketing to patients is a trend that is part of the epidemic of prescription medication. In 2015 alone, the industry spent a record-breaking $5.4 billion on direct-to-consumer ads to sell their drugs. The same year, Americans spent over $450 billion on prescription drugs. *Direct-to-consumer marketing remains a controversial practice*; there are dozens of drug advertisements per hour on TV. They are not trying to help you become healthier; they are trying to sell you a product. The American Medical Association has put out a call to ban advertising to consumers. The ban, however, does not extend to promotion aimed at doctors, which is seven times the investment on television. "Direct-to-consumer advertising inflates demand for new and more expensive drugs, even when those drugs may not be appropriate," quoted by AMA Board Chair-elect Patrice Harris. The United States and New Zealand are the only two countries where it is legal for direct-to-consumer advertising of prescription drugs.

According to the White House Office of National Drug Control Policy, prescription drugs are second to marijuana as the recreational drug of choice for today's teens. In fact, seven of the top 10 drugs used by 12th-graders were prescription drugs. And this only addresses recreational prescription drug use. In a June 2010 report in the Journal of General Internal Medicine, study authors said that in looking over records that spanned from 1976 to 2006 (the most recent year available), they found that almost a quarter million deaths out of 62 million death certificates, were coded as having occurred in a hospital setting due to medication errors. It is impossible to determine which prescriptions out of the 2 -12 different prescriptions a person may take has caused the cascade of counterproductive effects on the body. (12)

There is no doubt that some medications save lives and there are people who cannot live without medical intervention for long term health challenges. A major issue however, is that there is very little connection made to the profound influence of nutrition on recovery and on the brain.

How did western medicine and the giant conglomerate of multinational pharmaceutical corporations (Big Pharma) become the mainstream medical system in the US and other first world nations? As far back as recorded history goes, indigenous peoples have practiced holistic systems of medicine. Their complex and sophisticated systems of medicine were effective promoters of health, disease prevention, treatment, and palliative care. Another old system of medicine, homeopathy, is practiced around the world today. Homeopathy in Europe is actively practiced and supported by modern medicine and medical doctors. The U.S. is attempting to outlaw Homeopathics in early 2018. The dominance of allopathic (or non-homeopathic) medicine is specific to North America, whereas holistic health still has a stronger presence everywhere else in the world. (13)

In the late 1800's John D. Rockefeller, one of the richest U.S. oil men in the world came up with the idea of using coal tar – a petroleum derivative – to make substances that affect the human mind, body and nervous system. These are called drugs, and they are excellent at masking or stopping symptoms, but overall do not cure the underlying cause of a disease. He decided to buy out part of the massive German pharmaceutical cartel, I.G. Farben (if you are interested, this company worked with Hitler to implement his eugenics-based vision of a New World Order founded on racial supremacy, by manufacturing chemicals and poisons for war) and created the new business of Western Medicine. Rockefeller was aware that there were many types of doctors and healing modalities in existence at that time, from chiropractic to naturopathy to homeopathy to holistic medicine to herbal medicine and more. Keep in mind these original early methods of healing already existed around the world; the split between these and "western medicine" only happened in the U.S.

Rockefeller wanted to eliminate the competitors of western medicine; the only modality which would propose drugs and radiation as treatment, thereby enriching himself as owner of the means to produce these treatments. He hired Abraham Flexner to submit a report to Congress in 1910. This report "concluded" that there were too many Naturopathic doctors and medical schools in America, and that all the natural healing modalities which had existed for hundreds or thousands of years were unscientific quackery. It called for the **standardization of medical education**, whereby only the allopathic-based AMA (American Medical Association) was allowed to grant medical school licenses in the US. Congress acted upon the conclusions and made them law. Incredibly, western medicine (allopathy) became the standard mainstream modality, even though its three main methods of treatment in the 1800s had been blood-letting, surgery and the injection of toxic heavy metals like lead and mercury to supposedly displace disease! It should be noted that hemp was also demonized and criminalized not long after this, not because there was anything dangerous about it, but because it was a huge threat (as both medicine and fuel) to the Rockefeller drug and oil industries. As part of the AMA code of ethics, they specifically prohibited its members from professional consultation with homeopathic doctors (Solberg, 2009). In 1900 there were 22 homeopathic medical schools, more than 100 homeopathic hospitals and 1,000+ homeopathic pharmacies in the U.S. and within 50 years they would all be closed. The AMA also lobbied and abolished the licensure law, preventing all homeopaths from legal licenses. (14)

By 1950 all the homeopathic colleges in the US were either closed or no longer teaching homeopathy. To clarify the threat to Modern Doctors, one of the more respected allopathic physicians said, "We must admit that we never fought the homeopath on matters of principles; we fought him because he came into the community and got the business." (15)

Rockefeller and another elite leader Carnegie used their tax-exempt Foundations, beginning in 1913, to offer huge grants to the best medical schools all over America – on the proviso that only an allopathic-based curriculum be taught, and that some of their agents be allowed to sit on the Board of Directors. They called this "efficient" philanthropy, which means they wanted a return on their investment. They systematically dismantled the curricula of these schools by removing any mention of the natural healing power of herbs and plants, or of the importance of diet to health. The result to this day is that schools produce doctors that are poorly educated in the realm of nutrition and grossly unaware of alternative ways of healing the body.

The Hill-Burton Act of 1946 gave grants for hospitals construction and modernization, financed by Big Pharma to further entrench western medicine into America. This was just the beginning of creating lifelong customers dependent on only one way of dealing with health problems: pharmaceuticals. The practice and knowledge of 10,000 years of natural medicine was lost. Analysis of prescription drugs today reveals that 25% contain synthetic plant ingredients and at least 119 chemical substances derived from 90 plant species. They are considered to be important drugs currently in use in many countries. *There is a huge difference, however, between taking a synthetically produced chemical derived from a plant and taking the whole plant with its synergistic properties.*

To date, 70,000 plant species have been screened for their medicinal use, and more than 50% of your prescriptions are synthetic reconstructions of original plant sources. Along with this fact is the propaganda campaign to convince the public that plants are not medicinal. In addition, herbs can be grown by anyone and the myth that you cannot take care of yourself is constantly asserted by the pharmaceutical and medical industries. Of course it is important to be careful and wise with plants as medicine. Seek out knowledgeable sources of this information including health care professionals with specific plant based medicinal knowledge or take herbology courses and learn about plants.

Remember, all these synthetic drugs are isolates. Many are derived from plant compounds, but because Nature cannot be patented and sold, Big Pharma has no interest in natural cures. What they do instead is engage in bio-piracy, research natural compounds, copy them (or modify them slightly) in a lab and then patent them. Once they have a patent, the pill is marketed as a wonder drug while suppressing and ignoring the whole plants benefits to health. Ironically, Homeopathy is the medicine of choice for the British Royal Family and the Rockefellers themselves despite their medical takeover. (16)

You may not be interested in this history lesson of how your health care system has evolved. I can tell you, however that your health and performance (and ultimately your success) IS based on what you put in your body in all forms. Now, more than ever before, your knowledge of the truth regarding your health is of the utmost importance.

It is essential for you to know that there are many options for maintaining your health, performance and survival. Medications can save lives and perhaps control symptoms and do help people cope with pain. However, in general they do not direct people toward a cure. Keep in mind that health care on all fronts today is big business. For example, isn't it hilarious that the western world is doing handstands over the discovery that marijuana has intrinsic medical value to treat a variety of diseases? Once again big business gets involved in something you can grow in your garden that has been recognized worldwide as a healer for a century or more.

People donate billions of dollars each year in search of a magic bullet to cure disease. At the same time, we are fed the very chemicals in our daily food that cause these illnesses in the first place. Information is essential to your best decision making. Gather information from medical journals, consult with doctors, and find out what your body needs and give it the building blocks to heal itself. Pharmaceutical companies profit when you are sick. Gather an understanding of what a corporation is. No doubt they are filled with hard working, good hearted people who have no influence on the governance of that corporation that is solely driven by greed. This may not be intentional but it is a consequence of people allowing corporations to control money, health, and food globally. They are orchestrating, through the medical industry, treatments with products that treat symptoms, not cures. Prevention is the key to longevity. Do not just focus on the illness, but rather on the conditions that must exist in the body for that illness to occur. Work to

41

change your inner 'ecosystem'. Do your own research, inform yourself of the latest information on any health issue you face. Find a combination of solutions that will serve to eradicate the illness and return you to a state of good health.

The new science of epigenetics shows that you control your genes when you control the environment and your perceptions. The condition of your blood which controls the environment of 50 trillion cells in your body is influenced primarily by nutrition. In a nut shell, the brain is the device of perception; it reads the environment, interprets what's going on and responds by releasing chemicals through the nervous system and into the blood. That chemistry goes to the cells and controls gene behavior. Genes are blueprints and have no on and off switch, they have no actions, they do not make any decisions. We have been led to believe that blueprints are self-active, that a gene turns on and off. If you asked an architect whether her blueprint was on or off, she'd look at you like you were crazy. What you add to the chemistry mix of your body determines the outcome. *The chemistry of fear is different from the chemistry of positive emotions.* Similarly the chemistry of good food differs from the chemistry of foods that contain toxins. The brain interprets the environment, it releases chemicals into the growth medium called blood and the blood is used to feed and influence the behavior of your 50 trillion cells. It's the environment that controls your own inner ecosystem. Nothing proves this more than when you are happy, experience love or feel joy. You release wonderful chemicals into the blood: dopamine/ pleasure, oxytocin/ bonding, vasopressin/ sexual activity, pheromones and growth hormone, all of which cause your cells to grow in vibrant ways. If you open your eyes and see something that scares you, a completely different set of chemicals are released: cortisol and norepinephrine/ stress hormones which are inflammatory agents. Serotonin is a tricky hormone, both good and bad; it can be so good that one becomes addicted, obsessive, and aggressive. A thousand years ago this served as a survival mechanism for raising a family in hostile and challenging environments.

"Nothing can stop the man with the right mental attitude from achieving his goal; nothing on earth can help the man with the wrong mental attitude." ~ Thomas Jefferson

Disease cannot live in an alkaline environment. The pH of your blood is tightly regulated by a complex system of buffers that are continuously at work to maintain a range of 7.35 to 7.45, which is slightly more alkaline than pure water. If the pH of your blood falls below 7.35, the result is a condition called acidosis, a state that leads to central nervous system depression. Fluids that have a pH below 7 - like pop and coffee - are considered to be acidic. And fluids that have a pH above 7 - like human blood and herbal teas - are considered to be alkaline. When you ingest foods and liquids, the end products of digestion and assimilation of nutrients often results in an acid or alkaline-forming effect. There are buffers built into the body to protect the pH of the blood, essential for life. However, if you spend years eating a poor diet that is mainly acid-forming, you will overwork the buffering systems to a point where you can create disease and inflammation. For example the overburdened acidic body will be forced to take calcium from the bones in an attempt to restore alkaline balance to the blood.

If you have health challenges, create your own experiment with dietary changes and exercise and discuss all the possibilities with your medical professionals. You are worth it and I can guarantee that after one week of simple dietary changes you will notice a positive difference. Just a week! I am not suggesting one week on a healthy diet will 100% cure the challenges you may face. I can guarantee that you will feel more energy, think more clearly and feel calmer simply by removing sugar and chemicals from your diet. Take an interest in your own body, simplify, eliminate sugar for 7 days, and you will change your life. It need not be a life sentence of abstinence, take a week or two and monitor what you eat, change what you eat, drink more good water – you will be amazed at how much more energy you will have, and how much clearer your thoughts. Unlike generations before you, today's youth needs to 'see it to believe it'. Rebel against the traditions and out-of- date assumptions of previous generations. *But don't rebel against the common sense of generations of healthy nutrition, kindness, practicality, success and honesty.* Guaranteed results come when you feed your body healthy food. If you continue to feed your body based on information from television, the internet, advertisements and food corporations, I guarantee you will become sick or stay sick.

In the not-so-distant future, healthy water and good food will be more valuable than gold. There are countries in the world where this is already the case. Even now you can still eat well at reasonable cost if you do your research. Find farmers markets and local growers, and buy organic grains and rice in bulk (may last you months) and good food from wholesale food cooperatives and whole food buying groups. Eat food grown or produced close to home.

All disease thrives in an acidic internal environment, and a diet high in sugar, carbohydrates and toxic additives and chemicals create an acidic internal environment. Changing what you eat can turn the internal environment to an alkaline and healthy state. It is time for you to psych yourself into being the best coach you can be by creating optimum health for yourself. Team up with a friend or several who shares the same goal. There is so much information at your fingertips, and I know sifting through the many options can be a challenge. However, if you employ your common sense to sort out one step at a time using your logical, rational thoughts, how to move forward toward health will become clear. Your choices have to make sense to you. I urge you to think critically. If you do, you will see that the mechanics of foundational health are really very simple. Some of you may be in a health crisis and need professional help to understand your situation and your direction toward health. Be sure to get second and third opinions and seek out great doctors and health care professionals. Absolutely everyone can benefit from better food choices, more good water and a better attitude. I have been assisting people with finding good health for 30 years. I believe with the right connections, information and determination there is a solution for everyone, regardless of any disease label given by the medical community.

Ask yourself what happened to your own thinking, your own ability to make good choices to support your body to deliver your best performance. Surely you will see that the 'age of influence of advertising' and corporations that insist you buy their brand influences your ability to decipher fact from fiction! The reality is that too many of you have become sugar and additive addicts, substances that do nothing but suck your energy wells dry. The taste buds in your tongue alone can easily become addicted to salt and sugar. The World Health Organization is so concerned about obesity and junk food addiction that they are proposing a new tax on sugar. They are trying to turn around the fact that vegetables cost more than junk food. The National Soft Drink Association reported that Americans spent a total of $65 billion on soda in 2012. Soft drinks are simply sugar and chemical flavored water. You have to know that all forms of addiction can rob you of opportunities for health, employment, relationships, and happiness. (17)

Now let's talk about your skin. It is a medically recognized fact that our body absorbs significant amounts of whatever we put on our skin within seconds of application. Your skin is the largest eliminatory organ you have assisting your body in detoxing. Your skin is porous and therefore absorbs everything you put on including water and light. A study published in the American Journal of Public Health looked into the skin's absorption rates of chemicals found in drinking water. It showed that the skin absorbed an average of 64% of total contaminant dosage. Other studies found the face to be several times more permeable than broad body surfaces and an absorption rate of 100% for underarms and genitalia. Another peer-reviewed study showed 100% absorption for fragrance ingredients. Therefore it is easy to see that what you use on your skin ends up inside your bodies. (18) (19)

More than 10,000 chemical ingredients are allowed for use in personal care products, and the average woman who wears makeup puts at least 515 of these chemicals on her skin every day. More than 90% have never been tested for their effects on human health, and complete toxicity data are available for only 7% of them. (20)

Of the small sample of chemicals that have been tested, many are now known or are strongly suspected of causing cancer, genetic mutation or birth defects. Here is another opportunity to act on correct knowledge and information and change your behavior for your highest good. Once you know something is toxic, choose to stop using it or replace it with something safe. *Knowledge is useful only when it is put into action.* It is self-destructive to suspect or know that a product (food or otherwise) is toxic, and use it anyway. The cumulative effect of these choices has potentially serious side effects. Some of you haven't experienced feeling fit, energized and healthy for a long time because of the slow cumulative effects of your food choices and behaviors.

A Press Release from the Cancer Prevention Coalition dated as long ago as June 17, 2002, states, "Cancer and health risk experts just concluded reviews that indicate mainstream cosmetics, and personal hygiene products pose the HIGHEST cancer risk to the general public, even higher than smoking." That was 16 years ago and they are still pushing the use of toxic sunscreen on babies and adults alike. An alternative solution is to throw on a shirt and a hat; but where is the fashion fun of that?

Sunscreens that contain Retinyl Palmitate may actually increase the growth of cancerous skin tumors and lesions. Most sunscreens aren't safe or protective against skin cancer and have a long list of toxic chemicals difficult to pronounce. Oxybenzone is commonly used in sunscreens and is an endocrine disruptor. This is also an ingredient absorbed directly through the scalp and is in common hair products. If you are going to be outside in the sun all day, there are organic products available, but you must research and seek them out. Simply wearing a light long sleeve shirt and a hat doesn't take away from beauty on the beach. Reading labels should become a regular habit with everything you eat and buy that goes in or on your body. Hawaii is debating banning the use of sunscreen because it is destroying the coral reefs that we now know are critical to the entire ocean ecosystem. If it kills life in the ocean, what do you think it is doing to your life over time? It is time to realize that our bodies are part of the earth's ecosystem.

Another study has found that topical applications of moisturizers such as Dermabase, Dermovan, Eucerin Original Moisturizing Cream, or Vanicream could increase skin cancer risk. (21)

We see gorgeous movie stars covering their bodies in Aveeno products that are labelled as all natural, while the fine print displays petroleum byproducts. Yes, petroleum is a 'natural' product but why would you put it on your whole body? Mineral oil has been linked to no less than twenty-three different diseases and health problems. Ingredients in body moisturizers can include arsenic, coal tars and mineral oils that have been linked to skin cancer. An alternative is organic, unrefined, cold pressed coconut oil, a proven health food for skin.

Deodorants contain petroleum products, aluminum, parabens, and triclosan, all linked to cancer. These prevalent toxins can make their homes in the fat cells of your breast and underarms, causing serious harm to your central nervous system, metabolic system, and endocrine system. Benzoyl peroxide is a topical treatment for oily skin or acne and can put you at risk for Melanoma. Skin lightening creams contain mercury in excess of the established safe allowable levels. Talcum Powder for babies and women contain fragrance and petroleum by products, while the commercials are so tender and heart- warming covering our baby's bottoms in toxic white powder. *If we had simply taught people to read labels, lives would be healthier and longer lived. (22) (23)*

The **mascara** you choose can contain toxic cancer-causing chemicals, such as toxic polymers, petroleum distillates, petrolatum, formaldehyde, aluminum, retinyl acetate, fragrance, and parabens that can increase the aging process and affect your eyesight.

Hair products contain chemicals that are environmentally risky. Rashes often appear on the forehead of women who use hairspray frequently. Common ingredients in hair products are shellac, phthalates, formaldehyde, denatured alcohol and propylene glycol. Hair products can potentially cause multiple chemical sensitivities and their noxious fumes can lead to lung damage.

The skin on your head, your scalp, is rich in blood vessels and contains more hair follicles and more sebaceous glands than any other part of your body. Here is the list of ingredients in Axe men's hair gel on a postage stamp-sized label that one simply cannot read without a magnifying glass. The ingredients include aqua, lanolin wax, propylene glycol, PVP, stearic acid, tribehenin, Ceteareth-25, tridecyl trimellitate, dipentaeythrityl hexacepelate, parfum, PEG 40 hydrogenated Castor Oil, DMOM hydrnatin, carbomer, triethanolamine, disodium EDTA, iodopropinyl butylcarbonate, C1 17200, and C1 42090.

If you care what is in the products you put on and in your body I trust you are interested in the companies that in 2017 are still testing cosmetics, etc. on live animals. These corporations are L'Oreal, Estee Lauder, Procter & Gamble, Clorox, Johnson & Johnson, S.C. Johnson, Colgate-Palmolive, Reckitt Benckiser, Church & Dwight, Unilever, and Dial/Henkel. These companies all have poor ethics when it comes to animal testing, and are making no efforts to change their policies. The majority of cosmetics, cleaning products, hair products, soaps, fragrances, even Pampers are involved in animal testing. There are websites that help you find cruelty free cosmetics and other products. (24)

Toothpaste ingredients can include fluorides, sodium lauryl sulfate, saccharin, propylene glycol and several colored dyes that have been linked to cancer and neurotoxicity. Propylene glycol is one of the most common ingredients found in thousands of cosmetics, processed foods and electronic cigarettes. Propylene glycol (often referred to as PG) is the third 'product' in a chemical process beginning with propene, a byproduct of fossil fuel (oil refining and natural gas processing) and also found in nature as a byproduct of fermentation. Propene is converted to propylene oxide, a volatile compound used frequently in the creation process of polyurethane plastics (and to create propylene glycol). Propylene oxide is considered a "probable carcinogen." Finally, through a hydrolyzation process (separating molecules by the addition of water), you get propylene glycol. A few of the risks with propylene glycol are skin allergies and toxicity to liver and kidneys. It is considered unsafe for pregnant women and has been associated with neurological symptoms. There continues to be a polarized debate over the dangers of fluoride in toothpastes and tap water. You can find healthy toothpastes, the fewer ingredients the better. You can make your own toothpaste with baking soda and coconut oil, which is solid at room temperatures and add peppermint oil for taste. (25)

Lipstick ingredients can include tar, lead, formaldehyde, petroleum distillates, propylparaben, polypropylene and more. It's ironic that Revlon has a campaign called "Kisses for the Cure" that urges women to buy lipstick to fight breast cancer that have these toxic chemicals in them. Remember, knowing how to read labels is essential. It is also ironic that our most famous and beautiful movie stars and singers, who propose adamantly to support the #metoo campaign and defend young women, flaunt the very toxic perfumes and makeup that are very bad choices for everyone in multi-million dollar advertisements on TV.

Since 1955 **Tylenol** has been a family favorite for headaches, fevers, and aches and pains. Science has determined that Tylenol (acetaminophen) is so toxic to the liver that it has been linked to liver damage. (26) Even short-term use of acetaminophen, if taken at the maximum recommended daily dose, stresses the liver. (27) The study concluded that acetaminophen use during the second and third trimesters of pregnancy is a direct cause of increased risk of multiple behavioral difficulties in children subjected to this drug in utero. (28)

A large study in 2014 that looked at 64,322 children and mothers, found that children whose mothers used acetaminophen during pregnancy were at higher risk of being on ADHD (attention deficit hyperactivity disorder) medication and of being diagnosed with Hyperkinetic Disorder (HKD), a particularly severe form of ADHD characterized by hyperactivity and difficulty concentrating. The association between taking acetaminophen while pregnant and having a child with ADHD or HKD was strongest for women who used acetaminophen during more than one trimester. The more frequently they used it, the greater the risk. (29)

Science is questioning whether Tylenol is effective at all for pain relief. Despite being the most recommended drug for back pain, double-blind research shows that acetaminophen is no better than a placebo for back pain. (30) On an entirely different problem associated with Tylenol, women who used acetaminophen for more than 6 years had a significant 9% (12% increase for men) increase in risk of hearing loss. (31) If you consider the huge number of people who use painkillers, a 9-10% increase in hearing loss affects a large number of people. There was a 21% increase in risk of hearing loss for other NSAIDs (non-steroidal anti-inflammatory drugs) and 22% increased risk for acetaminophen. For NSAIDs and acetaminophen, the risk increased the longer the men used them. For men the risk went up 33% with aspirin, 61% for other NSAIDs and 99% for acetaminophen. (32)

It is highly likely that you have parents or grandparents taking statins for cholesterol and high blood pressure concerns. *Statins are* the largest selling class of drugs currently taken by patients throughout the world. Current sales for this one class of drugs are $29 billion. Today, an estimated 30 million people worldwide are taking statins.

In 2015, statins were proven to be a potential cause of heart disease. Did you get that? The following year saw a massive promotion of statins worldwide, even though recent research warned doctors of its' use. The Japanese study abstract posted in the March 2015 journal Expert Review of Clinical Pharmacology titled "Statins stimulate atherosclerosis and heart failure: pharmacological mechanisms" was summarized by Dr. Dean. "The epidemic of heart failure and atherosclerosis that plagues the modern world may paradoxically be aggravated by the pervasive use of statin drugs. We propose that current statin treatment guidelines be critically reevaluated." (33)

Further back in 2013, a study in Ireland, "The Ugly Side of Statins" concluded; "These finding[s] on statin major adverse effects had been under-reported and the way in which they withheld from the public, and even concealed, is a scientific farce." (34)

The challenge for everyone is to make decisions not only based on correct science, but more importantly on correct diagnosis and health choices that enhance rather than prohibit recovery.

I would suggest that you consider and research some of the 'belief systems' of our present society such as 'you must drink milk daily' and 'animal protein is essential for strength and growth'. Humans are omnivores and good healthy meat, harvested with respect and care may be a staple and work well for you. However the rule of moderation always applies. Milk is for calves. The protein, fat and carbohydrate ratio in **cows' milk** is perfect to grow a 1,000 lb. animal quickly. The AMA now recommends that no animal milk from any source be fed to babies less than 1 year of age. The side effects on human health caused by the over-consumption of factory farmed dairy products are staggering. You might think as hunter/gatherers that meat and milk is our heritage. Actually the staple for thousands of years was the gathering of root vegetables and plants and berries, meat was not a constant food and was highly celebrated when luck and skill were on the hunter's side. Less than 30% of a hunter gatherer's diet was supplied by meat.

Professor Mark Thomas, UCL Genetics, Evolution and Environment, says: "Most adults worldwide do not produce the enzyme lactase and so are unable to digest the milk sugar lactose. However, most Europeans continue to produce lactase throughout their life, a characteristic known as lactase persistence, based on a single genetic change that evolved 7,500 years ago when goat milk was first fermented to make yoghurt, butter and cheese, and not drunk fresh. This evolved to provide a source of vitamin D (though there is only 40 IU in a liter of cow's milk) for people in northern Europe where exposure to the sun was limited. "(35)

Whether you believe in the power of milk or not, be aware that milk and meat in general today are contaminated with pesticides, growth hormones, dyes and preservatives. According to research done by The International Journal of Dairy Science; "Chemical contaminants in milk comprise chemical hazards that may be introduced during milk production, dairy processing or packaging. Veterinary drugs, heavy metals, radionuclides, mycotoxins and pesticides are chemical contaminants that can enter into animal feed and they have some residues in milk. The most contentious residues that occur in milk are antimicrobial drugs. They have some hazards for humans who consume milk and dairy products. Government and producer must apply some methods and plans for prevention and control of chemical contaminants in milk and dairy products." (36) (37)

In the past the animal's humans consumed were hunted, not factory raised. There is a direct correlation between the consumption of dairy products and asthma and respiratory problems mainly due to the body's excessive production of mucus as a result of two factors. Humans generally have an inability to digest casein, a protein found in dairy, which is divided into two types - A1 and A2. Only cow's milk in the western world contains A1, due

49

to an evolution of the protein over the years as cows were bred to be larger and produce greater quantities of milk. All other milk, including human, goat and sheep milk, contains A2 casein, which is more easily digested. (38)

In the 1950's breastfeeding was discouraged in hospitals and new moms were given free dairy formula for their newborns. This began a generation of people that were not breastfed and that lay the foundation for all sorts of long term digestive and health problems in later years. The colostrum and immunity given to babies via their mothers' milk is the most valuable food for humans consumed during their entire life. Farmers are vigilant about this for cattle, horses and all mammals in their care. How is it that humans dropped the ball on something so instinctual? Of course there are women who can't breastfeed. There can be challenges and there are situations when babies need supplementation and the important thing would be to read the ingredients on the formula and choose wisely. (39)

Exercise is the fountain of youth, making us look better, feel better, and live longer. Have fun, play, skip, dance or whatever movement works for you and preferably combine it with time spent in nature. The technology revolution has displaced play and outdoor activity and you pay a huge price for ignoring this fact. Your body is designed to move. From thousands of years of foraging and hunting and moving with the seasons, we are now slouching in front of a computer or phone for literally hours every day. This will slowly (or quickly) age you dramatically. There are plenty of studies available that prove eyestrain from looking at screens and smartphones, poor posture that affects longevity and mobility over time and avoidance of movement have negative impacts on youth and may create future health problems.

Based in Chicago, the **American Pain Society** (APS) is a multidisciplinary community that brings together a diverse group of scientists, clinicians and other professionals to increase the knowledge of pain and transform public policy and clinical practice to reduce pain-related suffering. There is sound research that proves that yoga and chronic pain have opposite effects on the brain gray matter. This of course doesn't diminish the importance of correct diagnosis and treatment of underlying causes of pain. *Yoga has been proven for centuries to have a positive influence on all parts of the body, mind and emotions and can be performed by all persons at any age.*

The studies correlate reduced gray matter and depression with increased physical pain. "Insula gray matter size correlates with increased pain tolerance, and increases in insula gray matter can result from ongoing yoga practice. The encouraging news for people with chronic pain is mind-body practices seem to exert a protective effect on brain gray matter that counteracts the neuroanatomical effects of chronic pain", states Dr. M. Catherine Bushnell, PhD. (40)

Often the bridge between hope and despair is a good nights' sleep. Fatigue is deceiving and will rob you of the best of each experience. Sleep deprivation was a torture technique in times past and the modern medical community considers extreme fatigue to be an underlying factor in illness. They consider the following symptoms to be directly associated with extreme fatigue; higher levels of anxiety, poor white blood cell health, impaired memory and ability to think and process information, greater risk of high blood pressure and stroke, higher levels of depression, increased risk of breast cancer and diabetes, unhealthy cravings, and higher risk of injury. (41)

While you sleep the flow of cerebrospinal fluid in the brain increases dramatically to flush out harmful toxins and waste protein that builds up during waking hours, a process that greatly reduces the risk of Alzheimer's. Prolonged lack of sleep can kill an animal or a person. A key purpose of sleep is to recalibrate the brain neurons that help solidify lessons learned and use them the next day. The human brain can only store so much information before it needs to recalibrate and science has shown this happens during sleep. When a neuron maxes out, it loses capacity to convey information, which stymies learning and memory. The researchers confirmed that sleep is a necessity for this homeostatic (the human body maintaining a constant internal temperature) scale-down process that can't be substituted. The bottom line is that sleep is not down time for the brain. On the contrary, it has important work to do and we are short-changing our own potential and lives by avoiding attention to sleep. Researchers also state that drugs that are known to prevent homeostatic scaling down, including benzodiazepines and other sedatives or sleep aids, interfere with learning and memory. (42)

Your *attitude* plays an enormous role in your health and your performance. *Spend time in nature,* a park in your neighborhood, a walk by a river or sit under a tree in your yard; find space, quiet your mind and listen. Every cell of your body responds to your attitude, so be aware that you are the source of your own discomfort most of the time. Have a quiet mind so you can listen for your own guidance from within.

Mindfulness means paying attention to the moment, focusing on the activity at hand with your full attention whether it is meditation, physical labor, walking in the woods, etc. A Mindfulness-Based Stress Reduction (MBSR) program was launched in 1979 at the University of Massachusetts Medical School and has been accepted in mainstream medicine as a protocol to deal with stress and healing.

Mindfulness also involves acceptance of the moment rather than rehashing the past or imagining the future. Thousands of studies have documented the physical and mental health benefits of mindfulness in general and stress reduction in particular, inspiring countless programs to adapt the

MBSR model for schools, prisons, hospitals, veterans centers, and beyond. Studies have shown that practicing mindfulness, even for just a few weeks, can bring a variety of physical, psychological, and social benefits. (43)

Actively take responsibility for your health because it is essential for your overall longevity and quality of life. Educate yourself in using natural remedies and treat any illness or injury at the first signs of discomfort. Of course in an emergency or health crisis seek medical care from trusted health care professionals and have a trusted advocate to listen with you and be your support.

Use conventional medicine if it rings true for you to do so and get second and third opinions from good doctors before you make major decisions about your life. Understand and research your illness/situation, have solid opinions and goals about your own journey back to optimum health, make your voice heard, and be involved. Be an informed patient; don't just Google your symptoms, but search out trusted sources and studies that legitimately inform you of the facts you seek. If you need the help of Medical Doctors, be sure to seek the help of Naturopathic Doctors, Herbalists, Physiotherapists, and other holistic practitioners as well to find a complete solution for the challenge you face. Don't, under any circumstances, make other people's demands and choices your choices, unless it makes sense in your big picture. *Conventional emergency medicine is excellent and critical if you need to be put back together after an accident or need a transplant; however, by its own admission modern medicine doesn't succeed at treating chronic illness.* If you have a chronic illness, educate yourself and seek other opinions. Gone are the days when previous generations gave their lives over to doctors to fix. Today, be your own doctor and be informed enough to get treatment for yourself from the right sources. When you got to doctors take your questions and be patient to fully understand what you are told. Don't be naive - the battle between alternative healing options and conventional medicine needs to end and the two sides need to work together for their patients good.

Know that at the root of any healing protocol are good food, clean water, and a healthy attitude. You may choose to take pharmaceutical medications or vitamins and herbal supplements to deal with severe symptoms and/or deficiencies; however, if you don't prioritize good food that fuels the body to heal, you will be spending a lot of money for the rest of your life on drugs or supplements. They may be helpful, but the best long term solution is optimum nutrition. Choose for yourself, and provide your body with the building blocks it requires to do its job and maintain optimum health, vitality and youthfulness.

I have encouraged you to do your own research, seek out trusted sources of information, seek out trusted health care professionals, and team up with friends, family members or groups and share information and support each other. There are very good sources of information available on the internet and most or all communities have people (elders, educated and self-taught professionals) that would be happy to share their knowledge. Books and encyclopedias of natural healing abound.

A balanced diet and physical activity are vital to academic performance. It has been said by many that the best six doctors you can have in your life are sunshine, water, rest, exercise, air and diet. Never forget that over time good health is a much greater prize than wealth. The World Health Organization states that "Health is a state of complete physical, mental and social well-being and not merely the absence of disease or infirmity." *Invest in yourself; invest in good food, good friends, good play and good health. You deserve it!*

Chapter 4

Your Extraordinary Brain

Your brain is your most valuable physical possession, the conductor of your entire being, your intelligence, your humanity, your personality, and your body. Nothing is more essential to your success than an optimally functioning brain. Brain cells are more sensitive than other body cells to nutrients and dietary chemicals which determine at any moment how your brain functions or malfunctions. Neurotransmitters that communicate within the brain are greatly affected by nutrition. When brain cells do not get the correct nutrients, neurotransmitters and processing is affected almost immediately and thought processes begin to slow down. If your diet is poor on a daily basis the brain will be chronically slowed down in all areas. On the other hand when the brain gets too much glucose (a primary brain nutrient) we experience an immediate sugar high and the body and brain go into overdrive, quickly followed by a crash in energy on all fronts. When glucose levels drop too low, long-term or chronic imbalances can lead to serious problems in attention and memory, as well as behavioral and emotional status. (1) Ideally, you want a steady delivery of glucose throughout the day for optimum performance, best delivered through a healthy diet as previously discussed in Chapter 3.

Teen behaviors such as binge drinking create abnormally high levels of the stress hormone cortisol; and this often leads to higher alcohol consumption and stress levels as an adult as compared to teens who don't binge drink.

Medicine used to believe that the brain reached full development around age 25 and then began to decline as we aged. The discovery was announced in 2005 that, throughout your life and into old age brain cells are continually changing, growing new dendrites and receptors and creating new synapses. *For the first time in human history, scientists have acknowledged that a person can influence the factors that control brain functioning.* The brain is highly elastic or changeable, and able to modify its structure and function in response to learning and memory. (1)

Considering your brain is your organic, internal computer, it is important to understand the natural internal cocktail of chemicals that fuel our consciousness. *Your brain is the boss of your body and is one of the largest and most complex organs in the human body.* Weighing about 3.3lbs (1.5kg), it runs the show and controls just about everything you do, even when you're asleep. Your brain contains 86 billion neurons (gray matter), billions of nerve fibers (axons and dendrites called the white matter) connected by trillions of synapses arranged in patterns that coordinate thought, emotion, behavior, movement and sensation. A complicated highway system of nerves connects your brain to the rest of your body and delivers cause and effect results in split seconds.

The endocrine system uses hormones produced in the pancreas, kidneys, heart, adrenal glands, gonads, thyroid, parathyroid, thymus, and even fat which all act on neurons in the brain and controls the pituitary gland (seated in the brain center). The pituitary gland is your master gland and orchestrates a feedback loop that secretes factors into the blood that act on the endocrine glands to either increase or decrease hormone production. *Obviously your overall performance and health are dependent on the health of all the players in this feedback loop.* These players activate and control basic behavioral activities, such as emotion, responses to stress, eating, sex, hydration, and the regulation of body functions, including growth, reproduction, energy use, and metabolism. By now you have come to realize the vital importance of nutrition, sleep, good water and attitude that via the brain delivers the results you want in your life. All of your self-care choices determine whether you win the race or not, whether you are full of vitality or just mediocre, healthy or sick.

Did you know there is one frequency that puts your brain in an optimal state of functioning, no matter what you're doing? Whenever you find yourself 'in the zone' at work, at school, playing sports or your favorite hobby, science would say you were in the gamma state. The gamma frequency (40-100Hx) is the super focused state of brain activity that promotes the flow state of peak performance. A University of Wisconsin study found that trained meditators (Buddhist monks) showed increased gamma wave production, as well as a simultaneous action in different brain regions. Picture a stadium full of people clapping their hands in perfect unison. The monks in the study were able to sustain this action for long periods of time, unlike the control group. The unique thing about gamma rays is that they have a remarkable ability to create 'neural synchrony.' This synchrony creates a more efficient interaction between different parts of the brain. The usual way that your brain makes decisions in unfamiliar situations is via your senses and then combines this data with information from your stored memories in order to have more understanding of the situation before you decide what to do next. If you are in a gamma state, the information is processed instantaneously and you achieve the best understanding of the situation in record time. Being in a gamma state means you have enhanced focus of the whole picture not just specific parts of the picture. Memories are recalled with ease and understanding is enhanced in all areas of your life. Investigate the value of meditation and enjoy peak mental and physical performance by increasing the amount of gamma wave activity in your brain.

The brain is the new frontier in medicine. **"The Future of the Brain"** (Princeton University Press, 2014), is a collection of essays by the world's top researchers expanding knowledge in understanding the brain. Two neuroscientists received the 2014 Nobel Prize in physiology or medicine for their discovery of the brain's navigational system, describing how the brain computes, or processes information.

The effect of nutrition on brain health may be the biggest discovery yet to be made by scientists, considering the 'epidemic' of autism (1 in 45 children in US, 2015) and children labeled with ADHD, ADD, schizophrenia and/or Asperger syndrome. These are all included in the statistics that 1 in 6 children in the U.S. have a developmental disability. Estimates of 10 million children in the U.S. alone have ADHD. With the globalization of **ADHD** (attention deficit hyperactivity disorder), the multinational pharmaceutical industry has promoted a synthetic stimulant to 'control' the brains of young people. Ritalin and similar drugs increase the amount of dopamine and norepinephrine in the brain, stimulating attention and motivational circuits that increase your ability to focus and complete tasks. They are a form of speed that stimulates the brain so much that it becomes exhausted and thereby making it a sedate brain. The use of Ritalin for a year would likely reduce a child's growth by three-quarters of an inch and there is also evidence that it can precipitate self-harming behavior. The long list of side effects that further complicate a young person's life include nervousness, trouble sleeping, loss of appetite, weight loss, dizziness, nausea, vomiting, or headaches. (2)

In Germany, for instance, prescription ADHD drugs increased from 10 million daily doses in 1998 to 53 million in 2008. In the UK, stimulant-treatment for ADHD increased from under 200,000 prescriptions in 1991 to 1.58 million in 1995. Currently in the U.S., some 11 percent of children and 4.4 percent of adults now have this diagnosis. Nearly a million prescriptions for Ritalin and related drugs for ADHD were dispensed in 2015 – more than double the number a decade before. Adderall and Ritalin are illegal in Japan, while both stimulants are used widely in N. America. We're defining kids more and more as having some kind of psychiatric disorder and while they may have some kind of difference from the majority, a difference isn't necessarily a disease or a disorder. Many clinical psychologists agree that the public should be concerned about explaining attention deficits as brain disorders. This really makes little sense considering the multitude of possibilities that affect a child's behavior. (3) The two primary causes of ADHD are diet and environmental toxins. A study published recently in the British medical journal The Lancet indicated that in at least 2/3 of all ADHD cases, food sensitivities were the cause. (3) (4)

Dr. Stephanie Seneff, Principal Research Scientist at MIT University states by 2025 one in two children will be autistic. Seneff presents a consistent correlation between the rising use of Roundup (with its active ingredient glyphosate) on crops and the rising rates of autism. Her research into the effects of glyphosate toxicity shows that they mimic the symptoms of autism. Recently, the group 'Moms Across America' visited with officials from the EPA (U.S. Environmental Protection Agency) to discuss a ban or restrictions on Roundup, in light of recent findings that the active ingredient glyphosate is found in the breast milk of American mothers at levels that are a dangerous 760 to 1600 times higher than allowable limits in European drinking water. In this particular case the group made its point loud and clear. However, the 100 studies provided for the EPA's review to oppose the request by 'Moms across America' were actually provided by the chemical companies themselves. (5)

Additional chemicals in the Roundup formulation (glyphosate) are untested because they're classified as "inert" but, according to a 2014 study in BioMed Research International, the added chemicals are amplifying the effects of Roundup. (6)

Regarding brain nutrition, it is known that a lack of a simple nutrient like **Vitamin B1** can be a cause of brain fog. If you compound that with the chemicals in food that mimic our own hormones and block receptors the brain can't possibly function correctly. This should be the first critical step in assessing brain health and nutrition before a brain disorder is diagnosed and treated with brain altering drugs. Assessing any deficiencies in the complex and essential balance of nutrients for brain health should be the first step toward solving any behavioral problem. It only makes sense to assess any nutrient deficiencies that may be the root cause of emotional, mental and physical disorders. However, modern medicine doesn't even consider this, whereas Naturopathic Doctors know that this is the first step in assessment of any illness. The catch is that the cost of these blood tests to assess any nutritional deficiencies can cost between $600 and $1000. Because of the conflicting division between Holistic Health care and Conventional Medicine these costs aren't covered by health care plans. Another confirmation that wealthy can equal healthy in our society. Those who are disadvantaged or poor will default to conventional medicine if drugs are covered by their health care plan. Those who have the resources may consider the expensive route through Naturopathic Doctors. Affordable health care from both sides of the medical fence should be affordable for all citizens.

The complex hormonal supply the brain requires for efficiency and health can be adversely affected by an excess of **sugar, chemicals and preservatives** and imbalanced nutrition that inevitably leads to impairment of brain function.

Serotonin (considered our happy hormone) is one of many vital messengers that nerve cells produce. This chemical sends signals between your nerve cells and is found mostly in the digestive system, although it's also in blood platelets and throughout the central nervous system. Serotonin is converted from the essential amino acid tryptophan. This amino acid that can only enter your body through your diet is commonly found in foods such as nuts, cheese, seeds, tofu, red meat, chicken, turkey, fish, oats, beans, lentils, and eggs. Tryptophan deficiency can lead to lower serotonin levels. This can result in mood disorders, such as anxiety or depression. Only through food can you provide this essential nutrient. **Serotonin impacts every part of your body, from your emotions to your motor skills**. Serotonin is considered a natural mood stabilizer and the chemical that aids in sleeping, eating, and digesting. Serotonin also helps reduce depression, regulates anxiety, heals wounds, and maintains bone health.

You have 100 billion neurons, interconnected via trillions of synapses that make up your brain and all are influenced either directly or indirectly by serotonin. If there are any biochemical glitches like a shortage of tryptophan, or a lack of receptor sites able to receive serotonin, or serotonin is unable to reach the receptor sites, then researchers say this can cause depression, as well as Obsessive Compulsive Disorders, anxiety, panic and excess anger. Many chemicals in your environment mimic the chemicals in your brain and block these receptors. No end of chaos can follow.

'The Mind-Gut Connection', written by Dr. Emeran Mayer states that 95% of the serotonin in your bodies resides within your gut. You may recall that 70% of your immune system resides in your gut. The brain and gut (called the emotional brain) communicate back and forth through the central nervous system and the gastrointestinal tract while Serotonin functions as a key neurotransmitter at both ends of this network.

Dreaming and sleep are affected by serotonin levels. The REM sleep cycle (during which most of our dreams occur) happens when the serotonin system shuts off during sleep. Melatonin (hormone made by the pineal gland in the brain) plays a supporting role to serotonin in this function because it prepares the body for darkness and sleep, regulating our circadian rhythm. Sleep disorders, moods, inability to focus, lack of alertness, and dreams are entwined with the level of serotonin in our brains. *I'll just remind you here that looking at screens within an hour of sleep prevents the body from producing melatonin and has serious long term consequences, affecting the quality of your sleep.* Put down your devices an hour before sleep or, if all else fails, read a book. Both are superior ways to put you to sleep and to stay asleep.

It is not so simple to determine the perfect amount of serotonin (feel good hormone) needed, because it appears that too much or too little can have both beneficial and detrimental effects. It does however seem that increasing ones serotonin levels will help with focus, energy, and mood if you are feeling low. Eating foods rich in tryptophan helps the body synthesize 5-HTP, which can then be turned into serotonin. These foods include but are not limited to: nuts, seeds, tofu, cheese, red meat, chicken, turkey, fish, oats, beans, lentils, and eggs. Research shows that serotonin production is a two-way street with mood. By doing things that elevate your mood, you will increase serotonin production which will get you in an even better mood as the cycle feeds on itself. Yoga and exercise have proven to be beneficial in mood elevation, especially when combined with being outdoors. There is evidence which suggests that exposure to bright light increases serotonin, and people often employ full-spectrum lights in the winter to prevent SAD (Seasonal Affective Disorder) during the darker months of the year.

Drinking water and brain function are integrally linked. Lack of water (dehydration) to the brain can cause numerous symptoms including problems with focus, memory, brain fatigue and brain fog, as well as headaches, sleep issues, anger, depression, and many more. Approximately 65 percent of your body is composed of water and every function in your body is dependent on water, including the activities of your brain and nervous system.

According to the Mayo Clinic, *the average adult loses more than 80 ounces of water every day through sweating, breathing, and eliminating wastes.* If you are drinking less than 80 ounces of water a day, what is the impact on your brain function considering the brain itself is 73% water? It means you are always working with a deficit. Water gives the brain the electrical energy for all brain functions, including thought and memory processes and water is needed for the brain's production of hormones and neurotransmitters. *When your brain is functioning on a full reserve of water, you will be able to think faster, be more focused, and experience greater clarity and creativity.* Keep in mind that, unlike the rest of the body the brain has no way to store water and therefore has no reserves to call upon during dehydration. You cannot live more than 3 days without water.

Studies have also demonstrated that people with brain dysfunctions which include, autism and mental disabilities drink almost no water and their symptoms are greatly aggravated as a result. With adequate hydration many disabilities can be ameliorated.

Drinking a large glass of water every morning shortly after rising enhances brain function for the day. Depending on your source of water you may want to invest in a filtering system or reverse osmosis water. There are economical ways to protect yourself from tap water if it is the only water available to you. Concerns for the safety of tap water have been debated for decades. The EPA (Environmental Protection Agency) estimates over 60,000 chemicals are used within the USA, however only 91 contaminants are regulated by the Safe Drinking Water Act. The five most dangerous chemicals prevalent in tap water throughout North America are lead, chlorine and chloramine, fluoride and chromium-6. There are 85 other possible chemical contaminants in your drinking water. The impact of any one of these chemicals on the brain can be devastating. Refer to Chapter 7 on 'Water' to understand this in more detail. Your brain is extremely sensitive to these chemicals and though subtle changes may occur in behavior and health now, over the long term in your later years the full impact of drinking contaminated tap water will be realized.

Seek out healthy food and water as a priority for your health. Find Farmer's markets and Co-ops where food grown on healthy soil is your best source of nutrition. The difference in how you think and how you behave will be extraordinary when you eliminate chemicals and additives and consume healthy food and water.

The better informed you are about your brain and how it functions the better success you will have in all areas of your life. Earlier I pointed out that studying the human brain is the new frontier in modern medicine. With the provision of healthy food and water, love and a rich cultural and intellectual environment, optimal brain health can be yours. Keep in mind your brain doesn't fully develop until the age of 25. Nurture problem-solving talents and creative abilities as you chart a path in your life.

Nothing in the known universe is more complex than the human brain. Its ability to communicate with billions of cells with the collective intent of the best life you can create for yourself is truly miraculous. The brain holds many mysteries, experiences, processes, interpretations of your entire life, your thoughts, emotions, language, memory, cognition, awareness, and consciousness- all the things that make you unique. The human brain allows mankind to experience the world, communicate, build civilizations, create great art and travel in space.

Oxygen is critical to efficient brain function and breathing in a conscious way will greatly enhance your ability to think. If you take 3 long, slow deep breaths in and out, you will fill your brain with oxygen and instantly calm down, no matter the challenge you face. It works every time. From there your brain can allow the answer, the solution, the first step necessary to move in a positive direction to rise above the brain fog. Use this practice when making tough decisions, solving problems and most importantly when you are resolving conflict.

There are many simple steps you can take to protect your brain which promotes good health on all other levels in your life. Prepare your brain for sleep and renewal by setting aside your digital devices for an hour before sleep, and use that time for more interesting activities like reading, writing, conversations about your day, or perhaps making plans for the next day. Good food and good water to feed and hydrate your brain and body will enhance your thinking and your performance in all aspects of your life. Practicing mindfulness and yoga help to improve the mind, body, and heart functions and improves efficiencies - in particular quieting the mind and giving you the ability to be calm throughout your day.

Norman Cousins, political journalist and peace advocate describes the brain in this way - "Not even the universe with all its countless billions of galaxies represents greater wonder or complexity than the human brain."

Chapter 5

Depression & Mental Health

Depression can manifest differently for everyone, some people feel lethargic, others tearful, or maybe you just lack your normal level of motivation. Sometimes it manifests as irritability or even numbness and in the extreme as suicidal tendencies. It is important to discuss these feelings or lack of feelings with someone you trust and you may need to get advice from someone who knows more than you do about depression. It is extremely helpful to take time to listen to your own inner voice which may help you sort out your thoughts to better resolve and deal with your own feelings. (1)

All of you have likely experienced depression in your life at some point, the ups and downs; the tragedy of loss and pain all take a toll on our mental attitude and our emotions. If loss of any kind or the death of someone you love is involved in your depression, know there are healthy and essential stages of grief that everyone must go through to fully process loss and systematically find a way to move forward. (2)

There are times when depression can assist you by pushing you to retreat from a situation so as to better understand what's going on. Sometimes depression protects you by forcing you into a reflective state to look deeper, to better choose the correct course of action for yourself.

Albert Camus was a philosopher during the early 1900's and is famous for his considerations and essays chasing the meaning of life; he contemplated "the demand for happiness and the patient quest for it" in his journal, and captured the essence of the meaningful life. *His observation was that we must master the ability to live with the present moment despite the knowledge that we are impermanent.* Nevertheless, embracing life and living passionately when one is despondent about existence is easier said than done. At times severely depressed individuals may wake up day after day asking the question, "Should I kill myself today?" While another person embraces the simple affirmation of life that brewing a great cup of coffee or tea, or going for a walk was a way to give value to life that day. Camus said that despair might ambush you on a street corner or a sun-blasted beach. And yet beauty and the happiness that life brings can also surprise you in any given moment. The cultivation of happiness and the eradication of its obstacles were Albert Camus' most persistent teachings.

The Diagnostic and Statistical Manual for Mental Wellbeing describes 3 different possibilities with depression, as listed below. (3)

Minor depression is characterized by having symptoms for 2 weeks or longer that do not meet full criteria for major depression as described below. If not addressed and resolved, people with minor depression may be at risk for developing major depressive disorder.

Major depressive disorder, or major depression, is characterized by a combination of symptoms that interfere with a person's ability to work, sleep, study, eat, and enjoy once-pleasurable activities. Major depression is disabling and prevents a person from functioning normally. Some people may experience only a single episode within their lifetime, but more often a person may have multiple episodes.

Dysthymic disorder, or dysthymia, is characterized by long-term (2 years or longer) symptoms that may not be severe enough to disable a person but can prevent normal functioning or feeling well. People with dysthymia may also experience one or more episodes of major depression during their lifetimes.

Joseph Coyle, a neuroscientist from Harvard Medical School, writes that "chemical imbalance is sort of last-century thinking. It's much more complicated than that." The belief that depression results from a chemical imbalance in the brain was an idea posed in the late 1950s and has since taken hold in the mainstream. It's the general idea that a deficiency of select neurotransmitters exists (chemical messengers) at critical points, like synapses. One of these neurotransmitters, for example, is serotonin; others include norepinephrine and dopamine. As Scientific American reports, "much of the general public seems to have accepted the chemical imbalance hypothesis uncritically," and that "it is very likely that depression stems from influences other than neurotransmitter abnormalities." (4)

Before I outline the statistics below let me first remind you that in no way do I want to minimize your feelings and your situation when I say that if you are depressed there is a way forward, a light at the end of the sorrow. There is always something to learn from all our experiences when we take the time to delve into the whole picture. *I truly believe that we are born with an innate capacity for joy and constantly returning to joy is a life-long journey.* Be resolved that whatever you feel now can change, and you can find a determined path back to joy, or discover joy for the first time.

As in the previous chapter understanding your brain will assist you in coming to terms with and having a better understanding of depression and how to move forward for yourself or for someone you care about. *Depression is more common in youth today than ever before in history.* In a study from the laboratory of long-time depression, researcher Eva Redei, presenter at the Neuroscience 2009 conference stated that stressful life events are a major cause of depression. The other is that an imbalance in neurotransmitters in the brain triggers depressive symptoms (Northwestern University Feinberg School of Medicine).

The traditional approach to treating depression is to balance certain neurotransmitters with drugs. If you are on medications for depression and you have found success in their ability to help you find balance and happiness in your life then that solution means success for you. Drugs have their place and have saved lives and may be the best and only solution for some people. However, so many of them fail and target symptoms but not the root cause of the problem. They may help in the short term, however to really solve the problem you need to approach the whole dilemma from a holistic point of view. Some essential key ingredients to pay attention to immediately are healthy food (in particular adequate protein), hydration, exercise, positivity, and sunlight all play a role in mood and energy levels. Eliminating chemicals and additives in water and food can immediately begin a shift toward brain health and alleviate depression in many people. *Anyone who is on medications for depression should be informed by their doctors that healthy food and water, in particular toxic chemical free food and water are essential for success.*

It is always important to begin with the basics and understand what your body may be missing as a first step to treating any depression. Magnesium is fundamentally involved in protein production, synthesis of nucleic acids, cell growth and division, and maintenance of the delicate electrolyte balance and composition of our cells. It also imparts stability to the membranes of the energy factories of our cells called mitochondria. Researchers state, "The physiological consequences of these biochemical activities include Magnesium's central role in the control of neuronal activity, cardiac excitability, neuromuscular transmission, muscular contraction, vasomotor tone, and blood pressure".

Magnesium deficiency is directly correlated with symptoms of depression. Magnesium deficiency is correlated with systemic inflammation. Magnesium is essential to regulation of sleep and vitamin D metabolism as well as neural plasticity and cognitive function. However, food processing and industrial agriculture, including monoculture crop practices and the use of magnesium-devoid fertilizers, have led to soil erosion and depletion of magnesium content in our food. Magnesium is likewise removed from most drinking water supplies, rendering magnesium deficiency inevitable. Our daily intake of magnesium has steadily declined from 500 milligrams (mg) per day to 175 mg per day over the past decade. The nutrient-poor, energy-dense dietary patterns which have come to dominate the industrialized landscape are also insufficient in the fiber-rich fruits and vegetables which contain magnesium. There are many recent studies that prove oral magnesium is effective for the treatment of depression. (5)

A helpful book is written by Alex Korb PhD, titled *'The Upward Spiral: Using Neuroscience to Reverse the Course of Depression, One Small Change at a Time.'* It is written in a style that demystifies the intricate brain processes that cause depression and offers practical and effective approaches to feeling better.

Prioritizing how you spend your time each day and determining for you what really matters is extremely helpful. It is highly probable that in retrospect you are going to regret how much time you spent on social media. Too often social media reinforces what isn't working in your life by showing you falsely how great everyone else's life is. Real connection and real life experiences are absolutely essential to crawl out of that place inside you that is making you sad or feeling unworthy. There is much yet to learn of the potential repercussions of such a high level of exposure to technology. Society always learns these lessons too late for many. Wherever you find yourself with people, look up and you will see how many are just like you, potentially depressed looking down at their phones. Of course not everyone who is looking at their phones is depressed; however they are still not looking up at the world they are walking through and the people they are with or passing by.

Don't forget: bad things happen to everyone in varying degrees; the most important awareness you must have is that your reaction to it will dictate

how severe the impact is on your life. Natural reactions happen within all of us to bad situations. Pay attention to your reactions. If you react badly, see it for what it is and move on, choosing to not let the impact linger. Your reactions daily or weekly or yearly accumulate and can be part of the root of depressive thoughts or habits.

Also, keep in mind that people do not think about you nearly as much as you think they do. Most people are obsessed with their own issues, just like you and barely notice other people's issues. Most people do not notice whatever you perceive your flaws to be. Everyone is in the same boat, your best choice is to step out of that boat and be your own person, and learn to love yourself and all your parts.

There is a strong link between depression and diet, hydration and attitude. Depression can be associated with emotions, a physical challenge, a medical crisis and a wide range of events in your life. Always assess any nutritional deficiencies and nurture yourself with good food, good water and exercise. **Some scientists think that depression may be a side effect of inflammation.** By treating the inflammatory symptoms of depression — rather than the neurological ones — researchers and doctors are opening up an exciting new dimension in the fight against what has become a global epidemic. This realization has led to new treatments for depression. Clinical trials have found that adding anti-inflammatory medicines to antidepressants not only improves symptoms, it also increases the proportion of people who respond to treatment. There is also evidence that Omega 3 and curcumin, an extract of the spice turmeric are effective in alleviating inflammation and have a positive effect on depressive symptoms.

A new focus of science on depression is suggesting we should re-brand depression altogether as an infectious disease. Carmine Pariante, a Kings College psychiatrist says that we're between five and ten years away from a blood test that can measure levels of inflammation in depressed people.

PTSD (Post Traumatic Stress Disorder) not only affects war Veterans. Victims of abuse and stress experience similar symptoms of PTSD, with depression identified as a primary symptom. Two million Americans have served in Iraq and Afghanistan, and it is estimated that 30 percent of them have returned with PTSD. Consider the wars around the globe and the numbers of affected individuals in this example alone. That means the Veterans Health Administration has been overwhelmed with more than 600,000 PTSD patients, and in response they are over-prescribing opiates. Despite treatment, in the U.S. alone an average of 22 veterans commit suicide each day. 2017 saw the first placebo-controlled, triple-blind, randomized crossover study on the effects of smoking marijuana on veterans with chronic, treatment-resistant PTSD. The results were extremely successful in alleviating much of the internalized stress of the Veterans in the study.

The U.S. Centre for Disease Control and Prevention recently announced that the suicide rate for children ages 10 to 14 had caught up to their death rate for traffic accidents. The first occurrence of the word suicide appeared in the Oxford English dictionary in 1651 and prior to that it was described as self-murder and to this day is considered a crime in many countries. In another context, such as ancient Rome or medieval Japan, suicide was seen as a defiant act of extreme personal freedom against perceived or actual tyrants. There are high suicide rates in veterans and epidemic rates in northern aboriginal communities. At least a million people die annually from suicide worldwide. Many more people, especially the young and middle-aged, attempt suicide. The World Health Organization (WHO) calls suicide a major global health problem. WHO, which is launching its first global report on suicide prevention, said more people die from suicide than from conflicts, wars and natural disasters combined. (6)

A contributing factor to what many call a suicide epidemic, is the pervasiveness of social networking where entire schools can witness someone's shame, mistake or flaw according to a misguided norm. And with continual access to technology, those pressures do not end when a child is away from school. Rachel Simmons, the author of "Odd Girl Out: The Hidden Culture of Aggression in Girls" describes social media as a new way to quantify friends and faults in actual numbers. *Social media exponentially amplifies humiliation, and an uninformed, vulnerable child who is humiliated is at much higher risk of suicide than would otherwise have been.* The National Institute for Mental Health also warns that reporting on suicide can lead to so-called suicide contagion, in which exposure to the mention of suicide within a person's family, peer group or in the media can lead to an increase in suicides.

According to "The New Pubert," a 2014 book that describes the phenomenon of girls getting their first period between age 10.5 and 12.5 on average, compared to age 16.6 in 1860. This means girls are becoming young women at an age when they are less equipped to deal with issues like sex and gender identity, peer relationships, sexual pressures and expectations, and more independence from family. Girls experience depression at twice the rate of boys in adolescence, with this a pattern continuing into adulthood. Suicide is just the tip of a broader iceberg of emotional trouble. One recent study of millions of injuries in American emergency departments found that rates of self-harm, including cutting, had more than tripled among 10 to 14 year olds. *If you need help with depression reach out to a friend or family member. There are help lines and resources in every community that are willing to help anyone who asks. Please don't get stuck, reach out and get help.* (7)

Too often we blame our relationships for our depression. Relationships are an extension of our happiness but not the basis of it, so focus on strengthening the relationship you have with yourself and all of the others will follow accordingly.

Getting to know yourself and understanding your own feelings and reactions to the people around you can be your greatest tool to alleviate stress before it manifests as depression. Reaching out to ask for help if necessary and finding someone to discuss openly your concerns is a critical step toward finding your way to inner calm.

Meditation has been shown to increase dopamine levels and feelings of happiness which alter serotonin levels in your brain, directing your energy and thoughts toward positive things. Meditation is simply the act of quieting the mind. Meditation is a simple practice of concentrated focus upon a sound, object, visualization, the breath, movement, or attention itself in order to increase awareness of the present moment, reduce stress, promote relaxation, and enhance personal and spiritual growth. You can walk in the woods and call it a meditation; you can listen to music that soothes your soul and call it meditation. Find out what works best for you. Other proven ways to increase serotonin may be through psychotherapeutic methods like cognitive behavioral therapy, and HeartMath training, which strengthens the part of the brain responsible for mood. (8)

We all know ***exercise*** is important and increasing your exposure to outdoor light has been proven to alleviate symptoms of depression and increase serotonin levels. ***Studies have shown exercise to be more effective and safer than antidepressants for people with mild depression.*** Exercise increases serotonin levels and the firing rates of serotonin neurons. Be sure to get enough Vitamin D, studies show that worldwide, an estimated 1 billion people have inadequate levels of vitamin D in their blood, and deficiencies can be found in all ethnicities and age groups. Vitamin D is a nutrient that is absorbed through the skin when exposed to sunlight and travels to the liver where it is activated into a hormone that plays a vital role in your health. Using sunscreen, along with the dangers of their toxic ingredients, reduces our ability to absorb vitamin D by more than 90 percent. The sun's ultraviolet B (UVB) rays, the rays that trigger the skin to produce vitamin D are stronger near the equator and weaker at higher latitudes. Most people in Canada and the northern US and Europe don't produce enough Vitamin D from interacting with the sun for more than half of the year. Supplementing with Vitamin D is highly advised today by the medical system. Presently a new Vitamin D and Omega-3 Trial (VITAL), is underway with 20,000 healthy men and women to determine if taking 2,000 IU of vitamin D or 1,000 mg of fish oil daily lowers the risk of cancer, heart disease, and stroke, as science has finally connected the dots between nutrition and disease. In previous generations kids were given cod liver oil every day to maintain healthy levels of vitamin D and Omega 3. Installing 1000 watt halogen lights helps in office settings and there are light therapy lamps commonly available today that reduce symptoms of Vitamin D deficiency.

The most effective way to increase serotonin levels in your brain and improve your mood is to eat healthy food. Changing the types and amounts of protein and good fats are critical to emotional wellbeing. Eating a diet high in saturated fats (butter, fat in meats, dairy and cheese) with the worst fat of all is oxidized artificial trans fats which are in junk food and fast foods *decreases your mental performance and is linked to depression and irritability.* These saturated fats are assimilated into your brain and other tissues and they replace omega 3 healthy fats that lead to a healthy brain. Sources of best omega 3 healthy fats are avocados, nuts, seeds, fish, seafood and algae. Including organic flax seed oil, organic coconut oil to every meal is an easy fix while diminishing toxic fats in your diet. It is important to eat a balance of saturated and unsaturated healthy fats each day.

Learn how to meditate and focus on positive thoughts, walk in nature, increase exercise and eat well. If you require professional assistance and/or are in a crisis reach out to the closest person to you to begin the process of unraveling your state. You can find a way back to joy, you truly can.

Mild depression or crankiness or that feeling that you are just not yourself takes energy away from your best experience. Learn to pay attention to what you feel and why, in order to have more control over your own emotional stability. Remember the chapter on your brain and hormones and health? It is no surprise that consuming foods contaminated with 'hormone' mimicking chemicals that block receptors in the brain, therefore preventing the correct hormones access to the receptors would have an enormous effect on behavior and thoughts. *It is only logical that a vehicle (the brain) filled with the wrong fuel (the food) will misfire.*

Understanding the correlation between how depressed you may feel today and the history of your race, your town or your country has never been more important. *An underlying and pervasive attitude throughout humanity of institutionalized racism is a disease of the heart and mind and no matter how you decipher depression; this history of bullying on a personal, political or spiritual level has reached cataclysmic levels in emotional instability for people around the world.* Institutionalized racism has become ingrained in our society through education and politics and is reflected in disparities regarding wealth, income, criminal justice, employment, housing, health care, political power and education, and a myriad of other ways. Whether implicitly or explicitly expressed, institutional racism occurs when a certain group is targeted and discriminated against based upon race, religion, gender or skin color.

Children are not born depressed, racist or a multitude of other emotional afflictions that people have. Yes emotional stability of parents while in utero can affect the emotional state of a child. The resilience and innate happiness of babies rebounds through countless unhappy moments. Racism and depression are taught to a child, whether by instruction or example: conditioning of attitudes and behaviors can be subtle, however it is up to each person to unravel these untruths and find their own humanity. You cannot blame your parents for your attitude now. Blame will block your ability to find reason and truth in your life. Forgiveness plays a critical role in letting go of blame. Read Chapter 12 on Emotions for tools to resolve these issues.

If a person is depressed, it is essential for that person to understand their society and how they fit or don't fit within it. We are now further away from global peace than at any time in the past fifty years creating what is termed a global 'peace inequality' gap. *If there is no peace how can there be contentment?*

The Global Peace Index (GPI) is a report produced by the Institute for Economics and Peace (IEP) and developed in consultation with an international panel of peace experts from peace institutes and think tanks with data collected and collated by the Economist Intelligence Unit. The Index was first launched in May 2007, with subsequent reports being released annually. It is claimed to be the first study to rank countries around the world according to their peacefulness. In 2017 it ranked 163 countries, up from 121 in 2007. In the past decade, the GPI has presented trends of increased global violence and less peacefulness. Presently there are 10 countries that meet the peace criteria out of 163 countries worldwide. The index gauges global peace using three broad themes: the level of safety and security in society, the extent of domestic and international conflict and the degree of militarization. The factors that determine these ratings are based on levels of violence and crime within the country and military expenditure and wars outside of the country. The Global Peace Index has been criticized for not including indicators specifically relating to violence against women and children, which of course is furthest from any idea of peace within a country or community. However, the global community needs to work on this in every country as violence and misconduct against women is widely recognized and hopefully being addressed today.

The WHO Mental Health Action Plan 2013–2020 was initiated in Europe aiming to reduce suicide rates by 10% overall by 2020 and among specific groups by age, sex and ethnicity.

There are communities in Northern Canada that have been in a declared state of emergency because of an epidemic of youth suicide. Suicide rates for aboriginal (First Nations, Metis and Inuit) young men are five times that for Caucasian young men. Considering the Shifting Baseline Syndrome how can this be a surprise to any nation? This generation of Youth has no landmarks or healthy baselines for their cultures that were decimated by economic hardships and the legacy of colonialism. After 10,000 years living in gratitude with the land, and hard work of sustaining families and then to lose their culture and their land in a mere 200 years, it comes as no surprise that a chronic state of depression exists for so many. Community leaders and Youth are fighting to solve this cultural crisis.

Of course suicide rates and depression for Youth today cross all cultural boundaries. Suicide among medical students and doctors has been a largely unacknowledged phenomenon for decades, obscured by secrecy and shame. The Association of American Medical Colleges recently addressed an escalating crisis of depression, burnout, and suicide among physicians and university students due to a "culture of abuse" too often characterized by bullying, harassment, and humiliation. The number of physicians who commit suicide every year in the U.S. is between 300 and 400. Male doctors are 1.4 times more likely to kill themselves than men in the general population, female physicians, 2.3 times more likely. These numbers are most likely higher as suicide is often not put on a death certificate. In one study of six medical schools, nearly 1 in 4 students reported clinically significant symptoms of depression and almost 7% had thought of ending their lives in the previous two weeks.

This is a prime example of how a dysfunctional society works. These are the very people we expect and insist heal us of our wounds and ailments, while the road for them to get there is absurdly stressful. The stress starts in medical school with the pressure to master an overwhelming amount of material, peer competition, sleep deprivation and withering criticism from faculty. There is little tolerance for ignorance, signs of weakness, or emotional displays. Once they are physicians they are immersed into human suffering, long work hours, high expectations and a great fear of making a mistake. The culture of professionals around the globe prohibits vulnerability amidst adapting to a rapidly changing health care environment globally. (9)

Youth need a purpose, activities and exercise that challenge their boredom and apathy. Nature is our greatest cure for so many troubles of the mind today. What else could we expect from Youth but apathy and levels of obvious and covert depression when around the world they have been handed a life full of political, financial and career deficits? Aboriginals around the globe have a long history of initiation into adulthood through nature. Since time immemorial, aboriginals have had an intricate, respectful, spiritually, and physically-dependent tie to the land. The relationship is one of stewardship and gratitude, not ownership. It is their responsibility for the land (and sea) and all of the creatures that inhabit the land with them, that is at the core of their existence. Their stewardship is intrinsically tied to the spirits of all aspects of the earth and traditional knowledge, languages, cultural practices and oral traditions built up over millennia. They are all connected to the land. It only makes sense that when that connection was severed, their spiritual well-being and their very lives can be at stake, as with all peoples.

Most anthropologists say that rites of passage exist in order to consolidate social ties, establish roles, and give members of a group a sense of purpose and placement. In a family of four, cohesion is built in; the smaller the group the easier it is to manage. The parents protect and the children listen and learn. Rites of passage are nearly universal throughout human cultures, both ancient and modern. It is a biological imperative. The larger the group or society becomes, the greater the need to establish roles and work cohesively together. We know of the world through our perceptions, our thoughts and our language. These are what form our world. Rites of passage for youth have long been forgotten in contemporary society. When opportunities to mark a rite of passage as important as moving from a child to adult are missing, a youth will take on the task himself. In the extreme, teenage girls may prove their fertility by getting pregnant and teenage boys may demonstrate their manhood by ritualized violence by joining a gang. Both sexes may mark themselves with particular clothing or scarification, such a tattoos or piercings.

The transition from adolescent to adulthood is biologically marked by puberty, though our conservative societies still have taboos around public discussion of such events. The secret, the embarrassment, the jokes around female menstruation are present in all western societies. Mentors are important at times like these to assist young people in shedding what has become too small, their childhood self, and forging into and with a changing body toward adulthood. To navigate these transitions of adolescence well, young people need adults who understand the tasks, difficulties, and opportunities of this stage in life. They need mentors who know how to mark transitions in meaningful and relevant ways. Today rites of passage often consist of getting your driver's license, social insurance/security number, Facebook friend lists and jobs. Youth must now rely on these to define them in the world.

Consider what a modern rite of passage would look like for you in your own unique situation. Consider rites of passage that are practical for the life you are living now. Because you no longer need to hunt or survive in the wilderness as in the past, investigate rites of passage that would symbolize your transition in your way. A rite of passage must offer a challenge as you step into a new phase, age or experience in your life. Consider challenges that will improve you as a person, teach you life skills that will serve your life for the greater good, learn a new language, travel or deal with what you know you must in your present circumstance. The key is to know yourself now and determine rites of passage for yourself as you move into adulthood, careers or relationships.

In terms of depression, western medicine has relied on drugs as an easy solution for too long. Antidepressant drugs are the most commonly prescribed drugs in N. America. According to the World Health Organization, the global depression drug market was valued at 14 billion U.S. dollars in 2014 and is expected to generate revenue of 16.8 billion by the end of 2020. Antipsychotics remain the top-selling therapeutic class of prescription drugs in the U.S.

Direct-to-consumer (DTC) advertising for drugs in the U.S. is now firmly entrenched, selling directly to the public. Historically, though, it was promoted only to doctors. In Europe, DTC is considered an inappropriate means for pharma companies to communicate with patients because it bypasses the healthcare professional. The over- advertising and promotion of drugs and the over-prescribing of all medications by doctors has created a new category called 'Death by Pharmaceuticals.' This includes the latest opioid crisis in N. America. Deaths from prescription drug use are increasing, according to the U.S. Centers for Disease Control and Prevention (CDC). *Seven of the top 10 recreational drugs of choice by 12th-graders in the U.S. are prescription drugs.*

The excessive prescribing of medications like Prozac, Paxil, and Zoloft is an issue, and their effectiveness is being challenged by science today. Because of the role the gut plays in serotonin levels science is now calling the gut the second brain, which is the enteric (intestinal) nervous system. . This part of the gut consists of sheaths of neurons embedded in the walls of the long tube of our alimentary canal, which runs from our throat to our rectum. *Much of our brain processes that are affected by mood are a direct result of our gut health.*

Youth of today will be the leaders of tomorrow. Society has valued greed and monetary gain above the wellbeing of Youth, the world's greatest hope and resource. Kids and youth's brains are rapidly changing and the human brain is not fully developed until the age of 25. Considering the uniqueness of each individual Youth, their circumstance and their rapid brain development, prescribing drugs should be the last possible treatment considered. When combined with significant or traumatic life events it is easy to understand the mood changes and challenges for Youth. There are numerous organizations around the globe trying to resolve and find solutions for this issue. (10)

"*The Cundill Centre for Child and Youth Depression* was launched in September 2015, thanks to a $15-million philanthropic gift from The Peter Cundill Foundation. This international Centre mobilizes a global network of scientists, clinicians and experts, who, in collaboration with youth and families with real-life experience, focuses on developing best practices for screening, prevention and treatment of child and youth depression, revolutionizing research, care and knowledge exchange. "

Whatever state you find yourself in, *ask for help* if you can't find a next step for yourself and for your safety. However, don't underestimate how simple steps can assist you in finding yourself again. *Create some kind of routine* for yourself that you practice every day, which gives structure to your day, no matter how simple the routine might be. *Set goals*. By setting small goals (like cooking a meal or taking a walk) you can push back against sadness or depression. Each goal met can help you set more daily goals. *Be patient with yourself*.

Exercise. A simple walk, or run or sporting activity temporarily boosts endorphins in the brain and regular exercise has been shown to help the brain rewire itself in positive ways. There is a long list of activities that take you out into nature that further enhances a healthy state of mind, like biking, skiing, snowshoeing, canoeing and exploring in nature on foot.

Eat healthy food. Eat nutritious food and drink lots of good water. A few examples science has shown us, along with common sense is that omega-3 fatty acids (flax seeds, salmon and tuna) and folic acid (spinach and avocado) can help ease depression. Make an effort at optimum nutrition before considering anti- depressant medications. Seek professional help if necessary and be mindful of their advice. The goal is to get at the root of the problem not medicate and mask it to make it invisible.

Get enough sleep. Plenty of studies have proven that sleep deprivation has a negative effect on mood. Make the necessary lifestyle changes and get to bed and get up at the same time every day, while avoiding screen time for an hour before bed to allow your body to produce melatonin which is essential to good sleep. On average we need 7 to 9 hours of sleep nightly. Difficult though this might be, commit to this lifestyle change for just 7 nights and you will notice a difference and hopefully choose to continue this positive practice.

Take on responsibilities and help others if you can. We all know people who need our help; instead of withdrawing, push yourself to reach out to help others. Even small responsibilities can give you a feeling of accomplishment and purpose.

Challenge your thoughts. The mind defaults to negative thoughts when depression persists. Most of our negative thoughts are not true and have no basis in reality. Keep in mind that good people do not waste their time thinking unkind thoughts about you. Meditation and mindfulness are great tools to counteract the negative thoughts.

Do something new. This can be as simple as buying a new book and reading it in the park or going to a museum or taking an interest in something new. Volunteer at an animal shelter. The best place for reinforcement of your value is to be loved by an animal and so many of them need your support. Know that you can alter the levels of dopamine in the brain when you choose to do things that give you pleasure, enjoyment, and exercise for your brain. Most people enjoy the sheer delight of holding a kitten or a puppy.

Try to have fun. If nothing seems fun anymore, remind yourself it is just a symptom, a curable symptom of depression. You must keep trying. The old adage 'fake it till you make it' certainly won't fix a serious medical depression. It will however lead you to thinking more positively if you tell yourself you are happy until it becomes so.

Determine what happiness is for you. After all, happiness is a combination of how satisfied you are with your life and how good you feel on a day-to-day basis. Your life changes, and your mood fluctuates, but your general happiness can be a stable foundation. Remember that with considerable practice you have the ability to control how you feel. With consistent practice and intent, you can form life-long habits for a more satisfying and fulfilling life.

You deserve to be happy. Happiness is not something you postpone for the future; it is something you design in your present. In 1759 Martha Washington, the first - First Lady of the United States said, "I am determined to be cheerful and happy in whatever situation I may find myself. For I have learned that the greater part of our misery or unhappiness is determined not by our circumstance but by our disposition. "

There are many resources and guides to consider when truly getting to the deep understanding of depression. Youth are different than adults in this regard and a teenager's guide to depression is a reasonable reference to have. (11)

Accepting your feelings and opening up about them with someone you trust will help you feel less alone. This can be the first step to create a plan for good health, better sleep, exercise, challenging your thoughts with meditation, trying something new, building friendship with those who share a similar experience and trying to have fun. For most of us 'this too shall pass' teaches us that change comes, time passes and there will be another experience that will lead you in a more positive direction. For those who are stuck, get the help you need. Many people care and are willing to offer what they can to help you find peace.

Gratitude has been said to have one of the strongest links with mental health of any character trait. The longest lasting effects of gratitude, from a number of research projects were due to the writing of "gratitude journals" wherein participants were asked to write down three things they were grateful for every day. These participant's happiness scores continued to increase each time they were periodically tested thereafter. In fact, the greatest benefits were usually found to occur around six months after journaling began. It was so successful that, although participants were only asked to continue the journal for a week, many participants continued to keep the journal going long after the study was over. Similar results have been found from studies conducted by Emmons and McCullough (2003) and Lyubomirsky et al (2005).

We are human beings and happiness is a vital part of our survival. You deserve to be happy because then you can be your true self realizing your own personal power and offering it to the world. When you are happy, you come alive and feel inspired. *People who know happiness fight the longest, love the strongest, and try the hardest*. When you are in that place within, with that sense of knowing who you are, you have the greatest capacity to do good things in the world and create change. What more could you ask of yourself than to be happy with who you are, and from there build the life you want and deserve.

Chapter 6

The Politics of Food

Food is the fuel your life runs on. *The food choices you make influence everything you think, say, feel and do*. Most of us have a sense of healthy food choices; we used to call them the basics. Fruits, nuts, seeds, vegetables, whole grains, meat, fish and eggs cover the real foods that will nourish you well.

What you are about to read may sound dismal in regard to the challenge of eating healthy food in today's world. Even though the information is troubling, it is of essential importance that you be informed in order to make good choices for your life. *You are what you eat*. You can find good food grown by good people that you can afford if you make connections and make an effort.

If you want to eat healthy food, generally you cannot eat what is offered in mainstream grocery stores and fast food outlets around the globe. Other than what may be available in the organic sections, you need to find your own sources of good food, grow your own, join food cooperatives and eat non-chemically grown food and only consume animals raised with respect and are hormone/pesticide/chemical fertilizer free. *After all if you believe that you are what you eat, then it is simply imperative for optimum performance that you consume optimal food and water.*

The truth is that once you admit that you want better health, you must be honest with yourself about what you are doing now and what you can do differently. If you don't want to know how sabotaged and compromised your food has become, then skip this section. In our complicated society today, *it's what you don't know that will undermine your success*. Simple and healthy food must be part of your plan for success. It is more fun to cook with two people or more so consider forming your own healthy food posse. If you can master a great burrito, filled with healthy protein and veggies and an avocado and salsa you can eat that every day and know that you are nourishing your body. You can mix up 10 different types of burritos and be well fed. The more creative you are and the more effort you put into what you feed your body, the more energy and clarity you will experience. Just don't complicate the cooking process, simple meals are good for you and as you create a routine for yourself you can work into more creative cooking if you desire.

What you eat and why you eat are equally important. Carrying too much weight for your body frame does affect efficiencies of your structural strength, internal organ systems and how your mind works. It is important for you to understand your relationship with food. You don't live to eat, you eat to live. Food is meant to be the fuel you run on, the nourishment that each cell of your body requires to deliver a productive and healthy life. Fitness in terms of being able to walk comfortably and fast if necessary and have an active lifestyle are far more important measuring sticks of your health than the number you may see on your scales. Consider the addictive nature of dyes, chemicals and trans-fats which lead to emotional addictions to foods, which presents a whole new challenge to changing your diet. The entire phenomena of a multi trillion dollar business in the diet industry is hugely assisted by people's emotional under-nourishment. When a person starts to feel more connected, better understood and more in touch with their own feelings they start to eat less and make better healthy food choices.

Collectively, our society advertises and speaks so much about food but not about what people really need. Perhaps what is most urgent is the longing to feast on understanding, tenderness, recognition, forgiveness and love.

Sadly, today's food no longer has the same quality as in your grandparent's day. With the commercialization and globalization of food and farming, nutrition has suffered greatly and processed foods dominate the shelves. Eighty percent of the food on the supermarket shelves didn't exist 100 years ago. Conventional food for the masses is now grown in denatured soil that does not support healthy microbes and soil fauna. Chemical fertilizers and pesticides are used annually in large quantities. Many of the foods are GMO's (genetically modified organisms), and growing them is dependent upon large inputs of chemicals. GMO foods are banned in 38 countries worldwide indicating that there are health and safety concerns with consumption of GMOs. Further, garlic is bleached, fruits are sprayed & waxed, herbs and spices and beef are irradiated and injected with dyes and shelf stabilizers. These are a few of many contradictions in food integrity. Fake food is a $50 billion business. A honey smuggling ring in the U.S. is mixing and cutting fructose corn syrup with honey and is worth $80 million annually. You can't tell real food from fake food because labels don't always indicate the actual ingredients. (1)

In 2010 research linked arsenic exposure to millions of deaths in Bangladesh where "the magnitude of the arsenic problem is 50 times worse than Chernobyl," said Richard Wilson, president of the nonprofit Arsenic Foundation and a physics professor emeritus at Harvard University. The World Health Organization (WHO) called the issue for 70 million people in Bangladesh the worst case of mass poisoning in the world. Arsenic poisoning in food and water affects some 70 countries, including the U.S., Chile, Vietnam and Cambodia, however the biggest problem by far is in Bangladesh, a country roughly the size of Iowa with about half the U.S. population crammed into it. Well water contamination was killing the populations of the poorest countries.

A very cool solution to this problem was presented in 2016 by the University of Calgary, Alberta, Canada. A group of Veterinary Researchers connected the dots between arsenic and lentils grown in Saskatchewan, which have high levels of selenium. When both arsenic and selenium are present, they bind together in the blood and can't move into other organs and tissues and cause damage. Instead the elements are metabolized and excreted through the liver and kidneys. Presently families in Bangladesh are eating Saskatchewan lentils, a daily staple of their Bangladeshi diet to neutralize the arsenic in their bodies. Eating selenium in lentils is effective at neutralizing the arsenic — a "whole food solution" — and is a far cheaper solution than replacing the water supply and trying to get millions of people to take selenium supplements every day of their lives. (2)

Sugar has been touted by the medical profession today to be one of the most addictive substances contributing to a long list of diseases. Sidney Mintz, wrote 'Sweetness and Power' in 1995 which has proven to be an authority on the history and addictive nature of sugar. Sugar causes pleasure with a price that can be paid immediately, while overconsumption over time equals long-term nutritive or medical consequences. Sugar influences the same region of the brain known as the "reward center" as does nicotine, cocaine, heroin and alcohol. Sugar has been refined from its original form to heighten its rush and concentrate its effects. *The more we consume sugar, the less dopamine we produce naturally in the brain and the result is that we need more of the drug to get the same pleasurable response.* You might think this transformation happens only because sugars and sweets taste good. The truth is that sugar took over our diets because the first taste, especially for children, is a kind of intoxication and the kindling of a lifelong craving. Sugar and high-fructose corn syrup are the primary causes of obesity, diabetes and insulin resistance, and are a dietary trigger for many other diseases as well.

One 12-ounce can of pop contains 50 grams (13 teaspoons) of added sugar. The small fruit flavored yogurt (that people have been convinced is a healthy choice) has 26 grams of sugar (often fructose from corn source). Other high sugar foods are salad dressings with 3 grams of sugar in 1 tablespoon of dressing and most frozen convenience foods, such as TV dinners and pizzas also have high fructose corn syrup content. According to the USDA National Nutrient Database, one slice of commercially prepared white bread has 1.4 grams of sugar, though most people don't consider bread to be a sweet food purchase. One cup of canned fruit can contain up to 44 grams of sugar, twice the amount found in a cup of whole, fresh fruit. Juice is one of the biggest sources of sugar in the American diet, especially among children. Coca Cola may have 140 calories and 40 grams of sugar (10 teaspoons) but the same amount of apple juice has 165 calories and 39 grams of sugar (9.8 teaspoons). It is always better to choose the whole fruit. Often parents choose commercial granola bars as a supposed healthy option to candy bars. The truth is the amounts of added sugar are very similar to the amounts found in some candy bars. Condiments and sauces are often high sources of sugar, for example 1 tablespoon of ketchup has 3 grams of sugar. Coffee creamers are made mostly of sugar in the form of high fructose corn syrup. The roots of the modern discussion on sugar and disease can be traced back to the early 1670s, which coincided with the first flow of sugar into England from its Caribbean colonies. A vital skill for you to practice is reading labels. The carbohydrate count on the label tells you the sugar content plus the simple carbohydrates that are transformed into sugar when consumed per serving. If the words on the label are not foods you recognize but are chemicals and additives and dyes, don't buy it.

The part of your body most affected by high sugar intake is your gut. Keep in mind that 70% of your immune system lives in your gut, called your second brain. One of the reasons why your gut has so much influence on your health is due to the 100 trillion healthy bacteria--about three pounds worth-- that line your intestinal tract. This is an extremely complex living system that aggressively protects your body from outside offenders. Many recent studies agree that sugar can promote the growth of bad bacteria in the gut, which destroy the good bacteria in the gut. This can easily manifest itself as an autoimmune response, ranging from allergies to skin conditions to severe colitis and leaky gut syndrome. There is now evidence suggesting depression is a result of your body's response to swelling in the gut due to damage to healthy bacteria. Artificial sweeteners are considered more detrimental to health than sugar. All artificial sweeteners can detrimentally influence the microbiota (your gut's bacteria). This loss of good bacteria can lead to glucose intolerance, which can lead to diabetes. (3)

In America every child between 4 and 10yrs of age, on average, consumes the equivalent of 15-18 cubes of sugar daily. And research has found that "eight out of 10 parents believed their children's breakfast was healthy." Advertising and labeling are controlling food choices for children who can't choose for themselves. Through advertising children influence their parents' choice of breakfast cereal. These simple bad breakfast habits become lifelong habits. *Reading labels is your first line of defense when buying food*. Most people make food choices without knowing or thinking what is actually in the food they are eating.

In the U.S. in June 2016 the Environmental Working Group (EWG) released a report stating that processed cereal is an "excessive source of added sugar in children's diets," which is supposed to be the most nutritious and important meal of the day. The other 4 items above cereal were things like ice cream and cookies, which are not part of a real food group to begin with. Choose to take an interest in the foods you are eating and read labels. There is political pressure around the world to force corporations to label their food products which at the very least gives consumers a choice.

In England, former chancellor Greg Osborne has recommended a sugar tax to begin in April of 2018 on drinks containing "more than 5g of sugar per 100ml," which most often means soft drinks. This is causing the Coca-Cola Corporation to begin another campaign of convincing people their drinks are healthy and now with zero sugar (full of artificial sweeteners, with a minor component of stevia (a natural plant sweetener) they are investing billions in maintaining an unhealthy status quo. Who could resist commercials that link romance, wealth and beauty to a zero calorie cola drink?

One can't talk about food without talking about Monsanto, the originator of the genetically modified food you eat and the largest supplier of pesticides to the world. Today Monsanto is known as Pharmacia LLC and they represent the largest corporation in the world controlling food production, agriculture, chemical use and pharmaceuticals. Monsanto currently has about 4,000 U.S. patents and over 7,000 patents worldwide, including plants, chemicals, processes and machines. Worldwide, 282 million acres are planted in Monsanto's GM crops, up from only 3 million in 1996, according to Food and Water Watch. One hundred and fifty one million acres in the U.S. are planted in Monsanto's crops. Of great concern for us all is the fact that Monsanto owns 1,676 seed patents and provide 95% of plantable seeds to local farmers that are not fertile. Therefore you would have to buy new seed every year. They also control 75% of the world's pesticide formulations. Seven companies now control 71 percent of the world's commercial seed market.

Monsanto developed genetically modified (GM) seeds that would resist its own herbicide, the glyphosate-based Roundup. If you are a farmer who buys the company's Roundup Ready seeds, you are required to sign an agreement promising not to save the seed produced after each harvest for re-planting, which locks the farmer into buying seed each year. You are also prohibited from selling the seed to other farmers. GE (genetically-engineered) crops require much more water to grow and have much higher requirements for fertilizers and pesticide. With the development of herbicide-resistant super weeds, similar to the antibiotic resistant superbug in humans, there is a greater demand for fertilizers and pesticides to continue farming. Air and rain samples are contaminated with glyphosate (the active ingredient in Roundup), while waterways in agricultural areas are contaminated with a GE bug-killing protein. There are no long-term safety studies on these GE crops. Biotech giants such as Monsanto are protected under copyright and proprietary information laws and regulatory assessments on GE crops only come from the corporations themselves. *GE foods have become so ubiquitous in the food chain that seven out of every 10 processed foods contain genetically engineered products*.

An FDA-registered food safety laboratory tested iconic American food for residues of glyphosate and independent research shows that probable harm to human health begins at low levels of exposure – at only 0.1 ppb of glyphosate. Many foods were found to have over 1,000 times this amount! This is well above what regulators throughout the world consider "safe". This chemical is ending up in processed foods. Just a few examples are Cheerios, Ritz Crackers, and Oreo cookies and are being consumed by humans around the world. (4)

Independent research links glyphosate to cancer and it has been deemed a probable human carcinogen by the World Health Organization's team of international cancer experts. The childhood cancer rate is steadily rising, as is cancer for all ages. Research indicates that glyphosate is an endocrine disruptor, which leads to reproductive problems, early onset puberty, obesity, diabetes, and some cancers. When it comes to endocrine disruptors, very small cumulative exposures are doing the damage. (5) (6) (7)

Glyphosate is also a broad-spectrum antibiotic killing the good bacteria in your gut. Poor gut health is linked to inflammation and a whole host of diseases. As GMOs laced with glyphosate are commonly fed to farm animals, this is contributing to antibiotic-resistant bacteria. Glyphosate binds with vital nutrients in the soil (like iron, calcium, manganese, zinc) and prevents plants from taking them up which is partly why food today is lacking essential nutrients for health. Glyphosate (Roundup) is used by the majority of conventional (non-organic) farmers as a drying agent on crops, such as oats and wheat and as a regular weed control. It is in the soil and in the food that we consume. Glyphosate use is so widespread that it has infiltrated our water, air, and soil. Roundup is used by millions of people and businesses in parks, on lawns and golf courses and other public spaces. The FDA found glyphosate in honey tested from mass produced honey and even organic mountain honey. (8) Some municipalities and cities have banned the use of glyphosate by homeowners for weed control. As of March 2018 more than 25 countries have banned the use of glyphosate. (9)

The Lancet Oncology, the world's premier scientific journal for cancer studies, recently published a paper by the World Health Organization's International Agency for Research on Cancer (IARC) that has classified glyphosate as a "probable carcinogenic," outlining scientific studies showing that it causes a range of cancers including non-Hodgkin's lymphoma, renal cancers, skin cancers and pancreatic cancer. It is time this highly dangerous chemical was banned. (10)

Steven M. Druker, a public interest attorney and the Executive Director of the Alliance for Bio-Integrity, initiated a lawsuit in 1998 that forced the U.S. Food and Drug Administration (FDA) to divulge its files on genetically engineered foods. He's recently published a book on the lawsuit (2015). In his book, called *'Altered Genes, Twisted Truth: How the Venture to Genetically Engineer Our Food Has Subverted Science, Corrupted Government, and Systematically Deceived the Public'* he summarizes his journey. The reviews by scientists of his book are impressive, while recommending it should be required reading in every university biology course. Druker has served on the food safety panels at conferences held by the National Research Council and the FDA, presented lectures at numerous universities, met with government officials throughout the world, and conferred at the White House Executive Offices with a task force of President Clinton's Council on Environmental Quality. By publishing this book and filing this lawsuit, Druker exposed how the agency covered up the warnings of its own scientists about the risks, lied about the facts, and then ushered these foods onto the market in violation of federal law. (11)

If you are concerned about the toxic ingredients in food then you don't want to overlook the toxicity in food packaging. If it looks good it must be good seems to be the mind-numbing behavior to encourage people to choose that which is harming them in food and drink. An example of this would be the new apple genetically engineered at Okanagan Specialty Fruits in Canada. They are called the non-browning apple that will not oxidize when sliced and exposed to the air. There is no way to tell the difference between these apples and non-GMO apples because they are *not labeled*. Apples look delicious and healthy, and eating them we assume would be a good choice to make. Unless that apple isn't what you think it is.

Recently the BPA bombshell was dropped, whereby the industry database revealed 16,000 foods with toxic chemicals in packaging. This doesn't even address the actual chemicals in the food, just the packaging.

Consumers have a right to know what's in their food,- especially when it comes to an ingredient, such as BPA (Bisphenol A) that has been linked to cancer, infertility, brain, nervous system and cardiovascular abnormalities, diabetes, obesity and other serious disorders. Many BPA plastics may leach harmful BPA-like chemicals into your body that mimic estrogen, a natural female hormone. Scientists from CertiChem, a private lab in Austin, tested 50 reusable BPA-free plastic containers. The researchers found that some products leached hormone-altering chemicals even before being exposed to conditions, such as heat from a dishwasher or microwave, that are now known to unlock potentially toxic chemicals inside plastic. More than 75% of the containers tested released synthetic estrogens.

While more than 38 countries around the world have completely banned the import or growth of genetically modified foods, people in America are just now demanding the labeling of genetically modified food products. But at least it's a start to give them back the choice.

In a long-term study conducted in November 2012 and reported in the Journal of Food and Chemical Toxicology, Gilles-Eric Seralini and his team of researchers at France's Caen University, studied the possible effects of a GMO maize diet treated with Monsanto's Roundup herbicide. The study found severe liver and kidney damage as well as hormonal disturbances in rats fed with GMO maize in conjunction with low levels of Roundup that were below those permitted in most drinking water across Europe. Results also indicated high rates of large tumors and mortality in most treatment groups. The study was retracted in N. America, but then republished in multiple journals in Europe, one of them including Environmental Sciences Europe.

The N. American retraction was the result of strong commercial pressure of N. American biotech companies, like Monsanto, but the re-published studies in Europe were even more up-to-date and put to rest its previous criticisms.

This is a great example of the politicization of modern day science. Also there are multiple studies to support an extreme bias towards non-GMO food for health and longevity. I do not ask you to believe my point of view on this matter. I simply want to encourage each of you to investigate this thoroughly yourselves and come to your own opinion, especially considering the possible consequences of remaining 'uninformed'.

Resistance to the advent of genetically-modified foods has been pronounced across Europe. The continent features some of the strictest regulations governing the use and cultivation of GMO products, and public skepticism about biotech foods is quite high. In response to this, the U.S. State Department outlined its "Biotechnology Outreach Strategy," to assure a place for genetically-modified agricultural products, through "education" programs, government lobbying, or outright coercion – and to strip down European Union regulations designed to protect the people. Here again I point out that N. American consumers are all too easily convinced by corporations that their way is good for them. (12)

A concern we should have is whether current testing and safety standards for GMO foods currently in place are stringent enough to protect the public from hidden ill effects.

Many people believe that GMO food production is the answer to world hunger. In fact world hunger is mostly due to a distribution problem and corporate control of the food source. The five reasons for world hunger noted by 'Concern Worldwide' a global organization investing in farmers, are war and conflict, weather and climate change, agricultural practices, population growth and poverty. *In every nation on earth where there is significant hunger, poverty and economic inequality, there is significant political inequality. The opposite is also true in the countries that do the best job of meeting the basic living needs of their residents and have political systems in which most citizens have an active and effective stake in their governments.*

There is criminality behind selling food that is contaminated with chemicals and plastics. When you take this situation seriously and inform yourself adequately, you hopefully will see how governments should be held accountable for approving and distributing toxic food. In a study led by Michael Antoniou and published in Nature (2016), in-depth proteomic (the large-scale study of proteins) and metabolomics (the scientific study of chemical processes involving metabolites) analysis showed differences in cell energy use and oxidative stress as well as increases in potentially toxic polyamines (an organic compound having two or more primary amino groups).

The substantial increase in both of these polyamines are a significant cause for concern as they can exhibit toxic effects on consumers, including enhancing the effects of histamine, which can cause severe allergic reactions, and initiating the development of carcinogenic nitrosamines (any of various organic compounds some of which are powerful carcinogens).

John Hopkins School of Medicine has done much research around the exponential increase of allergies in people over the past 2 decades. Toxins and chemicals in food and industrialization are the primary cause while the hygiene hypothesis has become an important theoretical framework for the study of allergic disorders. This theory is based on how sanitized developed countries have become for children, limiting their immune system development and strength. They have determined that the developing immune system in children must receive stimuli (from infectious agents, dirt and dust in their environment, or symbiotic bacteria) in order to adequately develop immune system regulatory T cells. Otherwise, they will be more susceptible to autoimmune and allergic diseases, because of insufficiently repressed Th1 and Th2 (helper cells to immune challenges) responses, respectively. This can translate into a valuable consideration of whether the body is truly allergic to a substance or the immune system is weak. (13)

An inexpensive fish at the grocer is tilapia fish and 80% of it sold in America comes from China, and is grown in farmed pens around the world for human consumption. (14) These fish are bottom feeders and are contaminated with traces of antibiotics and environmental toxins. The United States imports up to 90 percent of its seafood, about half of which are grown in aquaculture. In 2014, it imported $2.9 billion worth of seafood from China, including large amounts of tilapia, salmon, cod, shrimp, tuna, oysters, and scallops. The FDA has found unsafe residues of antimicrobial agents, growth hormones and the antibiotics nitrofuran, malachite green, and gentian violet which were shown to cause cancer after long-term exposure, as well as fluoroquinolones which could cause antibiotic resistance. The FDA inspects less than 3 percent of imports, and tests only 0.1 percent for chemical residues. Another market absurdity is that some seafood, like certain squid and Alaskan salmon, are caught in the United States, but sent to China for inexpensive processing in questionable conditions, before import back to the United States.

Apple juice from China is contaminated with pesticides that are not legal to use in N. America. The processed mushrooms market from China is worth $40 million, and is highly contaminated with pesticides. The latest effort in 2017 for China to get a handle on toxins in their food has been worded by the government to the farmer in the form of a request to not use poisonous or highly-toxic pesticides to control sanitary insect pests and aquatic plant pests. (15)

Eighty percent of imported garlic worldwide comes from China, and in 2014, 65,000 tons were shipped to the U.S. They use pesticides to increase their production of garlic, some of which include bug-killing parathion, phorate and methyl bromide. Garlic also contains sulfites and lead, is exposed to cold temperatures, and is treated with growth inhibitors. As well, Chinese garlic is bleached to whiten it, stop it from sprouting, and to kill insects. One of the reports made by the government in 2014 claims the severe pollution of Chinese land is caused by heavy metals such as arsenic and cadmium, and the unsustainably high and health-damaging amounts of fertilizers and pesticides. (16)

What concerns me the most is the present threat to global food supplies and the challenge in urban areas where, in many countries in the world, more than 80% of the population resides. *Too many citizens cannot afford nor find nutritious, life promoting food on a daily basis.* Forming food cooperatives in your communities may be your best opportunity to work together and buy food at reduced cost in bulk, as there is a recent resurgence of small and large productions of healthy food and local farmers markets. *If you chose to be the leader in this area in your community and do the research, I guarantee you will find people to invest with you. The cost of food is on everyone's mind today.*

As part of your daily food vigilance for health keep in mind the benefits of essential life-giving water in your diet. Skin elasticity, muscle efficiency, body regulation and brain function, balancing mood and emotions, temperature control, memory function, joint lubrication, healthy bowel function, and immune function are all essential daily tasks facilitated for your wellbeing by good water.

Discover the fun and flavor of good food in your life; have fun with variety and color and feed yourself as you might love yourself. The power to transform your life is greatly supported by the food you eat and the water you drink. Truly, it is that simple. Your taste buds will adjust as you eliminate the addictive foods that are toxic for your health and eventually you will not be able to go back. The sweet taste of an organic strawberry or blueberry, the rich flavors of garden vegetables and the discovery of grains, nuts and beans that fill your body with energy will become the new you.

Milk commercials and billboards would convince you that you must have cow's milk to be healthy and vibrant. Cow's milk is designed to grow 1000 lb. calves quickly. Though there might be 300mg of calcium per cup, humans barely absorb the calcium in cow's milk (especially if pasteurized), and consuming cow's milk actually increases calcium loss from the bones. Like all animal protein, milk acidifies the body pH which in turn triggers a biological correction. Calcium is an excellent acid neutralizer and the biggest storage of calcium in the body is in the bones. With daily consumption of cow's milk calcium is pulled out of the bones to neutralize the acidifying effect of milk. Therefore the net result of consuming cow's milk is an actual calcium deficit and depending on how much dairy you consume can lead to osteoporosis in the long term. It's not a coincidence that approximately 65 to 75 percent of the total human population has a reduced ability to digest lactose after infancy and in some countries, more than 90 percent of the adult population is lactose intolerant. Every other mammalian species weans their young off milk and then never drinks milk again for the rest of their lives.

Calcium of course is found in many foods such as dried fruits and nuts, broccoli, beans, oranges, dark leafy vegetables, chia and sesame seeds. These foods are loaded with minerals and nutrients in addition to calcium. Dr. Sofia Pineda Ochoa's research states; *"Not only has the body of scientific evidence been found inadequate to support the idea that dairy consumption promotes bone health, but numerous large-scale studies have found that consuming dairy may actually be detrimental to bone health. In fact, there is substantial data linking higher milk intake with significantly increased risk of bone fractures."*

Why do countries with the highest daily milk intake have the highest rates of hip fractures, a key indicator of osteoporosis, and countries where the average daily milk intake is extremely low, have a very low incidence of bone fractures?

Vitamin D is essential for thyroid health and overall health and most of us assume we receive this from our skins interaction with the sun. An estimated 50% of all people worldwide are deficient in Vitamin D. That is 1 in 2 people lacking enough Vitamin D that directly modulates almost every single cell in the body. With the over use of toxic sunscreens and the underuse of covering up in the sun with light clothing Vitamin D deficiencies have become near epidemic. Fatty fish, egg yolks and cod liver oil provide excellent sources of Vitamin D. Chapter 22, 'Nutrition' expands a great deal on food and health.

Food Democracy Now is a grassroots community dedicated to building a sustainable food system that protects our natural environment, sustains farmers and nourishes families. "Our food system is fundamentally broken. A few companies dominate the market, prioritizing profits over people and our planet. Government policies put the interests of corporate agribusiness over the livelihoods of farm families. Farm workers (often migrant workers) toil in unsafe conditions for minimal wages. School children lack access to healthy foods--as do millions of Americans living in poverty. From rising childhood and adult obesity to issues of food safety, air and water pollution, worker's rights and global warming, our current food system is presently unsustainable, and not looking promising for the future."

'Food Democracy Now' members have a different vision. "We know we can build a food system that gives our communities equal access to healthy food, and respects the dignity of the farmers who produce it. We believe in re-creating regional food systems, supporting the growth of humane, natural and organic farms, and protecting the environment. We value our children's health, worker's rights, conservation, and animal welfare over corporate profits. And we believe that working together, we can make this vision a reality in our lifetimes." (17)

As with so many issues today the contradictions in individual and collective points of view obscure the truth that matters and thereby prevents solutions and success for health and global peace. The anti-GMO'er is vocal and volatile against the industry and yet would trust that same corrupt industry with their life and the lives of their loved ones if they happen to get a cancer diagnosis. The anti-vaxxer (those against vaccinations) who feeds their kids chocolate coco puffs for breakfast is another example of the contradictions that can influence our lives and choices.

We are surrounded with contradictions in our own lives and politics and medicine around the globe. The challenge is to investigate, be curious, and recognize that there are right choices to be made in every area of your life for your own good and the good of future generations.

Take it upon yourself to source out supplies of good organic food grown sustainably. If there are no growers in your community, start your own grassroots food network to provide what you need where you live. Join food buying groups or cooperatives who buy from local and regional farmers that nurture and steward the land that provides the bounty of nutrition your body needs.

It is time for a Paradigm Shift in how Youth think about food. How food is grown, processed, shipped and packaged, contributes to poverty, hunger, obesity, diabetes, cancer, deforestation, water pollution and soil erosion around the world. When people make informed choices they choose healthy food, support healthy environments and make the connection between healthy food, healthy planet, healthy people. No matter how unfair it may be that you have inherited a damaged planet, unhealthy food and bad politics, there is much promise in each individual choice you make for a better life.

Chapter 7

Water: Essential for All Life

The Earth has a finite amount of water. The water that is here today is the same water that will be here in 20 years or 20 million years' time. Water is constantly recycled through the Earth's system via a process called the water cycle and is the most important ingredient in health, wellness and performance for the human body. Water covers 70% of our planet, however only 3% of the world's water is fresh water, and two-thirds of that is stored in frozen glaciers or otherwise unavailable for our use. Climate change is thawing the glaciers of the world at unprecedented rates, and contamination of fresh water has become a global crisis. 1.1 billion people worldwide lack access to clean drinking or potable water, and a total of 2.7 billion find water scarce for at least one month of the year.

By 2025 (just around the corner), two-thirds of the world's population will face water shortages, and ecosystems and wildlife around the world will suffer even more. Day Zero 2018, approaches in South Africa when the taps will be turned off in every home and business. Severe droughts in other parts of Africa have led to famines for tens of millions of people. California has experienced a 10 year drought and the threat to the breadbasket of the U.S. is extreme. Every inhabited continent, to varying degrees, faces extremely high water stress. 54% of India faces high to extreme water stress. Spain, Mesopotamia, China and south eastern Brazil are facing droughts that have severe impacts on food production and health.

A human can go for more than three weeks without food (Mahatma Gandhi survived 21 days without food), but *one cannot survive more than 3 days without water*. At least 60% of the adult body is made of water and every living cell in the body needs it to keep functioning.

Peak performance depends on adequate hydration of your 50 trillion cells to win the race, pass the exam, or stay focused on your tasks throughout the day. Keeping your brain hydrated is essential to help you get out of bed in the morning or make the decision that might even save your life. To underestimate the role water plays in your life is unwise. In some organisms, up to 90% of their body weight comes from water. In a human adult the brain and heart are composed of 73% water and the lungs are composed of about 83% water.

As previously mentioned good food and good water will be the most valued commodities in the near future. Contamination of ground water worldwide, by industry and human waste has finally come to the attention of people in power. During the world-wide Great Depression in the 1930's, in the U.S. and central Canada, the breadbasket of the nation, states of emergency were declared in both countries. In 1929 Wall Street and the stock market crashed, known as Black Friday, to the tune of $40 billion. 15 million Americans were unemployed and half the banks in America failed. Franklin D Roosevelt, the U.S. President at the time coined the phrase 'we have nothing to fear but fear itself', while families went hungry. It took the Second World War to pull the country out of poverty and unemployment, and so began the heart-wrenching economics of war. In Canada the depression was called 'The Dirty Thirties', because the dustbowl of the western prairies, the breadbasket of Canada, lost 90% of the topsoil from drought and winds.

Many regions around the world are experiencing higher air temperatures, drier air, and more severe or frequent droughts and storms. African countries have had droughts and famines for decades killing over 4 million people in the past 65 years. We can't grow food and feed ourselves without water, while we waste billions of gallons mining with water, fracking gas from the earth with water and chemicals and poisoning the water with arsenic. The World Bank estimates the potential water market at $800 billion. The World Bank is transforming the scarcity of water in the world and privatizing water, while establishing trade in water with Monsanto Corp. Soon enough water will be more valuable than gold. Water has become big business for global corporations that see limitless markets in the growing scarcity and growing demand for water. Today in the Maquiladora zone of Mexico, drinking water is so scarce that babies and children drink Coca-Cola and Pepsi. Water scarcity is clearly a source of corporate profits. Coca-Cola's products sell in 195 counties, generating revenues of $16 billion, with endless shelf life and no nutritional value. Actually some of the ingredients in coca cola, including caffeine are diuretics; therefore your body loses water when consuming these products.

The Natural Resource Defense Council studied 103 brands of bottled water to find that bottled water is often no safer than tap water. One-third of the brands contained arsenic and E. coli; one-quarter contained merely bottled tap water. In some countries around the world, governments have privatized town and community watersheds leading to a tripling of water costs to citizens and a monopoly on how the water is used and by whom. Water wars in Bolivia are an example of corporations vs. citizens. Presently 'Water is Life' and 'Bless the Water' are movements around the globe for people to have access to clean water and prevent corporations from control of and polluting water. *And what about the animals we share this planet with which all require safe water to live?*

Nestlé S.A. is a Swiss transnational food and drink company headquartered in Vevey, Vaud, Switzerland. It has been the largest food company in the world, measured by revenues and other metrics, for 2014, 2015, and 2016. In Canada, Nestlé pumps more than four million liters of groundwater every day from an aquifer near Guelph, Ontario. Nestlé pays just $3.71 per one million liters (less than $15 per day) for this water and then ships it out of the community in hundreds of millions of single-use plastic bottles for sale around the world at astronomically marked up prices. Nestlé's operations in British Columbia have also stirred up opposition from communities trying to protect their water. Despite the 2015 drought, Nestlé continues to extract 265 million liters from a well in Hope, BC located in Sto:lo Territory (S'olh Temexw is the traditional territory of the Stó:lō people). The well connects to an aquifer that approximately 6,000 nearby residents in Hope rely on. Between 2011 and 2015 the aquifer that supplies the main Nestlé production well dropped about 1.5 meters, while Nestlé's water extraction increased 33 percent over the same period. This is an example of corporate greed capitalizing on a necessity of life, water, not unlike food corporate control. And this is at the expense of people and the planet. Governments have allowed this for decades and laws need to change to protect water and people.

Groundwater resources are finite. Droughts, climate change and over-extraction continue to impact our limited water sources. At this pace, few will have enough for future needs and wars over water will be common in the future.

It is never too late to wake up to what is going on in your world. Change must happen now to protect water. This is your world. Take an interest in Climate Change and observe the month by month dramatic changes in extreme weather patterns, extreme fire events, ocean behavior, glacier and ice cap melting around the world that bring about great loss of life. It is important to be part of the solution to ensure that the earth remains habitable for you and your future generations.

Adapt or die works one way or another every time. Charles Darwin taught the world a great deal about evolution through geology, biology and science in the early 1800's. One of his famous quotes is "It is not the strongest of the species that survives, nor the most intelligent that survives. It is the one that is most adaptable to change". Another of his quotes that most applies to Youth today, "In the long history of humankind (and animal kind, too) those who learned to collaborate and improvise most effectively have prevailed".

Now that you realize the importance of water in your life and the life of your planet let's talk about what is in your tap water. You can easily get a report from your municipality of what is in the tap water you drink. There are 12 toxins that appear in most water taps in varying degrees; fluoride, chlorine, lead, mercury, PCBs, arsenic, perchlorate, dioxins, DDT, HCB, dachthal (herbicide contaminant) and McTB (methyl tertiary-butyl ether) is a gasoline additive. I have intelligent people debate with me that the concentration in ppm (parts per million) of these toxins is so low that it shouldn't matter. The entire answer to this argument is in the finite balance of nutrients and hormones and enzymes within your body that are in minute doses to maintain good health for you. An imbalance imposed by toxic chemicals in minute amounts can be significant to short and long term health. However all of the listed contaminants have LD (lethal dose) statistics for humans. Dioxins and PCBs alone are highly toxic and can cause cancer, reproductive and developmental problems, damage to the immune system, and can interfere with hormones. The cumulative effect and the fact that many of these toxins are stored in the fat cells in the body and in the brain, dictate the common sense in avoiding the consumption of any of these substances.

Water fluoridation is a peculiarly N. American phenomenon. It started at a time when asbestos lined our pipes, lead was added to gasoline, PCBs filled our transformers and DDT was deemed so "safe and effective" that officials felt no qualms spraying kids in school classrooms and seated at picnic tables. One by one all these chemicals have been banned, but fluoridation remains untouched. Around 1945, local water treatment facilities in N.A. began to add sodium fluoride to the domestic water supply. For over 50 years N.A.

government officials have confidently and enthusiastically claimed that fluoridation is "safe and effective." If you are interested in the politics and absurdity of adding fluoride to drinking water please go to this reference, it is well researched and follows the timeline from then to now regarding fluoride. (1) Most of the western world, including the vast majority of Western Europe, does not fluoridate its water supply, while the U.S. and many cities in Canada do.

The debate about adding fluoride to drinking water has been raging for decades. Fluoride has repeatedly been linked to reduced IQ, by an average of 7 points, even at supposedly "safe" water fluoride levels of less than 4 mg/L (EPA's "safe" level). The EPA (Environmental Protection Agency) has recently been served with a petition that includes more than 2,500 pages of scientific documentation detailing the risks of water fluoridation to human health. Fluoride Action Network (FAN) is among a coalition of environmental, medical and health groups urging the EPA to ban the addition of fluoride to public drinking water supplies. The petition notes, "The amount of fluoride now regularly consumed by millions of Americans in fluoridated areas exceeds the doses repeatedly linked to IQ loss and other neurotoxic effects." The EPA is authorized, under the Toxic Substances Control Act (TSCA) to prohibit the use of a chemical that poses an unreasonable risk to the general public or particularly vulnerable populations.

"Neurodevelopmental disabilities, including autism, attention-deficit hyperactivity disorder, dyslexia, and other cognitive impairments, affect millions of children worldwide, and some diagnoses seem to be increasing in frequency. Industrial chemicals that injure the developing brain are among the known causes for this rise in prevalence. In 2006, we did a systematic review and identified five industrial chemicals as developmental neurotoxicants: lead, methylmercury, polychlorinated biphenyls, arsenic, and toluene. Since 2006, epidemiological studies have documented six additional developmental neurotoxicants—manganese, fluoride, chlorpyrifos, dichlorodiphenyl trichloroethane, tetrachloroethylene, and the polybrominated diphenyl ethers. Authors from the Lancet journal postulate that even more neurotoxicants remain undiscovered. *To control the pandemic of developmental neurotoxicity, we propose a global prevention strategy*. Untested chemicals should not be presumed to be safe to brain development, and chemicals in existing use and all new chemicals must therefore be tested for developmental neurotoxicity. To coordinate these efforts and to accelerate translation of science into prevention, we propose the urgent formation of a new international clearinghouse." (2)

If you have access to good water then this is not an issue for you, however 75% of North Americans live in urban areas where water is treated.

It is not easy to take a stand, the most important decision you make is to inform yourself of what is best for you and your family. There is plenty of research that you can access to best inform yourself.

Fluoride's effects on the brain were again confirmed in 2014, when the Lancet Neurology released a study, authored by a Harvard doctor, among others, that classified fluoride as a developmental neurotoxin. (3)

Fluoride's neurotoxicity, delivered in drinking water, is an especially unreasonable risk, because fluoride's predominant effect on tooth decay is related to topical application, not oral ingestion. Dental fluorosis, a condition in which your tooth enamel becomes progressively discolored and mottled, is one of the most significant adverse effects of consuming too much fluoride. According to the Centers for Disease Control and Prevention (CDC), 41 percent of American adolescents now have dental fluorosis. Even the National Research Council reviewed the evidence, at the EPA's request, and concluded in 2006 that fluoride has the ability to interfere with brain function. Nearly 200 fluoride/brain studies have been conducted since, and research published in Lancet Neurology classified fluoride as one of 12 chemicals known to cause developmental neurotoxicity in humans (others include lead (lipstick), mercury(flu vaccines) and PCBs (milk, eggs, other dairy products, poultry fat, fish, shellfish, and infant foods).

At daily doses ranging from 0.7 to 2.3 mg/L/ day of fluoride, adverse effects including reduced IQ, behavioral alterations, neurochemical changes, hypothyroidism and ADHD have been demonstrated. **Fluoride has the same chemical structure as iodine and is one of the culprits that blocks thyroid receptors that prevent iodine from being utilized by the thyroid leading to one of the highest density diseases of the thyroid today (hypo or hyperthyroidism).**

The vast majority (97%) of Western Europe has rejected water fluoridation. In fact, most countries fluoridate neither their water nor iodize their salt, but according to the World Health Organization (WHO), tooth decay in 12-year-olds is coming down as fast, if not faster, in non-fluoridated countries as it is in fluoridated countries. (4) In contrast, in the U.S. 200 million Americans live in areas where water is fluoridated. From city to city, debates over whether to start or end water fluoridation continue.

Data from India's Union Health and Family Welfare Ministry indicate that nearly 49 million people are living in areas where naturally occurring fluoride levels in water are above the permissible levels. Exposure to levels above 10 mg/L may cause crippling skeletal fluorosis, as well as abdominal pain, nausea, vomiting, seizures and muscle spasms.

Chlorine added to drinking water used to reduce the risk of infectious disease and was believed to be safe. Now, however it is recognized as a substantial portion of the cancer risk associated with drinking water. In recent years, halogenated organic compounds such as chloroform, were identified in chlorinated drinking water supplies and are common in water supplies throughout the United States. These concerns about cancer risks associated with chemical contamination from chlorination by-products have resulted in numerous epidemiological studies. These studies support the notion that by-products of chlorination are associated with increased cancer risks. Chlorine is used to combat microbial contamination, but it can react with organic matter in the water and form dangerous, carcinogenic Trihalomethanes.   According to Dr. Joseph M. Price, MD, in Moseby's Medical Dictionary, "Chlorine is the greatest crippler and killer of modern times. It is an insidious poison". (5)

In a 1992 study that made front-page headlines, and was reported in the July issue of the American Journal of Public Health, researchers at the Medical College of Wisconsin in Milwaukee found that people who regularly drink tap water containing high levels of chlorine by-products have a greater risk of developing bladder and rectal cancers than people who drink unchlorinated water. (6)

If your choices are limited and tap water is all that you have available, invest in a water filter. There are excellent affordable water filters available and you need to research what application is best for your situation. There is great technology available now for travelers to filter water wherever they find themselves.

With your pursuit of finding good water to incorporate into your daily life, it is critical to recall that your body is made up of a minimum of 60% water. Hydration is essential for good health and brain function. Brain fog, fatigue, the inability to detox, poor flexibility and motion are all potential results of dehydration. In light of the consumption of coffee and sugar sodas, which leach water from the cells in the body, too many people are suffering from dehydration while thinking they may be suffering from a long list of other problems. *Drinking 8-10 glasses of good water every day will improve digestion, promote healthy skin and hair and assist your body in performing the millions of tasks of delivering nutrients and cleansing.* Thinking clearly and counteracting fatigue are equally enhanced by adequate hydration. Again here is a simple choice to make great strides in your health and performance.

Klaus Kummerer at the University of Luneburg, Germany says, "We don't know what it means if you have a lifelong uptake of drugs at very low concentration." Anna Fels, a psychiatrist and professor at Weill Cornell Medical College in New York City, wrote in a New York Times op-ed that lithium, an antimanic drug that decreases abnormal brain activity, is present in varying levels in the water supply and "has been largely ignored for over half a century." Surprisingly, lithium was also included in early recipes of the soda

7Up. "These drugs have been individually approved, but we haven't studied what it means when they're together in the same soup," says Mae Wu at the National Resources Defense Council, a U.S. advocacy group. Besides pharmaceuticals, there are varieties of dioxins, insecticides, herbicides, pesticides, chemical additives and heavy metals in our water supply, which when combined, create a toxic cocktail affecting every system in the body, even at extremely low concentrations," said Clarke Brubaker, environmental toxicologist.

No matter how controversial and/or negative some of this information sounds to you, not knowing what you are drinking and eating has enormous risk for you and your loved ones. I make no apologies for bringing the bad news to your attention. It should be considered criminal that our governments have allowed and approved the toxins in our food and water supplies around the world.

Scientists won't know what will happen with small children exposed to low levels of pharmaceuticals in drinking water for a generation. Paul Bradley of the U.S. Geological Survey and his team checked streams in the eastern U.S. for 108 chemicals, a drop in the bucket of the 3000 drug compounds in use. One river alone had 45 different drug compounds. Ninety-five per cent of the streams had the anti-diabetic drug metformin, probably from street run-off or leaky sewage pipes. The Environmental Science & Technology Journal states, "The number of chemicals we are exposed to is very, very large, and we don't understand those impacts."

Pharmaceutical and personal care products, or PPCP's, are being flushed into rivers from sewage treatment plants or leaching into groundwater from septic systems. According to the Environmental Protection Agency, researchers have found these substances, called "emerging contaminants," everywhere they have looked for them. Drugs given to animals are also entering the water supply. *One study found that 10 percent of the steroids given to cattle pass directly through their bodies; while another study found that steroid concentrations in the water downstream of a Nebraska feedlot were four times as high as the water upstream*. Male fish downstream of the feedlot were found to have depressed levels of testosterone and smaller than normal heads, due to the pharmaceutical contamination in their water. There are so many reports of contamination with pharmaceutical residues how can it be ignored considering the high rate of disease in N. America today? In 2004, the British government reported that eight commonly used drugs had been detected in rivers receiving effluent from sewage treatment plants. *Antibiotics are showing up in our drinking water, which should be very alarming considering that 65,000 Americans die per year from antibiotic resistant bacteria*. Some of the drugs have even been linked with diabetes, breast cancer, and kidney problems. Don't overlook the fact that healthcare facilities dump about 250 million pounds per year, which could end up in our water supply, and which include hazardous chemicals such as oncology drugs and toxic pain killers.

Take an interest locally in what industry and activities affect your local watersheds, rivers, and ground water and understand if corporations are doing their part to protect your water. Marine based fish farms, feed lots and many industries pollute fresh water to varying degrees. Many large cities in N.A. are flushing partially treated and in some cases raw sewage into aquatic environments. Victoria (Canada) pumps an average of 82 million liters of raw sewage daily into waters just off Victoria's harbor. In Feb. 2018 Quebec City dumped 42 million liters of raw sewage into the St. Lawrence River. Pouring untreated sewage into the world's seas and oceans is polluting the water and coastlines, and endangering the health and welfare of all people on the planet. The oceans are choking on our junk: soda bottles, everything plastic, and tons of cigarette butts, just to name a few. Distant spots in the ocean — called garbage gyres — have become vortexes where humanity's trash bobs atop the water for miles on end. According to Ocean Conservancy only 5% of the trash is visible on the surface with the other 95 percent submerged beneath, where it strangles underwater creatures, is consumed by them, and destroys marine ecosystems. Join an organization to help clean up our oceans, and at least be careful with your own garbage and get all recyclable materials to appropriate facilities (engine oil, paints, plastics, glass, etc. —recycle all that you can in your community). (7)

Clean, safe drinking water is scarce. Presently, nearly one billion people in the developing world don't have access to it, while in developed countries we take it for granted, waste it, and worse yet pollute it and drink it out of expensive and polluting plastic bottles. ***Water is the foundation of life*** and around the world today many people spend their entire day searching, collecting and carrying it. People from many communities walk miles just to fetch water each day. This consumes a major part of people's lives in water-poor areas. In fact globally, "women spend over 200 million woman-hours every day collecting water." (8)

March 22nd is World Water Day. Most often in literature, water represents cleansing, life and freedom. Water has often been referred to as the life blood of the planet, similar in purpose and volume to the blood that serves the same purpose in the human body. Here are 12 ways you can protect water for yourself and future generations: dispose of chemicals properly, take used motor oil to a recycling center, limit the amount of organic fertilizer used on plants, take short showers, shut water off while brushing teeth, keep a pitcher of drinking water in the refrigerator and get involved in water education.

More in depth actions our society needs to undertake are: prevent deforestation and destruction of grasslands which are nature's water filters; restore forests and grasslands that have already been lost or damaged and are eroding into our waters; equip farmers with practical ways to keep harmful run-off out of our waters; restore floodplains that act as sponges and send water down into groundwater supplies and filter pollution out of rivers, and help create new science that pinpoints the greatest threats to our waters and the most effective ways to combat them.

Most important of all, find a good source of clean water for yourself and be mindful of the value of water in your life. If you are unable to have access to clean water (reverse osmosis, verified spring water) research the best filter to assure you are drinking safe water.

Remember that fresh water is a finite resource on the planet and true value of water needs to be recognized for its interconnectedness to all life around the globe. Protect water everywhere and do not waste it.

Chapter 8

Life Goals

When you free yourself from certain fixed concepts about the way the world is, you will become aware of more options and choices because you have stopped thinking there are limited options for your life. If you don't believe success and happiness are possible for you, it most definitely won't be. *Make a decision to live an extraordinary life, and take control of your thoughts which will determine whether you achieve that extraordinary life or remain mediocre living up to other people's expectations and definitions of success. Your life is shaped by your decisions, not your circumstances.*

Decide what you want in every area of your life because you cannot hit a target that you cannot see. Many people go through life on autopilot. True living is being present in every moment — no matter how mundane. Consider facing a new fear each day, celebrating past and present relationships with friends and family members, exploring and enjoying the outdoors, setting and meeting new goals, and living charitably so others may grow to understand the abundant nature of the universe.

The following advice from a 24 year old young man who has been informed he has months left to live has great value for everyone. *"Don't waste your time* on work that you don't enjoy. It's stupid to be afraid of others' opinions. Fear weakens and paralyzes you. *Take control of your life.* Take full responsibility for the things that happen to you. Let your life be shaped by decisions you made, not by the ones you didn't. *Appreciate the people around you.* It is difficult for me to fully express my feelings about the importance of these simple realizations, but I hope that you will listen to someone who has experienced how valuable time is. I believe that we all have potential, but it also takes a lot of courage to realize it. You can float through a life created by circumstances, missing day after day, hour after hour. Or, you can fight for what you believe in and write the great story of your life. Leave a mark in this world. *Have a meaningful life*, whatever definition it has for you. Go towards it!"

Many expectations and attitudes toward youth by previous generations and educational institutions contributed to the rebellious nature of Youth. Life has changed so dramatically for Youth today that sometimes the challenge is to find a reason to be inspired. When one is inspired there is less forcing and pushing and a lot more enthusiasm. For all past generations there was a predicted and planned life for Youth. Either you took over your Dad's business, went into the armed forces or got married and had kids amongst many other expectations. As society shifts with the advancing technological revolution, expanding urban populations, shifting work force, globalization, competition, and climate change, for the majority of Youth there needs to be new perspective with new opportunities for health and success. (1)

If you are paying attention to your life, you are learning every day. In the past the mantras of work hard, raise families, and stick together in times of trouble were essential for survival. Today there is a challenge between reaping the benefits of and being grateful for past generations and challenging the political and corporate institutions that fail to support the health of your family, community and your country.

Dramatic changes to the economy and culture shape the choices and attitudes of Youth today. Previous generations are hardly in a position to judge Youth today, with stagnating wages, the expansion of part time employment, student debt, rapid technological change, soaring housing prices, the difficulties of making a dual-earner relationship work, the exorbitant cost of post-secondary education, and the overall uncertainty of our economies and labor markets.

Too often, young adults are judged for adapting to these negative conditions. Surveys show that 20- and 30-somethings are looking for more than just a job. They want work that is meaningful and consistent with their social and environmental values. For university students today the stress of debt and job market uncertainty is very high. With the shift from permanent jobs to a high percentage of part time work without benefits, even for the highly educated, the challenge of finding work that allows them to feel like they are contributing to something bigger than themselves persists. Many youth have decided if they can't find a meaningful job they will find a job that requires a minimum amount of their energy and time. Then they would have the freedom to find purpose and contribute to society outside of paid employment, and/or focus on play and recreating.

The challenge is to sort through the noise and do what lights you up, what you love, what you are enthused about. *You have to know your talents and*

put them to good use. You will be a lot more useful in your life and your neighborhood if you know your own skills, talents and sources of joy. Spend some time analyzing your interests; list the pros and cons of your favorite activities and your goals. Put it on paper.

Take time to fully understand what might be holding you back; question your fear, challenge yourself to do better and be better, face your limiting beliefs and behaviors. Don't forget to make sure that what you are trying to achieve is what truly matters to you. Know what moves you. We each have so much to contribute; it is our job to decipher what we are good at, and what inspires us. Keep in mind that if you want to be a singer and can't sing, or a mountain climber and are afraid of heights or an artist and can't draw then success may be further down the road than you thought. Not to say you can't learn to sing or paint or climb, just be sure it's what you really want. Know yourself and identify what you are good at and what you love to do.

Make lists, ask yourself many questions, have a plan and change it every day if necessary to move forward in your life. Make connections with people who share your interests, find 'older' folks who have already succeeded at something that interests you and approach them for guidance. Ninety-nine percent of the time they are willing to help and support you.

The bright side of your effort is that you have the chance to re-member and re-connect to yourself and the universe at large. **It is also important to keep your dreams to yourself, and choose wisely with whom you share your goals and plans.** Sabotage is everywhere, especially if you share your life with people who may want your dream to fail because of jealousy or dysfunction in their own lives. **Thoughts are energy in action** and if you throw your vision out into the world, be aware that there are people who want to keep you at their level of mediocrity. Be careful; protect your vision and plan for your own life. Some people may be afraid you will leave them behind as you succeed, and that is possible if you follow your dreams. You have to be prepared to move on, let go and trust that you will find others elsewhere who share your vision, your common ground, and your joy of discovery.

Why are people so reluctant to give up a wrong position, even while sensing how it injures them? **Be honest with yourself, you too can become your own saboteur making it easier to stay the same than to change**. What is familiar, what becomes a habit may be your downfall. Shake it off and start again, and be willing to start anew.

Imagine if people got as passionate about their happiness, their day, and their goals as they do about sports, for example. Ask yourself why you are not enthused, inspired and participating fully in your own life and then **be quiet and listen**. It is up to you after all; no one, absolutely no one can fix your life for you. And most importantly be patient with yourself. You may flip a switch and change directions or you may take one step at a time in order to find the correct direction for you. *Be patient*!

Don't overlook small details. Remember that the universe and everything in it are made from tiny atoms. If you take care of the little things, the big things will often take care of themselves. Sometimes overlooking small details can create big problems later. Keep in mind that taking care of a number of small details may open the door to an opportunity you might not have been expecting. You can avoid the consequences of procrastination (of which we all have experience) and be less hard on yourself for your own neglect, if you take care of the details as you go. If this annoys you or you easily put off these tasks, you must discipline yourself and set aside a specific time each day or week to deal with them.

Know your own mindset and change it or manage it to conjure up enthusiasm for necessary tasks because in many ways, thought is more important than lifestyle. *Attitude is everything*. Science has proven that if a person is told lies, or tells themselves lies long enough they eventually believe them. Do your best to be aware of what is really going on in the world around you, both close to home and in the greater world. All species except man instinctively live their lives based on their own natural cycles. Collectively, man has moved away from the natural cycles of the seasons, as an agricultural society. Be prepared with what you need to be well and work hard.

Identify your goals while keeping in mind they must be flexible for when circumstances change. Detailed plans are important as long as you are open to opportunity that might step in your way. Fulfillment of plans comes in all shapes and sizes and there are times when what you most want passes you by. Then you might find what is standing right in front of you, is something you hadn't been planning; but it fits perfectly into your life at that particular time.

Do your best to bring your dreams to life, not unrealistic fantasies. It is a lot of fun to bring imagination to the task of seeing yourself where you want to be. *Your mind works in images*, the first step to creating something in your life is to be able to see it in your mind. Don't forget to include all the details you might want. Divide your vision into Career, Friends and Family, Physical Environment, Health, Personal Growth, Money, Significant Other, Fun and Recreation, including all that you value for your life plan.

Again, pay attention to detail! Once you know what you want, it is essential that you break each goal down into smaller ones that you can work towards on a daily basis. Don't be resistant to making the effort to detail your goal, it doesn't need to be complex and most likely common sense and attention to detail is all that you need. For example, if you wish to be healthy

103

enough to run a marathon next year, you may need to start with a daily walk, faster paced as you build muscle and energy to meet that goal. Of course, along with learning and mastering whatever exercise you choose, you also need to pay attention to eating healthy food, good hydration, getting adequate sleep and managing your time to fit in your daily run. Approach your big goals the same way to lead you to your preferred outcome.

There are many resources out there to assist you in learning how to create a plan or take action on a plan already in place. The books 'Project Life Mastery', 'Mind of a Winner' and 'Life Planning Strategies' are just a few examples out there for you to investigate. You will find a list of books that will inspire and assist you as well in the Book Ideas in the back of the book. (2) (3) (4)

There are too many lives spent at jobs that take up a lot of time and energy just to look forward to a two week annual vacation. Don't forget to play and incorporate it whenever and wherever you can into each day because this is where you find the freedom to create and laugh and be happy. Attitude is everything and being happy daily is critical to success. This kind of success follows people who work at what they love and are inspired by their work. Though many may define success in dollars and acquisitions, I can guarantee that a truly successful life is recalled through adventure and happy times and spending time with people you care about.

Make a conscious effort to not feel overwhelmed when goals and plans and work intersect to create chaos and stress. When this happens, be realistic and perhaps allow motivation to simmer for a while. Don't ask too much of yourself. If we break down any kind of overwhelming experience into parts we can tackle our reaction and response one step at a time. It is often the attitude we have towards the task that creates a highly stressful day or a reasonable day. On days that may appear to not have a minute to spare, keep flexibility in mind and this will assist you in adjusting your schedule when necessary. Flexibility is a way to control your plan rather than letting your plan control you. At the end of a particularly full week it is fun or at least interesting to review how you handled it and this can give you an opportunity to revise the next day or week to better manage your success. *Keep in mind that somehow you managed to get to the place you are in right now*. Of course there can be authentic and extreme stress around some life situations, but a good attitude and flexibility will always assist you in taking the best course of action. As mentioned in other chapters if you are fearful, in crisis and/or don't know what to do, ask for help.

With any plan it is important to be willing to reconsider and perhaps redesign your plan because, after all, it is YOUR plan and life is in constant motion. Be honest with yourself, rethink your plans if necessary and renegotiate a change of direction if required. This process will assist you in assessing whether you can achieve the goals you have set. *The most important relationship you will ever have in your life is with yourself.*

If you find yourself disappointed with your efforts you can consider hiring a coach. You may need financial advice, a fitness trainer, a family planner, or an education advisor. There is great wisdom in getting sound advice from someone you trust and respect in order to move forward. The best coaches would offer you a sample session to determine if you fit together well enough to solve whatever dilemma you bring to the table. Shop around and pick someone that you feel comfortable with. If finances prevent this then set up a shared communication with a trusted friend and help each other sort out the next step for each of your plans.

A traditional example of making plans is New Year's resolutions. The goals people generally set on New Year's Eve are solid plans with the best of intentions for health, happiness and wealth. Statistics are fairly abysmal for these resolutions but it is never too late to dust them off and make a realistic plan to achieve them. These resolutions are essentially goals which always increase a person's well-being because they force you to consider what you value most. Make resolutions that matter. Knowing that each time you follow through you are a better person for having accomplished them. Consider perhaps 12 resolutions that are within your ability to manifest over the course of a year, one per month. This also can help you structure your time and meet monthly goals, all to your benefit. Perhaps take dinner to a senior you know, foster a dog, donate your time, service or things, volunteer at an animal shelter, become a big brother or sister, donate blood or help out the homeless. If you just look around in your daily life you will see where and who could benefit from your assistance.

You can accomplish anything you desire. If you can imagine it, you can create it. Don't let obstacles stand in your way because for the most part they all can be overcome. Creativity, desire and passion may enable you to achieve things you never thought possible. Dream Big! The Desiderata, is a prose poem written in 1927 by American writer Max Ehrmann and is one of the most inspiring poems of the 20th century.

Life is about change - biological, environmental and psychological change. Adapting to change is the key to survival. Prioritizing what is your most urgent and important goal is a first step to success. In order to make that particular goal number one you must know why it is important and why you want to achieve it. If you have chosen well, it will come with inspiration because of its importance. Take immediate action small or large towards achieving that goal. Remember, success is always an accumulation of small steps in a particular direction; all journeys begin with one step.

Desiderata, by Max Ehrmann (1927)

Go placidly amid the noise and haste, and remember what peace there may
be in silence.
As far as possible without surrender, be on good terms with all persons.
Speak your truth quietly and clearly; and listen to others,
even the dull and the ignorant, they too have their story.

Avoid loud and aggressive persons, they are vexations to the spirit.
If you compare yourself with others, you may become vain and bitter;
for always there will be greater and lesser persons than yourself.
Enjoy your achievements as well as your plans.

Keep interested in your own career, however humble;
it is a real possession in the changing fortunes of time.
Exercise caution in your business affairs, for the world is full of trickery.
But let this not blind you to what virtue there is;
many persons strive for high ideals, and everywhere life is full of heroism.

Be yourself. Especially, do not feign affection.
Neither be cynical about love; for in the face of all aridity and disenchantment
it is as perennial as the grass.

Take kindly the counsel of the years, gracefully surrendering the things of
youth.
Nurture strength of spirit to shield you in sudden misfortune.
But do not distress yourself with dark imaginings.
Many fears are born of fatigue and loneliness.
Beyond a wholesome discipline, be gentle with yourself.

You are a child of the universe, no less than the trees and the stars;
you have a right to be here.
And whether or not it is clear to you, no doubt the universe is unfolding as it
should.

Therefore be at peace with God, whatever you conceive Him to be,
and whatever your labors and aspirations,
in the noisy confusion of life keep peace with your soul.

With all its sham, drudgery, and broken dreams,
it is still a beautiful world. Be cheerful.
Strive to be happy.

Chapter 9

Education

Every child is born curious and hungry to learn. Every child is a genius according to the meanings of the word genius, which are: 'to give birth' and 'to be zestful or joyous'. The real meaning of genius is to 'give birth to the joy' that is within each child. It is imperative that educators and parents help preserve these genius characteristics. Cities, towns, and communities are built by trades people, bakers, teachers, health care professionals, farmers etc., and it is a highly valued gift to learn a skill well and serve your community and prosper.

A new poll released by the firm 'Research America' illustrates that 81% of Americans are unable to name a single living scientist. When asked by pollsters, the results were: "Of the 19 percent who could correctly identify a scientist, 27 percent named Stephen Hawking, 19 percent named Neil deGrasse Tyson, and 5 percent named Bill Nye. Other answers that scored less than 5 percent included Richard Dawkins, Jane Goodall, and Michio Kaku." Dr. Jane Goodall is not just a celebrity who loves chimpanzees; she is a British primatologist, ethnologist, anthropologist, and UN Messenger of Peace and still is the world's foremost expert on chimpanzees. Additionally only 33 percent of Americans could correctly identify a health or medical research institution. (1) (2) As mentioned in many chapters, much of your reality is shaped by populism, Hollywood, social media, and politics. It is essential that your generation reach out to science and learn as much as you can about good science and learn to research thoroughly whatever questions you seek answers for.

Education is often discussed only in terms of schooling, and yet life itself presents opportunities every day for learning. Every event that you witness in nature is an ongoing opportunity to understand the world you live in. The more informed you are, the better decisions you will make and the more confidence you will have. A great part of the modern education system is filled with propaganda that only benefits the elite. Many people grow up thinking that N. America was founded by the British beginning in 1607 with colonization, or by Columbus in 1492. In reality, when the Europeans took over America, it represented perhaps the greatest genocide in history. American anthropologist and ethno historian Henry F. Dobyns estimated that more than 100 million First Nation people inhabited the Americas prior to Europe's arrival. How can any sensible person see this as a foundation for a just society knowing that our current education does not tell the truth of our own history?

A new study from Stanford University shows that Danish kids who postponed kindergarten for up to one year showed dramatically higher levels of self-control. The decisions made at the very beginning of a child's education can shape that child's experience over time. "We found that delaying kindergarten for one year reduced inattention and hyperactivity by 73% for an average child at age 11," states Thomas Dee, one of the co-authors and a Stanford Graduate School of Education professor. The results showed waiting one year virtually eliminated the chance that an average kid at age 11 would have higher-than-normal scores in hyperactivity and inattention.

Inattention and hyperactivity—the traits of Attention Deficit Hyperactivity Disorder (ADHD)—weaken a child's self-control. Finland and Germany start students in school relatively late and they score well in international tests for 15-year-olds. Educators and parents think of this as lost time in educational pursuits for children, while really this time is called childhood. Having children should equal a belief in the future, the next generation and prosperity. Their education is critical to shape and influence that future. But sadly, there is the reality that young parents may not have the luxury of keeping children at home because they are working two jobs to pay the high cost of living including childcare in N. America.

Quality education is at risk when our institutions of education, medicine, religion and politics become so corrupt and controlled by corporations and greed that they begin to implode on themselves. What happens when the information you read or hear does not reflect your reality? What happens when scientists are not able to speak freely? What happens if the safety of food in the grocery store is suspect or when the water you drink has been fluoridated and chlorinated? What does it mean when it is recommended that between 6 months and 6 years of age a child receive 30 plus vaccinations? What does it mean when genetically engineered GMO's, canola and sugar are found in most foods in the grocery store? Why have 38 other countries banned GMO's, while in N. America the biotech industry says it is nutritious and safe? All of the above is happening right now. I would love to convince you that they are robbing you of a super life, stealing your future but I said I wouldn't do that. I can, however, ask you, beg you, to be open-minded and educate yourself on all these subjects.

Of the 236 countries in the world today, the U.S. ranks third in population after China and India. Therefore, the influence of the people of one of the largest and most powerful countries in the world can significantly impact the future for all. According to a 2006 survey by National Geographic, nearly half of Americans between the ages of 18 and 24 did not think it necessary to know the location of other countries in which important news is being made. (3)

In N. American schools, the culture exalts the athlete and good-looking cheerleader. Well-educated and intellectual students are commonly referred to in public schools and the media as "nerds," "dweebs," "dorks," and "geeks". These anti-intellectual attitudes are not reflected in students in most European or Asian countries, whose educational levels have now equaled and will surpass that of the U.S. Most TV shows or movies such as The Big Bang Theory depict intellectuals as being socially inept geeks.

Oklahoma Educator Rob Miller blogs about 'hugging a porcupine' while explaining complicated young people today. *So many young people in schools today are smart and bright and kind and troubled and hurt and angry all at the same time.* For your entire time spent in school too many of you have struggled to overcome trauma, despair, learning challenges, and a self-defeating mentality. There is no doubt that most young people wrestle within to stay balanced, to calm inner turmoil, to make friends, to trust adults, to show compassion, to love themselves, and to learn with any consistency. I can tell you if you have patience and compassion for yourself and reach out to people around you with the same, the relationships that you build will serve you throughout your life.

John W. Traphagan, Professor of Religious Studies at the University of Texas, argues the problem is that Asian countries have core cultural values that are more akin to a culture of intelligence and education than a culture of ignorance and anti-intellectualism. In Japan, for example, teachers are held in high esteem and normally viewed as among the most important members of a community. Teachers in Japan typically are paid significantly more than their peers in N. America and the profession of teaching is one that is seen as being of central value in Japanese society. Also in Japan there is not a prevalence of religious schools that are designed to shield children from knowledge about basic tenets of science and accepted understandings of history and evolution. The reason for this is because in general *Japanese value education, value the work of intellectuals, and see a well-educated public with a basic common knowledge in areas of scientific fact, math, history, literature, etc. as being an essential foundation to a successful society*.

Recently the New York Times posted an article saying we are creating a world of angry dummies who feel they have the right, the authority and the need not only to comment on everything, but drag down any opposing views through personal attacks, loud repetition and confrontation. You have all observed how the herd mentality takes over online; the anti-intellectuals become the metaphorical equivalent of an angry lynch mob when anyone either challenges one of the mob beliefs or posts anything outside the mob's self-limiting set of values. *The virtual world on line directs people towards trivia, the inconsequential, towards unquestioning and blatant consumerism*. Psychology Today sums up that people accept without questioning, believe without weighing the choices, and join the pack because in a culture where personal agendas become the norm, real individualism requires too much effort. Thinking takes too much time and gets in the way of the immediacy of the online experience. *Whatever you do, resist becoming a participant in the powerful new strain of fact resisting humans. Become an active, conscientious evaluator of information*.

Daniel Levitin wrote; 'A Field Guide to Lies; Critical Thinking in the Information Age' (2017). He writes that we have created more information in the last five years than in all our preceding history. Along with the endless stream of information comes a profusion of misinformation, half-truths and un-truths. With new forms of media we need a new form of literacy; much of the misinformation is based on misunderstanding and emotion. Levitin writes - the age of screens has "no central authority to prevent people from making claims that are untrue." And so his book calls for independent analysis; anyone who consumes easy, cheap, fast information must understand how to verify that information themselves. It should be clear by now that nobody else is doing it for you. The truth is lost when artful quotations alter the original work and the new concept of something going 'viral' supersedes the value of a story based on truth. Levitin's book is a great start to realize how important it is to question what you read and learn how to check sources and facts. *Otherwise, you may get lost in loops of false data, political rhetoric, spin, and drama*.

Do not blindly accept the opinions of others without using your own intelligence and experience to determine fact from fiction. Education can also distract you from what is most valuable to your community and democracy. William Shockley was awarded the Nobel Prize in physics in 1956, and he was also an unrepentant racist. What is education if it is used to support a set of racist ideas? Prejudice, biases of all kinds, and racism are embedded in text books and attitudes throughout education today. Simply changing curricula and policy is insufficient because the problems are embedded in the social consciousness. The hidden curriculum, language and teaching practice perpetuate racism in subtle ways. The absence of the truth of history alone supports racist attitudes and lies. The hidden curriculum is a reflection of the sociocultural and economic-political structure of society. It is therefore easy for teachers, without intention to do so, to encourage existing power inequities by reinforcing social attitudes through their own prejudices and stereotypical assumptions about student capabilities and cultural behavior. For example if a teacher has low expectations of a student or unconscious assumptions about race, this can have an enormous impact on a student's life. Teachers can empower or disadvantage different students unless teachers examine their own values. *Multicultural education is often taught as having tolerance for others*. Acceptance of others holds far more truth than mere tolerance. Education must challenge the idea of white privilege and begin to recognize differences without categorizing people by race.

In a transcultural, well-travelled world our concepts of education and schooling need to evolve. Students need to be better prepared for the world of work; they need to be taught how to develop their emotional self to nurture cultural wealth and a healthy inner being; and equally important, they need to be taught how to create a civil society. The morality of education and the pursuit of social justice are needed to provide a foundation for each student to build a life on. (4)

Somehow rhetoric has replaced discussion and instead of productive communication and debate we live in times when having a difference of opinion has become a crime. Some of the issues are so polarized that one must be wholly in one camp or the other which is never where the truth lies. I am not exaggerating when I say your life and your future children's lives depend on your ability to form your own opinions, educate yourself and find the truth. You can and you must, if you want to live long and prosper. It isn't rocket science; it is simply you educating and thinking for yourself. Learn to question what isn't serving you or your community. Do the research and inform yourself because it matters, your future health depends on your awareness and your willingness to decide for yourself. We live in an age when access to information is the easiest it has ever been. *Whether your source is an educational institution or the internet or the library, your challenge is to be able to check sources and verify that what you are reading is true, based on good science and observation.* Greed and money have become the currency of information today, especially if it involves corporations that profit from their medications, oil companies that profit from their exploitation of resources and banks and governments that trade the health and livelihoods of their own citizens to play the games of politics and war. (5)

Humility, says Levitin, is one of the most important parts of critical thinking. We must do better than default to outrage, and trade our opinions and facts as if it doesn't matter. We must educate ourselves partly by becoming critical of our deepest-set beliefs and learn to recognize fact from fiction.

Dr. Richard Horton is the current editor-in-chief of the Lancet, which is considered to be one of the most well respected peer-reviewed medical journals in the world. Dr. Horton stated in 2015, "The case against science is straightforward, much of the scientific literature, perhaps half, may simply be untrue. Afflicted by studies with small sample sizes, tiny effects, invalid exploratory analyses, and flagrant conflicts of interest, together with an obsession for pursuing fashionable trends of dubious importance, science has taken a turn towards darkness." It takes tenacity and time to thoroughly investigate the truth. I have had many debates with young scientists who refuse to accept that there is an influence of money and conflict of interest on science. When pharmaceutical and other big corporations financially support and influence universities, and research, one is left struggling to find authenticity in research. *The greatest challenge really is for you each to determine who and what to believe.* (6)

Surely you must wonder about global leadership today simply because of the widespread poverty, severe inequality and perpetual insurgence of war around the globe. *If countries honestly focused on the health and welfare of their own citizens, the world would turn toward peace and a hopeful future.* It makes no sense to me, with the challenges we face globally, that anyone can afford the distraction, destruction, loss of life, and cost of war. However, that is exactly why wars will continue, fighting over dwindling global resources financed by tax payers and profited by countries and corporations and their greed. *Educate yourself on priorities at the local level in your community, your city, or your region and evaluate them in the context of global priorities.* Food, shelter, clean water and safety have remained the same basic priorities since the beginning of man's time on the earth. War has become a tool for corporations and governments to fight and profit over resources and land, while the majority of people in the world want to live a peaceable life.

Your bank makes multiple billions of dollars in profits annually on the backs of its customers paying the customer low rates of returns for their investments and making exorbitant profits off customer's investments for shareholders. Banks should be paying customers better returns to justify the enormous wealth of all banks.

For centuries, education was reserved only for men. Women in Canada were given the right to vote in 1917, Britain in 1918 and the United States in 1920. Late adopters to women's right to vote in Europe included Spain in 1931, France in 1944, Italy in 1946, Greece in 1952, Switzerland, as well as several small countries in 1971. Not long ago young women in high schools throughout N. America were told to be nurses or secretaries, certainly not doctors or lawyers. Harvard Medical School accepted its first female enrollees in 1945 — though a woman first applied almost 100 years earlier, in 1847. Women began petitioning Harvard Law School for admittance in 1871. It took the School 79 years to finally open its doors to women in 1950. The patriarchal imbalance in rights and freedoms between men and women has shaped everything about your society, your education and your politics. Your generation is really the first to benefit from significantly greater possibilities for women if they have the desire, and passion and funds to pursue them.

Parents have always wanted the best for their children, for them to have more opportunity than they had in their own lives. It only makes sense that society invest in the next generation. After all, who will be boss when the boss retires? Who will teach and who will govern when the rule makers get old? In N. America, student debt is fairly unbelievable. The Association of American Medical Colleges (AAMC) summarized that 84% of medical students graduate with a debt of between $170,000 and $200,000. In the United States, student debt totals an astronomically high $1.2-trillion (USD) and plagues some people all through their working lives and into retirement. Statistics Canada reported in 2012 that $28.3-billion was owed in student loans. Many countries in Europe offer free post-secondary education. In 2017, New York became the first state in the U.S. to make tuition free for middle class students at both two- and four-year public colleges. The reality that some countries outlaw women from attending school and/or university still baffles western thinking.

There are well over 25 prominent nations, which continue to discriminate against females and prevent them from acquiring an education. Equal education, is a basic human right, and essential for social change. Investing in education for women generates high social and economic return, and increases economic growth and sustainable development. India values virginity and purity over education for women. In Cambodia, where the entire educated class was eradicated in the 1970s by the Khmer Rouge uprising, only

15% of women are able to seek higher education today. The education rate for Pakistani women is among the lowest in the world. In Nepal, only seven percent of students actually make it to the tenth grade, and many Nepalese young women are sold into bonded servitude or raised to learn to run a household.

Afghanistan is one of the hardest countries in the world to be a woman. Nine out of 10 women are illiterate; 40 percent of Afghan girls attend elementary school and only one in 20 girls attending school beyond the sixth grade.

Chadian women face cultural and social challenges and have one of the highest rates of underage marriages in the world, with their husbands controlling every facet of their lives.

In Papua New Guinea, 60 percent of females are illiterate and that number is even higher in rural areas. Primary education is neither free nor compulsory, while violence against women is common place.

In Haiti, one-third of girls over the age of six never go to school with numbers even more staggering for those living in remote areas and 38 percent of the country cannot read or write.

The Thomas Reuters Foundation declared Egypt to be the worst Arab state for women in the world. After the Islamist political party Muslim Brotherhood came into power in 2012, women's rights have been drastically reduced, including their right to an education. And yet before the 2011 revolution, Egypt was one of the better countries in the Middle East for education rights for women.

Morocco, Yemen, Guatemala, Iraq, Rwanda, Benin, Tajikistan, Bangladesh, Malawi, Bhutan, Niger, Ethiopia, Mali, Gabon, and Palestine have extremely limited access to education for girls and women and high illiteracy rates.

Access to education is a basic human right for all genders, races and ethnicities. Though there is still more work to be done, residual and often blatant patriarchal influences around the world are still the main reasons peace and raising and feeding children have yet to be prioritized over war.

Travelling throughout your neighborhood or exploring the globe has long been recognized as one of the greatest educational pursuits. Building character, personal strength and wisdom are what you gain through adventure on any scale. Travelling is defined as going anywhere on foot or any other form of transportation. Exploring the environment where you live and beyond teaches you about culture, politics and diversifies your repertoire of choices in thought and action that make your life better in all ways.

As with all things in life it is valuable to be well informed of the choices you make when you travel. Believe it or not there are some countries you may travel to today where unbeknownst to travelers; the entire cabin of the plane with you in it will be sprayed with pesticides. You will have no choice to disembark and avoid this. Check before you fly if this concerns you or you could always carry a portable mask to prevent breathing it in. You might also shower and change clothes as soon as you reach your destination.

On top of that there is also a phenomena called Aerotoxic Syndrome, or fume events that occur in 1 flight in 100. Simply put it is a little known term used to describe exposure to contaminated air. There is a documentary called "The Truth about Aerotoxic Syndrome". Not only is this of concern for flight attendants and pilots on the plane, but passengers as well. Some people may suffer neurological effects. Compromising the neurological fitness of pilots should be of concern to passengers and airline companies. Because of the constant presence of fumes and the fact that modern jet aircraft have no chemical sensors installed and only visible smoke is officially reported in the flight log, there is cause for concern and safety for all on and around the plane. Background levels of contamination may not be detectable by smell at all. Likely the most toxic of the hundreds of chemicals present in the bleed air, the organophosphate TCOP, is in fact, odorless.

Presently there are only a few airlines worldwide that are investing in new technology to test air quality in airplane cabins. Passengers take for granted they are safe, however following hundreds of incidents, some causing death in March 2016, a debate in the British parliament resulted in MPs calling for a public inquiry.

Dare to think for yourself. How badly do you want to live a great life and have a future that is bright and rewarding? The escalating environmental damage of climate change, ocean pollution & acidification, species loss, water shortage, soil exhaustion, resource depletion and ubiquitous pollution may be sufficient to undermine the foundations of our modern civilization. *It is a truth that, as we have given our authority to governments they have done a poor job of it so far.* All of this is happening because of the lack of foresight and wisdom of all the institutions we have allowed to decide for us. Choose your own future. *It is never too late to be educated, make a change and become part of a solution for your life and the world in which you live.*

Education is simply the process of receiving and giving information. For some it may be through university or college, for others it may be travelling, for most of us it is through living each day questioning the status quo, finding answers to all our concerns and fulfilling our own mandate for our best life. Caring for your family and others in your communities, as you solve problems and make life better for those around you, is an integral part of your education.

There is more information available to more people most of the time than ever before, while innate intelligence is diminishing by the year and the experts say technology is dumbing us down. You must master the ability to decipher truth from fiction in what you read and study. This means not settling for the first documents you encounter that happen to agree with your point of view. Keep digging; keep searching for the whole truth in order to best teach yourself and then pass it on for the betterment of others.

Keep in mind that for some very significant scientists and visionaries who have come before you, at the end of their lives what really mattered to them was that they were a good human on a vibrant planet, learning and teaching on their journey. Put a high value on critical thinking, humility and keeping an open mind. Seek the truth and apply it in the context of humanity globally and invest in your future through quality education.

Chapter 10

Truth is the New Frontier

If politicians, religious leaders, military leaders and teachers were allowed or were courageous enough to tell the truth the world would be very different. Many who tell the truth are ostracized or fired or imprisoned by the very institution they represent. Governments around the world speak through a complicated and contrived matrix of misinformation and misdirection (called political spin) which of course has kept the world at war for centuries. If truth were spoken the problems of hunger, disease, clean water and the need for healthy food would be solved. Through capitalism and corporations, and government corruption, these institutions via the patriarchy have maintained power over the masses for too long. When the truth is buried how can peace ever prevail?

The question of 'What is truth?' has been debated for thousands of years. Man has always sought the meaning of life, and there can be no meaning without some ultimate truth. Many people believe that ultimate truth is related to the existence of God. Those who would deny the existence of God say there is no absolute truth and that everything is relative, which then must vary from one opinion to the next. Truth is often held to be opposite to falsehood. Perhaps rather than define truth, it is easier to determine how one would recognize truth when it confronts you in a life experience or decision that you must make. Here are four factors that determine truthfulness: 1) congruence (it fits the facts), 2) consistency (it has no contradictions within itself), 3) coherence (it confirms your established knowledge), and, 4) usefulness (your actions are successful when you apply truth). (1)

Truth must be more than true or false, black or white or a purely rational and logical way of looking at things. There is much more to truth than might meet the eye. Cultivate your personal understanding of truth and include your moral compass, your compassion and greater vision for humanity while knowing that reason is the only means by which truth can be established or known. When you incorporate your whole self into determining the truth you utilize your human intellect, your rational understanding, your ever increasing knowledge and your humanity towards all life.

What follows truth is action. Truth without action is a daydream, while action without truth can be a nightmare. Mahatma Gandhi said a long time ago, "You must **BE** the change you want to see in the world."

Truth is simple. Learning to hear the truth in your own life can be a great challenge. Your own thoughts may be the only battle many of you will ever fight. There are many tools available to help us learn to listen to Truth within our minds. Though Mindfulness has existed for centuries, science has finally brought it into the mainstream as a tool to quiet the mind, eliminate stress and manage the thoughts that make people victims. Instincts, inner knowing, the Truth will get you successfully through any challenge you face or decision you have to make. If you have been loved and nurtured you already know what is in your highest best interest most of the time. If you have not been loved and cared for you have a hunger for it and must always listen to your inner voice until you find it. **Whether you are in the midst of your most challenging or simplest moments, Truth is all that matters.** Truth doesn't change, ever. Nature has a finite law that maintains balance and harmony. I have heard too many times 'your truth' and 'my truth' but; all are simple disguises for differing opinions. Though we are each on separate paths that may cross periodically, the truth simply **IS. There is a correct action and a correct choice to make in all situations, whether personal or political.** Therefore have a keen eye and an open heart. Pay attention to relationships and what goes on in your environment every day. Much can happen in a day to distort your view and conflict your truth. You never want to give in to tantrums and emotional craziness because as soon as you are overcome by drama you totally lose the ability to hear or see the truth of the problem. **You cannot solve a problem at the same level that the problem exists.**

You get to choose, you really do - if you listen to your own inner voice. **It is absolutely true that what is in your highest best interest is always in everyone else's highest best interest and the earth's highest best interest and your relationships highest best interests, whether the people you are involved with are willing to admit it or not.** Though people around you may resist your choice, if it is for **your** highest good then it is for theirs as well - if they are willing to see it. Some people in your life may want to keep you at their level of mediocrity because your success is a threat. Some people might be afraid to lose you if you rise to your best life, and it may be true that living your own true life will leave some people behind. We all choose and we have to believe that our choice matters for us.

Truth can be lost if there is willful blindness, complacency, or simply by choosing to be a bystander. We must participate in our life. This doesn't necessarily mean taking high risks or action to intervene on other people's behalf, but sometimes action is necessary for us to fulfil our own purpose and take care of each other.

Truth can sometimes create fear when what is revealed is challenging. Humor is a powerful tool that breaks fear and has been utilized by many to influence change and awareness. "Blueprint for Revolution" is a successful movement teaching how to stand up for oneself and one's community with the help of humor to expose the truth. "Blueprint for Revolution: How to use Rice Pudding, Lego Men, and Other Nonviolent Techniques to Galvanize Communities, Overthrow Dictators, or Simply Change the World" is a brilliant handbook written by Srdja Popovic and Matthew Miller for anyone who wants to effectively (and peacefully) improve your neighborhood, make a difference in your community, or change the world. (2)

Cosmic intelligence exists in every cell of your body through evolution, and exists in all of nature and the universe at large. The planet you live on thrives and balances, and co-creates based on cosmic intelligence every minute of every day. You are part of that greater world. Paying attention and intending right action leads to right action.

Mark Twain told us, "When a lie is already half way around the world the truth is just getting its socks on." Filtering through enormous amounts of data to decipher fact from fiction can be exhausting compared to accepting what's presented to you. We have all seen the drama of politics, family conflict and lack of money, love, food or shelter. Often the drama becomes the reality and the merry-go-round becomes the societal norm. *But, by accepting the simple version of Truth, you can have peace in your life every day.* Though you may not at this moment influence world politics or solve the world's bigger problems, by observing cause and effect in your own life choices and actions, you harness a powerful teacher of Truth. You only get out of life what you put into it; make your contribution count for your own safety, happiness and success.

Remember, for every action there is a reaction. So make informed decisions based on truth and reality. Believe in every action and choice you make. Know and understand the truth and you will succeed and find peace in a world that appears to be circling with chaos.

Truth is the foundation for a fair and just society.   In court, we require witnesses to swear to tell 'the truth, the whole truth and nothing but the truth', because only that way can justice be delivered. When you choose to not be honest, stress and negativity will follow. You came to this life with the best of intentions to be honest with yourself and fulfill your own purpose. What is in your truthful best interest is always in the best interest of all others in your life.

Be authentic and live your life according to measures of honesty and compassion and you will be drawn to those who believe the same.

Chapter 11

Family

Consider yourself blessed if you have a family that loves you and supports you. It is the absolute best start and foundation for creating a good life. If you have a family that you feel didn't give you that foundation, no matter the reasons or circumstance, then you simply must create a circle of people in your life who will become your family. I am sure you have heard it said that people do the best they can with what they know. If their experience was based on lack rather than abundance of love and nurturing, the limitations may seem endless. Learn how to deal with people who push your buttons, especially if they are family, and you will create an essential skill to break free and live your life, your way.

The first step is to identify your own buttons. Take the time to honestly assess each of your relationships, and decide if they serve your best self. When someone pushes your buttons, it presents you with an opportunity to know yourself better. Anytime someone 'pushes your buttons', a phrase that means someone has provoked you into a response or strong feeling, it gives you an opportunity to look inside yourself and understand why you are reacting and how to resolve that conflict within. Most often these conflicting reactions that encourage arguments and more conflict come from a place of fear, insecurity, and or a lack of self-esteem or self-worth. When you feel these strong reactions to what others say or do, consider them as signals or reminders for your own internal assessment and renewal. This is where success in relationships and solving problems begins. How can you assess another's influence in your life if you don't know your own issues and resistance, your own fears and challenges? You can learn to be gracious in your response to conflict with family and friends, or at least be calm and quiet. We can assess who honestly supports us, gives us good advice and doesn't demand from us what we cannot give. We simply must learn who to walk away from and who to walk towards. Family can be the solid foundation from which you build a life encouraged with love and support. Family can also assert a hold over you and possibly guilt you into your loyalty and obligations to them. In generations past (and still in many countries around the word), obligation to family was essential to survival. Just living through a season together took a team effort. As with the wolf pack each relied on the other for survival.

We are all grateful to be here, grateful to those who made our lives possible. Today we determine our loyalties based on mutual respect, love and common good. We can be grateful to be part of a successful and loving family. We can also walk away from families that do not support our dream and we can find people to become our new family. It is no easy decision to leave people behind. You need to examine loyalty and love and understand that what is in your best interest, is truly in the best interest of everyone, even if that means you are moving on without them. You can also be grateful for all your family has given you, remain in their lives with generosity and kindness, but keep your distance. *Mastering the art of telling the Truth in relationships that matter to you is the gift that keeps on giving.* If drama surrounds you, keep telling the truth even if it is uncomfortable, knowing that change is inevitable when you stand up for yourself.

I have had clients make a stop sign for themselves. The stop sign is simply a way of giving yourself permission to stop the destructive behavior: the thoughts, the argument or fight, the worrying/wondering/making excuses for someone/blaming self/and on and on. The stop sign simply brings an end to the conflict in the moment. It allows everyone to take two or three breaths and find a calm place within. It doesn't mean that you wipe the slate clean. It means you pause, resolve or take action, and move forward without the pain that prevents your happiness. Resolving family conflict is a strengthening experience that can remind us of the resilience of the human spirit and how much stronger relationships can become through strife and determination at reconciliation. Remember though that, for some people resolution is not possible.

Many of us have to decide to stay or go and that decision must be made with a quiet mind and honest analysis. Moving on from relationship conflict doesn't always mean you will never see that person again. You can have a relationship from a distance based on mutual respect and in whatever capacity you choose. It no longer matters that they may or may not move forward or want the same things you do in life. Their lives are up to them. You can find the words and tell them that you need to stop the conflict because of the huge difference between both of your opinions and behaviors. In the moment there are many ways to stand up for oneself with truth, respect and compassion. There can be a fine balance between negotiating and telling the truth. As discussed in Chapter 16 (Relationships) and Chapter 29 (Politics), non-violent communication is a proven and successful tool that teaches how peaceful communication can create compassionate connections with family, friends, co-workers and even politicians to create healthy environments for solving problems. (1)

There are so many people to truly connect with, so many people who want what you want in action and words and fun. Finding a way to protect yourself in a challenging situation is a skill you must develop. People might be shocked and surprised by your approach to telling the truth with compassion. You must be committed to moving forward with or without people who want to hold you back.

When people tell you who they are, believe them. When someone shows you who they are believe them. Stop making excuses for others or for yourself. Pay attention to the red flags in relationships that people too often ignore or convince themselves the other person will change or worse yet that you will fix them.

The human family in all its eccentricities can be a wondrous and creative endeavor. We all know the brilliance that comes to each of us when we witness a crisis. Most of us willingly engage in helping those in need and give of ourselves, our homes and our resources in an emergency. This same reserve of generosity and care must infiltrate your daily life. With the knowledge that we can rise up and give of ourselves we can make our daily relationships better. **Now is what matters.** Our lives are a collection of the moments we have right now. Each new moment is guided by our behavior, thoughts and actions.

The Nigerian proverb "It takes a village to raise a child" reminds us that children are a blessing. When a neighborhood or community or family takes a responsible role in raising a child, in supporting a child, everyone wins. A child has the best chance to become a healthy adult if people care during their growing years. Life is easier when you are part of a network of family, friends, extended family and neighbors.

The U.S. Census Bureau still defines "family" as consisting of two or more people related by birth, marriage, or adoption residing in the same housing unit. *A new definition of family is simply a close-knit unit of individuals joined together without distinction of race, ethnicity, biology, sexual orientation, age, generation, or presence in households, cemented through bonds of love and respect.*

'The Four Agreements: A Practical Guide to Personal Freedom' written by Don Miguel Ruiz reveals the source of self-limiting beliefs that rob us of joy and create needless suffering. Based on ancient Toltec wisdom, The Four Agreements offer a powerful code of conduct that can rapidly transform your life to a new experience of freedom, true happiness, and love. The four agreements are simply; be impeccable with your word, don't take anything personally, don't make assumptions and always do your best.

The concept of family has changed rapidly in the past few decades and with that in mind build a family of your own wherever you find yourself whether for the short term or the long term. *Be true to yourself and be true to them and you will find support and love on your journey.*

Chapter 12

Emotions

We are here to be happy, inspired and creative in our lives, our jobs and in all of our choices. If you are not happy, take the time to understand what you are actually feeling and why. In most cases of unhappiness, or sadness or depression, you can look into your thoughts and see that you would never allow anyone else to treat you the way you treat yourself. Too often we get used to being 'hard' on ourselves, expecting more of ourselves than others and repeating thoughts and words in our head that can drive us deeper into sadness or failure. Even with all the campaigns against bullying, too many people continue to bully themselves. *Vibrant physical and spiritual health, inner wholeness, self-command, self-decency, and kindness are virtues that we must first experience for ourselves before honestly offering them to others*.

   As in every chapter I remind you that good nutrition, good water and adequate sleep are foundational ingredients that must be present for emotional well-being. What you put in your mouth every day equals attitude, resilience and mental clarity or lack thereof. What comes out of your mouth in words is greatly affected by those three ingredients for good health. Words have power; words do create and influence your reality. Be mindful of your words. 'The Four Agreements: A Practical Guide to Personal Freedom' as mentioned in Chapter 11 Family offers the simplest of guidelines to assist you in maintaining emotional health. Always worth repeating are the 4 agreements; 'Be impeccable with your word', 'Don't take anything personally', 'Do not make assumptions' and 'Always do your best'.

New research by UCLA neuroscientists has revealed surprising information to help us understand our emotions better. *Science now shows us that guilt and shame activate the brain's reward center*. Despite their differences, pride, shame, and guilt all activate similar neural circuits, including the dorsomedial prefrontal cortex, amygdala, insula, and the nucleus accumbens. Pride is the most powerful of these emotions at triggering activity in these brain regions — except in the nucleus accumbens, where guilt and shame win out. This explains why you might too easily heap guilt and shame on yourself because you are activating the brain's reward center with your thoughts. Even more surprising, worrying can help calm the limbic system by increasing activity in the medial prefrontal cortex and decreasing activity in the amygdala. That might seem counterintuitive; if you are feeling anxiety, worrying at least tells the brain you are doing something about the anxiety. We absolutely all agree that guilt, shame, and worry are not helpful for long-term health.

The good news is that science also shows us that the benefits of gratitude start with the dopamine system, because feeling grateful activates the brain stem region that produces dopamine. Gratitude toward others increases activity in social dopamine circuits, which makes social interactions more enjoyable. The most important key to finding gratitude is to remember to look for it in the first place. *Remembering to be grateful is a form of emotional intelligence*. One study found that it actually affected neuron density in both the ventromedial and lateral prefrontal cortex. These density changes suggest that as emotional intelligence increases, the neurons in these areas become more efficient. With higher emotional intelligence, gratitude comes easily. *Gratitude is also responsible for creating a positive feedback loop in your relationships.*

Science also shows us what happens when negative emotions take over and become so overwhelming that we get stuck. In one of the studies described in Alex Korb's book 'The Upward Spiral: Using Neuroscience to Reverse the Course of Depression', titled "putting feelings into words" participants viewed pictures of people with emotional facial expressions. Predictably, each participant's amygdala activated to the emotions in the picture. But when they were asked to name the emotion, the ventrolateral prefrontal cortex activated and reduced the emotional amygdala reactivity. Consciously recognizing the emotions reduced their impact. (1) *Studies also found that people who tried to suppress a negative emotional experience failed to do so.* While they thought they looked fine outwardly, inwardly their

126

limbic system was just as aroused as without suppression, and in some cases, even more aroused. Kevin Ochsner, at Columbia, repeated these findings using an fMRI (functional Magnetic Resonance Imaging) and determined that trying not to feel something doesn't work, and in some cases even backfires.

To reduce arousal of the limbic system, you need to use just a few words to describe an emotion or experience. This requires you to activate your prefrontal cortex, which reduces the arousal in the limbic system. *What this means is that by describing a negative emotion in just one or two words helps reduce the emotion.*

If you find yourself in an emotional and/or challenging situation, try to *become the observer in your own life.* Visualize a version of yourself in your mind watching and listening to the thoughts, actions, and words surrounding you. This takes the emotion out of the scenario and helps you truly observe yourself and get a better handle on what your next word or step should be. It is a common tool in meditation to simply observe the thoughts travelling through your mind. By not focusing on a negative thought you can more easily ignore it and choose to move on from there. It works in actions and in thoughts and is a great tool to help maintain emotional sobriety and balance.

Emotional sobriety is not being addicted to drama. It may be different for each person. Like recovery from other addictions, there are phases and step programs to help the body adjust and be free. We all know how much drama surrounds us. Become an observer first and take steps to maintain a healthy emotional balance. Of course feel anger, and regret and sadness whenever it arises; just don't stay stuck there. Move through to balance. The crisis likely still exists. However, if you insist on emotional sobriety you will find the grace to solve most of your dilemmas. Being restored to a reasonable and sane state doesn't always result in actual happiness or joy. It is essential, however, to move in that direction. You can't go anywhere productive in the midst of drama unless you separate yourself from it.

Meditation has used this principle for centuries and it is often labeled a fundamental tool of mindfulness. Putting a name or label to an emotion is an important way to get out of drama.

It is important to put up red flags in your mind when you feel out of balance. Hunger, anger, loneliness and fatigue significantly affect your wellbeing, your decision-making and your success. Be aware of them. The commercials about people not being themselves and needing a chocolate bar are very clear-cut. Eating well to maintain balanced blood sugar level (instead of hypo or hyperglycemia) can be the difference between creating an accident and getting home safely. An obvious example is children throwing a tantrum in a grocery store, the solution could have been as simple as giving that child something to eat. Adults are really no different, no matter how grown up you think you are. Symptoms of low blood sugar can be sweating, shaking, nausea, dizziness, headaches, blurred vision, irrationality, irritability and a multitude of more extreme symptoms.

Often in families, individuals can hold onto grudges for decades. In many different relationships it can seem easier to hold a grudge than to let go of the stressful thoughts. One grudge alone can displace you from accessing your own personal happiness and your ability to make the right choice. And on the mild side, your day can be infused with a feeling of fatigue, inattention and lack of focus.

Recent studies tell us that a human brain takes 25 yrs. to fully develop. So give yourself a break and create a daily plan that incorporates intentional joy, active imagination and self-nourishment.

We can save ourselves so much grief if we learn to say NO and not make a big deal out of it. The ability to say no is closely linked to self-confidence. People with low self-confidence and self-esteem often feel nervous about antagonizing others and would rather say yes than have to deal with whatever fallout comes with saying 'no'. Instead of defaulting to a yes you can ask for more time using words like 'I'll get back to you' and then you can take time to carefully weigh your options. Often saying no is confused with rejection, while it is a simple refusal of a certain task or request. Learning to say no is an essential life skill to learn in order to experience your own exciting life adventure, not someone else's. Don't fear the word 'no', it may seem an intimidating two letter word but it is very liberating for your personal development. It can be used with grace and efficiency and when you are honest with another person you will earn their respect.

The age of selflessness when generations were taught that everyone else comes first and we are selfish if we come first has shifted. Now we know that the better we care for ourselves the more we have to give others. *Place a priority on making your well-being a top priority*. If you have not considered priorities in your life, then practice on simple daily chores. *Prioritize a good sleep, a good breakfast, a good thought for the day; these are all ways to learn prioritizing the best for you.* If you learn to prioritize your own health and wellbeing, great things will happen in your life and in your relationships.

Invest some time in understanding the role fear may or may not play in your life, your decisions and your personal relationships. Sometimes fear shows up on your face and can't be denied, while other times it disguises itself as anger or perhaps lethargy. Many have said there are only two emotions, love and fear. Fear is often disguised as anger, guilt or shame. However at its root the real emotion may simply be fear. Fear of being judged, fear of being not enough, fear of the truth, fear of loneliness and on and on buried so deep that anger is often the only emotion visible. All the thousands of words for varying emotions that are negative are simply disguises for the root cause which is fear. All the thousands of words for good emotions are simply various ways of expressing love. You have likely been given a lot of advice about fear throughout your life. Fear is not always simple, it can be a multi-dimensional character that may take time and effort to decipher and understand.

Physical fear has served all animals and mankind well since man first walked the earth. There is *warning fear* that rises from the gut to direct you to avoid injury or harm. This fear is a valuable protector. There is *ego fear* whose job it is to keep your fragile inner self safe. This fear can lead to a slippery slope of intolerance to those who are different, convincing you that race, religion, sexuality and belief systems that differ from yours are inferior or to be judged. These feelings create separateness and make others less than equal. Essentially, we are all equal. This kind of fear must be deconstructed within yourself so it doesn't control you. Wars around the globe and within communities have been perpetuated for generations because of this kind of destructive fear.

Invitational fear is the kind of feeling you get, almost a physical trembling that is a message from your body to step into something important and life changing. It's an invitation rather than a warning and can lead you into right action.

Lastly there is *trauma fear* that has a way of embedding fear so deeply into your body that you can barely understand it or control it. This trauma can change a person so fundamentally that it has been known to alter DNA. Some trauma fear has been inherited from generations before you or traumatic events in your life. This kind of fear can be so irrational that it can flare up at the slightest trigger causing a fight, flight or freezing reaction that nobody watching can understand. With this kind of fear you must seek assistance from health care professionals or trusted mentors to understand, cope and heal.

Whenever you sense fear of any kind (unless you need to run to save your life) take time to listen to your inner voice and consider your next step. Our greatest tool to live a fantastic life is to understand and know ourselves. Listening to your body and your inner voice is the pathway to do this. Your body understands things your brain doesn't know how to process, so learn to listen and pay attention.

Do your best to avoid feeling sorry for yourself. Self-pity is an addictive drug. The more you allow yourself to indulge in it, the more you will require. Once self-pity becomes a habit, it can be so debilitating that you become immobile. If you can retrace the clues, step by step by following them backwards to get a clear and honest picture of how this happened, you can show yourself a path to heal. You must stop feeling helpless and choose to find your way to clarity with or without help. Sometimes in the midst of pain, fear or anger you must have the patience to wait for the dust to settle in order to begin the process of understanding. *It is critical to accept how you feel rather than deny how you feel.* Fight or flight saved your life a time or two generations ago when running from a wild animal. There is only one letter difference between the words fight or flight, a fine line between running and holding your ground, physically or emotionally. *Sometimes fear protects us and sometimes fear drives us into the abyss.* Understanding stress and managing your health and in particular the health of your adrenal glands is essential in managing fear. Your adrenal glands (tiny pea sized glands one on the top of each kidney) produce hormones that help the body control blood sugar, burn protein and fat, react to stressors like a major illness or injury, and regulate blood pressure. Two of the most important adrenal hormones are cortisol and aldosterone.

I have a friend who is in a negative situation, and he's hanging on for dear life because he wants to be brave and tough it out. He told me, "Giving up is not an option," which so many believe. But when holding on to something hurts your health and potential to be happy, you have to look closely at why you're choosing to stay. If you are too young to change your circumstances, ask for help. If you are old enough to start over and are afraid to leave, ask for help. Asking for help can be the first and foremost crucial step to your freedom.

Life is a balance of holding on and letting go. Romance, friendships, jobs, even places we live may have an expiration date. Perhaps our greatest fear is the unknown, which is why so many of us grasp, hold on to and manipulate our situations trying to control our surroundings. But the outcome is often the same - more pain, immense frustration and potential guilt and blame. *Avoid the toxic effects of staying in situations that no longer serve you.*

Nelson Mandela spent 27 years in a prison in South Africa because of his efforts to bring harmony and equality to South Africa. While in prison, his inspiration was a poem titled 'Invictus' by William Henley. Throughout his imprisonment he never lost sight of the poems message; "I am the master of my fate - I am the captain of my soul. " Whatever trials and tribulations are in your life, you too can find within yourself, the reservoir of strength you require to maintain wisdom, common sense and value for yourself.

Consider what is possible. In Virginia, a 22-year-old woman saved her father's life when the BMW he was working on slipped off the jack and landed on his chest, crushing him. With no time to wait for help, the young woman lifted the car and moved it off her father, then performed CPR to keep him breathing. In Georgia, another car jack slipped and landed a 1,350 kilogram (3,000 lb.) Chevy Impala on a young man. Without any assistance, his mother,

Angela Cavallo, picked up the car and held it for five minutes until neighbors could pull her son to safety.

In World War II, Joe Rollino served in the Pacific and was given a Bronze and Silver Star for his bravery in the line of duty, plus three Purple Hearts for his battle injuries, which landed him in the hospital for a combined 24 months. He is best remembered for pulling his comrades from the battlefield, one comrade under each arm, then going back into the line of fire to carry more of his wounded brothers to safety.

A semi-trailer truck careens over the edge of a cliff in the dead of night. The cab of the large truck groans to a stop while dangling perilously above the gorge below, with the driver trapped inside. A young man comes to the rescue, smashing out the window and pulling the driver to safety with his bare hands. This is not a scene from an action movie, but an actual event that happened in New Zealand at the Waioeka Gorge on October 5, 2008. The hero, 18-year-old Peter Hanne, was in his home when he heard the crash. Without thinking of his own safety, he climbed onto the teetering vehicle, dropped into the narrow gap between the cab and the trailer, and smashed through the cab's rear window. He then carefully helped the injured driver climb to safety as the truck creaked and swayed beneath their feet. In 2011, Hanne was awarded the New Zealand Bravery Medal for his heroic act.

These examples of superior strength and brilliance in times of need, tells us that reserve is within us moment by moment, day after day. When you learn to tap into it you will discover that limitless possibilities for your life exist within you. Never underestimate yourself. Knowing that reservoir is within, you can learn to use that energy and direct it towards your success. (2)

Emotional health is inextricably linked to physical health. It has already been accepted by conventional medicine that stress has a noticeable effect on heart disease and obesity rates. For example, your constant worry over finances may be causing your stomach upset or your spleen to become depleted of energy, thereby limiting your body's immune response.

A Dutch study surveyed over 4,500 people enduring stressful life events, including the death of a loved one, serious illness, or financial hardship. The people who lived within 3 kilometers of green space reported higher levels of well-being and fewer health complaints in the face of their struggles than those who lived elsewhere. Nature provides a more oxygen rich environment. Sitting in a park or taking a stroll among trees and flowers after a stressful day has been proven to lower blood pressure and heart rates, as well as reduce cortisol levels.

Science has established a unified theory of the universe and yet the most powerful unseen force is love. *Love is Light that enlightens those who give and receive it.* Love is gravity, because it makes some people feel attracted to others. Love is power, because it multiplies the best we have. For love we live and die. The power of Love is unlimited.

Love is the ultimate cure-all and most important of all, the love of the self, is where love of others begins. You might consider that a parent will love their child whether they love themselves or not. Consider the quality and immensity of love that a parent who loves themselves has to offer. So much more capacity for truth and generosity in raising that child exists when love comes from a place of self-love.

Some of the habits people too easily fall into regarding their own emotional health is failing to realize that there will always be people who will dislike you and/or people who will try to offend you. *Be truthful about people you spend time with.* Disruptions happen in all relationships. However, a return to encouragement and support must be the foundation for the relationship to prosper. *Don't waste time trying to please others.*

Keep in mind that blaming others takes an enormous toll on your emotional wellbeing. **Blaming makes you weaker and prevents you from taking responsibility for your actions and decisions.** Taking responsibility may come with consequences; however it is the only way to build a life based on honesty. A life built on honesty gives you strength down the road for bigger challenges, should they occur.

Value yourself for yourself, not based on how other people perceive you. Most of what you 'think' are other people's observations of your appearance, behavior, or choices do not occur. This is most often over-thinking and self-consciousness. Over-thinking is a trap that feeds the cycle of self-judgment. Most people don't think about you at all, unless they are close friends or colleagues that interact with you regularly. In truth, we obsess about others when most of the time they are not thinking about us at all. Most people are so concerned with their own inadequacies, that they don't have time to consider yours. *Remember, fear is the absence of love.*

Always remember that true happiness and emotional wellbeing come from within you, and can never be fully realized through a relationship with another. Through caring relationships with others you can build on your already solid center of happiness within you. *No one will complete you; you must complete yourself and be whole in order to find what you seek. And of course it is absolutely true that we become better and more whole people because of the good relationships we have in our lives.*

Consider a checklist that might keep you on your toes emotionally. Be aware of your emotions and your reactions. Learn to express your feelings in appropriate ways. Think before you act, consider giving yourself 60 seconds before reacting to be sure you are on track for an appropriate response. Manage your stress. Strive for balance between work and play and rest.

Always make your health a priority and remember exercise, adequate sleep, good food & hydration are essential ingredients in emotional stability. You are a social being, connect with others. Keep your eye on the prize of your goals and what is most important in your life. When you focus on the good people and things in your life you will attract more of the same. Keep in mind the greatest gift you can give another is the work you do on yourself.

Value yourself, love yourself, do your own personal work, remember the four agreements, don't be afraid to say no or let go and move on.

Chapter 13

Spirituality/Religion

"Real religion is the transformation of anxiety into laughter." Alan Watts
True faith is the opposite of clinging to belief. The underlying principle to any correct spiritual practice or teaching is to *do no harm*. Conventional religions are man's interpretations of the 'good book', no matter the culture or the book or the scroll. Though there is great wisdom in many spiritual writings today, most were written by man, generated many centuries ago and based on observations of life more than 2000 years ago. It is always in your best interest to form your own ideas of the wondrous wisdom of ages gone by. No longer does it serve you to believe another person's interpretation without your own personal questioning and understanding. *At the root of all spiritual teachings must be kindness, generosity, Truth and compassion.*

A spiritual principle is either true or it isn't. *Use common sense and make your life right with whatever divine principle rings true for you.* If you belong to a traditional religion be sure you are truly able to hold to your own spiritual truth without surrender. I have no desire to criticize religions. Good churches, synagogues, mosques, fire pits, etc. are places that create unity in community, and make people feel welcome and safe and are important parts of our social fabric.

Historically and still today the world has been at war over man's distorted views of religion for centuries. Can anyone in good conscience consider that fighting a war over religious differences makes sense at all? *Dare to think for yourself.* No matter how worrisome the information, the news, the latest catastrophe, no matter how bad it may seem, we as individuals can find a way through to see the light at the end of the tunnel. Change starts with your own life and understanding of your inner divine truth.

Religion and Spirituality mean different things to different people. My intentions are to summarize briefly what religions are in the world today. Over the centuries, millions of people have died for their religion, or because of religion. "Religion must have cause for the common good of man and nature and its loyalty must not be limited by national or racial boundaries", writes John Boodin in 'The Function of Religion, The Biblical World'.

Recent studies suggest a paradigm shift for Youth around the world from conventional religion to a personal spirituality around their belief in God. In a survey called 'Europe's Young Adults and Religion' published through St. Mary's University in London (2014), 16 -29 year olds were interviewed. The Czech Republic turned out to be the least religious country in Europe, with 91% of that age group saying they have no religious affiliation. Between 70% and 80% of young adults in Estonia, Sweden and the Netherlands also categorize themselves as non-religious. Just next door, Poland is noted as the most religious country where 83% of young adults identify as religious. 70% of young people in the U.K. identify as non-religious and in France, Belgium, and Spain, between 56 and 60% said they never go to church. (1) Along with the diminishing association with formal religions there is a study that summarizes 18 – 24 years old in sixteen of the dominant countries in the world who have a strong belief in God, whether they are associated with a religion or not. In Sweden, France and Great Britain 40 – 60% believe in God. 60 – 80% believe in God in Spain, Russia, Taiwan, and Canada. 80-100% believe in God in the United States, Italy, Mexico, Brazil, Poland, Iran, Egypt, Indonesia and Pakistan. (2)

Over centuries of debate theologians and scholars have determined that there are two forms of religions: conventional religion and true religion. *The first category refers to the three major religions of the world: Judaism, Christianity and Islam.* These are called the three 'monotheistic religions' or the 'Abrahamic religions'. They are called 'prophetic' because they believe in divine guidance revealed to their Prophets directly from God. The two things that all conventional religions hold as truth are that humanity is separate from God, and that humanity needs to be reconciled with God. The differences come in how that reconciliation is acquired. (3)

The origins of Islam come from the Qur'an (their Bible) which was verbally revealed by God to Muhammad through the angel Gabriel, gradually over a period of approximately 23 years, beginning on 22 December 609 CE (after Christ), when Muhammad was 40, and concluding in 632, the year of his death. (4)

The origins of Judaism are within the books that constitute the Torah, the Five Books of Moses, both written and oral, were given by God through the prophet Moses. The oldest texts come from the 11th or 10th centuries BCE (before Christ or before Common Era of man). They are edited works, and are collections of various sources woven together. (5)

Christianity originated in Roman occupied Jerusalem, a predominantly Jewish society, with traditional philosophies distinct from the Classical Greek thought which was dominant in the greater Roman Empire at the time. Christianity developed out of Judaism in the 1st century C.E. (after Christ). It is founded on the life, teachings, death, and resurrection of Jesus Christ, and those who follow him are called "Christians." The sacred text of Christianity is the Bible, including both the Hebrew Scriptures (also known as the Old Testament) and the New Testament. The Christian Bible was written over a span of 1500 years, by 40 writers. (6)

Conventional religion, as in the case of Judaism and early Christianity, assimilated many forms and symbols of paganism. Christianity accommodated pagan points of view and some practice as a way of adopting or forcing pagans into the Christian church. Paganism refers to the authentic religions of ancient Greece and Rome as well as surrounding areas. It originated from the Neolithic (Stone Age) era. The term, pagan, means country dweller. Pagans usually worship many gods, goddesses, and deities. They believe that everything has a spirit; therefore there are gods and goddesses of the forest, sea, and all aspects of nature. (7) (8)

The second category includes the other major religions (considered non-prophetic): Hinduism, Buddhism, Sikhism (a branch of Hinduism), and Zoroastrianism. These are considered non-prophetic, while there is the unsubstantiated claim that Zoroastrianism has a divine origin. The vast majority of believers in non-prophetic religions acknowledge the fact that their sacred scriptures are not authentic divine revelations, but rather the collections, writings, meditations, compilations, and sayings of revered men, passed down from one generation to another. These are considered to be 'true religions' because humanity and the common good of all man is their foundation. They profess to have no national or race boundaries and are loyal to humanity because man's entire destiny is interlinked. (9)

The Religious Right of the world teaches rigid, one-sided opinions of how women should live their lives, how men should treat women and how children should not think for themselves. Christian right or religious right is a term used mainly in the United States to label conservative Christian political factions that are characterized by their strong support of socially conservative policies. (10) In the U.S., the Christian right is an informal coalition formed around a core of evangelical Protestants and Roman Catholics.

The birth of the New Christian Right is traced to a 1979 meeting where televangelist Jerry Falwell was urged to create a "Moral Majority" organization. Prior to this date a person's faith had little impact on the way they voted. The Christian Right (the moral majority) focused on taking political action and began a strong union between the Republican Party and many culturally conservative Christians. The Moral Majority became a general term for the conservative political activism of evangelists and fundamentalists. (11)

Historically the U.S. separation of church and state was the cornerstone of democracy. "Religion and Government are certainly very different things, instituted for different ends; the design of one being to promote our temporal happiness; the design of the other to procure the favor of God, and thereby the salvation of our souls. While these are kept distinct and apart, the peace and welfare of society is preserved, and the ends of both are answered. By mixing them together, feuds, animosities and persecutions have been raised, which have deluged the world in blood, and disgraced human nature." (John Dickinson, Pennsylvania Journal on May 12, 1768).

"The new era of Religious Right politicians share a brand of Christianity, which is historically racist, homophobic, xenophobic, dangerously nationalistic, and exclusive. It is a form of Christian Sharia law, which forces those who believe differently into strict adherence to their version of "religious freedom." writes Tim Rymel, M.Ed., author and educator.

The confusion lies in the fact that most Americans support gay marriage and abortion rights, and recognizes and wants to change inequality and racist behaviors in American. And yet the politics of today in the U.S. are actively opposing freedom of choice for all Americans. Fundamentalist ideologies whether Christian, Islam, or any other, do not contribute to social progress. The new religious right endorses anti-science which threatens the world's environment, weakens education, and the lack of common sense and good leadership will negatively impact world stability and trust.

Be part of any religion, but please don't lose your personal truth and knowledge of what is right for yourself and the world. Instead, embrace the good parts and reject the bad. Know that each individual can have a powerful and loving relationship with the divine on their own terms.

Spirituality is a more personal approach to recognizing the miracle that you are. Many of the greatest scientists of our time realized in their later years that the divine spark exists and there is no explaining or proving it so.

There is faith that we are part of something greater than ourselves. *Our earth, ourselves, our combined relationships, our beating hearts, all represents a sacred truth of some kind*. Understand your own feeling in this matter and live up to it.

Einstein said that the most incredible thing isn't the existence of the universe but our awareness of its existence. We have been raised and educated to see only the linear drama of human existence. Make awareness the focus of your actions and choices. The challenge is to clear the slate of theological beliefs, faith-based concepts, and imaginary anticipations of a heaven or hell and investigate 'wonder'. Simple wonder at the very existence of the world, that nature is spectacular, magnificent and sacred, and let the sunrise and sunset inspire your heart and mind.

Jack Haas wrote 'The Way of Wonder' and reminds us that all is magnificent, all is marvelous and all is mysterious. He doesn't in any way suggest we give up the mind or the physical reality in which we live and breathe. He simply suggests we give up the assumption of 'understanding' what we are, what life is, and how we must therefore live it. We can rekindle the depth and simplicity of wonder. Babies and children experience wonder and discovery each moment and that wonder fills their lives. *This wonder might be the essence of Spirituality at the core of your being.*

Nature has been a focus of spirituality since the beginning of man on the earth. Nature is a place where we seek solitude, rejuvenation, reconnecting with plants, animals, ocean and freedom. The Earth provides our food, the trees provide our oxygen, and the planetary system provides us with the water of life. Ancient wisdom describes human beings as having five layers of experience: the environment, the physical body, the mind, the intuition and our self or spirit. If our environment is clean and positive, it has a positive impact on all the other layers of our existence. It is only logical that when we move away from our connection to nature, we begin polluting and destroying the very environment that sustains us.

Care and concern for the Earth is essential to our very existence. Strive to live in harmony with Nature locally and globally and you will foster respect and compassion for all human and non-human living beings on this earth. How is it even conceivable to not value the earth, your home? You know the value you put on your physical home, car, possessions even neighborhoods. How can that not apply to the natural world that feeds and nourishes you? We and all animal inhabitants are in this together. We all succeed and thrive or not, and your choices can influence this for better or worse.

However you phrase divinity, whether you use words like God, Nature, Buddha, the Divine, Allah, and so on, once you recognize that you are part of everything, your entire life view will change. Religions are man's many different interpretations of the spiritual realm. There is no suggestion here that you abandon a spiritual practice that may have been handed down to you for generations. *My suggestion is simply to fully understand, to question the worth and the influence of that practice so that it aligns with the Truth and does no harm.* There are a thousand names for God and many of us speak of greater intelligence, the source of all that is and all that is greater than what we now know.

Connect yourself to the greater intelligence that simply must exist in this glorious universe. To accept that man is not the top of the food chain of intelligence in the universe is a critical first step. Be open to that possibility and you will empower the good in your life.

Chapter 14

Society & History

As a whole, societies can consist of all people of all ethnicities, living in different places, speaking different languages, practicing different religions and are of different ages, genders, and sexual orientations. A healthy society makes it easy to live in balance with one another and nature. Any group of people can create a society in small neighborhoods or larger global communities through common interests, traditions or needs.

In poor countries of the world, 60% of the present population is under 25 years of age. It is a prerequisite for peaceful global development that the rights of children and young people be respected. Where there is war and conflict, there is often violation of children which leads to the continuation of violence from generation to generation. *The Nobel Peace Prize in 2014 was given to 17 year old Malala Yousafzay for her struggle to bring education and peace to children*. She reminds us - "Let us remember: One book, one pen, one child, and one teacher can change the world." How is it that countries sell weapons and invest in war, but cannot feed their own children?

General characteristics of a healthy society include economic security, ecological integrity, social equity and wellbeing, citizen engagement, and accountability. Look around you and assess the society you are participating in. It is time to create societies that enhance the quality of our living rather than the quantity of our consumption, and with that choice society moves simultaneously toward sustainability and a better life for the majority of society members. In today's world it is extremely challenging to have healthy societies when 93% of the world's money is in the bank accounts of 8 global families. With such extreme economic inequity comes social inequity making it very difficult to build a healthy society. The ever widening gap between the rich and the poor is almost incomprehensible.

Free thought requires a free society in which a clear line separates speech and actions, one in which violence can never be a justified response to speech. *'Blueprint for Revolution by Design'* written by Srjdja Popovic reflects how he brought down a Serbian dictatorship. His twin sources of inspiration are Tolkien and Monty Python. Popovic states, "If I had to choose one book to call my scripture, it would be Lord of the Rings (activists are hobbits, ordinary folk allying with a motley collection of unusual suspects – dwarves, elves etc. – to take down the Dark Lord) and Monty Python (dictators can't handle humor, and it makes being an activist fun). " He shows respect for national roots and differences and uses power analysis, quick wins, and clear narratives, identifies champions, allies, blockers and the undecided. This is a great and fun read considering the subject is revolution. *This book can teach you how to have grace and humor within your own life in areas you need to revolutionize*, for example dealing with bullies, conflict in families, and applying humor to your own conflicting thoughts. This is a great read and gets you out into the world with global information.

Consider wolf packs, bee societies and elephant herds where the primary value is always the health and protection of the young. Consider our human societies and the millions of hungry children, biased education, corporate control of food and medicine and the despair of the elderly. Some countries do better than others. However there is no point in trying to sugar coat any of today's reality for you. You get to choose what to believe, you get to inform yourself and make better choices.

Modern-day slavery exists around the world today in developed countries of the world as well as undeveloped countries. Modern slavery generates $150 billion for traffickers each year. Researchers estimate 40 million people are enslaved today around the world. Fifty percent are in labor slavery, 37.5% are in forced marriage slavery, 12.5% are in sex slavery, and 25% of slaves today are under the age of 18. The shock is that this happens in the open, where people can go to a farmhouse, place a bid and end up 'owning' a male laborer for $400 or paying more for a female person. India has the largest concentration of slavery in the world today. Millions are in debt bondage, where loans illegally enslave laborers. In Asia, Africa and the Americas and in every country around the world, people are working for little or no pay, controlled by threats, debt, and violence and though it can be called by many names, it is in fact modern slavery.

After 600 years of discrimination, racism and colonization around the world there is a price to be paid. Foreigners invaded other people's lands and took the resources and got rich with not only zero revenue sharing with the transfer of resources but the intentional destruction of the peoples that lived there. There are currently around 194 countries in the world and more than 90% of them were colonized. All the countries were colonized at some point in time by the UK, France, Spain, Portugal, Sweden, U.S., Denmark, Germany, China and Japan. The extreme consequences of colonization and inequality in all its aspects influenced conquered countries to then become colonizers themselves in neighboring countries. The melting pot of violence and poverty for the conquered represents billions of suffering humanity today.

Dr. Alberto Villoldo has travelled 7 continents over decades and written of Indigenous peoples around the world. In his book Shaman, Healer, Sage he describes the three sets of beliefs that Europeans and Conquistadors brought to the Americas that were incomprehensible to Indigenous peoples. "The first was that all of the food of the world belonged by divine right to humans – specifically the Europeans – who were masters over the animals and plants of the Earth. The second belief was that humans could not speak to the rivers, to the animals, to the mountains, or to God. And the third was that humankind had to wait until the end of all time before tasting paradise. Nothing could have seemed more absurd to the Indigenous Peoples of the Land. While the Europeans believed they had been cast out of the Garden of Eden, the Indigenous peoples understood they were the stewards and caretakers of that very same Garden. In addition to the silence of the European God, the American Indians were confounded by His gender. The conquistadors brought with them a patriarchal mythology that intimidated the North American feminine traditions. Before the arrival of the Spanish, Mother Earth and her feminine forms – the caves, lagoons, and other openings into the earth – represented divine principles. The Europeans imposed the masculine divine principle – the phallus, or tree of life. Church steeples rose to heaven. The feminine Earth was no longer worshiped or respected. The trees, animals and forests were available for plunder."

The challenge, the enormous challenge for your generation is to know the truth, be wise and build a safer reality and future for all. I suppose in reality this has been the task for each new generation before you, however the stakes have never been higher as now and the consequences dire given the over population and rampant chaos.

Youth today don't understand their own history and institutionalized racism is a disease of heart and mind. For example 95% of the population of

North America are settlers or descendants of settlers. Archaeologists believe that the Aboriginals first came to the Australian continent around 45,000 years ago. The first fleet of British convict ships invaded Australia a mere 200 years ago and the population of aboriginals over the next hundred years was decimated from an estimated one million to 60,000 who were then imprisoned in camps and their lands stolen. Just imagine that a so called civilized country, like Britain, shipped 164,000 convicts to Australia. Robert Hughes in his book 'The Fatal Shore' describes the majority of the criminals as starving women and children convicted of stealing cheese and other menial crimes. The last convict ship, the Hougoumont, left Britain in 1867 and arrived in Western Australia on 10 January 1868. In all, about 164,000 convicts were transported to the Australian colonies between 1788 and 1868 on board 806 ships. Knowing our global history can be traumatizing in its horror and violence; it's up to you to decide whether you need to know this history or not. Indigenous peoples around the world suffered the same fate. One of the greatest flaws in our humanity is that somehow history is forgotten, and then repeated. *If we collectively remember the devastation and violence of our species history would we not choose differently for our future, for the future of our children?* Aldous Huxley wrote in his essay "A Case of Voluntary Ignorance" in 1959; 'That men do not learn very much from the lessons of history is the most important of all the lessons that history has to teach.'

Decolonization is a goal for those who have been colonized today. Decolonization restores the Indigenous world view, restores culture and traditional ways, and replaces Western interpretations of history with Indigenous perspectives of history. It was once viewed as the formal process of handing over the instruments of government to the peoples who were colonized and today is recognized as a long-term process involving the bureaucratic, cultural, linguistic and psychological divesting of colonial power.

Indigenization recognizes validity of Indigenous worldviews, knowledge and perspectives, identifies opportunities for indigeneity to be expressed and incorporates Indigenous ways of knowing and doing. *Dignity can be defined as the power to control one's own life*. It must be acknowledged that there is not a homogenous Indigenous worldview, and that each Indigenous nation or community will have their own unique worldview.

Both decolonization and indigenization require the cooperation of Indigenous and non-Indigenous people, governments, organizations and institutions.

In previous chapters I have noted that inherited views and cultural rules can be outdated and you can be faced with a great challenge to decipher what is correct for you and your life in the complex societies we are all immersed in. *In 1929 Jung pointed out 'inherited presuppositions' can shape your thoughts* and actions throughout your life. *Jung points out that racism and prejudices are taught and inherited from parents and institutions of education and authority.* We all must stop racism and violence against and amongst each other. While not forgetting the past and using the lessons of the past to move forward there is a great deal for all of us to let go of and allow, in order to improve our societies and neighborhoods.

There are volumes of research on the negative impacts of watching violence on television, video games and other forms of social media. There is always vicarious trauma to the viewer who witnesses violence, whether in person or viewed on a screen. Studies have shown that children who view violence on a screen or play violent games, become less sensitive to the pain and suffering of others, are more fearful of the world around them and may be more likely to behave in aggressive or harmful ways toward others. When it comes to violence in the media and its influence on violent behavior, it is a risk factor for crime.

Carl Jung states, "The collective unconscious comprises in itself the psychic life of our ancestor's right back to the earliest beginnings. It is the matrix of all conscious psychic occurrences, and hence it exerts an influence that compromises the freedom of consciousness in the highest degree, since it is continually striving to lead all conscious processes back into the old paths." *In simpler terms, herd mentality, mob mentality, or gang mentality describe how people are influenced by their peers to adopt certain adverse behaviors that an individual without influence might not choose.*

The Dalai Lama writes, *"Since armies are legal, we feel that war is acceptable.* In general, nobody feels that war is criminal or that accepting it is a criminal attitude. In fact, we have been brainwashed. We have been trained to be impassive to the horrors of war. Some former soldiers have told me that when they shot their first person they felt uncomfortable but as they continued to kill it began to feel quite normal. In time, we can get used to anything." It may be true that some wars in the past were necessary to preserve safe societies, and it is absolutely true that we honor the brave men and women who fought for our freedom. *In the year 2018 it is time to collectively work toward peace on all fronts.*

Did you know that only a handful of corporations, six to be exact, control over 90 percent of the media? Thirty years ago 90% of media was held by 50 different companies. Today 6 companies are in control of your media and they are General Electric (GE), News-Corp (own the top 3 newspapers on 3 continents), Disney, Viacom, Comcost, and CBS with a total revenue in 2010 of $275.5 billion.

While rules in your home, at work and in your society may keep you safer, there can be a cost to rules. As Charles Eisenstein discusses in 'Ascent of Humanity', even sidewalks result in an illusion of safety with greater risk to the pedestrian who walks alongside cars travelling at high speeds assuming the safety of the street-sidewalk contract while neglecting any real responsibility to pay attention to potential risks. This sidewalk/street contract is a far greater risk today with so many people staring at their cellphones while walking.

The choice you get to make is to be part of the solution in a healthy society that is supportive and encouraging and prioritizes peace and wellness. If you begin with yourself and a friend, your small family unit, your work team or neighborhood, you will begin the change that is essential for your success and the success of the society around you. *As an individual you have a great deal of power to shape the society you live in.* Use your intelligence and your generous heart to be part of a healthy community from which a healthy future can grow.

A popular Community Poster summarizes many of the choices you can make: Turn off your TV. Leave your house. Know your neighbors. Look up when you are walking. Greet people. Sit on your stoop. Plant flowers. Use your library. Play together. Buy from local merchants. Share what you have. Help a lost dog. Take children to the park. Garden together. Support neighborhood schools. Fix it even if you didn't break it. Have potlucks. Honor elders. Pick up litter. Read stories aloud. Dance in the street. Talk to the mail carrier. Listen to the birds. Put up a swing. Help carry something heavy. Barter for your goods. Start a tradition. Ask a question. Hire young people for odd jobs. Organize a block party. Bake extra and share. Ask for help when you need it. Open your shades. Sing together. Share your skills. Take back the night. Turn up the music. Turn down the music. Listen before you react to anger. Mediate a conflict. Seek to understand. Learn from new and uncomfortable angles. Know that no one is silent although many are not heard. Work to change this. (1)

In the new media age, everyone is an expert and those who think they know the most are the least to be trusted. Television has become a virtual reality for so many. The majority of the world's population in developed countries now lives in urban areas. Rural living has become impossible for so many small communities where work is limited and schools are closed. Moving to the big city is the new reality, even though research shows higher happiness levels in rural areas. Research also shows us the longer the commute to work the lower the happiness levels. Commuting has become a way of life for millions of people due to housing shortages and high cost of living in greater metropolitan cities. In N. America millions of families have moved to bigger cities because of weakened economies in rural towns and communities.

It is absolutely true that when you make better choices for yourself, and when you care for yourself you are doing a great service to your society. Helping yourself first changes your life and the lives of those close to you for the better. That in turn offers an opportunity for others to learn from your example. It is obvious that loving oneself and being mindful of self-care creates a more positive output to give others. Make an effort to have fun and be better, faster, stronger, healthier and wiser all the while knowing that what is in your best interest is in the best interest of your community and society.

The greatest challenge and greatest opportunity for Youth today is to explore the history of our species and decide how humanity best serves life now. The vast majority of the 7.5 billion humans on this planet are focused primarily on living their lives as best they can under the circumstances they were born into. Most of us fall easily, some reluctantly, into a nature of generosity, compassion and pragmatism. Food, shelter, and as much comfort as can be mustered in these times are the focus for most people. Historically (and presently) the authority of the minority influences our simple and most basic needs, along with promoting consumerism and conflict around the globe. Just living is a full time job for most. The influence of the 'minority with authority' goes unnoticed, until freedom and choices for common folk become limited or are taken away. With the world's eight richest billionaires controlling the same amount of wealth as 3.8 billion of the poorest people, Oxfam warns that this ever-increasing and dangerous concentration of wealth is a great threat to world peace.

Human history has been influenced by conflict, great and small, since man first walked the earth. It serves you well to take an interest in our history and its impact on the life you are living now. Too many history books have left out vital information to represent the truth of how our different societies have evolved. Consider the Shifting Baseline Syndrome; if we are not aware of atrocities of the past that shape our future, how can we possibly correct the path we are on? You get to choose who you support or elect, the actions you support, the direction you take and the decision to believe enough in yourself and your loved ones to work this democracy of ours. *Consensus means to work together at home, at work or at play to allow for everyone to be safe and free. Democracy is defined as the control of an organization or group by the majority of its members. Which do you think is better or possible?*

Somehow memory has failed our species. If the horror and pain of war were truly remembered how or why would a country again go to war? There are countries today who are global bullies, countries who compromise all good sense in their quest for resources in places other than their own lands, and we still have countries that meddle in the elections and politics of other countries because it serves their best interest of greed and corruption. Citizens in these affected countries are just struggling to make a living and care for their families. The time has come for the safety of all to take the power out of the hands of the few who never fight their own battles or go to war themselves. They send youth to war instead of investing in shared common goals and peaceful solutions. *Creativity and genius are everywhere; we need to stop believing that violence is the answer to anything.*

Take, for example, hierarchies of the past and their preoccupation with Cura Mulierum, the care of women. Of course, in order to control and take care of women, it was first necessary to make both men and women believe that women couldn't care for themselves. The care of women has always presented a problem for governments or religions in the past. Handling surplus populations in the past has been a perpetual challenge. In order for authority to keep control, populations need to be best managed for productivity and acquiescence. Handling surplus men hasn't been difficult in the past as war, dangerous work, lethal rites of passage or taking over a new frontier have been easy ways to decrease the population of young men for thousands of years. The nature of man was straight forward in that a gang chief or general simply talked them into frenzy and sent them into battle; the promise of honor and a medal was sufficient. This is history and in no way negates the honor and gratitude that we hold for men and women who have given their lives for our freedom. If you research the history of our great wars, the facts that led up to the wars, the politics and greed underlying the transfer of power and weapons to the evil warmongers of the past, you will find that power and greed were the primary motivations. Knowing your history is critical to building a healthy future. The evolution of the working man was factory-driven. Employers generally got men to use up their lives in a factory job providing for families; when old and worn out they were set aside with inadequate pensions. *Men are generally team players and team spirit is a tool that authority has used to direct entire populations of males for centuries.*

Women were convinced that they could not provide for themselves, because a long, long time ago women were perceived to be poor team players. Our culture has been carefully orchestrated to keep women in competition with each other and isolated doing their biological duty of bearing and raising children. The multi-billion dollar fashion and cosmetic business today is to keep women in competition with each other. This is not to suggest that fashion and beauty and feeling 'dressed for the occasion' isn't important. We each celebrate our beauty in personal and sometimes elaborate ways. The truth is, men are easily impressed, whereas women, consciously or unconsciously, are in constant competition with each other. The strategies of control through the centuries are well documented. **One example of many is Purdah, the practice among women in certain Muslim and Hindu societies, of living in a separate room or behind a curtain, or of dressing in all-enveloping clothes to stay out of the sight of men or strangers.** Purdah always worked well, as long as no one ever saw your wife or daughters. It was easy for men to be at the center of all power as long as women were separated and isolated. Purdah is an agent in service to a system that insures women's subjugation. In no way do I suggest that women who choose societal clothing to match their religious beliefs are incorrect on any level. You choose what works for you and best supports your true self.

A few examples of bizarre society ideas *are women in China binding their feet* until they could barely walk. Beginning at about the age of five a girl's foot was virtually folded in two and a 10-foot long bandage was wrapped tightly around it to force the toes down toward the heel as far as possible. Eventually the feet lost all blood supply turning the skin blue; portions of the soles and toes sometimes actually dropped off. This led to women shuffling instead of walking, frail and unstable. The definition of 'mincing' is to walk or move with short, affectedly dainty steps. The practice has died out in China, however in Jo Farrell's historical photography book 'Living History' there are many women alive today whose feet were bound 50 – 60 years ago. Over the past century in China, as a result of female infanticide and sex-selected abortion, there are an estimated 30-40 million more men than women.

From the past to the present the most efficient strategy to control women has been economic. Our societies are based on these old attitudes that led to paying women so little that they couldn't survive or not hiring them at all because 'women belong in the home.' The wisest, most prosperous and hard-working women in the offices of CEO's and politicians today still work harder than men in the same job for one-third less pay. The 10,000 plus years of the patriarchy have kept women enslaved to men's ownership and control and only recently have women found some success through determination and creativity to become more free in their own societies. Any opposition to equal freedoms and rights for gender, race or religion should not be tolerated. Gender equality is good for everyone. Privilege is invisible to those who have it. We all need to understand class and race and gender and how it pertains to each of us and the truth about inequality. Objectivity in discussion is always challenged if a woman is speaking of gender inequality, and if a man is speaking of it then somehow he is accepted as more objective. There are many men who still see gender equality as detrimental to men.

Michael Kimmel, in his Ted Talk on Women said, "Without confronting men's sense of entitlement we will never understand why so many men resist gender equality." Gender equality is in the best interest of men. If we listen to what most men want in their lives, gender equality is the way for them to get what they want in their lives. Studies have shown that companies who have gender equality have higher success, less job turnover, a happier and healthier workforce and higher rates of productivity. Studies have also shown that gender inequality is extremely expensive and the economics alone of gender equality should convince businesses and corporations that this should be a goal. Gender equality is good for business.

Thankfully most young men today want this change in their lives and in the businesses they are involved in. Generally young men want equality with their coworkers, their friends and their spouses. This is a tremendous shift for a better future for all. Younger men today are demanding balance between work and family, are taking parental child care leave with the birth of their children and have equity in decision making with their partners. Data shows that when men share in housework and childcare their children do better in school, have lower rates of absenteeism, are less likely to be labeled with ADHD, and their children and partners are healthier and happier. Men want this. Gender equality benefits households, businesses, countries and the world. *One hundred years ago, during the suffragette movement when women demanded the right to vote, New York writer Floyd Dell helped start the Men's League for Woman Suffrage by writing "Feminism will make it possible for the first time in history for men to be free." He also published 'Women as World Builders' in 1913. (3)*

From the 16th century to the 19th century fashion in Europe and N.A. dictated women wear corsets that made the waist so tiny women actually broke ribs and suffocated wearing them. Hollywood's ideal female figure in the 1940's was Marilyn Monroe measuring 36:24:36. For the previous 300 years a corset forced the waist measurement as low as 18". With 'tight-lacing' that 24 - 30 inch natural waistline would be shrunk by many inches. Then and now corsets have evolved to girdles, compression lingerie and constricting under garments. The corset expressed contradictory messages: constriction and freedom, dominance and submission, femininity and power. In 1966 'Twiggy' became the model icon weighing 112lbs at 5'6" tall. The current culture that dictates women shape their body to suit current trends reflects social values of violence, war, sex, nostalgia and conservatism.

Around the world the 4-6 inch stiletto high heels of today can lead to abnormally lengthened calf muscles, stretched spines and chronic back pain. There are so many more absurd examples of compromise and control of women by the patriarchy of the past and present. Keep in mind that men's shoes are basically designed in the shape of a human foot. A similar contradiction in common sense was an obsession in the past by the taste of Northern Copper Eskimo women for a style of boot that let in snow but was

149

attractive to men because of the waddle it inflicted on the wearer—a fashion statement not unlike the ancient Chinese custom of foot binding or the 20th-century high heel shoe. Of course the argument is easy to make that women love to wear high heels, though the corset and binding of feet might be out of fashion, it doesn't change the fact that it is painful and damaging to ones' own body and health.

Some *Burmese women stretch necks with brass rings* and thus depend on them to hold up their heads as the spine weakens. From as young as five years old, Kayan girls are given up to ten neck rings to wear, and add a new one approximately every year until adulthood. The practice, which gives them a giraffe-like appearance, painfully compresses their shoulders and collarbones, rather than actually stretching their necks. *Lips are enlarged with disks in Brazil. In Central Africa the Mangbettu tightly wrapped the heads of female infants* in pieces of giraffe hide to attain the elongated, cone-shaped heads that were considered a sign of beauty and intelligence.

Whether vanity or low self-esteem, or societal dictates, one constant factor remains that most cultures through the centuries have wanted women to be thin. Anorexia may seem to be a uniquely late-20th century disease, but being thin is nothing new. Robin Henig in her book *'Civilizations'* states "In ancient Greece, mothers wrapped their baby daughters tightly in bands of wool or linen for the first six months or more in hopes of elongating their proportions to the willowy, slim ideal of the time. In England in 1665 a health pamphlet taught that overweight women should be bled 'largely twice a year, an eerie predecessor to today's binging-and-purging syndrome known as bulimia. In the 1930s women actually swallowed tapeworms to lose weight." There are countries today where being an overweight woman is a sign of prosperity, particularly where a long history of droughts and famine exist. Tahiti, a tropical paradise in French Polynesia is known for celebrating the well-rounded female form. The Tahitian appreciation of ample body shape goes back to the traditional practice of ha'apori. Literally meaning "to fatten," according to this ritual, young women were made to put on weight so as to be presented to the chief for beauty and fertility inspection.

Modern cosmetic surgery is also a method to increase a woman's 'market value'. There are many industries that thrive on women's insecurities that strive to convince them that their face and body are not adequate and need a boost that only their products can provide. In the Elizabethan Age many women in search of skin that looked like porcelain whitened their faces using ceruse, a potentially lethal combination of vinegar and lead - ladies who wanted to achieve the porcelain look 'naturally' took to swallowing whitening potions made of vinegar, chalk or arsenic, the latter of which is poisonous even in tiny amounts.

Are these male defined forms of beauty? What is at the root of these self-deceptions, and on some level dissatisfaction for whom you are born to be? This is an interesting and enlightening history to better understand for sure.

Society expectations of men over centuries are absurd as well in their complexities and conditions for manhood. Men have been expected to fight and win at all cost since the days of the cave man. A number of other gender expectations of men are the expectations of competition, of status consciousness, of financial success, strength and athleticism, leadership skills, mechanical skills, easy erectile functionality, a dehumanizing attitude towards women, and the message that to be manly you must be tall. What can a person ever do about the height they were born to be? Men have been taught to not feel, not cry and to bury or set aside grief for too long.

Gender roles are taught and learned, and research shows that people treat infants they think are female differently from infants they think are male. Youth today are shedding these society expectations and warped views of gender.

Beauty is not about distorting who you are, how you walk, what you eat or how you fit into society's version of constructed beauty. According to recent surveys, men's view of beauty in a woman is condensed into these points: intelligence, confidence, the character of her smile, optimism, her ability to understand things that men cannot, the sound of her laughter, and her acceptance of her body as beautiful. There are eight traits, both physical and behavioral, that actual scientific research has found that women find attractive in men. They are: a sense of humor, leadership skills, compassion, emotional stability, maturity, loyalty, intelligence and physically attractive. From Wikipedia, 'Beauty is a characteristic of an animal, idea, object, person or place that provides a perceptual experience of pleasure or satisfaction." Because physical beauty changes with time and experience, true beauty of the heart and the mind last a lifetime. In essence, beauty is in the eye of the beholder, so be kind to yourself and others in this regard. (4)

It is long overdue that young men and young women must challenge the aggressiveness and control of patriarchal culture. Why? Because it lacks the quality of excellence humans ought to aspire to. The #metoo campaign has raised the bar for conversations about gender and violence. It is inspiring to observe so many people waking up to this reality and actually considering the changes necessary for our society to become healthier in regard to gender equality. There are many opinions and sides to this entire debate and at the very best it is in the public forum for all to discuss. The pendulum always swings to the extreme opposite before finding middle ground between opposing opinions where the solutions wait. Measured against the present circumstances around the world, we must build new life-possibilities for ourselves and for society. With careful understanding we must all examine contemporary culture, traditional religion and popular culture, in order to build a better and more equitable future for all. Choose to keep the big picture in mind as you move forward in your life. *Working together, talking about the truth of our collective history, and actively letting go of shame and guilt that is not yours to bear will help to change the world.*

Understanding colonialism and the immeasurable negative impact on Indigenous cultures around the globe is a critical step toward positive change. *We are all in this together. If we don't come to terms with our differences of race, religion and gender; then war, poverty, contaminated food and water and a planet under siege will continue to unravel societies.* Considering the global climatic changes, there is much to be done in preparation for the new future we will all share.

In the past 50 years society has changed more than over the previous 10,000 years of human history. The digital revolution impacts lives on a much more personal level, by creating little or no space for private lives to escape from social and work pressures. Some of the benefits of the digital revolution have been expanded access to information enabling political, social, and economic engagement, as well as further democratizing access to education and capital. *Only recently are the stresses of the digital revolution being considered by medical establishments.* Information overload, fewer filters, and increased distribution speeds have people spinning to keep up with access to data and social media. There has been a loss of privacy at all levels of life with the invasion of technology. The historical division between work at home and work at work has been erased. With multiple digital connections there is a frenetic pace to life that prevents down time, and time spent for recreation and human interaction. Because we live in a consumerism society, everyone wants the newest iPhone, the latest pair of Nikes, so much so that this generation of teenagers is looking almost like clones of each other. *It is important to know how much of what you wear or eat is not because you chose it but because you were convinced that you needed it.*

As previously stated, take yourself seriously and know in your heart what is best for you and for the society in which you live. *Believe nothing, no matter who said it or supposedly said it; unless it agrees with your own reason and common sense and you have fact checked it*. We often think in terms of languages and images which are not our own, but which were given to us by our society. Learning to listen critically may be the most important first step to take when deciding where you fit into your society and what role you want to play.

We come from generations of people who put themselves last, due to either gender inequality, or patriarchal attitudes imposed often by the

church. Think of saving a drowning person. Your strength and ability to carry yourself and that person to shore are essential for survival of both. A mother of 5 young ones must be in good health to take care of all the children. The adult partner in that family must be in good health to continue to work and feed the family and keep everyone safe. It is common sense to take care of oneself in order to take care of each other.

'*The Dark Mountain Manifesto*', written by Paul Kingsnorth and Dougald Hine in 2009, states that "much of humanity is either inert with ignorance or numb with indifference to the deepening environmental crisis. Many are buoyed to optimism by their faith in the redemptive power of technology. Some continue to resist the notion that our collective behavior is unraveling the stability of ecologies essential to our civilizations comfortable survival." This manifesto is an excellent treatise. (5)

The concern of your generation is that the choices made today will leave fewer choices for your own children and grandchildren. This should concern you greatly.

In the animal kingdom power and strength are the rules for the best genetic opportunity for herd survival. With humans, the "might makes right" statute is challenged by conscience and is better described as "knowledge is power." Any show of personal power is simply a desire to dominate. We continually defend our arguments and justify our actions based on animal instincts that no longer serve us. The best leadership is not with words but actions and, from there; people have a better chance of making decisions based on common sense without drama. If you make good choices in your own life, you automatically show those around you that you have wisdom, which can lead to you being a leader in your community or job. This all creates a healthier society.

For generations societies have had an attitude towards youth that is unjust in many ways. Youthful rebellion is misunderstood by most. *Rebellion represents an important developmental stage for youth.* Challenging the status quo and practicing independence and personal choice all lead to more capable young adults. Youth that are not taught to think for themselves too often become victims of society laws and are punished. The penal system isolates and ostracizes youth instead of taking on the initiative to teach and support youth through resolution and hard work. A behavioral problem is far better rehabilitated and solved in youth than in later years through the criminal justice system.

The Stanford experiment of 1971 shockingly revealed the ease with which regular people, if given too much power, could transform into ruthless oppressors. The results show that we act as we think we are expected to act, especially if that expectation comes from authority. The lesson of Stanford isn't that any random human being is capable of descending into sadism and tyranny. What is more critical to understand is that misguided authority and certain institutions and environments can breed behaviors of self-defense and tyranny.

It is impossible to have hope for restoring democracy through governments who have surrendered all power to corporations. With hijacked electoral processes, corrupt judiciary, sensationalism in a biased press and a public that is wallowing in electronic over information, it is extremely challenging for people who seek nonviolent and profound change. With dysfunctional governments there is no one you can trust for support. There are no checks and balances on the structures of power, and society cannot move forward toward justice. Many modern day reform movements are battling for universal health care, development of alternative energy, strong environmental protection policies and financial regulation, with a deep desire to put a permanent end to the war economy worldwide. Yet they are confronted with opposition on all fronts from corporations and governments.

There are enormous challenges that come with change in societies; however, rebellion against all that is 'not' good is fundamental to our survival. Opposing the corporate reality is still deemed as subversive, while the majority of good rebels today fight for health, safety, food and shelter for all and most importantly a sustainable life on a vibrant planet.

"The Power to Change", is a documentary that is perhaps one of the most relevant films of our time. It has a clear message - a complete turnaround in energy policy towards 100 percent renewables. Considering that corporations that control our economy are mostly based on the petroleum industry, this film shows a way to change the course of our future. The opponents of this film would have you believe in only their way, however to change the future we have to want it enough, and fight for it. This film has a strong story, breathtaking cinematography and a great musical score that will offer you an insight into how the renewable energy revolution can be achieved and gives concrete examples of what it will look like. (6) (7)

Learning and doing must become inseparable in the face of conditions that force us to find solutions. *The many human cultures of the earth are mixing more rapidly than ever before*. To preserve social harmony we need to discover new cultural references. Considering conditions today the futures of law, medicine, philosophy, engineering, agriculture and every other field need to be re-evaluated by your generation.

Theodore Roosevelt said, 'In any moment of decision the best thing you can do is the right thing, the next best thing is the wrong thing and the worst thing you can do is nothing.' Perhaps you can picture yourself in 25 years on your current trajectory. You know what you want and can plan how to get there. Far too many have forgotten our collective past, our place in the present and our responsibility for the future. *It seems to me that society's ego-based state of consciousness is on a mission to seduce you into a reality of unconscious consumerism, an inauthentic lifestyle, and an unsustainable materialistic mindset.*

Another example of how your choices shape your society is described in a new short film called "The River Blue", a documentary about blue jeans. Following international river conservationist, Mark Angelo, The River Blue spans the globe to infiltrate one of the world's most polluting industries — fashion and more specifically blue jeans. Narrated by clean water supporter Jason Priestley, this groundbreaking documentary examines the destruction of our rivers, its effect on humanity, and the solutions that inspire hope for a sustainable future. The River Blue brings awareness to the destruction of some of the world's most vital rivers through the manufacture of our clothing, but will also act as a demand for significant change in the textile industry from the top fashion brands that can make a difference. This film points to one of your favorite articles of clothing, blue jeans, as a primary cause of chemical-intensive washes, dying processes, bleaching, and fabric printing involving heavy metals (including lead and mercury) which factories often discharge into rivers. The wastewater changes both the color and smell of rivers, sometimes into a reeking, oozing mass, completely toxic to life, usually in poor countries where labor is cheap.

There are rising stars for change in the blue jean industry. Everlane is an emerging start-up disrupting the fashion industry by being "radically transparent." The company wants to share with its customers details for each item of clothing including what factories a piece was made in and its various cost components. Everlane's value proposition is high quality at a lower price than traditional fashion brands, and, it also appears to start and end with ethical manufacturing processes.

In a society that demands your attention at every turn, through multiple devices seemingly designed to keep people in constant competition with each other you must tell yourself that 'You are enough'. You were born with your own unique and specialized skill set to live an awesome life and if you stay the course of your own dreams and potential, so it shall be. If you focus on what is missing in your life, you will continually live in a deficit. If you focus on optimism and possibilities then you will attract the same. *You can predict what a Society would be like if populated by either optimists or pessimists.*

Whether we speak of an individual life or the life of a society, both success and failure are largely the results of habit. It takes effort to change a habit in action or thought. This change however, can mean that every setback is temporary and every limitation can be overcome.

You are an organism composed of a complex system of trillions of cells all working together, through body intelligence, communicating and responding to deliver an inspiring life for your pleasure and performance. If you can master yourself, just imagine a society of individuals who have taken the time and effort to maximize their potential. That is the world you want to build and be part of.

We are all in this together regardless of race, religion, gender, or our place in society, and if we don't come to terms with our differences, war, poverty, disease and natural disasters will continue to unravel society.

Your societal masterpiece may be a handful of people, a neighborhood, a school, a government or several of these. Whenever you decide you want to live in a free society or in a healthy community take a step in that direction. The more you reach out the more your personal society will evolve.

Peggy L. Chinn wrote "Peace and Power: New Direction for Building Community" and reminds us of powerful and simple actions to take to encourage peace within the self and peace in our communities. A few simple suggestions are: plant and nurture something that grows, practice the fine art of yielding—in your car, in conversation, etc., do at least one thing to simplify your life and reduce your consumption of disposable products and natural resources, learn and practice ways to reduce hostile interactions with others, help three friends learn three things on this list, and many others.

Alan Watts, philosopher and writer predicted much of the state of the world today, fifty years ago. He spoke often of the danger of damaging the biosphere of our planet that supports all life. He often writes of the homeostasis of nature, which is the natural balance and order of life on the planet when humans don't disrupt it. Eventually, nature will find a way to return to that balance over time with or without the human race and so participating and assisting nature in finding balance again is our absolute best choice for society survival. All societies on the earth in plant and animal kingdoms live in balance with each other over time. Watts would tell us that as a species on earth, we know we are going in the wrong direction but simply don't know how to stop, or change. He suggests that we have created a system of language and calculations that have confused the simplicity of the solutions we must create. For example confusing money with wealth, happiness with status, and more importantly we have confused ourselves with our personalities. Our personality is our image of ourselves and each other which has very little to do with our interconnectedness to all life. He would tell us that the solution lies in our ability to come back from our constructed personalities to a sane view of our life in terms of an organism functioning within the whole environment instead of separate from it, nature within versus nature outside of ourselves. All of his books are great teaching tools for opening minds to a greater view of the self and the world. *As mentioned numerous times throughout this book, if you and the Youth of the world take a keen interest in finding purpose and learning about life, the world will be safer and the future more bright.*

Oxfam International has written a treatise titled "It's time to support Youth as agents of their own future." (8)

"Young people possess the energy, creativity and passion to take on the intractable problems they have inherited from their elders. Less imprisoned by ideological and institutional strictures, they have demonstrated the ability to think outside the box and develop innovative solutions." Around the world Youth are demanding political representation and a say in their government policies. Start the discussion in your own life with people who are enthused about change for the better.

Chapter 15

Decisions

There may not always be one right answer to solve life's problems. However there are always many considerations and steps that can lead you to a solution. Often your options are many and varied and the challenge lies in choosing the best action from among many in a reasonable time frame. *If you devote yourself to making small decisions promptly, you will find it much easier to be decisive when the stakes are high.* You'll find making decisions and acting on them far easier if you have practiced decision-making on a daily basis, so don't procrastinate.

Create priorities and keep track of what you need to do to succeed. If you face a challenging decision it is helpful to create a pro and con list in writing. Be practical and passionate about whatever it is you need to decide. Repeating this process usually leads to a solid decision that moves you forward. Writing down your thoughts, and creating a pro and con list for decision making also will help to stop the overthinking and take it out of your brain where the thoughts go round and round. Once you create your list, get input from friends or colleagues and when the decisions become clear you will free up your mind for other things.

Your decisions often affect important people in your life. *With serious consideration, you can almost always find a way to ameliorate the impacts your decisions may have on those you love.* It is not easy to prioritize yourself when others want your time or commitments. However, this presents an opportunity for honest communication about what is important for you. You will find that most people will totally support your dreams, choices and actions if they are well informed as to your reasoning. Not that you must share your dreams with everyone; it just makes sense to share certain details about your choices with people that matter to promote harmony around you.

Making decisions includes creating intentions and setting goals — all three of these brain activities are part of the same neural circuitry and engage the prefrontal cortex in a positive way, reducing worry and anxiety. Making decisions also helps overcome the pull toward negative impulses and routines. Finally, making decisions and finding solutions changes your perception of the world by calming anxiety that may surround choices you feel you must make.

Make an effort to have enough money for what matters. **Poverty is the greatest threat today to wellness and opportunity.** However, many people don't think twice about buying a $7 latte which is an investment in nothing while overthinking spending a couple hundred dollars on something that may be life changing. Many make financial decisions every day that limit their long term abundance.

Deciding can be hard. Don't worry about making the absolute best decision; make a 'good' decision. **Worrying and trying to make perfect decisions overwhelms your brain and can make you feel out of control.** Choosing and making a decision causes changes in attention circuits and increases dopamine activity. **It's important to like your own choices**. Ensure that your decisions fit with your overall plan of intentions, goals, and of course is in your own best interest.

There are decisions you may make that could change your life forever. Deciding not to use a condom, just once, could lead to an unplanned pregnancy. This situation would change the course of your life forever in one way or another. Unplanned pregnancy can be a gift of course, however teenage pregnancy presents challenging and heartfelt turmoil on all levels and the life of the child yet to be born is in your hands. Deciding to continue with the pregnancy and raise a child involves significant decisions and discussions for the future father and mother, and will radically change your life. To be faced with having to consider an abortion can be the toughest decision of all in the circumstances. Remember you are responsible for every decision and choice you make and the consequences that may follow. To make decisions wisely, courage is needed, the courage to say no, and the courage to say yes. Be ready and informed for small and big decisions.

Find ways to be involved in your community's decision-making processes and it will begin to recognize the measurable benefits you have to offer your entire community. In a world of constant change, setting long-term goals doesn't always make much sense for youth. If you have a goal set for yourself, move toward it one step at a time while knowing it is dynamic and that things can change as you move forward. Your goal needs to be flexible as long as you are moving forward with the best of yourself. Sometimes long term goals can set you up for failure or disappointment, but also they could lead you to great things. Always keep in mind that each day matters and goals will manifest as you are ready for them.

Good decision making is one of the most important life skills to have. Observe in your own life how many decisions you make every day, from the color and style of the clothing you wear, the next job interview or the courses you choose in University. There are so many decisions you make each day, such as the foods you prepare, decisions at school or work, your daily decisions for personal and social media time or the time spent with friends and family. *The more you consciously make decisions and choose your actions with purpose the more ease you will have on the journey toward meeting your goals*. As you meet your goals and fulfill what is best for your life, the society around you starts to shift for the better.

Write your own creed in regard to how you will make choices. I choose to live by choice, not by chance. I choose to make changes, not excuses. I choose to be motivated, not manipulated. I choose to be useful, not used. I choose to excel, not compete. I choose self-esteem, not self-pity. I choose to listen to my inner voice, not the random opinions of others.

Spend time defining and clarifying the decision you have to make in detail and you will save yourself a great deal of time searching for the right information to assist you. Be aware of your emotions that are connected to the decision you are about to make. If it is a simple decision to buy one thing or another, be rational, think it through calmly. If the decision you have to make is more complex or a matter of the heart trust intuition and your gut. Use the emotions you feel to assist you in choosing one course or another. If a decision is challenging, tough or emotional the old advice to 'sleep on it' can help you see more clearly in the morning what choice to make. Remember that brain science shows that making decisions reduces worry and anxiety.

Always reflect on what you have with gratitude, be grateful for the good decisions you have made in the past and know that an attitude of gratitude will assist you in making good decisions.

Chapter 16

Relationships

You can manage what you can measure. Whether your relationship is with yourself, a friend, a life partner, a boss or teacher, observe the details of that relationship clearly and honestly in order to master your own behavior and maintain direction.

Understand that finding fault or blaming someone else for your situation is never part of a solution. If you had or have an alcoholic parent, it is not your fault that this happened however it is absolutely correct that it is your responsibility to figure out how to live your own life correctly without blame or anger. Being stuck in anger or blame traps you into victim mode where no solutions exist for your life. In whatever circumstance you find yourself, your love life, work life or your family life, if you have been wronged or hurt take responsibility for how you feel. Otherwise the cycle continues, the anger wins and you miss out on the opportunities that happiness can offer.

In science, the Law of Attraction in the universe is based on the principle that all matter is made up of pure energy, which is in a constant state of vibration and spin. Thoughts and emotions are also energy, each having a unique energy signature. Every energetic frequency is in a constant state of attraction or repulsion with other energies. With new advances in quantum mechanics, this notion has been largely supported at a micro level.

The Law of Attraction states that "like attracts like." We are continually interacting with the fabric of reality (or quantum field), through thought and emotional energy. *What we focus on is likely to manifest. What we focus on expands. In relationship terms what we put out is what we will attract.*

Your belief systems can play havoc with creating relationships you deeply desire. If you try to think your way into something that you don't believe, your emotional reaction will support your unconscious beliefs more than your conscious thoughts. The most important relationship you will ever have that influences all relationships in your future is the relationship you have with yourself. Love yourself, respect yourself, believe in yourself first, which will attract the same in work, love, business and friendship. If you affirm that you will be financially abundant, yet on a deeper level you have a belief in poverty based on your upbringing, the latter is likely keeping you from achieving that financial abundance.

Renowned behavioral development specialist Dr. DeMartini discovered that we all have an inherent set of values that is largely governing our behavior. DeMartini states, *"All of our actions are strategies to align with our values as efficiently as possible."* Therefore, be sure your highest values align with your best success for happiness.

The law of attraction responds to everything, without exception. If you are confused in your emotions it will slow the process. The more detailed and confident you are in what you want in a relationship, the faster you will attract relationships that work best for you.

Ego plays an enormous role in the success or failure of all relationships in your life. We live in a culture that is obsessed with physical appearance. "I have to look good to feel good," is a common expression today. There are times when this is important however most of the time this is ego, self-consciousness and a distorted perception of what social media and fashion are imposing on you. The best approach is to accept the social pressure as reality and then choose to be your best self, based on common sense, intelligence and your own style. Come to terms with the idea that your personality and your ego are constructs in the image of what society expects of you. Your authentic self will attract healthy, like minded relationships that will reward you beyond measure.

Get to a point where fashion and social expectations are playful and fun to participate in when it suits your desire to express yourself. Don't base your personal healthy self-expression on other peoples' opinions. Each time you exercise healthy and fun choices for yourself you are retraining your brain and neurons to believe in your best self, not society's version of you. This will begin to give you the freedom to play with your self-expressions and lose the stress of fitting in.

Victims of bullying and societal pressure come in all shapes, sizes, ages and backgrounds. Too easily a person who is insecure or shy or afraid may reward the bully by crying, giving over their possessions, or running away in fear. We all want to learn to show self-confidence, respond with assertiveness, and get help and support when necessary. At the root of both sides of the bullying and victim scenario is lack of self-love and the imperative to teach young people how to care for and respect themselves is more important now than ever before.

I must address the importance of awareness and warning around the subject of inappropriate touching, sexual harassment and aggression in the work place, schools, churches, on the street or anywhere two people or more gather. This is addressed and discussed elsewhere in the chapters on Emotions, Dating and Society accenting the #metoo movement along with the multitude of cases of abuse through churches around the world. The clinical definition of child sexual abuse is inappropriately exposing or subjecting a child to sexual contact, activity or behavior. If you have been victim to inappropriate behavior none of it was ever your fault and reaching out for help is very important to assist you in resolving the problem and finding safety and support. Gone are the days when teachers could hug children or wrestle in fun, as safe boundaries have been crossed too many times. Along with these new restrictions comes the concern of how to show appropriate affection for others.

Marianne Williamson's quote gives us tremendous insight into our true selves and reminds us all that we have within us the power and ability to rise up out of victimhood and bullying.

"Our deepest fear is not that we are inadequate. Our deepest fear is that we are powerful beyond measure. It is our light, not our darkness, that most frightens us. We ask ourselves, who am I to be brilliant, gorgeous, talented, or fabulous? Actually, who are you not to be? Your playing small doesn't serve the world. There's nothing enlightened about shrinking so that other people won't feel insecure around you. We are all meant to shine, as children do. It's not just in some of us; it's in everyone. And as we let our own light shine, we subconsciously give other people permission to do the same. As we're liberated from our own fear, our presence automatically liberates others." Marianne Williamson (1992), author of 'A Return to Love: Reflections on the Principles of a Course in Miracles.'

Bullies are made, not born. Most people struggle to feel compassion for them. Of course it is complicated and very circumstantial how we behave in response to bullies. The victims of bullies themselves travel a rough and rocky road and in many ways face the same internal struggles as those who bully them. In most societies where politeness is a primary objective, would-be bullies can lose their voice, except when they're behaving like bullies. The expression 'the greater the yin the greater the yang' means that the more aggressive a person behaves outwardly suggests internally they are full of the opposite which is fear (at the root of all anger), and to cover up their insecurity they push people around in all sorts of ways. People who are labeled as "bullies" are often punished, but rarely asked what they want or how they feel. There is support, recognition and trauma treatment for those whose behavior is a result of tragedy and pain and suffering in their own lives that can manifest as bullies. An absence of love as a child can be the root of being a bully later on in years, searching in a dysfunctional way for the love and attention he or she never received in younger years, or to overcompensate for great feelings of inadequacy.

If you know that you must ask forgiveness or give forgiveness for your behavior or that of another, consider the social weight and implications of speaking of forgiveness. If you are or have been a bully a straight up request for forgiveness without excuses or lengthy explanations is an essential first step to forgiving yourself. Canadians seem to have a global reputation for saying 'I'm sorry' to the point that many use the phrase constantly. For the person offended according to Wikipedia, 'Forgiveness is the intentional and voluntary process by which a victim undergoes a change in feelings and attitude regarding an offense, or lets go of negative emotions such as vengefulness, with an increased ability to wish the offender well.' (1)

It can also be possible that one asks for forgiveness of others who have wronged them as a reflection of having blamed themselves for years for 'not' being the wise person they are today back 'then' when the incident occurred. It can be complicated that victims too easily blame themselves when people of significance in their life, an abusive parent, sibling, teacher, spouse, etc. have hurt them in the past or present. We know that our own personal strength and wisdom would instantly come into play if someone we love is being bullied; however we don't easily stand up in that way for ourselves, especially as children which is often when the initiation of abuse began. I am not simply reflecting on the old 'hind sight is 20/20' idea. I am speaking of the limitless possibilities and that the majority of persons of your generation and those before you were not taught to stand up for themselves. Forgiveness is powerful and essential. It may also be important to forgive yourself for not being that warrior, so young, so naive, so untaught and so vulnerable. *Forgiveness on all fronts will assist you in finding a way to peace, where neither winning nor losing exist, only peace.*

In Chinese philosophy, yin and yang (literally light-dark and positive-negative) describe how opposite or contrary forces may actually be complementary, interconnected and interdependent in the natural world.

Many tangible dualities, light and dark, fire and water, expanding and contracting, are physical manifestations of the duality of yin and yang. Yin and Yang make up the whole of the One of each of us. This also explains the paradox of loving someone and being annoyed, or loving family and being taken for granted (consciously or unconsciously). When we believe and understand balance within each of us it is much easier in every relationship we have to observe when yin and yang are out of balance. Bullies and victims are a perfect example, as they both have the same imbalance within, that of fear and insecurity expressed in opposite ways. A shadow cannot exist without light, opposites could be thought of as complementary (rather than opposing) forces. In nature there is an expression that the whole is greater than that of the assembled parts, creating synergy. So the goal is balance between all the inner aspects of us as we forge and manage relationships with others. In Taoist metaphysics, distinctions between good and bad, along with other moral judgments are perceptual, not real, so the duality of yin and yang is an indivisible whole for us to ponder.

The greatest reason for relationship collapse or conflict is unmet expectations. Expectation is the mother of all frustration. I'm sure you can recall examples when what you imagined might happen and what actually happened were very different. The point is to be aware that life is fluid, and when things don't meet your expectations, observe what changed, how it changed and assess the validity of the outcome. This is the best way to be flexible and non-resistant when your expectation of a perfect picture didn't turn out.

We live in increasingly polarized times, with people from opposite ends of the social and political spectrum making it more and more difficult to understand each other. *One of the missing ingredients in misunderstanding each other is often the listening.* You have two ears and one mouth, it is always wise to listen twice as much as you talk. The challenge is to have the compassion for others that we want them to have for us. It is essential to find common ground for our own good, the good of each other, and ultimately the good of our neighborhoods and society. Emotional correctness is the tone that goes with the listening and is far more important than the social political correctness that too many people currently focus on. When you make connections with the people you disagree with, you can actually start the conversations that lead to change. There is a big difference between listening to simply respond with your point of view and listening to understand.

The most important relationship that will shape each day and determine your future is the relationship you have with yourself. Most were not taught this all-important detail in how to build a life. Most people expend huge amounts of energy trying to impress people and mold themselves into the expectations of others.   When you care deeply for yourself all your relationships become more honest and easier to manage. If you know who you truly are and what you want, it follows that honest and open communication in work, family or romantic relationships is in everyone's best interest. Always keep in mind that listening is the most powerful part of communication. Too many of us don't pay attention and then start talking without reflecting on what the other person just told us. Communication is an art form well worth mastering to assure you of healthy relationships.

William Arthur Ward said *"**Gratitude can transform common days into thanksgivings, turn routine jobs into joy, and change ordinary opportunities into blessings.**"* The sooner you are grateful for the gifts you were born with, the talents you nurture and present to the world, the sooner you will find yourself in healthy work, friendship and love relationships.

In order to preserve traditions and standards decided long ago, cultures around the world have manipulated youth since societies first began. On the one hand, love is steadfast, faithful and forever; on the other hand, love is selfish, fickle and fueled with emotion. The push-back of Youth today against these standards for love and relationship is to stop idolizing romance. Women and men can live fulfilled and satisfying lives without the dependence on a romantic partnership to make that happen.   Marriage in the past had legal boundaries that protected children and property and served a great purpose for society security and the future. Today the boundaries are less legal and more invisible. They are, however, still important to protect love and allow relationships to flourish and thrive. *Though the old school thought of 'follow your heart' still holds some value - be sure to follow your intelligence and common sense along with the emotions that lead your heart in a particular direction.*

Society puts a lot of pressure on anyone not in a relationship. The assumption that being single is sad and that if you are not in a relationship then you must want to be in one is also expressed by family and friends too often. Live your life according to your own personal needs and desires with integrity and grace. Don't pay attention to what others insist is best for you. Though as humans we need to feel love and acceptance from others, be extremely particular about whom you trust with those feelings. Neuroscientists did a study where people played a ball-tossing video game. The subjects were told that the characters in the video game tossing the ball back were controlled by real people.   When the video game went from playing nice to not sharing the ball, subject's brains responded as if they experienced physical pain. Rejection doesn't just hurt like a broken heart. Your brain registers that pain. Five simple ways to deal with rejection are to name the emotions, treat yourself with compassion, do not let rejection define you, learn what you can from rejection because most of the time it simply means that you did not fit into the expectations of that job or person or social experience. Rejection can often be an opportunity to look at oneself more clearly, be better prepared, and to have a plan for escape or resolution that will serve you in the future.

In fact, as demonstrated in an fMRI experiment, social exclusion activates the same circuitry as physical pain. This small change was enough to elicit feelings of social exclusion, and it activated the anterior cingulate and insula, just like physical pain would.

Oxytocin is a powerful hormone that acts as a neurotransmitter in the brain. It regulates social interaction and sexual reproduction, playing a role in behaviors from maternal-infant bonding and milk release to empathy, generosity, and orgasm. One of the primary ways to release oxytocin is through touching, or as simple as a hug or a handshake. Oxytocin release is first experienced at birth when we are held by parents and when a child experiences affection throughout childhood and beyond. Handshakes and pats on the back also send a positive and respectful message. For people you are close to, affection is extremely important. Touching is powerful; it makes you more persuasive, increases team performance, and even boosts math skills. Holding hands with someone can help comfort you and your brain through painful situations. Research shows getting five hugs a day for four weeks increases happiness.

If you don't have anyone to hug, a massage boosts your serotonin by as much as 30 percent. Massage also decreases stress hormones and raises dopamine levels, which helps you create new good habits. Massage reduces pain because the oxytocin system activates painkilling endorphins, improves sleep, and reduces fatigue by increasing serotonin and dopamine and decreasing the stress hormone cortisol.

I'm sorry to inform you that texting as a form of communication is not enough on which to build a relationship. When you put people in a stressful situation and then let them visit loved ones or talk to them on the phone, they feel better. *Neuroscience demonstrates that, when they texted regarding the stressful situation, their bodies responded the same as if they had no support at all.* The text-message group had cortisol and oxytocin levels similar to the no-contact group.

The movie 'The Perks of Being a Wallflower', brilliantly demonstrates relationships with self and others and the deeper problems and powerful solutions we can find with each other's support. *'We accept the love we feel we deserve' is a line from the movie that answers all the questions that arise for each of us as we 'forget' to love ourselves first.*

There are 10,000 years of history based on survival of the fittest that has shaped the present behavior of humanity and that may no longer serve humanity's best interest. In the past 100 years human behavior has changed dramatically with the industrial revolution and more recently with the digital/tech revolution. It has been less than 100 years since women fought for and earned the right to vote in N. America. And there are still too many countries in the world where women can't go to school, drive a car, walk in public, wear what they want and a myriad of other limitations too many to list. I hope the absurdity of these and any other limitations on anyone's freedom of choice will lead all of you to be part of the solution for change. Have an understanding of the history that shaped your sisters, mothers and grandmother's lives and brothers, fathers and grandfathers too. With the long and sordid history of conflict between men, women, minorities and the disabled, creating solid relationships with anyone requires compassion and an understanding of this history. Most of us are at least partially aware of outrageous human rights challenges for women in some countries in the world today. Even in the most prosperous of developed countries equality is still not a reality. The last lynching of an African American in the U.S. was in 1953. I only address these atrocities because it is our human history; we are a product of the biases, prejudices, wars and angers of generations before us. Educate yourselves on what racism really means. Very few of us escape attitudes or views based in racism. *This only speaks more strongly to the fact that we must each separate ourselves from the imprints and influences of the past and present, which can imprison us with their anger and hatred.*

As you stand up for yourself and your desire for equality and harmony around you, as you tell the truth in your relationships, don't forget to care enough for others to allow them to be who they choose to be.

People will never do more for you than they can do for themselves. Always look to your role models. By paying attention to the success and happiness in the lives of your role models, you will be able to predict your own future. If you choose to follow other's advice or example, be sure their lives reflect your high standards of equality, compassion and truth. Some of you may have to change role models realizing that the current ones no longer fit the new direction of your life.

'Masterminding' may be defined as: "coordination of knowledge and effort in a spirit of harmony, between two or more people, for the attainment of a definite purpose." (Napoleon Hill, Think and Grow Rich). Hill uses ideas from physics to illustrate the synergy that occurs between like-minded individuals. He also warns of the danger to the mastermind group of any single member who thinks negatively. Another key insight from Hill is that knowledge is not power – it is only potential power. He defines power as

"...organized knowledge, expressed through intelligent efforts." The mastermind group makes this happen.

Making assumptions about anyone or any situation is naïve. Assuming people are who they say they are is naïve. It is very positive and optimistic to look for the truth in people, places and experiences you have. However it is only when you come from a place of truth, that you will know what is right for you or wrong for you. If most of the people around you are guessing at success, negative about their lives, and not aware that they are missing happiness, can they have answers for your life?

It is an interesting part of human nature that some people see opportunities, while others only see obstacles or problems. Know yourself and don't be naïve about who you are and know that all things are possible for you. Ten thousand plus years of oppositional roles for males and females continues to sabotage the possibility of long lasting love and joy between any two people. It is my understanding that the differences that matter between men and women are simply biological. Again we have been so sculpted by history and our different societies that we have surrendered to the roles imposed upon us. The greatest gift we can offer another is the work we do on ourselves. Because we enter into most relationships with a societal view of how that relationship should progress and develop, we may initiate a path of struggle and possible collapse. Most long term relationships begin with love and joy and celebration and very quickly can become peppered with stress and misunderstanding. If children present themselves quickly in a relationship then the divide is even greater as the children consume all the attention and time of primarily the mother, though there is a new generation of both parents sharing the tasks of raising their young.

To know oneself first, to have a solid, joyful and rewarding relationship with yourself before considering a relationship with another will assist you profoundly in finding friendship and love. You have all the time you need. Pay attention because distraction will keep you from the truth and you may miss the opportunity. Be grateful every day, at every opportunity. Feed and hydrate yourself as if it really matters, and it does! *Your performance and your ability to have successful relationships is a byproduct of good water, good food and a good attitude.* Many wise people have written that attitude is even more important than the food you eat. There is truth in this; however, I want to emphasis the importance of both.

Stop searching for goodness in a badly behaved person. It is simply too dangerous to associate with bad behavior. Many people want and need you to stay inside their drama; without that codependent relationship with you; they might have to see themselves as they truly are.

169

It is often true that if you are annoyed or angry with someone else's behavior, you are possibly frustrated with those same tendencies within yourself. Know the difference between ridiculous behavior in people who just want to annoy you and behavior you can make better in a relationship. Take an introspective look inside yourself the next time you are annoyed or angered. It's a great way to learn more about yourself and increase control of your own emotions.

Even though it can be challenging to 'stop' the mind from negativity or fear or anger, it is an important skill to master. Make a stop sign for yourself in your hand or in your mind. Just stop it! Don't go there! It's an addiction to resist what is best for you. I see many people having temper tantrums day after day. How would we treat a child in a tantrum? Ideally, we would stop the behavior, not tolerate the behavior, give them a time out, and certainly not participate in the tantrum. Some still do of course, and that's when the screaming conflicts and arguments happen. I have seen many people remain in adult temper tantrums for long periods of time, sometimes for years. Just because we think we are being adults and don't want to see ourselves as acting like juveniles, that's exactly what a temper tantrum is. Giving someone the silent treatment, ignoring them or the problem is still a type of temper tantrum and a display of immature behavior.

Kindness glues relationships together. Research has shown that kindness (along with emotional stability) is the most important predictor of satisfaction in a relationship. Who would have thought? Here is another example of science proving that common sense prevails yet again. Instead of thinking that you either have kindness in you or you don't; think instead of kindness as a muscle. You have to exercise it to keep it in shape. *Your first response in a conflict situation should be informed by kindness.* However, if a situation is extreme or dangerous, it is important to call for help and remove yourself from that person or that relationship. In every community today, there is somewhere you can call to be rescued, or receive assistance as you may require. Reach out!

If you believe something is true about yourself, good or bad, eventually it will be true. Believe that you are a good person and you will be good. The brain is a brilliant computer that believes what you think and say and puts it into action very efficiently. Because the brain is the new frontier in medicine, we now know that what you think, you become. The brain is where success or failure is planted in your life. Children who are told they are stupid in their youth will likely believe they are stupid throughout their whole lives. *If you think you are poor, unattractive, and sad or any other negative thought, you will attract the same to you.* The law of attraction, and what you focus on expands, are brilliant reminders of how to create good relationships in your life.

Humans are social creatures and yet this technological age has been referred to as the age of loneliness. Isolation has become a signature of the technological revolution. There are plenty of research papers identifying an age of technological loneliness that is killing the drive, inspiration and happiness of this generation and the next. *In this moment youth are being radicalized in their living rooms through technology and media without any direct connection to what they rally against.* It is highly dangerous that in the absence of human interaction and personal discussion, people take sides in serious debates from their homes through a small device that is potentially full of misinformation and propaganda.

Simple though this may sound try to remember people's names! We all make excuses for ourselves, but you could make it a point of personal pride to pay attention and remember peoples' names. Someone just told you their name, pay attention, listen and focus, remember their name. It is not just a common courtesy; it is what you would want for yourself. Another common courtesy is to let people know when you are going to be late. Social interaction between different generations is an excellent way to help each other out. Volunteer for worthy causes and learn from elders and colleagues to expand your point of view at every opportunity.

Does technology get in the way of your relationship? There are numerous ads on television and social media that show groups of friends out for dinner, all on their electronic devices, sometimes even talking to each other through their smart phones instead of actually talking to each other. These habits are difficult to change but if you want freedom, if you want exciting and adventurous relationships, it can only happen in person, face to face. Have the courage to be the first in your circle to put your phone down, and talk about this with your friends. Though it is cool to be on your device all day long, you don't have to commit to that. Look around you, it only makes sense to stay connected to people, rather than a device. So, put your devices down for a specific number of hours a day and see how your life feels. Just do it! *Live your life through your body, heart and mind, not your device.*

What you focus on expands so focus on all the good in your life and you will attract more of it. Align your actions with your values. Taking care of yourself will assist you in every relationship you have and loving yourself will best prepare you for a love relationship with another. *Be grateful every day. Take time away from digital devices and have fun.*

Chapter 17

The Inevitability of Change

There is a Buddhist precept that change is constant. In all relationships, we need to pay attention and adapt and grow through change.

Ask yourself these questions. Are your thoughts more in the past than the present? Do you feel more sadness than joy in your daily life? Are you resentful of a person in your life or apathetic about your situation? Do you feel alone, bullied or overlooked? Do you find yourself hoping that one day things will get better? Do you feel empty emotionally, spiritually or physically? Do you compromise who you know yourself to be in order to stay where you are? Do you tell yourself this is as good as it gets? Do you have a mask that you present to the world pretending all is well when it isn't? Does fear of the unknown keep you stuck where you are? Do you sometimes imagine how wonderful it might feel to be free? Do you believe in a better life for yourself?

If you found yourself saying yes to any of these questions, it is most definitely time for you to reevaluate where you are. *It is true that when we see a situation differently, the situation changes.* Plan to step forward with care and kindness for yourself and those with whom you are involved. Cultivate a measure of faith and trust in yourself that you can do it. If you are able to free yourself, your future will find you.

One small change can lead to other changes that, in turn, lead you to the ultimate potential your life holds for you. This is the domino effect.

Pain and discomfort, fear and doubt can become habits to which we are attached and in which we feel secure. Being free of the pain can seem too great to imagine. Feeling that you don't deserve happiness or that turning your back on the pain may leave you with nothing is a great force to overcome. You must believe you deserve to be free.

I know some of you are afraid for your life, some of you are afraid for people you love, while others of you are ready to leap straight into the possibilities of your life. What is most important is to move in a direction that fits for you. Listen well to yourself as you do know what's best for you. You truly do!

Fear can reach out and influence all aspects of your life. To undo fear you must break it down into manageable parts. Repetition of any emotion creates fixed patterns in the brain. To override worry you must have the awareness that fear isn't real. Every cell of your body has an innate intelligence. Within your body trillions of cells live together, cooperate, sense each other and constantly communicate and perform complex functions. If a single cell goes rogue, the immune system will intervene. Unlike early man when existence was defined by opposition and self-defense, today we can and must override thought patterns that are no longer relevant. Often fear or misunderstanding influences how we deal with conflict in discussions or debates about important topics. *There is a huge difference between listening with a closed mind and listening with an honest desire to understand ideas that may differ from yours.*

A Zen Proverb, 'Let go or be dragged' paints a great picture of the freedom to be gained by letting go. The losing battle of holding on to anger or pain when there is nothing to be gained is another example of letting go. For some it may be terrifying because of violence, hunger or pain; in those circumstances you simply must reach out to someone for help. For many it may be simple laziness and the habit of going along with or being dragged by someone else's life and direction. No matter which, you deserve freedom. You have a life of your own to live. *Name it, go after it, and live it.*

You find out how strong you are in the moments of uncertainty that inevitably come your way. The unplanned events – accidents, layoffs, death of a close friend or relative, disease, and crisis – can come crashing into your world at any moment. If you initiate personal choice and integrity in small decisions you make, in small changes that you incorporate into your life, you will be better prepared for any unplanned events. *It is from our reserve of trusting in ourselves that we rise up when we must to deal with tough situations.* It is much easier to deal with what you can measure. Of course in serious matters, in sorrow and loss there are important steps you must follow. There are landmarks in grieving that you simply must allow yourself to go through in order to become whole again. We are changed by grief forever. However, that change over time can become a gift of love. A movie in 2017 called 'Collateral Beauty' is a brilliant summary of the grace and gifts that will come from loss and grief if we allow them. There is life and death all around us; it is part of the circle of life that is at the root of change. Reach out to those you trust and share in the grieving process. 'Grief shared is divided, while joy shared is multiplied.' Go with the flow. You can do it and still maintain your integrity and highest best self as you proceed along your chosen path.

Opportunities rarely come when we are 100% ready to seize them. They are more likely to knock on your door when you feel insecure with your preparation, knowledge and skills. But that doesn't mean you should be ignoring them until you feel ready. *Most of your lifetime opportunities force you to grow both emotionally and intellectually.* They push you to give the best of yourself, even if that means leaving your comfort zones. Sacrificing your comfort will give you an opportunity for personal growth. If you want to change your life for the better, open yourself to the opportunities that arise, even if you don't feel ready.

There are brilliant examples of change in nature that teach you the many phases and changes you may encounter in your life. The four stages of the butterfly from egg, to larvae, to pupae, to adult butterfly; all encapsulate a wondrous imagery of struggle and change with the end result being beauty and flight.

Great opportunities to help others seldom come but small opportunities to help others surround you every day.

Change can bring glorious celebration or sometimes despair and devastation. It is all part of the circle of life that you work through every single day. Build yourself a life that will sustain you through good times and bad and assure yourself the best outcome. Remember attitude is everything! Your attitude leads you to your desired outcome and brings forth your hidden talents. A positive attitude instills positive energy into your actions and choices and most definitely attracts positive people into your life.

When change comes your way don't be complacent, pay attention and take action when necessary. Take a step back and assess your situation. Plan to shift your perspective, prepare, prioritize, consider all the options, and persevere until you have settled into the change and made it fit into your life.

Believe that you can change. If you look ahead and create a picture of a successful change you want to make in your life, let that end picture determine the first step you take in that direction. When dealing with any change in your life align your desires and flexibility with your innate body intelligence and trust in the process. *Your body is a brilliant and masterful example of coping, adjusting and thriving through change every minute of every day.*

Chapter 18

Dating/Sex/Birth Control

There has been enormous change in the evolution of dating over the past 3 generations. Far enough back in time, forming a couple was based on survival of the species. The strongest was the best choice for both mates: strong hunters and protectors, strong hips for child bearing, and hard working. Survival was often based on loyalty and endurance, the luxury was not there for love and romance. For today's generation, long term relationships are not prerequisites for living your individual and unique life because individuals can take care of themselves and support themselves more independently than in the past. *'We accept the love we feel we deserve'* would be a great motto for building a foundation within yourself first and then in relationship with another. Too many people undervalue who they are and overvalue who they are not.

Only a couple generations back, especially for most of your grandparents there was a post-war boom as society replaced the millions lost through war and the industrial revolution was celebrated. There was a lot more going on than just falling in love. Today there is on-line dating that has replaced the dating game for all ages. There is a new family concept, multiple possibilities of partnering and raising a family or not raising a family. Dating and sex have gone from taboo to casual.

Understanding between the different sexes is essential to make good decisions and move forward with or without relationships that are best for you. *There is a Yin-and-Yang dynamic, a masculine and feminine dynamic to be understood that may not be reflected at all in conventional ways of male and female bodies.* Biologically we all come from a father and a mother and therefore we cannot isolate one from the other within us completely. Masculinity is in crisis around the world because it is out of balance and it can only be out of balance with respect to the feminine, which is manifest in all of us. The masculine and feminine aspects of our collective psyche are out of balance and if we want to see a change in its outward manifestation, we have to address this imbalance from the inside.

It is my intention to direct all the information in this chapter to both young men and young women. Whether the subject is the long and detailed subject of birth control or sexually transmitted disease it is equally as important for men as women to fully understand the options, concerns and choices.

The very recent *#MeToo campaign* has highlighted a surprising fact that nearly every woman, girl and many young men have had an experience, ranging from awkward to horrifying, in which they felt sexually intimidated or harassed or worse. Many might argue this is over dramatized, however we all know that many men in work places, on the street, in bars and clubs, and in homes around the world comment and show inappropriate behavior toward women, in mild and extreme forms. This behavior has been socially acceptable for too long. The taboo of silence and shame is being erased by these women speaking up and men are now responding with their own stories. Many men are admitting to being bystanders to this kind of typical behavior and are reflecting on the importance of change and respect. The previous paragraph addresses the imbalance between the sexes, between the masculine and feminine within each of us and this new conversation around sexual harassment and sexual misconduct offers a brilliant opportunity to address and resolve imbalances within each of us.

The *#HowIWillChange* campaign is one of men's responses to this new conversation and their personal observations of changing their own behaviors is equally important. Childhood bullies need to be stood up to and taught better behavior and choices, as they too may need help as a result of abuses they have suffered in childhood. Those who perpetrate sexual harassment and assault must also be reported and identified by every woman and man. The old adage 'boys will be boys' and 'just being a man' need to be taught to young people as examples of misogyny that has existed for centuries in all cultures. The 'no means no' campaign is around the subject of giving consent for sexual interactions. The power given to men so long ago over women, in particular in the arena of consent is baffling and frightening. All this conflict presumably over an orgasm. Bottom line is, one person wants something the other doesn't want to give. No means No right? How is a man's orgasm so highly valued that he will force it on someone unwilling? It just doesn't make sense when they could take care of their own orgasm any time they want on their own. Men and women need to put an end to the rape culture, and the attitude that women resisting sex is part of the chase, and as in the animal kingdom need to be forcibly overtaken.

Humans have used force to get what they want throughout history. Wars have been fought over possession of land, resources, people and money. The old adage 'taking candy from a baby' sums up the ease with which people take what they want from others. Is this the same psyche behind forcing women to have sex and the long history of domestic violence? Men are also victims of domestic violence. Statistics say that women attack their partners more often than men but do less physical harm, and it generally is not reported.

Recent studies involving American college students found that 1-in-3 collegiate males admitted they would force a woman into sexual intercourse, but many would not consider that rape. The study, "Denying Rape but Endorsing Forceful Intercourse: Exploring Differences among Responders," was published in the peer-reviewed journal 'Violence and Gender' in December 2017. University of North Dakota psychology professor Sarah R. Edwards was the lead researcher, and reported "the No. 1 point is there are people that will say they would force a woman to have sex but would deny they would rape a woman." This must point to the history of men dominating and oppressing women. It is shocking on one hand that reasonable, educated men in our society do not consider forcing women to have sex as wrong. Men have had power over women for so long and historically consent or asking permission was not necessary. There has been little research on differences between individuals who endorse a behaviorally descriptive item like coercion but refuse the label of rape. "The present study uses discriminant function analysis to separate men who do not report intentions to be sexually coercive, those who endorse behaviorally descriptive intentions but deny it when the word rape is used, and those who endorse intentions to rape outright. Results indicated that participants can be differentiated into three groups based on scores from scales on hyper masculinity and hostility toward women." (1)

Desiring relationship and intimacy is part of our human biology. These lingering effects of the patriarchy when women/children/men were considered possessions, and dominance and power over was the norm, need to be erased from men and women's minds. I am not implying this should be forgotten but it must cease to influence the behavior of people today.

In 2013 numerous examples were publicized of Universities in N. America where freshman orientation included chants that encouraged sexual violence against women along with multiple rape cases. The public response to these events was widespread with instant condemnation of what had been happening for decades in universities but was not brought to public awareness so concisely. The Canadian Federation of Students developed the "No Means No" campaign to raise awareness and to reduce the occurrence of sexual assault, acquaintance rape, and dating violence. There is a great deal of material and research on the incidences of sexual violence in Canada and ways to eliminate it. Students have a right to feel safe and secure on the street and in particular on their campus, and that right is taken away when sexualized violence continues to happen. *The evolution of sex should be loving, tender, compassionate and pleasurable for both partners. Women and men need not settle for less.*

Meaningful change starts in the home. Fathers and grandfathers can teach sons to honor and respect women and themselves. Men can learn more about this issue and history instead of expecting women to explain to them why they are impacted by misogyny. There is no doubt there are countless good and honest men, young and old who respect women. For those men this campaign presents them with an opportunity to no longer be a bystander. Hopefully, for those that are less respectful, this movement will have been enlightening. If a person is not part of the solution then they are part of the problem.

Information about safe sex is taught in school from grade 4 and up and protection against disease and preventing pregnancy are details that most young people are aware of. Pro-choice in matters that pertain to your body and your life is crucial for freedom and equality. In many places around the world today, people do not get to choose either their own sexual orientation or birth control. The U.S. has more laws regulating sexual behavior than all the European countries combined. These laws and behaviors are archaic and destructive. Many laws continue to exist from a time when governments and mobs burned women at the stake, practiced open infanticide, and made eunuchs of men.

Birth Control has a long and sordid history. Men and women alike need to be informed of the options and actions of birth control in order to better understand each other regarding this essential topic. In 1965, the Supreme Court gave only married couples the right to use birth control under the landmark court case Griswold v. Connecticut. It would be another seven years before birth control would be legal for all people to use. *Birth control must be a shared responsibility for both parties in a relationship*. Overpopulation, poverty and hunger in many countries, along with the enormous efforts of women have brought birth control to most countries in the world. It is obvious that a woman can only give birth and care optimally for her and a small number of children. Even with a good partner providing much of what is needed for health; pregnancy and giving birth remains high risk today. The World Health Organization estimates that approximately 830 women die every day because of complications during pregnancy and childbirth – and that statistic is actually a 44% reduction since 1990. I include this alarming statistic because in general people around the world assume that popping out a baby is the most natural thing to do. The medical community began investigating risk in childbirth and came up with the 'obstetrical dilemma'. When our hominin ancestors evolved to walk upright, to walk on two legs efficiently, the hominin skeleton had to be pushed and pulled into a new configuration, and that affected the pelvis. In most primates the birth canal in the pelvis is relatively straight. In hominins, hips became relatively narrow and the birth canal became distorted – a cylinder that varied in size and shape along its length, making birth a far more difficult and risky task. Then about two million years ago, our hominin ancestors began to change again with bigger brains, taller bodies and shorter arms. Female hominins had to maintain a narrow pelvis with a constricted birth canal in order to walk efficiently on two legs, while the babies they carried were evolving to have larger heads, hence a tighter and tighter fit through that narrow pelvis. (2) (3)

Safe birth control is essential to prevent unwanted pregnancy and unwanted risk. The birth control pill and the condom are the universal quick fix for preventing pregnancy. There isn't a convenient substitute at the moment for the Pill. The effort required to prevent pregnancy requires vigilance and attention to a lot of factors that young people may not be inclined to accept. However the serious side effects of the pill need to be made public. As you read about the consequences of taking the Pill, I don't ever suggest you reject it's use, though that may be the best choice for you, but consider all the alternatives and the huge responsibility you and your partner have in regard to fertility. How you manage your fertility determines the direction your life takes. If you throw the Pill out without being responsible for 'not getting pregnant' then you compromise everything. If you consider the Pill your only option then be sure to explore the deficiencies that it may cause and be preventative with supplementation and correct diet to make up for the depletion of essential nutrients that may be affecting your health. In no way do I suggest that women should stop taking the Pill, however I do seriously believe every woman should know the ingredients, the biology and the side effects to best make a decision for her own safety, longevity and health.

Currently over 100 million women are on the Pill worldwide, not long ago 300 million women were on the Pill. Tens of millions more use injectables, patches, and implants which contain similar levels of hormones. Girls as young as 12 are prescribed the Pill not only for contraception: but also as a treatment for heavy periods, acne, and 'hormone imbalances.' The Pill earns pharmaceutical companies billions in profits each year.

The Pill works by keeping women's bodies in a constant state of pregnancy, by keeping your hormone levels at a high point tricking your body into thinking that it's already pregnant, so pregnancy can't occur. These levels are 3-4 times higher than they naturally occur at the peak of your cycle.

You can't absorb nutrients properly on the Pill because taking the Pill every day places a heavy load on your liver, which has to metabolize all the synthetic hormones. Your ability to absorb vitamins B2, B6, B12, C, riboflavin, thiamine, and folic acid is compromised and leads to a depletion of the minerals zinc, copper, selenium, potassium, and magnesium. Sometimes it takes months or years before the effects of this malnutrition become apparent, beginning with multiple symptoms of insomnia, cravings, skin infections, headaches, weight gain, anxiety, fatigue, constipation, and irritability.

The Pill suppresses testosterone, which all women have and science has shown that women on the Pill produce up to seven times more of a sex hormone-binding globulin, a protein which binds with testosterone and takes it out of circulation. Lack of testosterone can equal lack of sex drive.

Depression symptoms double as a side-effect when taking the Pill. Studies show that women 18 years and older on the Pill, with no clinical history of depression, were twice as likely to suffer from depression as those not taking the birth control pill. New studies from Denmark looked at data from over a million women during a 19-year study, comparing the rates at which those who used hormonal contraceptive pills, but also other methods including hormonal implants, were diagnosed with depression or began taking antidepressants. The results are most dramatic for teenagers. Women between the ages of 15 and 19 who took oral contraceptives were 80% more likely to end up depressed without any history of depression. Those who took a progestin-only form of contraception, which contains one hormone instead of two, were more than twice as likely to be depressed. It's not rocket science when women's hormones have been associated with emotional states for a century (where do you think the word hysterectomy originated – from the word hysteria) that ingesting a high daily dose of synthetic hormones would have a serious effect on emotional wellbeing. (4)

Your risk of breast cancer, cervical cancer, stroke, bone density depletion, blood clots, and ovarian cancer is increased due to the hormonal changes and nutrient deficiencies.

The Pill is linked to infertility and the inability to become pregnant after taking the pill forcing the body to be in a constant state of 'pregnancy'. Even beyond the risk to women's health, Britain has determined a serious problem of fish dying off due to pollution in the water mainly due to human urinary birth control pill excretions.

The Pill changes your cervical mucus production, which over time can cause the mucus-producing cells to atrophy which effectively ages your cervix and narrows the cervical canal. The Pill alters 150 bodily functions, and affects all your organs.

There are new, 'no period' pills being released in the U.S that have no break intervals – the long-term effects of these have not yet been properly tested.

A new contraceptive pill for men has been announced in 2018 by the National Institute of Health and the University of Washington. Ironically, one of the side effects of the new birth control pill (dimethandrolone undecanoate) for men is weight gain, something women have struggled with since the Pill became popular. More choices for women and their partners are essential for family planning. Men would then have to decide whether their choice of birth control was worth the impact it may have on their physical and emotional wellbeing. On top of the potential health risks women are confronted with by taking 'the Pill' there is also the stress that women have endured for centuries regarding the burden of responsibility to prevent pregnancy. Perhaps this male birth control pill will be a reminder for men who have had the luxury of a particular kind of privilege and freedom regarding pregnancy prevention, of the burden that women have carried all along.

On an over populated planet women's ability to control fertility has been an enormous challenge since humans began on this planet. The Pill has become the cheap and accepted primary tool for women. With all the documented health risks pertaining to the Pill, choices for women and fertility are extremely challenging.

Parents of teenagers and the medical establishment would greatly oppose my suggesting that natural birth control is a logical option. Of course unwanted babies have and continue to be a sad and complicated part of humanity. However, there also exists the belief that youth can't decide this for themselves, and can't have the personal care and attention to pull off natural forms of contraception. Still this information is offered for you to understand the entire challenge you face with contraception.

There are natural forms of contraception that do not require drugs. Of course there is more effort and diligence required with non-drug birth control methods. Natural fertility, practiced with care and attention, has a 97% success rate and requires no devices. There are new tools such as the "Lady-Comp" and newly released "Leaf" necklace from Bellabeat that make tracking your ovulation down to the exact day easier. This method of birth control requires planning and attention to detail and parents of young people might not support this option because unplanned pregnancy changes lives forever. It all depends on how seriously you take your own life choices and have the maturity to realize the implications of unwanted pregnancy.

Fertility is determined by ovulation, when a mature egg is released from one of the ovaries, which usually takes place near the 14th day of a 28-day cycle. The 14th day is only an average. In a 28-day cycle a woman may ovulate on one of the days between the 11th and 21st cycle day (the first day of your period is cycle day 1). This is called your "fertility window." The two to three days prior to ovulation, and the day of ovulation itself, are your most fertile days. Getting pregnant after ovulation is possible, but is limited to the 12-24 hours after your egg has been released. Cervical mucus helps sperm live up to 5 days in a woman's body, and it takes around 6 hours for active sperm to reach the fallopian tubes. If the sperm is there when or shortly after an egg is released, you can become pregnant in the day after ovulation. Thorough understanding of your own biology is necessary to use natural birth control methods and there is plenty of information available for you to investigate. Some women have highly irregular cycles, due to poor diet and health issues and therefore cannot follow their cycles. However an irregular menstrual cycle is in itself a puzzle to solve. Your emotional wellbeing can be directly linked to the regularity of your menstrual cycle and getting to the root of that problem will give you a great boost in health and wellbeing. (3) Generally, an erratic menstrual cycle and the emotional stress and physical symptoms that can come with it are indicative of health imbalances that can and must be solved for your overall wellbeing. 'Natural Birth Control Made Simple' by Barbara Kass-Annese is one good example of the many books available on women and fertility.

Barrier methods such as diaphragms or cervical caps are reusable, and can be worn in advance to allow some spontaneity. Even the condom has been recognized as one more potentially toxic cog in the wheel of choices people have to make every day. There are **new condoms on the market** that are nitrosamine free, which is a better choice for both partners in a sexual relationship. (5) (6) (7) (8) (9) (10) (11) There is a great deal more information on condoms and health in Chapter 3, Health and Performance.

Sexually transmitted diseases (STD's) like gonorrhea, syphilis, chlamydia and HIV are the only STD's that are required by law to be reported to the Centre for Disease Control (CDC) by doctors. However, when you include herpes and more than a dozen other diseases that are transmitted sexually but are not reported, the statistics are extremely low for STD incidents in America. The CDC estimates there are more than *20 million new cases of STDs in the United States each year* and at least half occur in young people ages 15 to 24.

One of the reasons so many STDs spread is because many people think they can only be infected if they have sexual intercourse. Many STDs, like herpes or genital warts, can be contracted through skin-to-skin contact with an infected area or sore. Kissing alone can be the vehicle that gives someone herpes. The viruses or bacteria that cause STDs can enter the body through tiny cuts or tears in the mouth as well as the genitals. The other troubling fact is that many people don't even know they have an STD and therefore can pass an infection on to their sexual partner without even realizing it. If untreated, STDs can cause permanent damage such as infertility and can lead to liver damage and in the case of HIV, immune collapse. (12)

People who have sexual contact with many different partners are more at risk than those who stay with the same partner. Condoms are the only form of birth control that reduce your risk of getting an STD, and must be used every time. Spermicides, diaphragms, the Pill and other birth control methods may prevent pregnancy, but they don't protect a person against STDs.

Don't let embarrassment or resistance to seeing a doctor prevent you from having a checkup if you have multiple sex partners and/or symptoms. The sooner you are diagnosed and get treatment the better, as less damage and other complications will occur. Waiting to see a doctor may allow a disease to progress and cause more harm, and of course if you are diagnosed with an STD then you must morally inform your sex partner or partners. (13)

Depth of feeling, the need for security, visions of family dancing in the head are no longer the deciding factors in choosing a sexual partner. All the wonderful and unique desires we have attract us to others. A Sapiosexual is defined as one who finds intelligence the most sexually attractive feature. More so today than in past generations, sex can be based on a casual hook up that may or may not benefit the individuals involved. *Intimate connections are made during casual sex.* Some say it is simply about pleasure and have no limits on who, when or how many people they might hook up with for sex. Some think that sex is to be savored only with someone of deep connection. Not wanting to judge either end of this spectrum, it is critical to know that there is a trigger point within us that is affected when sex happens with another. Create a standard for yourself with intentions and goals in the form of respect and pleasure, patience and honesty no matter how casual the connection. *When we reveal our most intimate body parts and strip down to our natural selves, we make ourselves vulnerable.* Just be sure that person deserves you, and that you will be respected and cared for, whatever you choose to experience.

The best dating relationship will be effortless when you can be the real you and feel appreciated and respected and not consumed by unnecessary details or worry about being judged. Friendship is always a good foundation for a long lasting relationship.

Whatever relationship you pursue, be sure it is not because you feel incomplete, or that you need someone else to validate your awesomeness. It has been proven time and again that not having a relationship is better than having a bad relationship. Never settle for less than what you deserve. We are here to encourage each other and lift each other up. Remember that it is your uniqueness that makes you attractive. Understanding yourself and being understood by another is a great gift.

Sexuality is unique to each person, yet the world is intent on minding the business of everyone in regard to sex and sexuality. So much residual tension and control still exists from a long history of patriarchy when women were possessions without minds of their own or authority over their own lives. Homosexuality was illegal for centuries, and men were tortured and executed because of it. The conundrum is that there were societies such as the Celts, the Chinese, the Greeks, the Romans, the Mayans in Central America and the Aztec, who identified with the god Zochipili, who was a patron of male homosexuality. Homosexuality was pervasive and highly visible in the Arab and Islamic worlds, all dating back to the 1st century BC. Depictions of homosexuality are found on the ancient San Rock paintings in the modern day Republic of Zimbabwe, from centuries long past. Laws have been present for centuries around the illegal status of LGBT (lesbian, gay, bisexual, transgender). Karl Heinrich Ulrichs (1825–1895), was a pioneer of LGBT rights. More recently the illegal status of homosexuality has been removed in many countries around the world. However, LGBT relationships are still illegal in 73 countries around the world and in 13 of those countries being gay or bisexual is punishable by death.

David F. Greenberg's 'The Construction of Homosexuality' (1988) provides a detailed, well researched history of homosexuality, both in terms of sexual practices and the attitudes of the society at large, from ancient and tribal societies to the present.

As Youth seek their own identity and expression of sexuality, the influences from the world can completely disrupt any natural evolution in a

185

young person's own version of sexuality and intimacy. Digital pornography has created a young oversexed generation of 6 to 12 year olds that will never know what it's like to grow through puberty with their own feelings and opinions on the matter. Every year 1.2 million children are sold into the sex trade with only one percent of them ever being rescued. A new film by Andrew Kooman called "She Has a Name" has been translated into many different languages, educating everyone on the crisis and horror of the child sex trade around the world. For most of us it is monstrous and unimaginable, and yet around the world, millions continue to suffer by the cruelty of others. (14)

It is impossible to fill this book with all that you need to know about the world you live in. Yet awareness is critical if you truly live in and care for the world and all her inhabitants. Be your healthy self, do no harm and help those in distress whenever you can. *There are too many bystanders who see and look the other way or suspect and tell no one.* For thousands of years sexuality has been influenced and corrupted by taboos, laws, religions, fashion, the patriarchy and corporations wanting you to look and behave a certain way.

It takes guts to be yourself! To resist all the pressure to fit into the mold of societal expectations takes courage and intention. This doesn't mean you cannot be your creative, fashionable self. Just make sure it is *your* preference; design your own look and have fun with it.

Unimaginable a decade ago, the intensely personal subject of gender identity has entered the public realm. Gender has become a subject with cultural, social, biological, and political significance. Gender is a social construct used to classify a person as a man, woman, or some other identity. There are presently 21 identified genders in the human species. On the cover of National Geographic January 2017 is the title "Gender Revolution", a special edition on the shifting landscape of gender. Can you imagine a world when gender is neither a plus nor a minus? Biology need not define your destiny no matter your gender. Anne Marie Slaughter wrote "The concept of gender fluidity remains alien, even abhorrent, to many people in Western society. *Once we recognize that gender identity and expression exist along a spectrum, why should we cling to the rigid categorization of men and women?* The ultimate goal, surely, is to let all people define themselves as human beings, to break out of assigned categories and challenge present day stereotypes." Historian Yuval Noah Harari, in his masterful account of how Homo sapiens evolved, writes; "If Homo sapiens advance because of the power of our imaginations, then we can imagine a world in which gender does not define a person any more than race or ethnicity does. Without the weight of gendered expectations, each of us can develop the full circle of ourselves."

Gloria Steinem writes that it is time to extend equality and opportunity to the entire human family.

Asia Kate Dillon made history as the first gender non-binary character on mainstream television and shared her research. "After doing some research, I understood, Oh, sex and identity are different. Female is a sex, and sex is between our legs and gender identity is between our ears," states Asia and further reminds us that the word non-binary, is an umbrella term for any number of gender identities falling outside the conventional terms of male and female. (15) (16)

In this chapter on sex and dating it is impossible to avoid addressing the subject of a global rape culture that is one of the worst aspects of humanity. Rape culture is defined as a society or environment whose prevailing social attitudes have the effect of normalizing or trivializing sexual assault and abuse. An example of the most bizarre and incomprehensible phenomena is that, during war, at times when circumstances of crisis lead to extreme scarcity of food, water, shelter, and loss of family and belongings, there is a plethora of documented evidence of both the invaders and the liberators raping the women and girls who survived the war. This is unconscionable behavior and seems impossible to understand for most of us on any level. Gloria Steinem is a writer, lecturer, political activist, and feminist organizer. She is particularly interested in the shared origins of sex and race caste systems, gender roles and child abuse as roots of violence, non-violent conflict resolution, the cultures of indigenous peoples, and organizing across boundaries for peace and justice. She has written a dozen excellent books on the subjects of gender, education and women's rights. (17)

WMC 'Women's Media Center' is an online database of media-experienced women experts who connect to journalists, bookers and producers to make it easier for journalists to include diverse women's voices around the world. There are many articles on gender conflict on their website. (18)

It is obvious that the attitudes towards men, women and sex passed down from previous generations can affect and shape views of youth today. *What we witness and hear at a young age becomes a standard for behavior*. Biology classes are no longer enough for teenagers navigating a world where porn, explicit music videos and online hook-ups are the norm. Understanding consent, boundaries and effective communication are essential to understanding how sexual violence works and how to prevent it. *Consent can no longer be defined as a simple yes or no answer*. To assist you in navigating all the possible circumstances affecting your ability to say yes or no, a deeper understanding of the role played by alcohol, drugs, peer pressure, coercion and boundaries is required. For many the concept of consent is straight forward and obvious.   However, the history of women as possessions can be traced back millennia and the residue of that entitlement is at the root of the repetitive demonstrations of some men's toxic attitudes toward women.

The Game of Thrones has been watched by a record 16 million people and from the first scene to the last has been inundated with extreme violence toward women and men.   Eighty two percent of viewers are young males watching reinforced ideals and behaviors based on violence and conquest of women and land. One would think there is some kind of strategy of the brain that should cause the viewer to be repulsed by the violence? What you watch on screens can radicalize (to cause someone to adopt radical positions on political or social issues) you to accept standards and behaviors far below your preferred moral compass. A dumbing down and becoming numb to what is around you are serious consequences of the influence of violent movies, games and entertainment.

As a result of social images in music, movies and pornography, men are depicted as the predators and women are depicted as the prey. Their expressions of fear and rejection, including defensive physical attacks are excused away as part of a coy game to be overcome. A culture in high school and university suggests that asking permission is a sign of weakness. Today there are sitcoms that easily support this hypothesis.   There are many great articles written by men on this subject who agree that, for every "No Means No" reminder, there are thousands of messages saying or implying that it's okay and sexy not to wait for consent. Many people (men and women alike) fall back on the old excuse "boys will be boys," which is license to behave like immature, taunting bullies or worse. There is much to learn about the male sex drive. Women rarely rape men. What is it about male sexuality that prevents them from interrupting their need or desire for orgasm at the request of their present partner? Where does the sense of entitlement come from that women must meet their needs? These alone are interesting and essential conversations to have.

As a result of the #MeToo movement, the Alianza Nacional de Campesinas in November 2017 wrote a letter of solidarity to the Hollywood women involved in exposing the sexual abuse allegations against Harvey Weinstein. The letter, published in Time Magazine, described experiences of assault and harassment among female farmworkers. The letter stated that it was written on behalf of the approximate 700,000 female farmworkers in the United States.

Following #MeToo, the #Time'sUp movement was announced in The New York Times on January 1, 2018. The new foundation announced three initiatives: a $13-million legal defense fund administered by the National Women's Law Center, to support lower-income women seeking justice for sexual harassment and assault in the workplace, advocating for legislation to punish companies that tolerate persistent harassment, and a movement toward gender parity in studio and talent agencies.

The challenge is to know where you personally draw the line for inappropriate behavior. There are obvious lines drawn regarding sexual assault and rape. With the maximum coverage and drama of the culture of Hollywood taking on hundreds of years of oppression of women, the challenge still falls to each person to choose to behave in a manner of respect and tolerance. Ten thousand years of patriarchal control around the world has left scars and damage on everyone.

Here is an opportunity, along with all the publicity from battles fought on the public stage, to simply reflect on your personal behavior toward men or women in the arena of flirting and partying and searching for love and attention. There is no doubt in the #metoo movement there will be innocent victims in the brawl of accusations and that is extremely sad. However, our penal system for hundreds of years has punished the innocent along with the guilty. In prisons in the US alone, studies suggest that 1 in 25 people on death row are innocent and of the 2 million people behind bars, 20,000 of them have been convicted of crimes they did not commit.

Be aware of your behavior and that of others. Friendship and love are good things, and most of us strive for both. The important thing is to be mindful of your behavior and other's behavior towards you and protect yourself and others in all circumstances.

In truth the whole scenario of sexual reproduction plays out around the world with millions of different species; while the female resists, the male demonstrates his physical superiority and the female acknowledges his suitability as a mate and willingly or unwillingly gives in. Perhaps we have simply not evolved past the cave man days regarding sex. However, women around the world are demanding attention to these very issues and taking back their right to say no. Good men can't conceive of being part of any of this conflict and are grateful to support women in their demand for individual autonomy.

It has been true in the past and is still true today that, for many women the quality of her life is overwhelmingly influenced by what kind of man she can attract. Ten thousand years of oppression is hard to withstand. Women married to capable men have had higher standards of living. Historically women compromised a great deal in order for them and their children to be safe and to be fed. Laws, religions, fashion, TV and movies have created an atmosphere wherein women culturally collude to keep the value of sex and female companionship high. To do this women compete with each other at great expense. Fashion and makeup are fundamentally here to keep women

189

in competition with each other. And if you go back in time you will learn that they were all created by men. All that high heeled discomfort, all that toxic makeup, all those diets and uncomfortable clothes create a platform where women compete with women.

Feminism and women's rights are often hijacked by Hollywood, corporations and celebrities. One could consider Walt Disney, beloved by so many families for decades as one of those hijackers. The premise is that a beautiful, innocent and intelligent girl is held captive by a beast, who is a 'good' man under a spell waiting for true love to release him. In true beast fashion he is violent and the tale epitomizes the classic 'Stockholm Syndrome" which is a condition that causes hostages to develop a psychological alliance with their captors as a survival strategy during captivity. There are plenty of real-life examples of this today whereby the hostage no longer seeks escape and will defend her captors if released. This is called the Stockholm syndrome. No matter how great the music, and delightful the teapot and candlestick performance, the underlying message is still that a woman can fall in love with a man with a big problem and it is up to her to fix it. This is at the root of so many domestic violence scenarios: woman marries damaged man with the intention of changing him and it proves impossible. Of course not all relationships begin this way. However, the history of domestic violence speaks for itself.

The present struggle to rise above the past and allow youth to come to their own opinions about truth, integrity and respect can be blamed on historic religious attitudes towards all things sexual. Many religions taught that eternal hellfire was the price you paid for sex outside of marriage, consensual intercourse before marriage, premarital hand jobs, oral sex at any time, homosexual sex, and masturbation, leaving no room for sexual expression or experience of any kind outside of marriage. Religious attitudes still have a lot of power, partly because these subjects are still not openly discussed and understood by most people today. (19) (20)

When women were property, had no legal rights, could not vote, could not leave the home or choose for themselves, men were under pressure to protect, fight and provide everything necessary for the family to continue. There was a time when manhood was defined by sex and assured procreation. *Though history has difficult stories to tell in the arena of dating and sex, we are here 'now' and we must learn from that history and work together to solve these huge social issues.*

Great strides have been made for women who have found communities to support and encourage their dreams, communities where men support women and women support women. The tide is turning.

I believe that most people are inherently good. The key is to be mindful of how easy it is to be part of this type of violence, either as a bystander or as a cat-calling jokester. There are many ways this slippery slope has so-called 'regular' people behaving badly toward each other. The 'No means No' campaigns are everywhere today, working to counter this rape, sexual abuse and misconduct culture. *(21)*

For a society that succeeds and values each and every member, 'do no harm' must be the bottom line for everyone. When you are your best self, only good choices are made. The most important priority, above all else, is to be safe, and protect yourself and your partner from sexually transmitted disease and unwanted pregnancy. Focus on loving, cooperative and compassionate relationships.

Identify your personal deal breakers; these can be your non-negotiables that you will not abide in a partner or relationship for your own well-being. These standards would apply to both one night stands and potential long term relationships. For past generations, differences in socio economics like religion, race, economic status or education were common deal breakers. Deal breakers today include substance abuse, addictions, bigotry, lying, infidelity, or a tendency towards violence or abusiveness. The greater number of deal breakers you have could equal a smaller pool of potential dates or partners. There must be bottom line deal breakers for each of you, however many successful relationships come from working through, compromising and evolving beyond limitations that you might have ruled out before the relationship could even exist. An excellent guiding principle for establishing deal breakers is to examine the deal breakers you have for your own behavior.

It's not rocket science to know people respond positively to respect, compassion, concern, gentleness, patience and understanding. Be yourself and don't lose sight of your moral compass when navigating the world of dating and sex.

Chapter 19

Happiness

Laughter is the best medicine. *Laughter is one of the most essential aspects of life, for happiness and more importantly for health. Science supports this.* Change your words and change your life!

Happiness is a very personal, individual state of being. People may describe their lives as busy, complex and interesting with moments of easily-described joy. If calm, content and grateful is your state of mind with intermittent noticeable points of happiness and joy then you are doing a great job of your life. 'Hap' is the Old Norse and Old English root of the word happiness, and it just means luck or chance, which puts another whole spin on the word happiness. The key is to know yourself and be willing to assess your state of mind to determine what, if any, work needs to be done to foster an attitude of happiness.

Laughing heals on so many levels. Laughter and negative emotions simply cannot exist in the brain at the same time. There is plenty of science that has determined the positive effects of laughter on the circulatory system, the heart, the production of good hormones in the brain, and the healing effects in relationships.

Laughter works wonders for the teenage brain, (brains of all ages of course,) and has been shown to greatly assist those with addictions and those in pain. Laughter lowers anxiety and improves personal performance and therefore significantly contributes to your health and wellbeing.

"Anatomy of Happiness", written by Martin Gumpert, describes the positive effect that happiness has in all areas of your life. *He proves to us that over-thinking is a cause of unhappiness*. "A History of Happiness" by Darrin M. McMahon, Ph.D. is an excellent reminder of the role happiness has played in our history. *The Smile Project* was created in 2012. Its mission is to promote random acts of kindness and spread happiness while raising money for various charitable organizations.

We lose touch too easily with what we loved as a child. Partly because of an acute awareness of how others might judge you, you avoid anything that could potentially embarrass you. So much laughter is missed by over-thinking. Be aware of your vulnerability to social pressure and herd mentality and actively choose that which makes you happy because this is essential for your individuality and persona to grow. Embracing embarrassment can be enlightening and humorous. There are limits, of course; however, feeling intimidated or fearful can greatly limit happiness, which in turn can limit success in whatever you endeavor to achieve.

Nothing new can happen if you don't push past your vulnerabilities and fears and try something new. Discovering what you're passionate about and what matters to you in life can be a process of trial and error. No one knows exactly how they feel about an activity until they actually do the activity.

Charles Montgomery's latest book, *"Happy City"*, looks at how lessons from psychology, neuroscience and design activism can help all of us fix broken cities and improve our lives. The book describes working with neighborhoods to promote wellbeing and happiness. *Stumbling on Happiness*, is a project in a neighborhood where different households and families shared weekly meals together and eventually took down fences and built a super park for their children. One mom died in the neighborhood and her child was slowly incorporated into the neighborhood and suffered far less from the loss of his mom. There are many happiness projects going on in every country in the world.

Your brain, with its billion nerve cells forming a trillion plus connections called synapses is in a constant dynamic state of remodeling in response to the world around you, and is the source of your observations and thoughts. The new frontier in medicine today is brain research and seeking to understand its limitless possibilities. If you wake up each day and want the same thing for breakfast that's what you will have. If you wake up and say I want something new for breakfast, this actually opens up a reservoir of creativity in your brain and new neurons are born to choose something new for breakfast. If you want to learn a new language or challenge yourself to a new skill your brain will deliver. The more you learn, the more you use your brain the higher the probability of success in all of your endeavors. Think of the possibilities if you are open to change, open to happiness. It is how your brain is wired. *Your creativity and curiosity are living, breathing, ever new inspirations that no computer can match.*

Who you are is enough. There is nothing wrong with you at all. You are each as much an extraordinary phenomenon of nature as another. It's true, its basic biology; you are extraordinary.

Stop the cycle of wishing things were different and take control of your thoughts and reactions. Realize that optimism is a choice, just as sadness and negativity are choices.

You are not born with a positive or negative attitude. It is something you create through your perspective of experiences. Very few situations are completely bad, although there are some that are; in those times scream for help, fight back or run as fast as you can to safety. Try to come up with three positives of any challenging situation you have been through. This is easier in retrospect and a great teaching tool to remind you to look for the positive in bad situations. Hang out with people who have fun and who have a positive attitude. Everyone feels better around positive and happy people.

Choose a signature phrase for yourself, like 'I feel great today!' and repeat it daily out loud or in your mind. Repeat it often. This is how you retrain your subconscious mind to be more positive. Louise Hay wrote 'You Can Heal Your Life' and it is full of affirmations for all occasions of stress or illness. Repeating affirmations can quite simply change your mind about how you view a situation. Nature creates uniqueness in all things, from flowers to birds to landscapes. We are all unique and so find your joy and be happy with who you are. The best way to find happiness or maintain happiness is to actively create balance in your life. Happiness is enhanced by a balance of good food and water, healthy relationships, physical activity, spiritual awareness and emotional well-being.

The absurdity of the human condition can be both very painful and very laughable. Albert Camus, (novelist, editor, philosopher, 1913 – 1960) argued that human beings could not escape asking the question, "What is the meaning of Life?" always seeking to understand life's purpose. Throughout each of our lives the natural world and the universe barely notice our presence or absence and the wheel of life keeps turning. The absurdity is easily visible in the enormous global inequality, poverty and starvation for billions and constant wars along with the millions of people who believe life after death has more value than the actual life they are living here and now.

The stark contrast is the staggering wealth of a minority of global citizens, in governments around the world so mired in corruption, bureaucracy, outdated laws and inner conflict that they can't feed and house the less fortunate in their own countries.

What to do with this conundrum? Laugh I say, laugh. Laugh in the face of adversity. As described in detail in other chapters, laughter is medicinal. Finding a balance between reality that may be intense and conflicting and simply submitting to laughter is a reasonable goal in dealing with the chaos of society today. Laughter stops you from over thinking, increases endorphin levels and reduces stress hormones like cortisol and adrenaline. After a good laugh the situation may be still intense and chaotic but you will see it and approach it and deal with in a totally different way after you have laughed. While life may seem like a roller coaster at times, cultivating a good sense of humor helps you ride the highs and lows with a great deal more grace.

Face problems head on and don't hide from them or try to pretend they don't exist. The sooner you deal with 'stuff' with a positive attitude, the sooner you can return to a state of calm and eventual happiness. Don't let failure or sorrow or pain stop you from returning to joy. The majority of challenges you face will pass and be behind you, change will come and with effort you will come out the other end looking forward to a brighter day.

Consider time before and time yet to come and, with the realization that our human existence is relatively short, make the absolute best you can of your life. A great many wise people teach us that by dismantling the power structures and seeing through the transparency of contrived society with intelligence, imagination and humor, you will be a free thinker. Fixed thinking weakens the imagination.

When things are not working the way you want and you have been robbed of your optimism and enthusiasm; remember that changing your perspective is imperative. Know that some good, will come of every mistake you have ever made, that is how the universe works. Rise to any occasion of conflict and have a bigger picture in mind, that being your happiness, and move towards it. Be vigilant for your own wellbeing.

Insist on happiness in your life! *Remember that humor is the place where joy and intelligence meet*.

In 2013 I wrote *'Handbook for Happiness'*, a concise pocketbook that offers ideas, information and protocols to assist you in finding more happiness in your life. There are many simple ways to pursue happiness, and most importantly within yourself. Honor your values and all that you know to be good in your world, hang out with people who make you smile, accept the good and imagine the best in your life in spite of some of the challenges you face, be open to change and do things that you love and have fun with, listen

195

to your heart and learn to measure happiness in small ways which accumulate to show you how much happiness you already have that you might not notice. Be grateful for what you have!

Happy people have younger hearts, younger arteries, and are younger in mind and body than other people the same age. Happy people recover more quickly from trauma, cope better with pain, have lower blood pressure, and have longer life expectancy than unhappy people. Studies show that happy people have stronger immune systems, are less likely to get colds and flu viruses, and when they do; their symptoms tend to be mild.

The brilliance of happiness is that it takes all aspects of your life, job, relationships, parenting, politics, etc., to the next level. We simply have to choose; that is where the first step lies on any journey. The best of positive habits will begin to flourish and the results will surprise you. *I am astounded to notice that happiness, joy and love have been placed so high on their pedestals that, to many, they seem forever out of reach.* Define what "happy" is to you and your life will begin to feel more stable and full of promise.

Chapter 20

Now is the only place your life exists

NOW is all you've got, yesterday and tomorrow don't exist. When you live in the moment, only then are you able to fully experience all that moment has to offer you. In other words most people are missing the moment and missing the potential for their own lives. Know yourself, and be aware of the cost of fatigue and procrastination, they are thieves of time.

I could put this quote from Lao Tzu in every chapter, *"If you want to awaken all of humanity, then awaken all of yourself. If you want to eliminate the suffering of the world, then eliminate all that is dark and negative inside of yourself. Truly the greatest gift you have to give is that of your own self-transformation."*

While multitasking is often viewed as a valued skill, focusing on one task at a time is much more efficient. Doing many things at once has been proven to slow down productivity and lower your work quality. According to MIT neuroscientist Earl Miller, "[Our brains are] not wired to multitask well...when people think they're multitasking, they're actually just switching from one task to another very rapidly. And every time they do, there's a cognitive cost." (1)

Dr. Daniel Leviton wrote "The Organized Mind, Thinking Straight in the Age of Information Overload" and shows you how to navigate the churning flood of information and organize your time, your home, your workplace and perhaps most importantly, your fun time.

Create a morning routine for yourself; a kick start to your day. Decide on a thought, a plan, an activity, or a ritual breakfast that will inspire not just you but your body to get going. Music helps. Figure out what motivates you and make it an important first start to the day. This always helps you be in the Now.

In the internet age, there are many Jacks Of All Trades - people who know a bit about many things, but have not mastered any one thing. This is unfortunate. Immense pleasure is derived from being absolutely badass at something. Mastery keeps us in the Now. Dance, music, math, sports, recreation, gardening, volunteering, communicating and even work – pick one that matches your passion and do it, everyone can be a master. Take up one idea, make that idea your focus, think of it, dream about it and live it daily. Let your brain, muscles, nerves, heart be full of that idea and you will find a way to success. **Passion and creativity keep us in the moment, in the Now, which is where your life really does exist.**

Realize and accept that other people may be looking through an entirely different lens than yours. The Power of Now is a book by Eckhart Tolle, intended to be a guide for day-to-day living, translated into 33 languages. He stresses the importance of living in the present moment and avoiding thoughts of the past or future. If you feel stuck in the past, spend too much time thinking about things instead of accomplishing things, and you feel like you are waiting around for happiness to fall in your lap, this book is for you. Pay attention to yourself and be aware if you find yourself complaining too often, or feel constant anxiety or worry day to day.

There is no better time than the present to get a job done, to make a change or consider that which makes you happy.

Unless you're a savant, you need to read, learn, and experience things multiple times for them to stick. Meditation has proven to be a tool that teaches you how to be fully present in the moment to live your life fully and completely. Sara Lazar, a neuroscientist at Massachusetts General Hospital and Harvard Medical School, was one of the first scientists to test the benefits of meditation and mindfulness in brain scans. What she found surprised her; through brain scans she proved that meditating can literally change your brain. Meditation and mindfulness are just like exercise. They are both forms of mental exercise and help us better handle stress, promote longevity, improve focus, creativity, relationships, enhance your immune system, and reduce physical and emotional pain.

In order to live fully in the moment it is important to recognize the opportunity that all experiences can offer. *People generally misinterpret the meaning of the word "failure"*. Failure is just as natural as success. One doesn't replace the other. In actuality, failure is simply the opportunity to try again with a better approach, materials and choices, and is a part of the circle of success.

Success isn't possible without action. Though knowledge is power it is useless without action. All of your mistakes teach you valuable lessons and can make you stronger and wiser. Likely the only mistake you will regret in your life is not taking action or not taking that step and opportunity to learn or do something new as a result.

Sometimes too many options can impair one's ability to make a decision, especially when it comes to determining a career or life path. Knowing your strengths and weaknesses and making your priority list are great tools to decide on the step or direction you want to take. It's important to remember that a youth today may have 5 or 6 different careers in their lifetime. Whatever you are doing right now be the best you can be at that task, and when you are ready move on to what will get you closer to your vision or the career path you are on.

It is important to find work/play/life balance. If your job is strictly for monetary gain then be sure to balance that with recreation and time spent in nature. If you have passion for your job and you are benefiting society then perhaps work is your play.

Here's a simple exercise to get you into the NOW and face any decision you have to make: breathe. Breathing consciously will bring you into the NOW faster than any other method. Most people shallow breathe. This is defined as "thoracic breathing, or chest breathing, which is the drawing of minimal breath into the lungs, usually by drawing air into the chest area using the intercostal muscles rather than throughout the lungs via the diaphragm" (Wikipedia). Oxygen is essential for every cellular activity that takes place in the body. The brain cannot function efficiently without the proper amount of oxygen. Diaphragmatic breathing, abdominal breathing, belly breathing or deep breathing involves slow and deep inhalation through the nose, filling the brain and body with oxygen.

The body has a physiological response to the breath. As the breath is regulated, chemicals in the brain become more balanced; the level of oxygen in cells increases and the heartbeat can slow down. Many people spend a huge amount of time stuck in the 'fight or flight' mechanism that served us well running from a predator generations ago. That continual level of hyper-awareness and stress exhausts the adrenal glands and eventually we become paralyzed by stress, unable to save our own lives.

Conscious breathing can slow down the mind. By making conscious breathing a habit, the brain begins a new pattern of behavior. Calm becomes the foundation from which we begin to make decisions and react to our lives. According to Ujjayi breathing in Yoga, "The quality of your breath is directly related to your state of mind, so when you are aware of your breath you can be aware of your inner state." (Yogajournal.com) Conscious breathing is a focus on the breath, a perfect way to be in the NOW.

Don't confuse success with happiness either, though both can exist together. "The monk who sold his Ferrari" by Robin Sharma is one of the most inspiring books to remind you that you can be happy as you choose one step at a time in a long life of accomplishments and choices.

Time is your existence measured in minutes, days or years, during which an action, process, or condition exists or continues. Time can be viewed as too much time but more likely not enough time for a given event or task or vacation.

To value your time, and to understand the value of time NOW, you might appreciate the top 5 regrets of those who are or were near the end of their physical lives.

- I wish I'd had the courage to live a life true to myself, not the life others expected of me.
- I wish I hadn't worked so hard.
- I wish I'd had the courage to express my feelings.
- I wish I had stayed in touch with my friends.
- I wish that I had let myself be happier.

The most important thing is to value every moment of every day and to be thankful for who you are and what you have NOW.

Chapter 21

Stress

There are times when you will be overwhelmed. There may be times when you must take action to save your own life or the lives of others. Your body is designed to manage extreme stress. Understanding the biology of stress will help you to de-stress when the crisis is over. Stress can also become so habitual and subliminal that you may not even think you are stressed. If in doubt, determine your stress levels by observing how calm, productive and light-hearted you feel. That would be one of the opposite stress determinants. You want to acknowledge stress in your life, examine the details, be willing to explore the contents and create a plan to deal with it.

There is healthy physical stress when the heart races and adrenaline pumps into muscles for explosions of energy necessary to run, escape or rescue someone. Healthy levels of stress can pump more adrenaline into your muscles to help you win the race. Hormones released during stress can sharpen the mind. Recognize what is going on in your body, focus on the best course of action, and choose to work with it rather than resist it. ***There is also chronic stress that can slowly kill over time***, and can trigger violence you had no idea you were capable of, or the opposite can occur and create cowardice, making you hide from your situation. Knowledge is power. Understanding stress is vital to living a healthy and long life.

Daily and repetitive stress shuts down the prefrontal cortex, the part of the brain responsible for decision making, correcting errors, and assessing situations. You can imagine the multitude of decisions and experiences you encounter in a day that could be greatly affected by stress. Whatever limitations you think you have, you are usually the one who imposes them on yourself. By setting higher expectations you enter a phase of higher functioning. For example if you constantly affirm that your memory isn't good, the brain accepts this and follows through with poor memory. The keys to overcoming stress are adaptability and changing your thoughts.

A most interesting aspect of brain chemistry is that you can change your biology with your thoughts and attitude. For example, gratitude has been noted as a great way to boost dopamine. Gratitude sets up a virtue-cycle, which encourages us to be grateful for what we have and work towards or seek more things that make us grateful while focusing on things that make us happy. A great practice in gratitude is to keep a gratitude journal that you write in and read each day. You can take it one step further by practicing the feeling of gratitude often throughout the day. Feelings of gratitude easily displace stress.

Research has shown that people who feel gratitude are happier, more satisfied with their lives and report less stress. Grateful people are less likely to be depressed, anxious, lonely, and neurotic. But it also appears that grateful people don't live in a world of denial. They don't ignore the negative parts of their lives. Psychologist Robert Emmons defines gratitude as "a felt sense of wonder, thankfulness, and appreciation for life." Gratitude can mean different things to different people. In its simplest form it is expressed as gratitude for your life, for your friends or family, for the love you have for yourself no matter what situation you find yourself in.

Change your mind about stress and you can change your body's response to stress. During healthy stress, the body is energized, preparing to meet the challenge. The heart rate increases, preparing for action. There is more rapid breathing, and increased oxygen to the brain. Stress hormones are produced by your pituitary gland. This is the biology of courage, creating resilience. There are many stories of people performing super-human feats of strength to help others during disasters.

Emotions associated with subliminal stress are like magnets which attract similar emotions, thoughts, actions and scenarios. As discussed previously with the law of attraction. Scientists working at the Institute of Neurology in London have discovered that people who visualize a better future are more likely to be able to bring that future into existence.

Researchers at the University of Exeter have published studies on constructive repetitive thought, finding that people who consistently tell themselves that they can meet a goal are more likely to secure a positive outcome. Positive affirmations are proven to help with recovery from trauma, improve anticipatory planning, aid treatment for depression, and boost physical health. When someone sees you radiating positivity, this same response is mirrored in the brain of the observer, drawing them to act positively towards you as well. Rumi said *'When you practice kindness and compassion, you are the first one to profit.'*

Whenever we are conflicted about what to do or not to do, we can explore the ramifications of the actions and, examine the toll the actions will take on our emotional and mental well-being. For instance, on a global scale there are economic wars about oil and resources, environmental wars, political wars, religious wars and so on with horrific costs to everyone involved. Governments are not examining the toll of all this on humanity and the earth. *Your personal conflict can be resolved if you take the time to understand what is at stake, what is to be gained and by whom, and how to proceed*. Everything you do is an opportunity for self-discovery.

In no way do I want to minimize the incredible struggles some of you may face - the hunger, pain, loss of self/family or home, the fear, and the chaos. If that is your present reality, your first step is to ask for help. If your life is in danger call 911! At the same time there are young people who have none of those obvious struggles, have wealth and opportunity at their disposal and yet may still feel lost with despair and loneliness. Whether wealthy or poor, fundamentally we are all the same; we want the same health and safety for ourselves and each other.

The biology of stress is discussed thoroughly under Chapter 3, 'Health and Performance'; however, it is essential to understand how your body responds to stress. Cortisol is often called the primary "stress hormone" because it's one of the main hormones we release when we're under any sort of pressure and our evolutionary-based "fight or flight response" kicks into gear. High Cortisol levels contribute to acne, high susceptibility to infections, high blood pressure, high anxiety and difficulty sleeping (that tired but wired feeling). It's also important to know that cortisol is natural to your body and it serves an essential role in your life. Cortisol helps keep you motivated, awake and responsive to your environment. Chronic stress, whether subliminal or acute, and the overuse of steroids are the biggest contributors to high cortisol. Lowering cortisol levels that are too high is essential to overall well-being and in some cases survival. Adaptogen herbs like Astragalus and Ashwaganda are very helpful, along with B vitamins and Vitamin C. A whole food, anti-inflammatory diet includes healthy fats and proteins with every meal and lots of organic fresh fruits, nuts and vegetables. The best foods are discussed thoroughly in Chapter 22 'Nutrition'.

Reducing stress may take effort to correct signals sent via the cortisol messengers that increase breathing, heart rate, pain and muscle tension. Sleep-related problems can put you at higher risk to skin inflammations and infections. Deep breathing exercises activate the body's natural relaxation response by activating the parasympathetic nervous system. Regular exercise helps bring cortisol back down to healthy levels. Remember getting enough sleep is your best way to control cortisol production. No matter how busy or how much fun you are having, science shows us that seven to nine hours of sleep per night will reset your circadian rhythms and bring hormones back in to balance. (1)

'The bridge between hope and despair may be a good night's sleep'. There are direct correlations between stress and lack of sleep. Your brain is not fully developed until 25 years of age. While all that growing is going on, an average of eight hours of sleep at night is essential for brain development, resilience and restoration from the day. This follows a pattern of alternating REM (rapid eye movement) and NREM (non-rapid eye movement) sleep throughout a typical night in a cycle that repeats itself about every 90 min. In a nutshell NREM is the deepest and most restorative sleep during which blood pressure drops, breathing becomes slower, muscles relax, blood supply to muscles increases, tissue growth and repair occurs and energy is restored. Hormones are released such as growth hormone, essential for growth and development including muscle development during the deepest part of your sleep as well.

REM first occurs about 90 minutes after falling asleep and recurs every 90 minutes getting longer later in the night. It provides energy to the brain and body, and supports daytime performance. Your brain is active and dreaming, your eyes dart back and forth, and your body becomes immobile and relaxed as muscles are turned off.

Science has now proven that technology has a negative effect on sleep. Not what you want to hear perhaps, but simple changes like putting your phone on airplane mode while you sleep and giving yourself time to wind down from technology with yoga or a walk or quiet time before you go to sleep assists your body in maximizing recovery overnight. You might be resistant to the idea of device down time before sleep but, think about it. *No one else can take care of your brain for you or manage your stress, so it truly is time to step up to the plate of your own life and take some actions to protect yourself.*

Your circadian rhythm is a 24-hour internal clock that is running in the background of your brain and cycles between sleepiness and alertness at regular intervals. It's also known as your sleep/wake cycle. A part of your hypothalamus (a portion of your brain) controls your circadian rhythm. When it's dark at night, your eyes send a signal to the hypothalamus that it's time to feel tired. Your brain, in turn, sends a signal to your body to release melatonin, which makes your body tired. Your circadian rhythm coincides with the cycles of day and night. This is partly why the challenge for shift workers to sleep during the day and stay awake at night can be very stressful. Regular sleep habits are important. Along with technology and all the reasons people are on their devices late into the night it is also important to understand the value of napping, in order to fill the gap and compensate for an overtired brain. Of course, the best choice is to put down the device, regulate your activities and get regular good sleeps. The value is immeasurable in health and mental alertness and clarity.

"We're moving toward a 24/7 culture ... life isn't as easy as it used to be," says William A. Anthony, PhD, author of the book 'The Art of Napping at Work'. His sleep studies provide evidence that napping reduces sleepiness while improving cognitive functioning, psychomotor performance, short-term memory and mood.

One study determined that only one-third of people actually take naps. Most sleep experts agree that if you want to have a quick jolt of alertness, vigor and/or decrease fatigue; take a 10 to 20-minute nap. Set an alarm so you don't over nap which can create challenges for getting your best sleep at night or feeling too tired after a too long nap. The 20 – 30 minute nap assists in recovery from fatigue and is specific for remembering information, facts, places and names and is an overall stress reducer. On days when you are not working, the 90 minute recover nap, best called REM (rapid eye movement) napping is when you reach your full sleeping cycle and dream. A 75 – 90 minute nap improves creativity and emotional and procedural memory such as learning a new skill. Experts say that the ideal time for a person to take a nap is between 1-4p.m. The short naps of 10 – 30 minutes are considered power naps whereas the 75 – 90 minute naps are recovery naps which are useful in overcoming sleep deficits. (2)

Science has now shown that the simple act of quieting the mind, breathing deeply and focusing, increases the production of the enzyme telomerase. Telomerase is your best defense against stress and resides at the end of every chromosome where telomeres protect DNA and it promotes anti-aging. Recent studies determined that telomerase should prevent healthy cells from becoming cancerous in the first place by preventing DNA damage. (3)

Deepak Chopra tells us humanity's new trend is survival of the wisest not survival of the fittest. Striving to be wise is your absolute best defense against stress.

When a person undergoes a stressful event, the effects often last beyond the event itself. Whether it's a traumatic loss like the death of a parent, friend or child, a violent event, or the rigors of combat, the resulting stress can last for years. It is not a well-understood mechanism in the brain. While many people can experience multiple stressful events and be fine, others might only have one instance of stress and feel repercussions for years. Some people appear to become resistant to stress like police officers, firefighters, first responders and others that have dangerous work. However, if they don't take care of themselves with the awareness of that stress in their lives, the problem multiplies over time. Post-Traumatic Stress Disorder (PTSD) is now considered a mental illness, but new research shows that there is a definite physical component in the brain as well. PTSD is a valid medical condition that may result from an abused childhood, a car accident and any other traumatic event that may occur or repeat in a person's life. (4)

Scientists in India have found that even just one severely stressful event can cause molecular changes in the brain, which leads to other physiological issues which can change that person's life, sometimes forever. Their most recent work shows that the actual architecture of the brain can be altered from a single stressful event.

A team of researchers led by Sumantra Chattarji from the National Centre for Biological Sciences (NCBS) published results of their research that shows electrical activity in the brain, specifically in the amygdala, occurs after a stressful event. *They also determined that the negative impact is often delayed as much as ten days after the event occurs*. The molecule involved is the N-Methyl-D-Aspartate Receptor (NMDA-R), an ion channel protein on nerve cells known to be heavily involved in the brain's processing of memory.

The amygdala is a small bundle of nerve cells in the brain located deep within the temporal lobe. It is responsible for some of the brain's major functions, including memory development, emotional reactions and decision-making. Anything that impacts these nerve cells will show up in the behavior of a person who has undergone trauma, exhibiting anxiety behaviors.

Stress also occurs when demands made on you at school, work or in relationships exceed your ability to cope. It is important to be able to determine if the stress is beneficial or not. At times stress can provide a boost to your energy and drive to meet a deadline or help someone out.

The bottom line is that you must recognize stress and make a decision to manage its impact in your life. Taking a break from the stressor and giving yourself permission to step away from the situation can give you a different perspective, a different view. *When you look at a problem from a different angle; the problem often changes*. Exercise is always part of the solution, a quiet walk, a vigorous walk or workout or sport, yoga, or any kind of movement is a good choice to make daily. Science has shown that a 20-minute walk, run, swim or dance session in the midst of a stressful time can give an immediate positive effect lasting for several hours.

Researcher Sheldon Cohen at Carnegie Mellon University conducted a groundbreaking series of studies looking at effects of stress on the common cold. Results showed that both the number of stressful life events and the perceived stress, each predicted a greater likelihood of developing a cold after viral exposure. Knowing that stress can cripple or weaken your immune system is critical awareness for you to better manage stress and take better care of yourself. The threat to health occurs when stress becomes chronic, when either the stress doesn't go away or you don't calm down when the physical stressor is gone. If chronic relationship stress, work stress, or threat of violence is always in the background, this will greatly interfere with sleep, concentration, physical health, healthy lifestyle, and relaxation. *Children exposed to violence, the unemployed, those heavily in debt, the chronically ill, and care givers of ill family members all get worn out from chronic stress and become vulnerable to a host of symptoms and diseases, ranging from muscle pain and slower wound healing to autoimmune diseases, depression, diabetes, asthma, heart disease, and possibly cancer.* Chronic stress creates a feedback loop that no matter how well you might think you are taking care of yourself, impacts of chronic stress on your immune system will catch up to you over time.

Most people show their emotions in their facial expressions. If you intentionally smile it truly does trigger a reaction in the brain and takes some of the tension out of the moment. Every time we share a concern or a feeling with another person it divides or diminishes the stress over any problem. People that care always want to help, so asking for help is the first step. *Just as joy is multiplied many times by sharing good news, it is also true that stress and grief are diminished and divided when we share the experience.*

Meditation and mindfulness help the mind and body relax and focus. Mindfulness can help people see new perspectives, develop self-compassion and forgiveness. When practicing a form of mindfulness, people can release those emotions that may have been causing the physical stress. Much like exercise, research has shown that even meditating briefly can reap immediate benefits.

HeartMath is a unique system of rigorous scientific research, validated techniques, leading-edge products and programs and advanced technologies for people interested in personal development and improved emotional,

mental and physical health.   HeartMath is internationally recognized for practical solutions that can transform the stress of change and uncertainty, and build people's heart coherence and energy reserves.

Researchers today hold that it is our perception of events, not the actual events themselves that cause most of our stress.

HeartMath teaches that you can understand your own stress and learn some simple and effective ways to reduce it, increase energy and resilience and renew your joy for life.   One of the tools that HearthMath teaches is personal coherence, also known as psychophysiological coherence, which refers to the synchronization of our physical, mental and emotional systems. It can be measured by our heart-rhythm patterns: the more balanced and smooth they are, the more in sync, or coherent we are. Stress levels recede, energy levels increase and our brain and our heart work together. It is a state of optimal clarity, perception and performance.   Twenty three years of research supports HeartMath tools and technology that may help you achieve personal mastery over stress. (5)

Coherence is the state of being logical and consistent. Raising coherence helps you feel, think and sleep better, do better at work and school and improve communication skills. It is of great benefit in all areas of your life when you realize that your heart is as smart as your brain and affects everything you do.

If you are struggling to pay off a debt, imagine the feeling of being debt-free.   Use your mind to visualize a future time when the stress is over. Remember the mind works in pictures. Create a mental image of yourself achieving your desired goal and celebrate it.

Resilient is the opposite of stressed. Diane Coutu eloquently explains in her luminous book 'How Resilience Works,' "Resilient people possess these characteristics — a staunch acceptance of reality, a deep belief, often buttressed by strongly held values, that life is meaningful, and an uncanny ability to improvise. You can bounce back from hardship with just one or two of these qualities, but you will only be truly resilient with all three. These three characteristics hold true for resilient people, companies and neighborhoods - face reality with staunchness, make meaning of hardship instead of crying out in despair, and improvise solutions from thin air." (6)

Be mindful of subliminal stress which may be in a variety of forms of anxiety from over-thinking to pressures that are so constant on our lives, such as finances and relationships, that we fail to notice the full impact on our health.

Recent studies reveal some easy ways to lift your spirits and lower your stress that actually create positive shifts in your brain and body. Rick Hanson, PhD, the author of 'Buddha's Brain' offers some simple science based suggestions to instantly improve your mood and lower your stress. Smile, it relaxes the tension and eases the stress, or warm your hands with a hot cup of tea which signals the nervous system to relax (when stressed the body redirects blood flow from the extremities to the larger muscles). *Researchers learned that those who gave even $5 to someone else felt measurably better than those who bought themselves a treat instead.* Digging in the garden or greenhouse soil with your hands increases serotonin levels or give yourself a hug which releases oxytocin and other biochemicals that promote well-being. We've talked about deep breathing in other chapters and when you take three long deep breaths and focus on the outbreath (taking twice as long to exhale), you influence your parasympathetic nervous system to slow down your heart rate. Even a short walk or just two minutes of exercise (if you raise your heart rate) is enough to change your mood and relax the nervous system. More specifically if you relax your tongue and jaw, you send a message to your brain stem and limbic system to turn off the stress hormones adrenaline and cortisol. Simply let your tongue go limp in your mouth, and then open your mouth slightly, which instantly loosens up your jaw. All these simple suggestions bring your parasympathetic nervous system online telling your body to rest and restore.

Most important of all is to pay attention to yourself, and be aware of stress, either obvious or subliminal. Only when you are aware of how you feel and why, can you take steps to alleviate stress and find calm in your life. Value yourself. Recognize and monitor stress on a daily basis and balance stressful situations with exercise and mediation. Practice mindfulness, get adequate rest, and or take power naps or recovery naps as required. Work on resilience, laughter and that sense of humor that can alleviate stressful situations in your life. Socialize with friends and family that make you laugh and practice gratitude and generosity every day. Good nutrition and hydration with good water are essential tools to manage stress and create wellness on all levels of your being.

The time and effort you spend relaxing and learning new stress management skills is always well-spent. Once you master stress in your life, moods become more stable, thoughts become clearer, relationships improve, and the risk of illness diminishes. Stress among children is estimated to have increased 45% over the past 30 years. The effort you make in assisting your younger siblings to learn to cope with stress builds emotional health and resilience and better prepares them for taking care of themselves. Remember to not stress at solving stress in your life; smooth is slow, slow is steady, steady is fast. Take your time and success will be yours in all areas of your life.

There are a number of Apps that can be super tools for you to master and manage stress in your life. Breathr is an app that provides opportunities for users to try out a variety of mindfulness practices, while also teaching them interesting facts about the brain science behind those practices. HabitBull is an app that helps you organize your life. You can customize, set goals and create positive habits and routines that can help you feel more in control of unwanted habits that cause you stress. 1Giant Mind app is for anyone who wants to feel less stressed, more calm and present, experience greater health and well-being, and learn to meditate in 12 easy steps.

Kindness is an antidote to stress. *It is a mark of great strength to maintain a kind heart in a chaotic world.*

Chapter 22

Nutrition

You are what you eat. You've heard this before, and it is so! Your resistance to illness, your longevity, your performance, your mood, your ability to cope with stress, your output in all ways every day is primarily based on what you feed your body. One of your best defenses against diminishing your potential performance is to literally read labels, find out where your food is grown, how the animals that you eat were raised and take an interest in fast food - what is real and what is fake food. *Alfred E. Newman said 'We are living in a world today where lemonade is made from artificial flavors and furniture polish is made from real lemons."* Some frozen chicken meals are only 15% protein derived from chicken, the rest is GMO soy products made to look like a chicken breast. How can food that is contaminated and diminished by factory farming, factory raised, and/or chemically polluted nourish you at all, not to mention the short and long-term consequences of consuming chemicals, pesticides and additives? This is all basic science. If food is no longer food then what are the biological effects on your body and your brain of eating nonfoods. If your diet is far less than optimal, a simple 7 day experiment choosing real food and good water will provide you with all the evidence you need. You will think, feel and behave in a more positive way and have more energy than you thought possible for yourself. 7 days! *You deserve to take this challenge.*

The western concept of three meals a day plus snacks may not be your personal recipe for health. Some people perform best with a protein breakfast while many benefit from a morning fast and eating later in the morning. Find your best scenario for meals and notice when you feel the most energy. Then create a plan for yourself. Typically, breakfast (breaking the fast of sleeping all night without eating) is the most important meal of the day. With a solid breakfast, that includes healthy protein and complex carbohydrates and healthy fats you elevate your blood sugar levels and boost your metabolism and start the day with energy. Hydrating first thing is the morning is equally as important. Starting each day 20 minutes before breakfast with 8 ounces of good water or greens kick starts your metabolism and rehydrates your brain after the fast of sleep.

Mankind has been hunter gatherers for more than 10,000 years and biologically we have changed very little. Along with healthy, whole foods that were acquired through great effort and social collaboration our bodies were always in motion. Today, many are living a sedentary lifestyle and their body's requirements for foods differ as a result. The physical consequence of sitting for too long is finally being recognized by the medical community. Our bodies are meant to move.

Uncontaminated vegetables, grains, beans, legumes and fruit are your best sources of nourishment, organic if possible. Although there are some specific allergies like nuts or shellfish that you cannot mess with, many people with whom I've consulted have grain allergies because of a weakened immune system as a result of the unhealthy diet they have been eating for years. Here again, knowledge is power. Take an interest in your food choices, know that the parents who raised you did the best they could with what they knew. The food industry is in the hands of corporations that are motivated by profits and this has changed everything in regard to your health and future. Thinking for yourself is always better than believing what corporations want you to believe. Rebelling against the status quo is essential to your health, performance and your very survival.

In 1958 Ancel Keys noted an association between variations in dietary patterns and the rates of heart disease. Instead of good dietary advice becoming mainstream 60 years ago, corporations got involved and promoted low fat and fat-free alternative foods to satisfy medical advice to cut back on fat. Instead, people simply added the low fat junk foods — and reduced the percent of calories we derived from fat by increasing our total calories. This has meant we have squandered decades of opportunity related to diet and health. Instead, populations in N. America find themselves fatter and sicker than ever. The proliferation of corporate alternative facts through the marketing of dietary non-foods, soft drinks and tobacco has sabotaged health for far too many people.

There are fundamental truths about diet and health, to say nothing about dietary choices on the planet, backed by a global consensus of multidisciplinary experts. All that stands in the way of applying good science to your health and well-being is corporate greed and influence to control food and food production around the globe.

Don't underestimate how tragic the cost and influence of alternative facts are in regard to nutrition alone. Not only are most people confused and in denial, but the greatest crime is that the truth about what is good and wholesome food has become suspect. People generally don't know what to believe anymore. The default is always to the multibillion dollar industry of advertising and manipulation to which most people fall victim, usually in regard to convenience.

There are countless examples around the world of mothers who would willingly die for their children, willingly take on their child's disease and suffer great consequences in the pursuit of safety and health for them. With this unavoidable instinct in most mothers to protect their children, our society has brainwashed them into feeding their children toxic food, hidden by the design of visually and tastefully perfect looking and convenient food. *Mothers have been forced to be complicit in what defies their own maternal instincts.*

Even if you have never been on a diet or consumed a diet drink or junk food in your life, the following example of Aspartame is a demonstration of who is making decisions for the health of the food you and your family consume. I'm sure you all know someone who has or is consuming diet drinks and sugar free foods.

The history of Aspartame, one of the earliest artificial sweeteners, is only one of many examples.(1) Aspartame was first developed by the pharmaceutical company G.D. Searle. Searle had difficulty getting their product approved by the Food and Drug Administration (FDA), considering the test monkeys and mice developed brain lesions, tumors, and seizures, and sometimes died. *The company's applications for approval were rejected for 16 years*, as noted by an FDA senior toxicologist, Dr. Adrian Gross, who told Congress, "Beyond a shadow of a doubt aspartame triggers brain tumors."

To win at all costs G.D. Searle, producer of aspartame, then made Donald Rumsfeld its CEO. President Ronald Reagan came on the scene and in 1977 made Donald Rumsfeld the new FDA commissioner and one of his first acts as head of the agency was to approve aspartame over the objections of the FDA scientific board. Another important bit of trivia - when aspartame was approved for use in carbonated beverages, the National Soft Drink Association itself objected, because aspartame is very unstable in liquid form and breaks down into, among other things, **formaldehyde when ingested**. Monsanto (Pesticide Conglomerate) bought G.D. Searle and Co. in 1985, and the NutraSweet Company operated as part of Monsanto until 2000, when Monsanto sold it to J.W. Childs Equity Partners, where it remains today. *During all this time, the FDA has compiled a list of 92 symptoms associated with aspartame consumption, including nausea, dizziness, blindness, deafness, weight gain, and even death*.

With all that, aspartame is still here. *The Aspartame Resource Center, at www.aboutaspartame.com, notes that it is found in more than 6,000 products worldwide*. To further implicate our law makers who are expected to watch over our wellbeing, the Aspartame Resource Center offers fact sheets such as the "Straight Answers about Aspartame." This was prepared by the American Dietetic Association and the Calorie Control Council, who are sponsored by Aspartame. You might think 'The Calorie Control Council' might be an official and judicious organization concerned with your well-being. In fact "The Calorie Control Council, established in 1966 represents 60 manufacturers and suppliers of low-calorie, low-fat and light foods and beverages, including the manufacturers and suppliers of more than a dozen different synthetic dietary sweeteners ."

To further shed light on the difference between truth and corporate greed and influence the American Society for Clinical Nutrition, aka *the American Society for Nutrition*, consists of "sustaining members," such as The National Cattlemen's Beef Associations, Cadbury, Schweppes, Campbell Soup Company, ConAgra Foods, Dannon, Eli Lilly, General Mills, Gerber, GlaxoSmithKline, Kellogg, Kraft, Mars, McCormick, Monsanto, The National Dairy Council, Nestle, PepsiCo, POM Wonderful, Procter & Gamble, The Sugar Association, Unilever and Wrigley and Wyeth.

Worse yet, the medical doctors on the American Society for Nutrition are consultants for the Department of Health & Human Services, the National Institutes of Health, (NIH) (sponsored by the list above), the National Research Council/National Academy of Sciences, the U.S. Congress, the USDA and the FDA, which must be considered a serious conflict of interest.

In 2010 the U.S. market for artificial sweeteners was $1.1 billion, while worldwide it was projected to be over $3 billion. Aspartame can also come with many different names such as Acesulfame potassium (K), AminoSweet®, Neotame®, Equal®, NutraSweet®, Blue Zero Calorie Sweetener Packets™, Advantame®, NutraSweet New Pink, Canderel®, Pal Sweet Diet®, and AminoSweet. It will turn up in children's vitamins, liquid antibiotics or even Metamucil, along with all your diet food products. *Your vigilance is the only thing standing between you and your unintended ingestion of dangerous products.*

I have argued against GMOs (Genetically Modified Organisms) for years with scientifically educated youth who defend the basic science of genetic manipulation of food as an answer to world hunger. They refuse to be open-minded and investigate both sides of the story. They too often side with the corporations that fund their universities, and their belief that all science is good science. I bring this up in this particular book because the shocking rise in disease in America is greatly attributed to food, pharmaceuticals and corporations who manufacture our food today and control the farming of the food on your plate. Along with the power of advertising most of you believe what you watch and what you are told. Terry O'Reilly has a show on CBC Radio podcasts called 'The Age of Influence' which is a brilliant summary of how advertising has shaped our culture and our decisions.

I am still wondering why youth have fallen for the corporations that have turned their food into industrial byproducts. I realize that those very corporations have mastered the chemicals of taste and have addicted generations of people to sugar, additives, dyes, and artificial flavors. Ask yourself why you are eating these non-food products every day, limiting your potential, affecting your brain and your physical health. *Bad food not only robs you of your future, but more importantly robs you of your potential today.*

I am not exaggerating. Monsanto published test results of GMO foods fed to rats after 90 day trials and that mere 90 days convinced governments in N. America to legalize their food take-over. Environmental Sciences Europe, published test results of two year studies where the same tests were repeated over a longer period of time. Severe liver damage, tumors and hormonal disruptions began to occur at 120 days and onward. *A great film to watch is 'Genetic Roulette' by Jeffry Smith if you are interested in knowing the whole story about the history of GMO's and the food you are eating.* (2)

In January 2017 two studies were published in the peer-reviewed journal Scientific Reports that cast new doubts on the safety of genetically modified foods and glyphosate herbicides. The first found that a genetically modified corn, NK 603, was deficit to a non-GMO counterpart, which is contrary to claims of GMO proponents. The second study found that glyphosate, the main ingredient in Monsanto's Roundup herbicide, can cause liver disease at doses thousands of times lower than that allowed by law. (3)

Dr. Antoniou, Head of the Gene Expression and Therapy Group at King's College London in the United Kingdom states: "I've maintained all along that when you take a look at the GMO transformation process—whether inserting genes or using newer methods, such as gene editing—and place these

215

methods in the context of new genetics, which tells us that no gene or its protein product works in isolation, then you can expect problems from these genetic engineering procedures. Genes and their protein products work together in a highly complex, interactive, and integrated network. From the holistic perspective of gene organization, control, and function, the GMO transformation process is technically and conceptually flawed. It's inevitable that there will be problems; it's just a matter of degree. This is what basic science tells us. And when GMOs are added to their associated pesticide residues, as a package, they become a potentially very harmful product." (4)

Technologies like genetic engineering in agriculture need to be re-evaluated for safety as science catches up with the corporate control of food and agriculture around the world.

We know that survival requires adaptation. There is no doubt that your generation is adapting on some level to this dramatic change in food that you eat every day. Of course those with stronger immune systems and more stable home environments (economics and food quality) have a huge advantage over those less fortunate. For a century, humans have thought that evolution takes place 'only' over extremely long periods of time; however, science is now demonstrating that evolution can be extremely fast with many species and changing environments. Why would it be any different with the human animal? Rapid evolution changes species in real time, as reported in Discovery magazine in 2015. (5)

Did you know that Aluminum is the most widely distributed metal on the planet? In fact aluminum is in a lot of day-to-day products such as drinking water, cookware, foil, baking soda, cake mixes, non-dairy creamers, vanilla powders, aspirin, many medications, flour, and even your deodorant. Food additives such as E173, E520, E521, E523 E541, E545, E554, E555 E556 and E559 contain aluminum compounds. The use of aluminum foil is common place at home, in grocery stores and restaurants for food storage.

Why aren't the Federal Drug Administration and Health Canada and equivalent government food protection agencies worldwide, looking out for us, especially considering the proven correlation between aluminum toxicity and Alzheimer's disease? Unlike iron and other vitamins and minerals, our body does not need aluminum; therefore you have no means of processing it in your body. It gets stored in our body and accumulates with time in our kidney, brain, lungs, liver and thyroid which potentially does damage to our health. If you use aluminum foil for reheating food, barbecuing baked potatoes, wrapping burritos, leftovers, etc. you are being exposed to this toxic mineral. There is also significant risk from aluminum cans used for carbonated and non-carbonated drinks.

Aluminum damages your central nervous system. Aluminum exposure in children has been linked to autism. In adults, aluminum exposure can lead to age-related neurological deficits resembling Alzheimer's. (6) It has also been implicated in dementia as well.

Aluminum can damage your brain. Research has demonstrated that aluminum can produce toxic, oxidative stress in the brain. Because your brain can store a lot of aluminum this can be a factor in a long list of diseases today, MS, chronic fatigue syndromes, epilepsy, ADD, Alzheimer's, Guillian-Barre' syndrome (a common post vaccination injury) and other neurological disorders.

Aluminum robs the body of magnesium, calcium and iron. "Trace aluminum levels cross the blood-brain barrier and progressively accumulate in large pyramidal neurons of the hippocampus, cortex, and other brain regions vulnerable in Alzheimer's disease. More aluminum enters the brain than is expelled, resulting in a net increase in intra-neuronal aluminum with advancing age. Aluminum is responsible for two main types of toxic damage in cells; as a pro-oxidant, aluminum causes oxidative damage both on its own and in synergy with iron. It also competes with, and substitutes for, essential metals, primarily magnesium, iron and calcium ions, in or on proteins and their co-factors." (7)

Aluminum accumulates in bone tissue, which results in weakened bones. It is also believed to be a contributing factor in osteoporosis. (8)

Foods that assist your body in removing heavy metals (stored in your body and brain tissues) are important to add to your diet. Onions, blue green algae, garlic, cilantro, burdock, bentonite (high grade), carrot juice, green tea, and chlorella are excellent foods that help remove metals and help the body rebuild nerve tissues.

Another common cookware in the kitchen that people use daily without considering the dangers are Teflon, non-stick pots and fry pans. Toxic fumes from the Teflon chemical released from pots and pans at high temperatures may kill pet birds and cause people to develop flu-like symptoms (called "Teflon Flu" or, as scientists describe it, "Polymer fume fever"). Manufacturers' labels often warn consumers to avoid high heat when cooking on Teflon. The Environment Working Group (EWG) commissioned tests conducted in 2003 which showed in just two to five minutes on a conventional stove top, cookware coated with Teflon and other non-stick surfaces could exceed temperatures at which the coating breaks apart and emits toxic particles and gases. In 2015, 226 scientists from 40 countries signed 'The Madrid Statement', which highlights the potential harm of PFAS chemicals, which are often used in the manufacture of non-stick pans, among many other items. (9)

At one time or another you may have seen the shredded appearance of the inside of an older frying pan with Teflon coating, which also then exposes the food you are cooking to the aluminum beneath the protective coating. (10) It is also best to store food in your refrigerator in glass containers considering that plastic containers can leach into the food being stored, especially if put into the container hot.

Stainless steel, glass, or ceramic cookware are your best choices for food preparation. This decision is vital to prevent unnecessary exposure to more chemicals and aluminum contamination in your body as well as your family. The old cast iron frying pan is still the best conductor of even heat for cooking, used for centuries in Europe and N. America. If you choose cast iron combine it with other cookware to assure that all your food is not solely cooked with cast iron. Cast iron is known to leach iron into food in the cooking process. We all need iron for good health and so it is up to you to know if you are getting too much with this cooking choice. Acidic foods, high moisture content, and long duration of cooking increase the release of iron significantly. The amount of iron you need daily depends on age, gender and whether a woman is pregnant and/or breastfeeding. You can have iron levels checked through your doctor easily. There are ceramic cookware and cooking tools that are safe and dependable. However, you have to be vigilant about using soft utensils because they scratch easily and can contaminate your food from the toxic subsurface materials if the ceramic coating is damaged.

There are nutritional choices you can make to enhance your wellness. Organic powdered greens, organically grown vegetables in powdered form sweetened with stevia and peppermint are a good start to your day in 6 − 8 ounces of good water. An organic vegetable juicing regime can heal much of what ails you. The challenge is compliance, affordability and ease of application that you have to figure out for yourself. Changing your diet and consuming organic greens for as little as 7 days will give you an improved sense of wellness that will inspire you to carry on with a change of lifestyle. Again, try and use organic vegetable and fruits that are home grown, from known local and regional growers, and or as organic as you can get them from the grocery store. The label organic (certified or not) has become less reliable because there are loopholes in the guidelines and people bend the rules. Many communities have box programs where you can get fruit and vegetables in season and more important than a certified organic label is knowing the grower and how the food is grown.

Check out 'SuperJuice Me' (11) wherein over 5 weeks, 8 clients with 22 diagnosed diseases using 52 different medications collectively participated in a cleanse. Their daily routine included fresh organically juiced vegetables five times a day, gentle yoga and walks. After 5 weeks, with medical doctors on site the entire time, they were reassessed down to 2 medications between all eight clients. The before and after interviews and the journey they each take was life-transforming. This is a perfect example of how quickly we can change our lives and our health. We have heard from the oldest people alive, who all agree that their health is more important than any amount of wealth. Don't be naïve to think that the resilience of youth will get you through. It is true that you can throw a lot of crap at your body and somehow keep that beautiful glow and vitality, but for how long? Everything we choose is cumulative over time, whether it is food, thoughts or actions; good or bad. (12) (13) (14)

"People are fed by the food industry that pays no attention to health and are treated by the health industry that pays no attention to food". **Wendell Berry**

Your body is designed to heal itself. So it is easy to understand the importance of giving your body the right building blocks for maintenance, repair and performance. Along with this is the critical role hormonal health plays in growing young people. The majority of cases of acne, hormonal stress and their ups and downs, menstrual complications, and behavioral challenges, can mostly be corrected or solved through diet and nutrition (based on better science than the Canada food guide or other country equivalents). It only makes sense to start with diet and nutrition; then whatever residual symptoms remain after a period of time may better define issues that actually need to be treated. I believe it should be a last resort to introduce drugs into growing bodies. Change what you eat for 7 days and see the difference. The body works on cycles of 7; make a change for 7 days and the body begins to respond differently. Your body intelligence actually recognizes that you are serious about quitting that bad habit or wanting wellness and the shift will happen. Try it!

For at least a century the rewards of childhood have often been candy treats. I find it ironic that dentist appointments for kids over many decades resulted in a candy sucker or ice cream as a treat. In 1971, Soviet scientists announced that Red No. 2 dye was potentially carcinogenic. In 1976, the Food and Drug Administration (FDA) in the U.S. concluded that, in high doses, Red No. 2 could cause cancer in female rats. Public outcry in the U.S. against the dye quickly gained such momentum that the Mars candy company temporarily stopped producing red M&Ms. Red candies were then reintroduced in 1983, though we will never know why or how that decision to reintroduce a chemical that is dangerous for children was made. These artificial colors have been referred to as "neurotoxic chemicals" by a Change.org petition in 2014 as well as a press release from Center for Science in the Public Interest (CSPI). (15)

What I find so challenging is that much of this research began back in 1975. Over 40 years ago they were talking about dyes and chemicals in food that adversely affect children's health and still these products are consumed every day by millions of children.

Kraft Macaroni and Cheese experienced a similar petition urging them to remove dangerous dyes Yellow #5 and Yellow #6. The CSPI has recommended that warning labels listing the risks of the eight approved FD&C food colors should be a requirement for all products containing these dangerous ingredients. The CSPI's Dr. Jacobson said: "The evidence that these petrochemicals worsen some children's behavior is convincing. I hope that the committee will advise the agency to both require warning notices and encourage companies to voluntarily switch to safer natural colorings." Everyone in the western world has experienced the post Halloween hysteria followed by the blues over past decades, but chronic issues prevail with everyday consumption of foods with these dyes in them.

For your interest, here is the ingredient list for M&M's. 'Milk chocolate (sugar, chocolate, cocoa butter, skim milk, milk fat, lactose, soy lecithin, salt, artificial color), sugar, corn starch, >1% corn syrup, dextrin, artificial colors (Blue 1 Lake, Red 40 Lake, Yellow 6, Yellow 5, Red 40, Blue 1, Blue 2 Lake, Yellow 6 Lake, Yellow 5 Lake, Blue 2), gum acacia.' Keep in mind that these candies are sugar and dyes, of no nutritional value whatsoever, and toxic as well. Also keep in mind it is not difficult to make homemade candy from healthy ingredients.

Let's move on from food to popular over-the-counter medications that people don't think twice about using on a daily basis. You might wonder how this fits under the chapter on Nutrition. Everything you put in your body becomes a piece in the puzzle your body must sort out and differentiate toxic chemicals from food every minute of every day. Another study has emerged linking Ibuprofen, the popular over-the counter pain-killer to harmful and life-threatening health effects in those with cardiac conditions. This time it's from researchers in Denmark, who found that taking the drug caused a 31% increased risk of cardiac arrest, among other things. It wasn't just Ibuprofen, but common painkillers that also fall under this category, known as non-steroidal anti-inflammatory drugs (NSAIDs). They found that other drugs in this category, like Tylenol, present an even higher risk with study results recently published in the European Heart Journal. (16)

NSAIDs are among the most commonly used drugs in the world and easily available to anybody. The amount of literature available on this subject can be overwhelming and we all need to question how over-the-counter drugs can be so accessible, and so potentially dangerous for our health.

Dr. Peter Gotzsche, co-founder of the Cochrane Collaboration (the world's most foremost body in assessing medical evidence), estimates that 100,000 people in the United States alone die each year from the side-effects of correctly-used prescription drugs. (17)

In 2012, following the release of a report discussing arsenic found in apple and grape juice and rice, Consumer Reports conducted numerous tests. "In virtually every product tested, we found measurable amounts of total arsenic in its two forms. We found significant levels of inorganic arsenic, which is a carcinogen, in almost every product category, along with organic arsenic, which is less toxic but still of concern." Foods tested included Kellogg's® Rice Krispies cereal, which had relatively low levels of arsenic at 2.3 to 2.6 micrograms per serving, and Trader Joe's Organic Brown Pasta Fusilli, which tested higher – from 5.9 to 6.9 micrograms per serving. Arsenic levels were also found in infant cereals for babies between 4 and 12 months old. (18) This is another reminder that organic foods grown in toxic soil cease to be organic.

"Inorganic arsenic, the predominant form of arsenic in most of the 65 rice products we analyzed, is ranked by the International Agency for Research on Cancer (IARC) as one of more than 100 substances that are Group 1 carcinogens. It is known to cause bladder, lung, and skin cancer in humans, with the liver, kidney, and prostate now considered potential targets of arsenic-induced cancers." (19)

You might be surprised to know there is a maximum allowable limit for the consumption of arsenic each day. (16) This is because arsenic in rice is due to the rice being grown in contaminated soils. Rice absorbs arsenic from soil or water much more efficiently than most plants. Partly because it is one of the only major crops grown in water-flooded conditions, which allow arsenic to be more easily taken up by its roots and stored in the grains. Areas where rice is now grown have a long history of producing cotton, a crop that was heavily treated with arsenical pesticides for decades.

Remember you have a lot of power as a consumer where you choose to spend your money. Whenever possible buy organic rice and check the source and grower certifications. Rice is an excellent staple and healthy food choice, depending on its source. If you buy your rice in 10kg or larger quantities the price will be very similar to or less than that of inorganic rice in small packages. The shelf life of uncooked rice is very long. Rice has sprouted that was found in ancient tombs in Egypt 5,000 years old.

Keep in mind that nutrition can be measured in all areas in your life. To nourish is defined as "to provide with the food or other substances necessary for growth, health, and good condition. " Therefore nourish yourself with good food and water, good company, good music, good exercise, art and quality friendships. Overall they will balance out your poor choices and actions. As you know 'attitude is everything', do the best you can with what you feed your body and to a degree a good attitude will balance out or help to balance out any adverse effects of other choices.

So many people wonder what to eat and how much to eat for good health. It is most certainly more about quality than quantity. Between 70 and 100 years ago ever since man left hunting and gathering and became more of an agricultural people, people grew their own food. There was little intentional chemical contamination of food and water. Food was wholesome, nutritious, and though perhaps lacking in variety, they supplemented with what grew wild, and with game and fish from the land. Ideally, this is the kind of food we should be striving to eat – whole food, as close to its original state, and not heavily processed. Finding whole foods that are not contaminated can be a challenge – but everywhere that food can be grown, you will find growers that are dedicated to producing food that is wholesome and nutritious. Even in urban areas, people are making an effort to grow fruits and vegetables that are as free of chemicals and contaminants, as much as possible.

Priorities are best put on good clean water and whole organic food, while assessing everything you put into or on your body to determine if it contributes to your health, performance and happiness. *Becoming a member of your local food cooperative can be fun and you will learn so much that will contribute to your well-being*. You may learn about food storage, how best to prepare food and you can build relationships with others who value their communities and the future of food as well. If you can grow your own food, do it, seek out growers young and old, and share and trade stories and skills. If you can't grow your own, seek out growers and families and companies that are dedicated to growing good food for you and others. Box programs in urban areas may be able to provide organic vegetables, free range eggs and meat from free range and grass fed animals.

Most important of all learn to cook with delicious and nourishing foods. Keep in mind your safest oil to fry with is butter or coconut oil as other vegetable oils become trans fats when exposed to high heat. Cooking is fun, delicious, extremely social and exciting to feed friends and gather around tables of good food.

Don't put anything on the outside of your body that you wouldn't put inside your body. In Chapter 3 on Health and Performance I discussed all the concerns and choices around deodorants and cosmetics and sunscreens. Keep them in mind as you would keep in mind healthy foods that you eat. By avoiding or minimizing consumption of foods that have no nutritional benefits such as sugar, soft drinks, candy, and junk food you will save yourself energy and illness now or later.

Find a local market or cooperative in your area that sells bulk good, quality foods and make a priority of valuing yourself by valuing the food you buy and consume. As consumers you have a lot of power collectively to support growers who care about the land to produce whole foods that nourish you and your family. The more people that support organic and whole food producers, the better the supply and the lower the prices.

Chapter 23

Music & Dance

Music informs a culture more than any other influence. Humans have danced and sung around fire circles since the beginning of man's time on this earth. Music continues to be the greatest force in building community, feeling freedom and love, finding inspiration and motivation, releasing fear and pain, showing love for each other and opening your minds to the beauty and possibilities in your world.

I hope all of you have access to music. Listen to what inspires you; don't waste time being faddish, or listening only to certain music because those around you do. *Find your own musical inspiration*.

Music aids brain function and has been proven over and over to improve performance and intellect. (1) Music influences the release of the chemical dopamine in the brain, the happy hormone that relieves anxiety, induces pleasure, joy and motivation, boosts your immune system and reduces pain.

Surgery patients who listen to music before, during and after their procedures require less pain medication and have speedier recoveries. When surgeons listen to their favorite music their surgical techniques and efficiency measurably improve. Studies also show that listening to music during a math test can improve your scores by 40%.

According to a new Canadian study led by the Rotman Research Institute (RRI) at Baycrest Health Sciences, starting formal lessons on a musical instrument prior to age 14 and continuing with music for up to a decade enhances key areas in the brain that support speech recognition. With seniors this proved to be evident in brain health decades longer than with those who didn't actively have music in their lives. There is plenty of evidence of brain neural plasticity from musical training proven to give young developing brains a cognitive boost with neural enhancements extending across their entire lifespan. Sadly, music programs in high schools have suffered cuts throughout N. America due to budget constraints, ignoring the profound benefits of music to healthy brain development.

The neuroscience of singing shows that when we sing, our neurotransmitters connect in new and different ways. Singing fires up the right temporal lobe of your brain, releasing endorphins that make you smarter, healthier, happier and more creative. When we sing with other people this effect is amplified. *The research suggests that creating music together evolved as a tool of social living.* Groups and tribes sang and danced together to build loyalty, transmit vital information and ward off enemies. What has not been understood until recently is that singing in groups triggers the communal release of serotonin and oxytocin, the bonding hormone, and even synchronizes heart beats. There is plenty of science behind the health effects of the release of endorphins and oxytocin, which in turn relieve anxiety and stress and are strongly linked to feelings of trust and bonding. People who sing regularly have reduced levels of cortisol, and therefore lower stress. (2) If you feel lonely or depressed consider joining a choir, or find friends to sing with. When many people sing together there is a level of anonymity and less pressure on your voice to be perfect.

US opera singer Katie Kat wishes to encourage everyone to sing far more often regardless of whether you think you can sing or not. It can take practice but the more you sing the better you sing. The vocal chords are a muscle. Singing increases self-awareness, self-confidence and your ability to communicate with others. It decreases stress, comforts you and helps you to forge your identity and influence your world. Society has somehow changed the value of the ancient art of singing. Mothers and fathers have sung to their children since the beginning of time. Plato, born 2500 years ago, founded the first institute of higher learning in Athens. Plato first pointed to the influence of music saying 'musical innovation is full of danger to the whole state, and ought to be prohibited. When modes of music change, the fundamental laws of the state always change with them.' Though Plato wrote this as a warning, considering a happy society may stand up for itself, this can be taken as a revolutionary statement that music is an important and powerful movement in the life and culture of all human beings, especially when living in community with each other.

Twenty five hundred years ago Pythagoras taught that music could be used "in the place of medicine". Music therapy is presently an established clinical discipline widely used to assist people to overcome physical, emotional, mental, social, and spiritual challenges.

"Music opens a path into the realm of silence," was the opinion of German philosopher Josef Pieper. Pieper wrote that the nature of music has been understood as nonverbal articulation of life experience, as wordless expressions of man's intrinsic dynamism of self-realization and a process understood as man's journey toward ethical personhood and love.

Aldous Huxley wrote *"after silence, that which comes nearest to expressing the inexpressible is music."*

Psychologists have for decades considered the healing music of Johann Sebastian Bach with the phrase 'Listen to Bach, Listen to Life'. Invest some time in listening to Bach and join the generations who have found comfort, solace, genius, and eternity in his music.

The Goldberg Variations is a work written by Bach for harpsichord, consisting of an aria and a set of 30 variations. First published in 1741, the work was commissioned by Count Keyserling to ease his headaches and insomnia. It was played for the Count by harpsichordist Goldberg, a 14-year-old pupil of Bach's and listening to the music cured the Count of his ailments over time. Music is a brilliant healer.

Great musicians today take their inspiration and instruction from the masters of music of the past. *The format for Adele's music is similar to the classics.* Her songs are based on a piano format, with verse-chorus, addressing the issue of love and romance and shaping the voice around that. Emotions are expressed; the length and the format are all intended for the listener to rise to their own occasion of greatness.

Human beings are naturally creative, musical and artistic. When you were a baby in your mother's womb you grew to the rhythm of your mother's heartbeat. You would hear and feel the sound and emotions of both parent's voices. After you were born you create your first sound, your voice. Laughter comes to your expressions around four months of age and by six months you respond and recognize songs with movement and dance. Before you learned to speak you used your voice to express feelings and learning patterns, pulse, rhyme and structure without the complication of language. Once you started to sing and dance to music you became totally absorbed in the physical fun of movement. Singing is also aerobic and improves the efficiency of the cardio-vascular system by increasing oxygenation in the blood. Singing and dancing have been linked to stress reduction, longevity and overall well-being.

When people sing together there is a bond created and their behavior improves, whatever the song or the language. Neurological studies from the UK, Germany and the U.S. have shown the increased development of parts of the brain involving music and language. Of course combining music and dance increases the benefits for development and joy all around. In many cultures around the world, music, singing and dance are seen as a whole activity and many countries don't differentiate singing from dancing. Through dance, children develop spatial awareness, become less clumsy and pay more attention to others sharing their space. By communicating freely with the voice, face, and body, children learn to express ideas with confidence, empathize with others from different cultures and backgrounds, and perhaps most importantly feel at home in their own skin.

Dancing can happen anywhere at any time so set aside your inhibitions and move your body to the music you love, from break dancing to a waltz and everything in between. For centuries communities have danced together around the fire, celebrating life, death, marriage, birth – all of the rights of passage; this has created unity and harmony that carries them through difficult times.

Expanding your experience in music can pose a challenge to a generation who may be listening to pop music that has been described as addictive, hypnotic and repetitive. *Reach for variety in music and experience music other than the latest craze.* Millions of people over the centuries have benefitted from the intuitive and healing power of music. You have music that inspires you, let that music be your guide to move forward and take affirmative action in your own life. Humans are naturally creative, musical and artistic. Dance develops confidence, body movements, flexibility, fitness and footwork that can be beneficial to pursuing any sport.

Ball room dancing is cool again! Prior to the polka which originated during the 19th century, folk dancing was not a 'couples' dance. However, when the waltz came into being during the Victorian era it was considered revolutionary and shocking because of its speed and the prolonged close embrace of the dancers. Though chaperoned, couples for the first time could embrace in public. And then along came the tango in the 20th century. The Tango was derived from two dances, a solo dance from Spain and an Argentinean courtship dance that was originally considered taboo among polite society in Argentina. The explosion of new cultural dances on the dance floor took off from there with the swing, cha-cha, rumba, fox trot and the sexy salsa. And with them came the intimacy of dancing in public.

Music and dance are expressions of art. They both help us to unwind and have fun, muscles release tension, gain strength and endurance and stress disappears. Dance is not only a universal art form; it has become a universal language. The amazing ability to communicate through dance between people who don't speak the same language is evidence of the universal language of dance, music and the connection we all share.

Listening to music continues to be one of Youths' favorite digital activities. Music has been central to young people's lives for generations, offering refuge during stressful times and connecting with peers through music. Confucius said 2500 years ago, "Music produces a kind of pleasure which human nature cannot do without." Maya Angelou, American poet, singer and civil rights activist said "Everything in the universe has rhythm. Everything dances."

Music therapy for seniors has been proven to help restore and maintain their health, as well as help them recall memories and fight depression. People with dementia and depression who listen to favorite music from their past have come fully to a conscious state, aware and happy to be reminded of better days and joy from their Youth. You all know seniors that you could share the gift of music with. You could talk to them about their favorite artists or musicians from their past, and bring music back into their lives. Sharing your personal favorites in music with a different generation can be fun and an adventure in itself. (3)

People love music and it can make many activities more enjoyable. Embrace music in your life and consider how much fun it would be to dance more. You will nurture a happier outlook on life if you include music and dance in your daily routine.

"Music is the universal language of mankind." — Henry Wadsworth Longfellow

Chapter 24

Dare We Discuss Vaccinations?

You might wonder why this chapter is in this book. *This subject is so extremely polarized and politicized that to even discuss the subject can carry risk and judgment.* There are provinces in Canada and states in the U.S. where vaccination is mandatory by law in order to attend school. The social landscape for discussion is so volatile and toxic that no measure of facts and information can enter a simple conversation on the subject without emotions dominating the discussion. My goal in discussing this topic with you is to highlight what is missing in most conversations. I do not have an opinion on whether you choose vaccination or not, however I value facts and information so highly that at the very least I would ask that you have all the information necessary to make an informed choice one way or the other.

The battle between pro-vaccinators and non-vaccinators is riddled with emotions and fear while sharing one common interest and that is the honest desire for good health for their families and themselves. People have been very misled about a lot of public health issues in our world. According to the graph above, in the Journal of Pediatrics "...the largest historical decrease in morbidity and mortality caused by infectious disease was experienced NOT with the modern antibiotic and vaccine era, but after the introduction of clean water and effective sewer systems. " (1)

This is not at all to say that vaccines are good or bad, this is simply to point out that they were not the pivotal intervention the majority of people believe they were in protecting people from infectious disease.

Vaccine hesitancy is the medical and pharmaceutical term used to describe anyone who raises any questions about vaccine safety (or effectiveness). Due to the well-funded medical-pharmaceutical-media

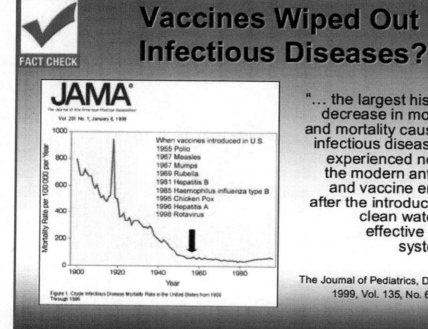

Vaccines Wiped Out Infectious Diseases?

FACT CHECK ✔

"... the largest historical decrease in morbidity and mortality caused by infectious disease was experienced not with the modern antibiotic and vaccine era, but after the introduction of clean water and effective sewer systems."

The Journal of Pediatrics, December 1999, Vol. 135, No. 6, p. 663

apparatus that insists that all vaccines are safe for all people all the time, it is presently impossible to ask common-sense questions about vaccine safety. While the debate about the correlation between autism and vaccinations has been raging for several decades, the contents of the vaccination, in particular mercury in flu vaccines (thimerosal), are now in the spotlight again. The international Science Journal of the Total Environment has just published a compelling study from the Republic of Korea, where autism prevalence is high. The study identifies a strong relationship between prenatal and early childhood exposure to mercury and autistic behaviors in five-year-olds. (2)

I have never advised anyone not to vaccinate or to vaccinate. I believe the political, social and medical opinions around the subject of vaccination have robbed the public of feeling informed enough to understand fully the whole subject of vaccination. This is not an easy debate. The most important point I want to make is that the subject has become so politicized and fear injected, that people do not make decisions based on their own research and understanding, but simply on the insistence of authority. *The ingredients in the vaccine, all vaccines, are a far more important subject of conversation than the one everyone is fighting about, 'to vaccinate or not to vaccinate.'*

Meredith Watman wrote 'The Vaccine Race' (2017), a well-researched book that is pro vaccination in the extreme. On the other hand Dr. Sherri Tenpenny, a veteran in the battle to raise awareness of the threats posed to human health by the ongoing vaccination assault, is also well researched and authentic. (3) It reminds me of the arms race, the race to the top and a multibillion dollar industry.

'The Vaccine Court' by Wayne Rohde documents the Vaccine Injury Compensation Program and billions spent through courts to pay families for death and damages. Keep in mind vaccines are supposed to be safe. Now many settlements occur out of court for publicity reasons. Also laws have been put in place to protect vaccine manufacturers, such as "No vaccine manufacturer shall be liable in a civil action for damages arising from a vaccine-related injury or death associated with the administration of a vaccine after October 1, 1988."(4) This is government protection as vaccines are usually produced by governments.

Well known educator Andrew Nikiforuk has written numerous books on the history of epidemics in the world and presents the opposite opinion of Watman in regard to vaccinations. The challenge is that you might read both these books and still be left in the middle, in no man's land where a decision is not made on common sense and science, but on the pressure of extremes and fear.

Perhaps at this point you are already angry because the previous paragraphs may include information you did not know. Persevere to the end of the chapter and formulate your own opinion. I ask that you have an informed opinion at the very least considering the enormity of this subject and do your own research if you need more information. Seek out reliable sources.

Stats on the Flu vaccines prove them to be the most ineffective vaccine on the market. (5) Global research determines that there is no reason to doubt that the vaccine contributed to more cases of flu infection than it prevented. And this is a fundamental flaw with all live vaccines, and even killed attenuated ones, that have been shown to "shed" and infect people in contact with the vaccinated persons, especially those with compromised immune systems. (6) (7)

In a world where the wellness of all really mattered, the decision to vaccinate or not to vaccinate should not be fueled by the profit motivation of pharmaceutical corporations that make the product and earn billions of dollars. *Today the vaccine market is worth close to $24 billion annually*. The report titled 'Global Human Vaccines Market 2016-2020' forecasts a market value for vaccines to be $61 billion in 2020. Presently the measles vaccine is still replicated from the original Hyfik aborted fetus cells on ice from 1960. Henrietta Lax is the mother of the aborted fetus and to this day has never won a court case (as the cells from her aborted fetus were taken without her permission) or been recognized for her contribution to science. That is near 60 years of cost free source for production and still the profits from repeating a simple vaccine is in the billions. Also there is continual debate with groups that object to abortion, raising ethical questions about Plotkin's rubella vaccine (and other vaccines developed with similar human cell strains) over the years.

Because of its position on abortion, members of the Catholic Church have asked for its moral guidance on the use of vaccines developed using cell strains started with fetal cells. This includes the vaccine against rubella as well as those against chickenpox and hepatitis A, and some of the rabies and mumps vaccines.

The world has recently been introduced to the 'Zika' virus, another multi-billion dollar opportunity for Big Pharma corporations worldwide. In 2016 $1.9 billion was offered to hasten vaccine success and Congress stalled in the U.S. and killed the bill for 9 months during which time 1500 babies were born with Zika and by 2020 they say a safe vaccine will be ready. The big news, for people paying attention, is still whether the symptoms in newborns are actually caused by the Zika virus carried by the mosquito. What you think you know that may not be correct is where the danger lies, often in all areas of one's life.

Amidst growing fear-based propaganda of the threat of Zika virus came an admission from health officials in Brazil that Zika alone may not be responsible for the rise in birth defects that plagued parts of the country. While there is evidence suggesting the Zika virus may be linked to the birth defect microcephaly, rates of the condition have only risen to very high levels in the northeast section of Brazil. Since the virus has spread throughout Brazil, but extremely high rates of microcephaly have not, officials are now being forced to admit that something else is a factor. Dr. Fatima Marinho, director of information and health analysis at Brazil's ministry of health, states "We suspect that something more than Zika virus is causing the high intensity and severity of cases." The outbreak occurred in NE Brazil in a largely poverty-stricken agricultural area of Brazil that uses large amounts of banned pesticides. NECSI (New England Complex Systems Institute) also suggested, "An alternative cause of microcephaly in Brazil could be the pesticide pyriproxyfen, which is cross-reactive with retinoic acid, which causes microcephaly, and is being used in drinking water." Between these factors and the lack of sanitation and widespread vitamin A and zinc deficiency, you have the basic framework for an increase in poor health outcomes among newborn infants in that area. Data is lacking to confirm the Zika-Microcephaly link and it's also been suggested that microcephaly may be the result of the Zika virus occurring alongside other infections, such as dengue and chikungunya.

Florence Fouque, a World Health Organization (WHO) expert on animals that carry viruses, called the public response to the Zika virus "completely hysterical." She blamed the overreaction on the findings that the virus affects pregnant women and can be sexually transmitted. Health officials in Brazil quietly announced in August 2016 that Zika alone may not be responsible for the rise in birth defects that predominantly plagued northeastern parts of the country. (8)

In August 2016, the National Institutes of Health (NIH) launched a clinical trial of a Zika vaccine. The University of Minnesota Center for Infectious Disease Research and Policy quoted concerns voiced by Dr. Philip K. Russell, the former director of the Walter Reed Army Institute of Research and commander of the U.S. Army Medical Research and Development Command, as well as founding president and chairman of the Sabin Vaccine Institute: "Russell said that the fact that Zika is occurring in areas where dengue fever has been endemic hints at a serious potential problem with ADE (antibody dependent enhancement) and Zika vaccine development. 'The current epidemic of Zika, which is usually a mild disease, is made a lot worse in these populations,' Russell said. 'I think there's a major effect, but the studies haven't been done yet to sort that out.'

Another troubling response to the hysteria was that many areas were ramping up pesticide spraying to combat the Zika virus. Use of pesticides to kill mosquitos creates another entire health risk along with the fact that birds and bats eat mosquitos and are at high risk to mortality from exposure to pesticides. A Clean Water Act permit is generally required to spray pesticides in areas where they might end up in water. The permit is intended to keep the toxic chemicals from contaminating water, but now the Zika virus has been used as an excuse to do away with this common-sense precaution. By removing requirements for permits when spraying pesticides near water, the use of these chemicals will skyrocket, including via aerial spraying. *As of Jan 2017 aerial spraying of pesticides is the number one tool to fight against the Zika virus.* The primary chemical weapons against Zika — Naled and Malathion — are both up for re-evaluation at the EPA under a special provision of the Endangered Species Act. If these chemicals are found to harm endangered species, they will be banned, however with the Zika panic and billions of dollars on the table for pesticide companies you can be sure they will continue to push for its use. There is even discussion to spray DDT against the mosquito, which DDT (a synthetic insecticide) has been illegal in the US for over 40 years. (9) (10)

In research presented at the Pediatric Academic Societies 2016 Meeting, aerial pesticide exposure was linked to an increased risk of developmental delays and autism spectrum disorder among children. The study compared children living in zip codes where aerial pesticide spraying was used each summer to combat mosquitoes that carry the eastern equine encephalitis virus with children living in non-aerial-spraying zip codes. Children exposed to the aerial pesticide spraying were about 25 percent more likely to be diagnosed with autism or have a documented developmental delay than those living in areas that used other methods of pesticide application (such as manual spreading of granules). If authorities use the supposed threat of Zika to increase aerial spraying, it could increase children's risk of brain and developmental disorders, which is the opposite of what anti-Zika campaigns are supposed to achieve.

I know there are many people who would be enraged by my discussion here primarily because they have never taken the time to investigate the impact of pesticides on children and the politics of supposed epidemics. There is a big profit to be made by corporations that keep the public uninformed and mislead with propaganda and fear tactics.

Even mosquito experts are questioning whether an emergency actually exists. Chris Barker, Ph.D., a mosquito-borne virus researcher at the University of California, Davis School of Veterinary Medicine, told WebMD: "I think the risk for Zika actually setting up transmission cycles that become established in the continental U.S. is near zero." Barker expects Zika to go the way of other tropical diseases spread by mosquitoes, such as dengue fever and chikungunya in the U.S. with small clusters of outbreaks in southern states and little activity elsewhere. You needn't go dousing your backyard in chemicals in an attempt to stay safe from Zika virus (whose connection to birth defects is still being explored)."

What stands out dramatically from my childhood is the increased number of vaccinations per child. In the 1960 – 70's there were 7 diseases children were vaccinated against in 3 different shots. Tetanus, Diphtheria and Pertussis (whooping cough) were in one DTP shot. The MMR shot covered Measles, Mumps and Rubella and there was a single shot for polio. As of 2014 the list includes Hepatitis B, Rotavirus, Diphtheria, tetanus, and Pertussis (combined DTaP vaccine), Hib (Haemophilus influenzae type b), Pneumococcal, Polio (inactivated vaccine), Influenza, Measles, Mumps, and Rubella (combined MMR vaccine), Varicella (chickenpox), Hepatitis A and

Meningococcal (certain high-risk groups only). In addition, the 7-18 year olds schedule recommends human papillomavirus (HPV) vaccination and meningococcal vaccination. From birth to aged 4 there are presently 31- 49 different vaccinations recommended. Why would anyone need to vaccinate a newborn shortly after birth and again a month later for hepatitis B? HepB is a sexually transmitted disease or by drug needle contamination. Less than 1% of Canada's population is infected with this virus. (11)

I am well aware of how volatile this issue is to simply discuss. *However, common sense would dictate that a person know what the ingredients are in the vaccination being injected into their or their child's blood.* The ingredients in the vaccinations that are injected into the bloodstream and the consequences of those additives and their combined effect on the immune system and the brain are worth understanding. These are just rational questions, especially if there is mercury (thimerosal) in the annual flu vaccine recommended for old people, pregnant women, people with diagnosed weakened immune systems and the general public. Thimerosal is an ethyl mercury-based preservative used in vials that contain more than one dose of a vaccine (multi-dose vials) to prevent germs, bacteria and/or fungi from contaminating the vaccine. (12)

Don't reject information because the general population doesn't question it. You have to think for yourself. There are billions of dollars invested by pharmaceutical companies (through universities and governments) and billions in profits through the sale of vaccinations. *If you are pro vaccination at the very least you should demand safe ingredients in that vaccine you inject into your own or child's body*. If you are anti-vaccination, you better have all your facts straight because you will be pressured, shamed and ostracized and told you are stupid (or worse a criminal) by the majority who are pro-vaccinators. There actually may come a time when you will go to jail for having this opposing view. (13)

We need to bring sanity back into the discussion of vaccinations and immunization. It's obvious that there are known cases of side effects—including death—from vaccines. However making blanket statements that vaccines cause this disease or that are not helpful either. In the case of Autism there are too many variables. It could be that vaccines don't cause Autism per se, but may trigger changes in some people that make the conditions for Autism ripe. For example, there's a lot of research coming out linking Autism to the gut biome. It's no secret that 70%+ of the immune system is located in the gut. Could the alteration of gut flora in a certain way (via various triggers, not just vaccines) create the conditions for the development of Autism? Who knows? Do you know? There are now more than 1000 chemical additives to common foods in the grocery store and some of the additives have been proven to have adverse effects on the immune system. With a weakened immune system, and in particular the presence of chemicals consumed on a daily basis that impair the immune system, is there any wonder why society is getting sicker and hence the perceived need for more vaccinations as our immune systems become inept. *The contradiction here is that vaccinations are not recommended for children with weakened immune systems*. Compare this with chemical contaminants of the air, water, home and workplace environment and there is great potential for compromised immune systems. The same manufacturers of vaccinations are the same manufacturers of chemicals and pesticides that end up in our food one way or the other. Corporate control is in the hands of a small number of mega companies that are managing what you eat, how it is grown, processed and packaged.

There is a total disconnect between healthy immune systems, resistance to disease (with or without vaccinations) and the toxic food, air and water that has become the norm in N. America. The only way to maintain a healthy gut biome (remember 70% of your immune system resides there) is with healthy food and clean water and of course a good attitude. Why fight so aggressively about vaccinations when the food you eat is not contributing to your overall wellbeing and your future health anyway? It is a fact that immune systems are collapsing within N. American populations as evidenced by the rise in chronic illness, cancer, and mental illness and depression. Why are we not fighting for affordable healthy food to feed our families? *It is baffling that the connection between food and health and immunity is not even on the table for discussion in the political and corporate control of what you inject into your body.*

To have an opinion contrary to the conventional medical opinion today can have serious consequences. A famous example of the consensus error is called the Semmelweis Reflex. Ignaz Semmelweis was a doctor who argued in the 1840's that hand-washing by doctors reduced childbed fever mortality rates ten-fold. It turns out that medical doctors used to perform autopsies and then see patients, including pregnant women, without washing their hands. This was the widely accepted practice at the time and Semmelweis objected to it. He was eventually shouted down and run into an insane asylum (literally where he died) by his peers for advocating for something that is blatantly obvious to us today. Because that was 170 years ago we also naively assume they weren't as smart as we are today because of how ridiculous it would be to perform an autopsy and then examine a pregnant woman without washing your hands. The truth is no midwife from hundreds of years ago to today would consider 'not' sterilizing hands before childbirth. *Common sense isn't an invention of today*. You may think this irrelevant today, however there are plenty of examples of medical actions that took a decade to truly determine if they were successful or not. The original measles vaccine created in the 1950's was tested on orphans, prison inmates, (in particular babies of prison inmates) and the mentally handicapped in asylums. The damage and death rate was very high with the first many trial runs of the measles vaccine. That was the common practice until 1966 when the law for informed consent for vaccine tests was passed. Now all the testing is on mammals and if the public were truly shown the true picture of that scenario there would be outrage yet again.

Language is extremely important in controversial discussions of this magnitude. The use of the word consensus and eradicate are misleading to common folk. The word 'eradicate' means to destroy completely and put an end to. According to the CDC (Center for Disease Control, U.S.), measles has never been eradicated, though the term is thrown around pretty loosely. It should also be noted that this is a global economy and bacteria and virus' arrive here from other countries. Perhaps even more significantly virus' have been found to travel the globe in high altitude winds and end up in high concentrations per square meter on the ground from countries on the other side of the planet. The CDC which many look to as a global source of current information on disease control is far from unbiased when it comes to vaccination. The CDC holds 20 patents for vaccinations and is in the business of administering vaccinations globally. "The CDC is a subsidiary of the pharmaceutical industry. The agency owns more than 20 vaccine patents and purchases and sells $4.1 billion in administering vaccines annually." (14)

There is presently, in 2017, a vaccine being tested in Africa to combat AIDS and in the worlds view that is fantastic news. The Bill & Melinda Gates Foundation and National Institutes of Health are joining forces with Johnson & Johnson to advance the potential prevention option, which is designed to be a "global vaccine" that could prevent a wide range of viral strains responsible for the HIV pandemic. "Developing a vaccine against HIV is a top priority and our best hope for a world without AIDS. Finding an effective HIV vaccine to protect people at risk has been a major scientific challenge, but today there is new optimism that we can get there," said Paul Stoffels, M.D., Chief Scientific Officer, Johnson & Johnson. "That's why we're joining forces with the worlds leading HIV researchers and global health advocates to help advance our experimental vaccine."

The new, large-scale study (HVTN 705/HPX2008), also known as "Imbokodo", will evaluate whether the investigational Janssen vaccine regimen is safe and able to reduce the incidence of HIV infection among 2,600 women in sub-Saharan Africa. The study aims to enroll 2,600 sexually-active women aged 18-35 in five southern African countries. (15)

What follows is information for you to consider. Though some of this information may offend pro- vaccinators the intent is solely to ask you to educate yourselves on the pros and cons and reality of the politics of vaccination. If the benefits outweigh the risks in your estimation then go ahead and vaccinate; at least you will make that decision as an informed choice.

"Vaccination is not immunization" written by Tim O'Shea (2013 3rd edition) and is not anti-vaccination however his subtitle is *'Educate before you vaccinate'*. Do you even know what Prevnar or Human Papilloma Virus, or MCV4 or DPT or Rotateq are? – do you even know what these vaccines are for? David Ayoub, MD, Clinical Radiologist, states of O'Shea's book, "It is impossible to estimate the true value of Dr. O'Shea's work. His review of the history of the vaccination industry is vastly more thorough than that taught in medical schools and decisively more balanced. Dr. O'Shea takes the reader through a thorough review of each "vaccine-preventable" disease and the risk/benefit of their vaccine counterpart. "

Not everyone advocates for vaccinating people against their will, but many do. One of the legitimate fears among those who don't vaccinate is that vaccine advocates will use the power of government to force vaccination compliance. Supporting forced vaccination directly contradicts your own beliefs about your body and your rights. Even though many people have never heard of the **Non-aggression Principle (NAP),** they agree with it when it's presented to them. Consider how confusing it can be when people have opinions on these matters. If you're "pro-choice" when it comes to abortion, then you can't be anti-choice when it comes to vaccines, as this would be counter intuitive or hypocritical. Whether you choose to vaccinate or not vaccinate I certainly hope you have done extensive research. Otherwise you are just allowing yourself or your loved ones to be injected with something you know relatively nothing about at the insistence of a group of people who are supported by the Big Pharma industry and their propaganda.

It is always important to keep in mind that vaccinated persons can carry the disease and spread it to others. So the fear mongering that one person's choice affects the survival of others is not considering this factor. A person who is vaccinated and carries the disease may get symptoms of the disease, though the symptoms may be diminished or not, as compared to a person not vaccinated. It is important to understand that herd immunity is based on protecting those who are not vaccinated. Therefore if you choose to be vaccinated there is no risk to you in regards to herd immunity as long as the vaccination is effective. Over a 14 year study the flu vaccine was found to be only 40% effective. (16)

There are examples in the past of the medical establishment universally recommending drugs that have had dire consequences for many people. A few examples are - cholesterol and statin drugs or the link between saturated fat and heart disease and the use of thalidomide drugs as an anti-nausea drug during pregnancy led to 20,000 births of children in the 1960's having deformed limbs. (17)

We are all forced to consider the suspicious relationship between governments and industry. 97–99% of medical journal advertising profits come from pharmaceutical companies, to the tune of hundreds of millions of dollars a year. Today, medical-journal editors estimate that 95 percent of the academic-medicine specialists who assess patented treatments have financial relationships with pharmaceutical companies, and even the prestigious New England Journal of Medicine gave up its search for objective reviewers in June 1992, announcing that it could find no reviewers that did not accept industry funds. *Unsafe things can be made to seem safe if the right amount of money or power lands in the right hands.* And if enough hands are involved, combined with doses of fear and paranoia, you the public have no idea what to believe or what is correct for you and your families.

Why are vaccine manufacturers themselves exempt from the consequences of putting out a potentially dangerous product? Government protects vaccine manufacturers from liability if something goes wrong or someone gets hurt. A U.S. Supreme Court decision has given drug companies total liability protection for injuries and deaths caused by government mandated vaccines. The National Vaccine Information Center (NVIC) called the decision a "betrayal" of the American consumer. (18) (19)

Meanwhile every other business is held liable for every possible outcome. The only way a true market works is if the manufacturers of products that harm people can be litigated against and are held accountable.

The death rate among those infected by measles is typically 0.2%, or close to equal that of your chances of dying in a car accident. The chance of being killed or injured by the measles vaccine still surpasses the chance of being killed or injured by measles itself. In 2004, research data suggested that the chances of dying from measles in the US in the late 1950's were probably closer to 1 in 10,000. (20) (21) (22)

There is also the herd immunity debate which is confusing because immunized children can carry the virus and infect others while minimizing symptoms for themselves. So herd protection isn't at risk solely based on those who are not vaccinated because immunized people can carry the virus and spread it to others. (23)

To be totally logical this is a debate about immunity, therefore proven immune boosters should be an objective of health care professionals, such as breast feeding for a minimum of 2 years, or vaginal birth, the two primary components of the development of a healthy immune system—an immune system that can reduce the chances and severity of disease along with reduced injury and death rates? Around the world, a C-section (surgical removal of a baby through the abdominal wall of the mother as a means of birthing) rate of approximately 19 percent seems to be average according to an analysis of childbirth in 194 countries published in The Journal of the American Medical Association. And yet In N. America, about one in three births (33%) happen by C-section, a rate that has risen dramatically over the past few decades. This is due largely to busy doctors and parents scheduling convenient birthing times. Yet again birthing a baby through C-section may be a lifesaving decision and best for baby and mom. Mostly I want to point to all the factors that are important to consider for healthy immune systems and resistance to illness.

No matter what side of the vaccine debate you fall on, HPV vaccines should give you reason to pause. These vaccines, marketed as a way to prevent cervical cancer, have twice the number of adverse health reactions as any other vaccine. (24) How is it justified to give all grade 6 boys and girls a vaccine against a virus that is only sexually transmitted while saying the vaccine may prevent other cancers in later years? There is no evidence to prove this. To vaccinate 11 year olds from cancer and sexually transmitted diseases that the likelihood of them contracting is extremely low is ill advised given the risks. Especially if you keep in mind the information on epigenetics which shows that most disease is a result of the environment in which your cells live. Therefore what all children truly need is good food, clean water and all that will keep them healthy. Dr. Diane Harper, one of the developers of the Gardasil vaccine warns publicly about the many possible negative side effects. The ingredients in the HPV vaccine include individual proteins from four types of HPV virus, which produce an immune response in your body. The vaccine also contains a small amount of an aluminum compound which acts as an adjuvant, strengthening and lengthening the immune response to the vaccine. The vaccine may contain a trace (a few millionths of a gram) of sodium borate (borax), used as an acidity regulator. Yeast is used in the production of Gardasil and doesn't address the number of youth with yeast infections and yeast sensitivities. Some of these ingredients can produce a rejection response in the body as the non-active ingredients are foreign to the blood and the body has to resist them to protect itself.

Hopefully you are able to understand that this isn't a 'vaccinate or not vaccinate' debate. There are valid concerns for the ingredients in vaccinations that are injected directly into your blood stream.

The fact that the divalent vaccine, Cervarix (HPV vaccine), is manufactured by the UK's GlaxoSmithKline (the second largest Big Pharma company in the world after Pfizer) should raise alarm bells.   Monsanto owns Pfizer! *The connection between Big Pharma and Big Biotech should be extremely alarming*.

Bill and Melinda Gates Foundations, with assets of $43.5 billion, is the largest charitable foundation in the world. There is no doubt that the Gates have been generous philanthropists for a better world. And yet they have also invested much in stocks in GlaxoSmithKline and Monsanto and this always suggests a double standard speaking of healthy water and food for the poor while making money investing with those who would poison the food and water they promote. The Bill and Melinda Gates Foundation also gave HPV vaccine to 16,000 young girls, aged 9-15 in India under the guise of 'well-being shots'? The girls gave no consent to being part of a human trial for the HPV vaccine. India is now, in fact, challenging Gates in the courts on accountability for vaccine crimes. (25)

These vaccines have an alarming track record. They have generated 20,000 recorded events in the UK and 39,000—including 227 deaths—in the US. The children in India fared no better. An estimated 14,000 tribal children were vaccinated with another brand of the HPV vaccine, Cervarix, manufactured by GlaxoSmitheKline (GSK), and some of them became infertile, suffered mood swings, and even endured epileptic seizures.

The first HPV vaccine became available in 2006. As of 2017, 71 countries include it in their routine vaccinations, at least for girls. They are on the World Health Organization's List of Essential Medicines. The wholesale cost in the developing world was about $47 U.S. a dose as of 2014. In the United States it cost more than $200 U.S.   HPV (human papillomavirus) is a sexually transmitted disease and the vaccine is promoted for ages 9 and up (boys and girls) and advertised aggressively to prevent all cervical cancers and a list of other sexual organ cancers. (26) There are a multitude of other potential causes for these cancers, unrelated to HPV.

The real challenge is for a young person to decide if this vaccine is in their best interest. It is impossible to state on any level that this vaccine will prevent any cancer anywhere in the body. To date, science has determined that there is no such thing as a specific cancer like breast cancer or cervical cancer. Science has now proven that all cancers are 'individual' cancers in whatever part of the body it chooses to manifest. The factors that influence cancer as an illness in anyone's life are many: lifestyle, stress, diet, addictions, and chemical exposures in food and water and environment and so on. So to choose to invade your developing immune system with an HPV vaccine would take a lot of convincing and a lot of science and evidence that to this day does not exist.

If you feel strongly about getting your children vaccinated, I encourage you to do extensive research on both sides of the debate regarding the HPV vaccine in particular.

The insistence of the scientific community is crystal clear on the importance and overall safety of vaccines. The same scientific bodies and institutions that proclaim GMO foods safe to eat also advise children to be fully immunized according to the standard pediatric schedule. Why do some people accept the consensus judgment of expert medical panels and scientific institutions on vaccines but not GMOs? (27)

How much do you know about your annual flu vaccine? In 2016, U.S. government officials admitted that, in most years, flu shots are, at best, 50 to 60 percent effective at preventing lab confirmed influenza requiring medical care. And down to 40% effective in the 2017 season. The Centers for Disease Control and Prevention (CDC) analysis of flu vaccine effectiveness revealed that, between 2005 and 2015, the influenza vaccine was less than 50 percent effective more than half of the time. Their pattern to mismatch the vaccine with the prevalent flu virus has proven to be one of the most expensive experiments in medicine over the last few years. In addition to the ineffectiveness of the flu shot, tests conducted at the Natural News Forensic Food Lab found that seasonal flu vaccines contain neurotoxic mercury. Thimerosal, a common vaccine additive and preservative, contains mercury and is on the ingredients label for flu vaccines. (28)

The greatest contradiction of all is that most doctors and even scientists today agree that prevention is the key and so those who eat well, sleep well, get adequate exercise and manage stress are not prone to getting the flu and/or if they do, the symptoms are short lived and mild. It is well short of common sense to still believe in a 'magic pill', which is what vaccines promise to be and ignore what everyone's body requires for a healthy immune system to resist not just the flu, but most diseases known today.

Pregnant women, young children and elderly are encouraged to take the flu vaccine while they have the highest risk to be detrimentally affected by the presence of mercury in their bloodstream. RxList.com, the "Internet Drug Index," has stated the following, that flu vaccines contained added mercury in the form of thimerosal: "Thimerosal, a mercury derivative, is added as a preservative. Each 0.5-mL dose contains 50 mcg (micrograms) thimerosal and less than 25 mcg mercury. Each 0.5-mL dose may also contain residual amounts of ovalbumin ([less than or equal to] 0.3 mcg), formaldehyde ([less than or equal to] 25 mcg) and sodium deoxycholate ([less than] 50 mcg) from the manufacturing process."

Just to put the 'mcg' (microgram) dosage in perspective, 'A List of Deadly Poisons' summarizes a range of chemicals and their relative toxicity to human health. It is cause for concern that mercury is highly toxic to an average human being, and taking into account the size of a child, mercury should not be present in any single flu shot. (29) Except for influenza (flu), thimerosal was removed from or reduced in all vaccines routinely recommended for children 6 years of age and under, manufactured for the U.S. market. And yet, there is still thimerosal in the flu vaccine today.

Each of these ingredients in the flu vaccine is a known neurotoxin, which will damage and destroy the tissues of your nervous system. Also, formaldehyde is a known carcinogen. Please keep in mind this is just information for you to consider. It is not up to me to decide for you, but I would strongly suggest that you inform yourself and decide for yourself, and not have that decision for your health made for you by others. *Also don't just rebel and reject a particular vaccination based on youthful rebellion and attitude, be informed, and be smart about your health and your choices.*

There is public concern over mercury toxicity from coal fired power plants, and fresh and salt water fish, even advising pregnant women to avoid or limit the consumption of canned tuna, which contains mercury and yet little public concern about mercury in vaccines. Your current opinion might be mostly based on propaganda and deception. Accurate and truthful information is power.

The concept of "herd immunity" first materialized in the 1930s, when Johns Hopkins University's Arthur Hedrich discovered that, after 55% of Baltimore's population acquired measles (and thus immunity to measles), the rest of the population, or "herd," became protected. This concept provides today's rationale for insisting that everyone be vaccinated. Measles outbreaks occur even when the vaccinated population exceeds 95%. The emotional debate within the general public and pushed by the medical establishment is, "If you only risked your own health by not getting vaccinated that would be your business. When your failure to get vaccinated endangers me or my child then that becomes my business." It's a powerful argument, except for one thing — herd immunity in vaccinated populations has been repeatedly disproven. In particular it is a fact that 'a vaccinated child is not at risk from an unvaccinated child.' It is also correct that if a child has a weak immune system and is not able to be vaccinated then they could be at risk from both a vaccinated and a non-vaccinated child because vaccinated children can still be carriers of the disease and pass it on.

In the original description of herd immunity, the protection to the population at large occurred only if people contracted the infections naturally. The reason for this is that naturally-acquired immunity lasts for a lifetime. The

243

vaccine proponents quickly latched onto this concept and applied it to vaccine-induced immunity. The one major problem in addition to 50% success rates is that vaccine-induced immunity lasted for only 2 to 10 years at most. And so what followed was the new profitable idea of imposing boosters for most vaccines, even the common childhood infections such as chickenpox, measles, mumps, and rubella. (30) (31)

I understand that these are challenging decisions for youth and parents to make amidst the chaos of campaigns and propaganda that push vaccinations and imply that all people who disagree are wrong. However, fully understanding this subject is important. Understanding herd immunity is important as well. If 100% of those vaccinated or not vaccinated can carry the virus or bacteria and pass it on how can herd immunity be reached? Those who make vaccines should be as concerned about the ingredients as those who are injected with vaccines.

Do your own research. Getting vaccinated is a personal choice that everyone has the right to make. But, as with all decisions regarding your health, it is VITAL to understand what you are doing to your body. Seek to understand the whole story behind the 'herd immunity' concept. There is plenty of research, misinformation and propaganda on both sides of the vaccination debate; be sure to research thoroughly and not just settle for research that supports your present personal opinion. You want the facts before you make decisions that affect not only your life but the life of loved ones in your care. Most importantly, remember that maintaining a healthy immune system is in your control and your best health defense. History and science has shown us that clean water and sanitation was the primary reason for the decline of infectious disease. Travel can present you with a different set of vaccination decisions. Indonesia, Thailand, India, Vietnam, Cambodia, and China all require or recommend vaccinations for typhoid, Hepatitis A and B, yellow fever, rabies or even cholera to name a few.

It is time to separate emotion, propaganda, and fear mongering from the debate. Educate yourself rationally, with patience and common sense, and good decisions will be made.

Chapter 25

Addiction and Recovery

There are endless lists of possibilities that may lead an individual to addictions of any type. According to the American Addiction Centre the compulsion to continually engage in an activity or behavior despite the negative impact on the person's ability to remain mentally and/or physically healthy and functional in the home and community defines behavioral addiction. A person may find the behavior rewarding psychologically or get a "high" while engaged in the activity but may later feel guilt, remorse, or even overwhelmed by the consequences of that continued choice. The varieties of addictions may fall into the categories of gambling, drug and alcohol abuse, food addiction, compulsive shopping, risky behavior addiction, cell phones, sex, pornography, video games addictions, etc.

Today, along with technology came the new phenomenon of behavioral addictions. Behavioral addictions are based on the idea that people were addicted to changes in the brain chemistry, rather than the drug itself. Addiction is a primary, chronic disease of brain reward, motivation, memory and related circuitry. This can be reflected in a person pathologically pursuing reward and/or relief by substance use and other behaviors.

Addiction is characterized by the inability to consistently abstain, impairment in behavioral control and craving, diminished recognition of significant problems with one's behaviors and interpersonal relationships, and a dysfunctional emotional response. Addiction often involves cycles of relapse and remission and may be identified as doing something in the short term but compulsively continuing the behavior in the long term which undermines your wellbeing.

We are engineered biologically in a way that the brain will release the neurotransmitter dopamine when the right buttons are pressed by a particular activity. The brain will respond the same way whether taking heroine or playing video games. With the flood of the feel good hormone dopamine, you will feel wonderful in the short term but in the long term will build up your tolerance levels and want more.

Loneliness in itself has been proven to decrease survival rates, increase anxiety, weaken the immune system and result in addictive behaviors.

According to data from the General Social Survey (GSS) the number of Americans who say that they have no close friends has roughly doubled since 1985. "Zero" is the most common response when applicants were asked how many close confidantes they have. This loneliness seems to be more prevalent in millennials partly due to social networking, which was originally meant as a tool to keep us connected and up-to-date with our community. Young people are avoiding real-life relationships in favor of internet friendships. Life can become a virtual reality while your 'in person' life is falling to pieces.

Dr. Robin Dunbar, evolutionary anthropologist and author wrote "How Many Friends Does One Person Need?" Dr. Dunbar has determined that the closest 15 individuals within your social circle, virtual or real are the most influential when it comes to your mental and physical health. The competitive number of friends on social media is meaningless in an individual's need for companionship, friendship and support.

Dr. Nicholas Christakis explains that loneliness can be contagious in social circles and there can be a cascade of loneliness that causes a disintegration of the social network. A 2009 study using data collected from 5,000 people found that since 1948 participants are 52% more likely to be lonely if someone that they're directly connected to is lonely. This includes family members, close friends, neighbors, and co-workers. That means that people who aren't lonely tend to become lonely when they spend time with lonely people. Loneliness itself can become contagious and an addiction.

If you are trapped in addiction or know someone who is, seek out the documentary or the book *'Wasted: An Alcoholic Therapist's Fight for Recovery in a Flawed Treatment System', by Michael Pond*. This will give you much needed information to understand your or their dilemma better.

Understanding the biology of addiction is critical to find a way through to wellness again. This book is brilliant, concise and highly valuable to help you move from 'assumptions' to understanding. Addiction is now classified as a disease of the brain and no longer has anything to do with the idea of being weak willed.

OxyContin (prescription pain killer) abuse has greatly damaged the lives of thousands of people in N. America. Families have been separated and lives have been lost because of the devastating effects from this dangerous drug. In fact, OxyContin's manufacturer faced criminal charges in the U.S. and pleaded guilty in 2007, after they proclaimed to doctors that this drug was less likely to cause addiction. In Canada, citizens have filed a class action lawsuit to hold Doctors accountable for the damage that they have caused. The complication that followed the realization that OxyContin is highly addictive is that Doctors stopped writing prescriptions which led to addicted patients going to the street for unsafe drugs contaminated today with fentanyl. After manufacturers earned more than $31 billion off the sale of OxyContin, it is time for compensation to reach people whose lives were negatively impacted by the use of this common painkiller.

Doctor prescribed opioid abuse and addiction is a much bigger problem than heroin addiction in the USA. In 2014 there were 11,000 overdose deaths from heroin; however, there were 19,000 overdose deaths from prescription opiates. Eighty percent of heroin users in the US reported that they began on prescription painkillers before progressing to heroin use, and 45 percent of heroin users are currently addicted to prescription painkillers. This problem largely starts in the doctor's office from over prescribing prescription drugs.

Tobacco has been growing wild in the Americas for nearly 8000 years. Around 2,000 years ago tobacco began to be chewed and smoked during cultural or religious ceremonies and events. Nicotine is the addictive substance in cigarette smoke. It is present in the tobacco leaf and when a cigarette is burnt, nicotine from the tobacco leaf is inhaled and reaches the brain in six seconds. Nicotine causes changes in the structure and function of the brain producing both positive experiences such as feelings of arousal, relaxation, and improved concentration and negative withdrawal symptoms such as nervousness, restlessness, irritability, anxiety and impaired concentration. Via the bloodstream and the lungs, nicotine reaches the brain within 6 seconds of inhalation. The risk of developing dependence following exposure to cigarettes is greater than the risk of developing dependence following the initial use of cocaine, alcohol or marijuana. 80 to 90 percent of lung cancer cases are caused by tobacco smoke. Further, tobacco is associated with over 400,000 annual deaths in the United States alone. Cigarette smoke contains over 4,000 chemicals, including 43 known cancer-causing (carcinogenic) compounds and 400 other toxins. These include nicotine, tar, and carbon monoxide, as well as formaldehyde, ammonia, hydrogen cyanide, arsenic, and DDT. Nicotine is highly addictive. (1)

Electronic cigarettes, commonly known as e-cigarettes or vaping, have become popular since 2006. A recent study by the CDC shows that from 2011 to 2013, the number of never-smoking youth who tried e-cigarettes tripled. E-cigarettes are marketed as a better alternative to traditional cigarettes, but as a new product there is no reliable data on its safety. Unlike traditional cigarettes, e-cigarettes are loaded with a vaporizable liquid. This fluid is made up of a number of chemicals, among them propylene glycol, glycerol, nicotine and a variety of flavoring substances. While these chemicals don't sound entirely appealing, the new research shows that the real danger may be in how these compounds change when heated. To use an e-cigarette, you load the liquid and apply electricity, heating the liquid until it vaporizes. At this temperature, the chemicals inside the fluid undergo a breakdown process and are converted into other chemicals. Using an advanced measurement system called nuclear magnetic resonance spectroscopy, scientists examined the new chemicals. When the e-cigarette liquid broke down, it produced both formaldehyde and formaldehyde-releasing agents, both are known carcinogens. *The results of their study state that the risk of developing cancer with e-cigarettes may be up to 15 times higher than actually smoking cigarettes.* (2)

Your brain isn't fully developed until the age of 25 and the impact that drugs, smoking and alcohol have on the underdeveloped brain are far more detrimental than the effects on a mature brain. Since teens generally lack the ability to adequately assess risk, this makes them more likely to overindulge in substances. It's this same lack that explains why people tend to be braver and more open to trying new experiences during teen years. This courage or naivety perhaps comes at a cost, as teens cannot adequately assess the risks of the substances they may be using.

Presentations from a program called DARE, or Drug Abuse Resistance Education, in high schools around N. America focused more on avoiding criminal behavior than protecting their bodies. There wasn't much focus on long-term effects of drug use. They always maintained that abstinence from drug use was best and that marijuana was the gateway drug. It has become obvious that alcohol is far more dangerous than marijuana. Though to be clear, neither, in any way, other than perhaps medical marijuana for specific health conditions preferably ingested rather than smoked, support healthy brain development in young people. Alcohol is readily available and easy to obtain, be it from parent's liquor cabinets or fridges, older siblings, or peers.

Teens are under tremendous pressure, from their parents, their teachers, and especially their peers. It is far too easy to default to fitting in and using alcohol or drugs as a coping mechanism for stress and perhaps bury what may be happening in your life. Have a plan in place if you are familiar with peer pressure situations. Saying no isn't always that easy, but changing the subject, hanging out with people who support your choices and use the buddy system if you bump into peer pressure regularly. Discuss your feelings with someone you trust, and its okay to give yourself permission to avoid people. It is extremely important to remember that you can't please everyone, so check in with your own feelings on some decisions you are asked to make. Does it feel right to you? Be prepared to stand up for others, (called the bystander intervention), if you see someone else is being pressured or bullied. This can be done with a sense of humor or insistence, whichever works best in each situation. If the risk is too great, call for help or dial 911. Whenever you stand up for someone else, you are also standing up for yourself.

According to an Icelandic psychologist, Gudberg Jonsson, just twenty years ago Icelandic teens were among the heaviest drinking youths in all of Europe. Apparently you couldn't even walk downtown in Reykjavik on a Friday night without being bothered by rowdy teenagers getting wasted. He says it felt unsafe. These days, Iceland has various after school classes in facilities that include heated swimming pools and clubs for music, dance, or art. (3) **Iceland now tops the European table for the cleanest living teens.** The percentage of 15- and 16-year-old teens who were drunk on a regular basis dropped from 42% in 1998 to 5% in 2016. The percentage of cannabis users dropped from 17% to 7%, and those smoking cigarettes every day fell from 23% to 3%. This country has been able to achieve such a successful turnaround thanks to what might best be described as enforced common sense. **"This is the most remarkably intense and profound study of stress in the lives of teenagers that I have ever seen,"** says Milkman with Project Self Discovery. "I'm just so impressed how well it's working." Milkman believes that if this model were adopted in other countries it could benefit the physical as well as psychological well-being of millions of kids worldwide.

Milkman helped develop the idea that people were addicted to changes in the brain chemistry, rather than the drug itself. "People can get addicted to drink, cars, money, sex, calories, cocaine – whatever. " The idea of behavioral addiction became a brilliant new way to understand addiction.

His idea to "orchestrate a social movement around natural highs, around people getting high on their own brain chemistry – because it seems obvious to me that people want to change their consciousness – without the deleterious effects of drugs?" With the help of the Icelandic government he began the Project Self-Discovery, which offered teens natural high alternatives to drugs and various crimes. Being addicted to dance is obviously a much better alternative than being addicted to drugs or alcohol. Building, creating, exploring, learning new skills are all more satisfying and fulfilling than any addiction to substances. ***Because drug education generally doesn't work, teaching the life skills to act on that information was extremely successful. A new national plan called "Youth in Iceland" has the attention of the world because of its huge success.*** Possibly the most important step to this plan was increasing state funding for organized sport, music, art, dance, and other activities. This allowed kids more ways to be able to bond with their peers and feel good and have fun, without resorting to drugs and alcohol. Lower income families also received a bonus for each child so that they too, could participate in these activities.

Many addicts cannot imagine life without their addictions, whether to heroin, crack, television, food, the internet, entitlement, or technology. The money behind the drug trade and the money spent on the 'war on drugs' adds up to billions. Portugal, with 1% of their population addicted to heroin, decided to spend drug money on secure housing, subsidized jobs and reconnecting people to the wider society. An independent study by the British Journal of Criminology found that in Portugal since total decriminalization, addiction has fallen, and injecting drug use is down by 50 percent. This is relevant to all of us. Human beings are bonding animals. A ***wise mantra for the twentieth century was E.M. Forster's -- "only connect."*** Behind so many addictions is the disconnection a person feels from those around them. A feeling of being cut off from society with no path, direction or future. British writer George Monbiot has called today **"the age of loneliness."** Bruce Alexander -- the creator of Rat Park —says that *we have talked exclusively about individual recovery from addiction, whereas we need now to talk about social recovery.*

What also goes along with most addictions is malnourishment and dehydration on a cellular level. Good food and water feed our brains and thus enable us to be more empowered to choose differently in our lives. Good food, hydration and improved health alone can be the foundation for change. (4)

Addictions can begin from habits gone wrong. It only makes sense that in a time of technology and isolation that a possible root cause of addiction just may be a lack of connection to people, to each other. (5)

Somehow people have come to believe that suffering is necessary and an addictive substance becomes the tool to cope with suffering. So much happens in a life from birth to the present moment that it helps to backtrack in your life to a place where you diverged from contentment to coping and eventually to not coping. If that is your present situation figure out how you got to here, it can help you remap a journey to wellbeing and help change your focus. *If you focus on the 99 things that don't work in your life, this becomes the trend,* however if you focus on the one thing that is working in your life (and you can find it if you look hard enough) the other 99 will eventually line up in a more positive direction with effort and patience.

Annie Dillard said 'How we spend our days is, of course, how we spend our lives.'

Much has been written about the effects of using alcohol and marijuana separately, but there is surprisingly little research on using them together. When people use alcohol and marijuana at the same time, it's often referred to as *"cross fading."* There are some pretty strange things that occur biologically when you mix pot and alcohol together. (6)

On its own, alcohol affects the central nervous system by altering the communication process of your neurons. This involves suppression of the excitatory neurotransmitter glutamate, and increasing the inhibitory neurotransmitter GABA. The end result for the user is less feeling, less recognition, and less recollection while you drink.

Weed, however, involves the active ingredient THC, which alters the cannabinoid receptors in the brain, causing neurons to fire continuously. This can result in your imagination and thoughts being intensely magnified and connected.

The connection between the two responses is glutamate inhibition. Glutamate is an essential part of the learning process, linking getting high and drunk at the same time to bad memory. Marijuana is often used as an effective anti-nausea treatment for those going through chemotherapy, and has taken front stage as a cancer cure and useful for many other health concerns. *There are serious cautions in regard to overdrinking while smoking marijuana.* Drinking too much often forces the body to vomit the excess poisonous alcohol from your system. If you are high and drinking excessively - getting "cross-faded"- THC levels in your blood plasma nearly double. With more THC hitting the brain thanks to the ethanol in alcoholic drinks, the usual effects of marijuana—like impaired judgment and increased heart rate—are stronger, which means accidents like drownings and car crashes could be more likely. It is important to note that the amounts of drugs approved for this research were lower than the levels that people often use while out partying. (7)

Any choice you make, you want your decision to be balanced and informed. Explore the upsides and downsides to cannabis. Most of the medicinal benefits of marijuana come from different methods of ingestion, not smoking. Heavy marijuana use is linked to lower dopamine levels in the brain. A number of studies have linked smoking cannabis to schizophrenia and psychosis. A fairly recent study found that schizophrenia plays a role in a person's likelihood of smoking weed. The study showed that genetic variants predicting schizophrenia can also be used to predict a person's tendency to smoke pot. Smoking marijuana changes your brain. Smoking anything harms the lungs. Smoking marijuana daily can increase your risk of serious cardiovascular disorders. (8) The occasional use of alcohol is socially acceptable and woven into the fabric of most societies. Common sense and balance are the keys to managing alcohol or marijuana in your life.

No matter your decision to combine the two or not, remember that all bodies respond differently to drugs. Let common sense and you paying attention be your rule. Our cultures have strayed from living an authentic life for many young people. Without authenticity in your immediate environment this can lead many people to drugs and alcohol to dull or distract them from all that is missing in their actual life. *Civilizations around the world have celebrated with fermented beverages since the beginning of man's time on the earth.* Be wise and celebrate with care if using drugs or alcohol and protect all your brain cells for use in other matters.

Cigarette smoking has been noted as one of the toughest habits to kick. The dangers of smoking cigarettes have been front and center for decades in media and with medical professionals. Most people are well aware of the risks, though even the knowledge that a habit is killing you is not enough for some people to choose to stop smoking. Be a support and friend to anyone attempting to quit smoking, it may mean the difference between success and failure for them. There are many organizations today that help those who want to quit. *'Quit Now' has a great track record*.

Acupuncture, studying your habits and changing behavior, healthy food and good water, lime instead of Nicorette®, creating replacement habits that are good for you will help a person quit. The tobacco industry has reaped financial rewards in the trillions over time. Cigarettes today are a far cry from the old school roll-your-own cigarettes that were mostly real tobacco decades ago. *The chemicals in cigarettes are toxic and many are known carcinogens.* There are way too many examples of toxic food, substances and medications that benefit corporations and bring in money in taxes with each sale to governments. *This makes no sense if you believe that governments are here to represent your best interests*!

It can't be stated often enough that taking responsibility for and caring for your self is key. Being confident and putting value on our own heart and intellect no matter the opinion of others is vital in order to change a lifestyle that causes you suffering. You can only do this for yourself, though you can assist each other by reminding those around you of their value and importance in the fabric of life.

Substance addiction and behavioral addictions are uniquely different though both can be severely destructive. Behavioral addiction is a form of addiction that involves a compulsion to engage in a rewarding non-drug-related behavior despite any negative consequences to the person's physical, mental, social or financial well-being. These behaviors can translate into food addiction, sex addictions, self-pity addictions, and so on. (9)

You don't recover from an addiction simply by no longer using. You recover by stopping and creating a new life where it is easier to not use. If you don't create a new life, then all the factors that brought you to your addiction will eventually catch up with you again.

You don't have to change everything in your life. Refer to your lists of wants and not wants, best case scenarios and opportunities you wish you had in your life. Decide to let go the behaviors that get you into trouble. The more you attempt to stay the same as your old life, the less chance you will recover and succeed with your goal to be free of addictions.

Avoid high-risk situations. Some addictions specialists use the term HALT which stands for hungry, angry, lonely or tired. At the end of a busy day you might not have eaten enough or you may be annoyed because of a tough day at work. If you are isolated you might feel lonely, exhausted or depressed. These are a few of the reasons why your strongest cravings usually occur at the end of the day. If alcohol is a challenge for you, avoid friends who drink and don't have alcohol in your house; this will require honesty and determination.

Decide on a new strategy. For example take a break from those that are not contributing to your wellness and people you may have conflict with. Decide to spend time with people who support and encourage you to be well. Find new places to hang out, safe places where you are distracted with more fun and challenging activities. This could be as simple as reading a book in the park, volunteer at animal rescues and take a dog for a walk, or seek out new friends you can trust. If you pay attention and are aware of your surroundings you can effectively avoid high risk situations and prevent small cravings from turning into major urges.

Take better care of yourself. Eat a healthier lunch so you're not as hungry at the end of the day. If you consume high sugar snacks during the day this will contribute to big swings in glucose levels in your blood which can cause similar swings in focus, energy and irritability. These swings can also lead to the use of stimulants to get you through the day. Coffee has been the fuel that keeps the world moving for decades. A cup or two of good coffee can be a reasonable choice. However, 4-6 plus cups of coffee a day is excessive caffeine intake. The new craze of caffeinated energy drinks like Red Bull ® or Rockstar® have a whole host of other ingredients as well. According to a recent study, caffeine is the only ingredient that actually works. Participants who drank only caffeinated water had the same brain activity and response times as those consuming 5 Hour Energy drinks. One Rockstar® energy drink can have 63 grams of sugar which is the same amount in two regular size Snickers candy bars and **equals 16 teaspoons of sugar**. These energy drinks along with all high sugar foods can cause a sugar crash that leaves you foggy and weak, which of course leads to searching for another energy source, another energy drink perhaps.

If your addictions control your life it may be necessary to join a 12 step program, addictions anonymous group or call a drug and alcohol help line for guidance so that you don't feel isolated. Learn how to relax so that you can let go of your anger and resentments. Develop better sleep habits so that you're less tired. Consider meditation, yoga and exercise to support your body's shift from craving to satisfaction with wellness in food and exercise. (10)   With good health there are five key ingredients; good food, good water, adequate sleep, good attitude and exercise.   These all help you to manage stress and cope with all the challenges life presents you with.

Recovery isn't about one big change.   It's about a domino effect of multiple little or big decisions you make that add up to a new life of your choosing.   Make a list of your high-risk situations.   Addiction is sneaky. Sometimes you won't see your high-risk situations until you're right in the middle of one. That's why it's important that you learn to look for them and maintain constant awareness.   Discuss with someone else who understands addiction and recovery so that you can spot situations that you might find yourself influenced by. Make a list and keep it with you. Some day that list may save your life.

A few of the reasons people use drugs and alcohol are to escape, relax, and reward themselves, which ultimately relieves tension and stress. You can now understand at the root of many addictions is the inability to relieve tension and stress. Just as stress affects your physical body you also know the impact of stress on your mind. Finding actions that calm your mind and your emotions is the most important step to take in overcoming addictions. Creating coping skills to lead you to a happy life will greatly assist you in finding peace within. Too many 'addicts' work hard and stop using for a while, but if they didn't learn to relax, the tension will build again. Tension and stress are the most common cause of relapse.

Research tells us that learning to relax has changed the life of many addicts. The general reason why people don't relax is because they think they're too busy to relax. If you consider how much time you spend on your addiction, only a fraction of that time spent relaxing could really pay off. Relaxation is essential to recovery. Do something every day to relax, walk, run, play sports, bike, get out in nature, sing, meditate and create a reward system that helps turn off the mind talk.

Equally important is to learn how to manage stress and change your thoughts to be more positive and calm. *Studies show that when a person is tense they tend to fall into familiar and incorrect behavior and it is more difficult to be open to change.* Especially when new behavior is critical to success, it is essential to change your thinking, because anxiety and depression often underlie addictions. (11)(12)

Nothing changes, if nothing changes. This is a common phrase used in Alcoholic Anonymous (AA). Honesty is essential with the people who love and support you if you want to create a new life for yourself. The 12 step program with AA was first formed in 1935 with 2 million members worldwide in 2015. The success rate for AA members is variable between 10% and 12% depending on the source you check. There are many new avenues, rehabilitation centers and help lines that may increase and improve your success.

When you're completely honest with yourself you don't give your addiction room to hide, however when you lie to yourself you leave the door open to relapse. You may have spent so much time learning how to lie that telling the truth, no matter how good it is for you, won't feel natural. Show common sense in who you share your journey with. People that care about you will be grateful you have told them the truth and will help in any way they can. *Shame is a trap that keeps a person stuck and thankfully this past decade has identified alcoholism and other addictions as diseases.* This at the very least is helping to remove the shame and stigma, while addressing the real life struggle of addictions.

Too many people sleep walk through life. If you are changing your life no matter how difficult that decision is, you will become acutely aware of what matters most and what you want your life to be. You may begin to deeply appreciate the simplicity of each breath and the healthy choices you make. Many successful recovering addicts will describe that their addiction helped them find an inner peace and tranquility that many non addicts crave and never find.

Whether you are an addict or you have a friend or someone you love who is an addict, it is extremely important to let go of needing to fix them or change them. In Chapter 16 on Relationships I discussed the difference between helping or fixing and serving. The difference is profound when compassion is your guide in either choosing to save your own life or serve another to save theirs.

Letting go of and avoiding people who have passively or actively supported your addictions is essential to your success of quitting. Though some of your best memories, whether you are the addict or love an addict, have been with people you love, (or think you love if the memories are immersed in addictions), you have to determine who is helping and who is holding you back. If the relationships are toxic, you have to let go of them. (13)

You've heard the phrase, 'misery loves company,' and nowhere is there more misery than in an active addiction. Somehow, from deep inside, see value in yourself. Even a glimmer may be all you need to move in a direction that will relieve some of your suffering. Gandhi said "If we could change ourselves, the tendencies in the world would also change. As a man changes his own nature, so does the attitude of the world change towards him. We need not wait to see what others do. "

There are so many experiences a person can have in a day that can challenge their equilibrium. Someone dies, someone leaves, something breaks, institutions and governments that are supposed to help you turn you away, jobs end, time flies and holding it all together becomes a daily struggle. Good job for getting through each and every day, for taking care of the menial but important tasks that make up your life. Perhaps you feel like you are treading water and getting nowhere. Know that you are holding your place with courage and strength until the table turns and there is a light at the end of your tunnel. It takes enormous courage to sustain yourself through the dark times and start to put it all back together when opportunities present themselves, no matter how small they may seem.

If you are lonely, change that by reaching out to family or friends or join a hiking, canoeing, or outdoor club -whatever activity you enjoy most, or try a new one where you can make new friends. No matter how strongly you feel unwanted or not able to fit in, trust that people will welcome you when you take that step. There are more people than you can imagine who are willing to include you and support you. *Instead of recreational drugs, find recreational activities that produce healthy hormonal responses in your body that make you feel good.* Active sports, dance, and aerobics encourage your body to detox and energize. Canoeing, hiking, backpacking, biking, & winter sports all reconnect you with nature where your mind and body can find peace. These all create natural highs and alter the chemistry of the brain in a good way without drugs.

Choose your social circle carefully and form new habits that improve your health each day and contribute to your overall wellbeing. Your defenses will get stronger every day and you will be more resilient and more able to resist the temptation of addiction.

Reach out and a hand will be there to help you. *May the beauty of Nature remind you of the Beauty within you.*

Chapter 26

Technologies

Two decades ago, a bold new hope for civilization came in the form of a technology revolution. Academics, commentators, and politicians prescribed that the Internet was going to free and democratize the world. It enabled the free flow of information and goods, it allowed users to change their identities, and resist older, fixed notions of personhood. Philosophers proclaimed that it began another grass roots movement that would oppose authoritarianism. Today much of that technology has been turned against us with surveillance, controls, hacking, and propaganda in absolute opposition to the expectation that technology would solve our problems. (1)

Your attention is extremely high priced these days. We live in an attention economy where billions are invested in influencing your attention, your interest and hooking you into spending money to benefit and support consumerism. *As persuasion goes up your ability to choose goes down.* The screen world is designed by some of the smartest, most creative minds on the planet and most young people don't get a chance to resist technology. There are yet unexamined consequences considering that there are more devices than people on the planet. In the 1960's, technology liberated humanity, and today humans have become servants or possibly slaves to their devices.

One of the many upsides of technology is published in Brain Research Journal. The study found that regular gaming may actually improve certain aspects of cognitive function, especially when it comes to working memory. This study found that young people who consider themselves to be avid gamers performed better on working memory tests than those who were not. The gamers had a more advanced response speed in completing tasks and they also demonstrated a superior ability to keep track of new and changing information.   When the task became more challenging, the gamer's brains were conditioned to become more active.   Keep in mind however; when gaming becomes an addiction and takes time away from other activities that are crucial for brain health such as sleep and exercise, the cognitive benefits of gaming are diminished.

Technology has increased multi-tasking in a big way. However there is plenty of research to suggest that fully focusing on one task is more efficient, the task is better accomplished and the brain is not over taxed.   Working with lists helps to complete tasks and move on to the next with higher success rates of productivity.   Video game skills were a better predictor of surgeon's success in performing laparoscopic surgery than actual laparoscopic surgery experience.   Visual intelligence has been rising globally for 50 years partly due to using technology.

In a new book, *"Irresistible: The Rise of Addictive Technology and the Business of Keeping Us Hooked,"* the social psychologist Adam Alter warns that many of us, youngsters, teenagers and adults are literally addicted to modern digital products.   In the past, addiction was mostly related to chemical substances like heroin, cocaine, alcohol or nicotine.

Keep in mind that the people who create video games wouldn't admit to creating addicts, they simply want you to spend as much time as possible with their products. However with the 'taking over of technology' you can be sure great minds are seeking to addict you to their products and are highly competitive for your attention and time. *Game producers pretest different versions of a new release to see which one is hardest to resist and which will keep your attention the longest*.

Today there are rehabilitation centers that specialize in treating young people with technology addictions.   Gaming and internet addiction is a serious problem throughout East Asia, and perhaps the world.   In China, there are millions of young addicts, and they have tech rehab camps where parents commit their children for months, and therapists treat them with a detox program from technology.

The main reason Adam Alter wrote his book 'Irresistible: The Rise of Addictive Technology and the Business of Keeping Us Hooked' was as a result of the late Steve Job saying in a 2010 interview that his own children didn't use iPads. *There are private schools in the Bay Area in California that don't allow any tech — no iPhones or iPads. The most interesting aspect about this school is that 75 percent of the parents are tech executives.*

Technology is designed to hook you with bottomless social media platforms like Facebook, Snapchat, Twitter and Instagram. Information of all kinds is available to you 24 hours a day 7 days a week.

The human brain doesn't fully develop until the age of 25 years. With that in mind there are many concerns that youth lack the skills in critical thinking and analysis for making the best choices for their individual lives according to research by Patricia Greenfield, (UCLA distinguished professor of psychology and director of the Children's Digital Media Center, Los Angeles). Learners have changed as a result of their exposure to technology, says Greenfield, who analyzed more than 50 studies on learning and technology, including research on multi-tasking and the use of computers, the Internet and video games. Youth today experience more images in one day than a 14th century youth would see in a lifetime.

Know yourself first and if you spend more time on your devices looking down than you do looking out at the world, make a decision to find balance. Youth are disconnected and isolated today. If you are interested, find the app (AntiSocial) that shows you how many hours you spend on all the different social media platforms and you will then perhaps be able to quantify and no longer ignore how much time you are 'not' living your life. (2)

More than 85 percent of video games contain violence, and multiple studies of violent video games have shown that they can produce negative effects, including aggressive behavior and desensitization to real-life violence. There are millions of video game players who believe they would never commit violence based on their gaming. It is likely those connected to both violent behavior and video games have a button within that gets triggered based on their unique life experience. Many gamers may never show aggressive behavior, however becoming numb to visual violence may be at the root of becoming a bystander to violence in the real world.

In the first chapter I discussed the 'Shifting Baseline Syndrome' and here is an example of how violence becomes normalized because it is a new baseline for games and entertainment. Nothing good will come of this accepted behavior and the new normal too easily forgets that kindness, compassion and caring for your family, neighbors, your community, and the world at large – this is why we are here.

There are downsides to information overload. The amount of time spent online by the masses has created a deficit in other important parts of a person's life. It is easy to get lost in following other people's ideas and methods while never attempting to create one of your own. Reality is highly subjective. *A high number of youth today have the opinion that they fail in real life and succeed in the virtual world.* Technology displaces natural human interactions, communication and contact and it is important to balance your technology time with nature and people.

When a social world revolves around a belief in rugged individualism and technological addictions, people will begin to feel separate and alone because that is what everyone else around them is doing. The outcome will be heightened anxiety and stress, a greater likelihood of depression and, in extreme cases, suicide. Humans think in terms of groups, and with the isolating impact of technology the individual becomes the group and this prevents healthy relationships with others.

The negative mental, emotional and biological impacts associated with the technology era we are all immersed in, are determined to be high and future research will reveal even greater threats to human health. Switzerland (Dr. Thomas Rau, 2009) started a petition and stated that "If you install mobile cellular phone towers near schools which radiate to the children, their intelligence and their brain capacity decreases. You will have more ADD children; with less brain function, which in the long-term reflects on the intelligence of children." We are now into generation 2 of people affected by the constant bombardment of electromagnetic fields (EMF).

When children play in nature, climb trees, build forts and explore in the woods they have less obesity, less ADD, less depression, less suicide, less alcohol and drug abuse and less bullying and actually have higher academic achievement. Robert Bateman wrote an article on Children and Nature and said that "Children's brains have been invaded by electronics, a virtual world. What will true happiness, freedom and brilliance look like for this screen trapped generation? TV played a major role in the 1960's to train a generation of consumers, and that has escalated to limitless electronics today, separating the natural world from the virtual world almost completely from young people's lives. "

Independent research links cell phone radiation to a myriad of adverse biological effects, such as DNA chain breaks, blood-brain barrier damage, and disruption of cell metabolism. These biological effects may translate into symptoms such as fatigue, irritability, headaches, and digestive disorders. Worse still these exposures may lead to disease. Thousands of independent studies now link these exposures to a long list of serious diseases.

A study published in 2016 by Kaiser Permanente researchers reported that pregnant women exposed to radio-frequency radiation from sources such as wireless devices and cell towers had nearly a threefold greater frequency of miscarriage. (3)

December 2017, California officially issued groundbreaking guidelines advising cell phone users to keep phones away from their bodies and limit use when reception is weak. State officials caution that studies link radiation from long-term cell phone use to an increased risk of brain cancer, lower sperm counts and other health problems, and note that children's developing brains could be at greater risk. The state Department of Public Health also recommended that parents consider reducing the amount of time their children use cellphones, and encourage kids to turn the devices off at night. (4)

Even the very conservative World Health Organization has classified radiation exposure from cell phones as a "possible Class 2B carcinogen." It would be highly beneficial if there was a way of knowing which phones emit the most (and least) radiation. The U.S. government, via the Federal Communications Commission (FCC), requires all cell phone models sold to be tested for their Specific Absorption Rate, or SAR. (5)

The SAR measures the maximum amount of microwave radiation absorbed by the head or the body. The SAR, measured in watts per kilogram (W/kg), represents the maximum amount of energy absorbed in any one gram of tissue in the test model. In the United States the legal limit is 1.60. That's to say all cell phones sold in the U.S. must have a SAR value of below 1.60 W/kg.

SAR values are measured at two levels, the head and the body. The SAR values are lower on phones sold in the European Union (EUR) than for the exact same models sold in the U.S. For comparison the Samsung Galaxy S6 has a SAR of 1.15 W/kg for the head and a SAR reading of 1.16 W/kg for the body and the other end of the spectrum is the Google Nexus 6 with a SAR reading of 0.86 W/kg for the head and a SAR reading of 0.36 W/kg for the body. (6) (7)

Ways to help minimize cell phone health risks are to use your phone on speaker mode as the amount of radiation absorbed by your head and body decreases dramatically with even a small distance. Don't put your phone in your pocket or clip it to your belt when turned on even when using your headset. When a phone is on and not in use it still sends out an intermittent signal to connect with nearby cell phone towers which means radiation exposure continues to occur. Text more and call less because phones emit less radiation when sending texts than voice communications. Call only when the signal is strong, fewer signal bars mean the phone must use remote power to broadcast its signal. Research shows that radiation exposure increases dramatically when cell phone signals are weak. We already have multiple case reports of young women with no family cancer history getting a diagnosis of breast cancer. Tumors were unusually located directly underneath the skin where patients placed cell phones in their bra. (8)

The debate around the emotional contagion experiment, for instance, is fundamentally a debate about what metaphor should guide our thinking about what the Facebook News Feed actually is. The Facebook experiment determined that emotional states can be transferred to others via emotional contagion, leading them to experience the same emotions as those around them. Emotional contagion is well established in laboratory experiments, in which people transfer positive and negative moods and emotions to others. Similarly, data from a large, real-world social network collected over a 20 year period suggests that longer-lasting moods (e.g., depression, happiness) can be transferred through networks as well. (9) This experiment defines the moral burden of social media networks and where the ethical onus truly lies.

The language of the internet about data streams, exhaust and mining and clouds uses metaphors that naturalize and depersonalize data and its collection. The current data metaphors mask the human behaviors, relationships, and communications that make up all that data that is being streamed and mined. As a result, it is easy to get lost in the quantity of the data and forget how personal so much of it is.

Digital historian Ian Milligan, warns of a digital dark age that is coming and may already be here. The enormous volume of personal information now solely digital can potentially be deleted at any time. He believes preserving digital history is imperative to saving our cultural history. Entire Geocity websites that have been on line for 10 years are being erased and the fragility of digital data is being ignored.

Loneliness often triggered by technology is a pandemic which has been identified as a cultural sickness that goes by the name 'Individualism'. *This belief is profoundly at odds with everything that is known about human nature*, yet it still persists and has been built into the social DNA of our modern world. People feel a strong foundational need for belonging. This need is so fundamental that newborn children who are not given physical contact are much more prone to immune failure. Sociologists agree that the fundamental unit of human existence is the small group and not the individual. A focus on materialism is an expected outcome of social isolation. If a person cannot find comfort in the affections of family or friends they will look for it outside of themselves and technology and consumerism becomes the substitute. Awareness is the key, and the first step is to recognize your disconnection, so you can interrupt it.

The recent expansion of man-made electromagnetic radiation exposure from modern appliances and technologies in your home, place of work, or school is something you might pay attention to. Many health problems including eczema, cancer, and chronic fatigue syndrome have been linked to electromagnetic fields (EMF) through dirty electricity and RF microwave radiation. Poor house wiring can cause strong electromagnetic fields. Home EMF hotspots are found close to electricity meters, not just Smart Meters. You can expect high EMF readings near main distribution panels or fuse boxes, transformers, battery chargers, back-up power supplies and inverters. These hotspots often extend up to 6 feet (1.9 meters) from their source before the EMF radiation fades to background levels. One simple way to limit exposure in your home is to switch things off when you are not using them. This can save on your electrical bill but perhaps more importantly interrupts the constant exposure of you and your family in your home to EMF pollution where you are meant to feel safe. Don't forget that low-frequency magnetic fields will pass through walls without any trouble, so if your hotspot source is close to a wall, pay attention to what is on the other side too. You might have to move your favorite chair to give you distance from the hotspots. Sleeping areas ideally should be located far from EMF hotspots.

Most of us are not well informed about the cause and effect of EMF. There are two components of electromagnetic radiation: electric and magnetic fields. The magnetic field is of particular concern, as it easily penetrates obstacles including thick walls, metal shields, or human bodies. Because it can penetrate a person's body, there is potential for it to harm the cells inside. With the speed of this technological revolution there haven't been enough studies to predict with long term exposure, how much damage could occur to a person's health. How a room is wired can create an envelope affect that leaves no escape for EMF that can damage your health. (10)

According to Wikipedia, ring circuits can generate strong unwanted magnetic fields. Other hotspots from installed electrical equipment such as florescent lights, light switches (particularly dimmer switches), heating panels, intercom base stations and air conditioning units usually have a shorter range. If wiring is well-designed and properly executed, background levels of low frequency EMF should be very low (less than 0.3mG on a Gauss meter), although there can be local hotspots substantially above this level in any house.

Keep in mind, people respond to exposure in different ways. The first cases of Electromagnetic Hypersensitivity (often referred to as electro-hypersensitivity or even EHS) were studied in the 1970s. The human body is more than just flesh and blood; but also a highly complex electromagnetic system. This also means that the human body interacts with external electromagnetic radiation (EMR). There are some people who are so sensitive to EMF that they experience an auto-immune response to exposure. There are so many factors that can contribute to this, such as stress and fatigue, and all of the health factors I have described in previous chapters that contribute to wellness. Each person needs to assess themselves as to whether sensitivity or exposure to EMF is a health risk for you. It is important enough to make choices that limit your exposure where possible. (11)

According to Vickie Warren, former Executive Director of the Bau-Biologie Group for the US, there are primary sources of dangerous EMF that surround you on a daily basis. These are the fields that emanate from anything that has voltage, basically anything electric, such as lamps, electrical wiring, outlets, extension cords, electrical appliances, and power outlets. Electric fields can affect the electrical communication in your body, such as your brainwaves, or the ability of your neurons to fire and communicate. It can also impede inter-cell communication anywhere in your body. Health problems that can manifest as a result of this type of exposure include neurological and behavioral changes, altered cell growth, cell mutations, fibromyalgia and chronic fatigue. It is also very important to always keep in mind when assessing your own health that there are a multitude of other influences in your life that can lead to illness and cell damage.

These fields can occur when there is an imbalance in the electrical wiring, and around electrical motors such as the compressor motor in your refrigerator. A major source of magnetic fields is next to the main power meter for your house. You definitely want to avoid sleeping up against a wall that has a power meter on the outside. Electric clock radios can also generate magnetic fields. The good news is the effect drops off dramatically with distance, so putting five or six feet between yourself and the source is usually sufficient to drastically reduce or eliminate the danger.

This EMF-Doc website is extremely well written and researched regarding EMF's (Electromagnetic Frequencies), their possible effects on your health, and ways you can protect your environment. (12)

The other sources that may surround you on a daily basis are power lines, whether above- or underground, metal plumbing (older metal plumbing can frequently carry a current) and wireless communications, which includes wireless power meters (Smart Meters), cell phones, cell towers, wireless routers, and cordless phones. These types of technologies expose you to both electric and magnetic fields.

Keep in mind cordless phone bases are a major source of exposure and should never be kept in your sleeping area. While the handset is a source of exposure while you're talking on the phone, the base transmits constantly, whether the phone is in use or not. Old school land lines do not present any of the same risks. In addition it's best to use the speaker phone or a headset when using a cordless phone because the thermal impact of the antenna can also cause problems, particularly if you're frequently on the phone or talk for long periods of time.

The thermal heat impact is what the SAR rating on the phone refers to. The radiation emitted by wireless communications decreases linearly, so you have to put space between yourself and the source to sufficiently reduce your exposure. There are reflective barriers such as metal/copper foil and certain types of metallic paint that are incorporated into new building codes to protect room to room contamination of EMF. Take the time to know the space you are living in and make an effort to create a safe zone in your home where you get a break from the constant barrage of EMR/EMF that surrounds our homes and cities today. Ideally, you'll want the cordless base station located at least three full rooms away from where you're sleeping. Keeping a cordless phone base on your desk is not recommended, as you'll be continuously affected by small amounts of radiation throughout your work day.

Across N. America hydro companies have begun installing a 'smart grid,' where utility meters transmit data on your household energy usage wirelessly to the utility company. Of course they want to expand this to include smart meters on each household smart appliance within your home, which would then individually transmit the usage data to the smart meter. (13)

According to research citations on the health hazards of electromagnetic fields (EMF"S), they've already seen a direct correlation between increasing health complaints in neighborhoods where smart meters have been installed. A great source of information on all matters EMF can be found at ElectromagneticHealth.org. and from Blake Levitt, author of 'Electromagnetic Fields', a long-time science writer on this topic, and Duncan Campbell, Esq., a visionary thinker on the future of utilities and new energy technologies.

The first health issues that may result from EMF long or short term exposure may be the inability to sleep, mood swings, and headaches. After all the effort of you investigating your own living space you will also need to be aware of the location of your neighbors 'smart meter' depending of course on how close to your home they are. In condos and townhouses, often the smarter meters are concentrated in one area of the complex. In Australia they are installing reflective barriers with smart meters to keep meter radiation from coming into the home.

EMR Australia is dedicated to creating EMR-safe living and working environments, offering a unique blend of technical expertise, knowledge about the effects of electromagnetic radiation and concern for people's welfare. The potential for electromagnetic radiation to cause harm has not only been identified in thousands of peer-reviewed scientific studies, but also by insurers, courts, groups of scientists and medical practitioners, and by many international authorities. Dr. Malka Halgamuge, PhD, Electrical Engineering is a respected and experienced expert in the field of electrical engineering who has an interest in the biological effects of electromagnetic radiation. She provides assessments of electromagnetic exposures for households and businesses. (14)

Vickie Warren has given us the perfect analogy of the dilemma of cigarette smoking and society and present day health concerns of second hand smoke. Over time perhaps there will be cell phone rooms where children aren't allowed because eventually the threat of EMF will be fully realized after so much damage has already been done. Unfortunately it takes two generations before current studies and wisdom recognizes and makes efforts to educate people to protect themselves and their loved ones. (15)

The science is not able to catch up to or inform us of the present safety of the all-pervasive uses of technology in our daily lives today, including the microwave oven. I have spoken at length to young scientists who defend microwave ovens and I lose any kind of serious debate regarding the impacts on nutrition and safety because unbiased science is lacking. I have an intuitive sense regarding concerns around safety and microwaves, while not forgetting that science has determined that they do leak radiation and so standing around watching your food cook is likely unwise. If you are a pregnant woman take appropriate precautions regarding EMF exposure near known electrical points in your home, EMR from laptops and potential radiation leakage from microwave ovens. It just doesn't make any sense to take those kinds of risks. So many people use their lap tops on their laps without any awareness of how sensitive your internal organs are to EMR exposure.

Before spending money on an EMF sensing device or a professional EMF engineer it is worth doing your own experiments in removing potential sources of electromagnetic pollution. As EMF is invisible to the eye and all-pervading you may even have to go outside the city into the country. In the extreme, remove yourself completely from electrical equipment, not just modern electronics but anything connected to the electricity grid and go camping. And for the sake of experiment when out in nature if you must take your mobile phone for emergencies make sure that you not only switch it off but also remove the battery.

There are countless reasons why you will feel better in the country, however if you feel much better by removing the EMF/EMRs in your life then become even more attuned to how you feel going back into your "normal" daily routine. Once you have enjoyed the peace and quiet of the country make an effort to go home and make your home as electromagnetically clean as possible. *And above all else, find green space and spend time with nature at every opportunity. The rewards are endless!*

Your world began with a technological revolution to rival no other. The latest Kaiser Foundation survey of technology use by young people ages 8 to

18 informs us that this age group spends more than seven-and-a-half hours a day engaged in non-school-related technology. This represented a 2-hour increase over the past two years. Technology plays a totally different role in young people's lives in places in the world where freedom, safety and medicine are nearly impossible to find. In countries like Africa, Vietnam, India, South America and poor communities around the world, technology and social media have, In fact empowered an entire generation of youth to get the help they need and meaningfully connect with their communities. While in N. America technology is blamed for isolating youth from reality, in so many countries around the world technology is bringing diverse people together around complicated social problems, breaking social stigmas caused by poverty, and helping youth to see themselves as part of a solution to their community's problems. Just as technology can build connections between troubled youth and the help they need, it can also connect youth to helping others, connecting them to employment and feeling empowered in countries where poverty is a constant companion. Harnessing technology and digital media can promote media literacy on a global scale, allow people to share personal opinions on world issues, tap into global knowledge networks, engage a global audience through online publishing, and bring emerging and developing nations into the global conversation.

The challenge for each and every one of you is to find balance between technology and time spent with people doing things you love in the real world. Be very aware of the overuse of technology and in particular your cell phone and how close you keep it to your body, or how long you talk on your cell phone by your ear. There are proven dangers to its overuse. Balance through good food, good water, good attitude and use of technology to enhance your life and learn and grow, is the goal for wellness.

According to Steve Jobs, "Technology is nothing. What's important is that you have faith in people, that they're basically good and smart, and if you give them tools, they'll do wonderful things with them.

Chapter 27

How NOT to get Cancer!

For the majority of people, the state of our health at 20 or 30 and older is the accumulated result of the food, air, water and attitude we have filtered through our trillions of cells over time. *The foundation for your health and the length of your life is mostly determined by the health of your immune system and your gut biome, and by your ability to be active and flexible.*

Be encouraged to know that prevention is the best medicine and what you eat, how you care for and protect yourself in the environment you live in are the primary determinants of whether cancer will be in your life or not. This should be very empowering news for each of you, if you take care of your biology, your bodies will live long and healthy lives. To understand the rise in cancer rates among all ages of people it is helpful to first understand the dramatic changes in the environment around you, including the air, water and food.

I do not in any way want to minimize the trauma and fear and pain of anyone experiencing cancer in their life. The challenge is always to step out of the fear and crisis to search for the correct direction for each and every individual, which may vary in a big way. As with so many subjects today it is critical to be able to discuss Cancer without fear and drama, but with good science and common sense.

To survive, our bodies must maintain a pH very close to 7.4. PH is a measure of acidity or alkalinity of water soluble substances; correct blood pH is the key to good health. Our pH is measured on a scale from 0 to 14, with 7.35 being alkaline (normal) and less than 7.35 is considered acidic (mild or extreme down the scale to 0). Your blood must always maintain a pH of approximately 7.35 so that it can continue to transport oxygen efficiently. The resilience of your body enables it to self-correct in the event of an imbalanced pH level via a buffer system. Foods like junk food, fast food, processed food, sugar and sodas, stress your body as it struggles to maintain the proper pH in the blood. Depending on your diet and excess of acidic foods you may deplete your alkaline reserves used to buffer acids in these situations. For example when the blood becomes too acidic your body will pull calcium from your bones to neutralize the pH imbalance.

When your buffering system is exhausted the excess acids are dumped into the tissues and when this accumulates, your tissues begin to deteriorate. The critical task of the body is to prevent the blood from becoming acidic, and so the body deposits acidic substances into cells. Though this tactic protects the blood from acidity it causes other tissues to become acidic and toxic. Hopefully these acidic cells die off, however some do adapt to the new environment. Some cells survive by becoming abnormal cells, which can be called 'malignant' cells. Malignant cells do not correspond with brain function or the DNA memory code and can grow indefinitely. This is one way that cancer can manifest. Therefore the key is to keep the pH in the proper range by eating mostly alkaline foods. A reasonable balance is to eat 20% acid foods and 80% alkaline foods. *Remember you are what you eat!* A list of alkaline-forming foods are most raw vegetables and fruits, figs, lima beans, olive oil, honey, molasses, apple cider vinegar, miso, tempeh, raw milk, raw cheese, stevia, green tea, most herbs, sprouted grains, sprouts, wheat grass, most nuts and barley grass. Foods such as yogurt, kefir, and butter are basically neutral. Foods that can create acidity are sugars, sodas, coffee, alcohol, chocolate, tobacco, aspartame, other artificial sweeteners, and highly processed meats and other foods. Foods that are nutritious and are best eaten in moderation are healthy meats, healthy fish, free range eggs, free range chicken, pasteurized organic milk, and organic nut butters.

Cancer is defined by cell cycle deregulation and uncontrolled growth. It is the second leading cause of death in the world. *Carcinophobia is the term used when the very word 'cancer' can cause fear and symptoms in many people.* Our cells are constantly replicating and as a result there will always be the potential for some cells to mutate and become cancerous. With a healthy immune system, however, our bodies have the ability to get rid of these cells. When our bodies do not recognize the cell as a cancer and because a weakened immune system can't destroy it, that cell may become a cancer.

This is a constant process in your body detecting damaged cells and destroying them; your immune system is designed for this very task.

For a long time medicine has explained the rapid increase in illness and cancer today as a result of better tools for diagnosis and detection. All of us have parents, grandparents and friends who have been affected by cancers, who have died from cancer or who are in treatment for cancer today. Childhood cancer today is the most common disease-related cause of death – more than asthma, diabetes, cystic fibrosis and AIDS combined. It is second only to injury-related deaths among children in N. America. An estimated two-thirds of childhood cancer survivors will have at least one chronic or long-term side effect from their cancer treatment during their lifetime.

Each year there are more new cases of skin cancer than the combined incidence of cancers of the breast, prostate, lung and colon. Over the past three decades, more people have had skin cancer than all other cancers combined worldwide. There is a 200% increase in cases worldwide from skin cancer. Ninety percent of non-melanoma skin cancers are associated with exposure to ultraviolet (UV) radiation from the sun and form in the upper and middle layers of the epidermis (skin) and rarely spread to other parts of the body. The annual cost of treating skin cancers in the U.S. alone is estimated at $8.1 billion. A person's risk for melanoma doubles if he or she has had more than five sunburns. Melanoma is the rarest form of skin cancer, with approximately 76,000 new cases diagnosed each year in the U.S. Melanoma begins in the melanocytes, which are the cells in the lowest layer of the epidermis (skin) and is most likely to spread to other parts of the body. *In spite of these distressing statistics skin cancer is the most preventable of all cancers.*

Keep in mind that your skin is the largest eliminatory organ you have. Whenever the organs of the body are stressed and overworked, the skin becomes the avenue of choice to eliminate toxins. This alone creates unhealthy skin which is potentially unable to produce Vitamin D and melanin adequate enough to defend against UV rays. Melanin is the natural substance that gives color or pigment to the skin, hair and iris of the eye. Cells called melanocytes, located just below the outer surface of the skin, produce melanin, which is in higher levels in people with darker skin. Melanin's primary function is to protect the skin from sun damage. In even the most light-skinned people, the body's melanocytes respond to sun exposure by producing more melanin, which creates the effect known as tanning. However, there is a limit to the degree of protection that melanin can provide, and melanin levels are significantly higher in people with naturally darker skin.

The International Agency for Research on Cancer, an affiliate of the World Health Organization, includes ultraviolet (UV) tanning devices in its

Group 1, a list of agents that are cancer-causing to humans. Group 1 also includes agents such as plutonium, cigarettes and solar UV radiation. Because the toxins in most sunscreens are carcinogenic in themselves, your best defense against UV rays is a light cover up on your upper body, a good sun hat, good sunglasses and an organic sunscreen if you are a red head or have fair skin. The Faculty of Pharmacy at the University of Manitoba, Canada, developed a method for assessing common sunscreen agents and the results indicate a significant penetration of all sunscreen agents into the skin, meaning all of these chemicals are entering multiple tissues within the body. These chemicals include oxybenzone, triclosan, parabens, phthalates, and more and they are carcinogenic. Read your ingredients labels and you will be shocked at the number of chemical ingredients that you are putting onto and therefore into your body, with mothers unknowingly lathering their babies with toxic chemicals. As mentioned elsewhere, Hawaii is considering a ban on these sunscreens because of the deadly impact on marine coral reefs.

Create a resilient internal healthy environment and your resistance to most cancers rises dramatically. (1)

As mentioned in previous chapters it is in your best interest to make the connection between a healthy immune system and the role it plays in combating any pathogens you may encounter. We are all unique in our responses to the environment around us. 'Epigenetics' as discussed in previous chapters demonstrates the correlation between your cellular function and behavior in response to your immediate environment, which includes food, air, water and attitude. For some individuals the choice is made for them in the womb that may create challenges throughout their life, with a disease or dysfunction. Yet even in those cases good clean food, air, water and a positive attitude matter and can ameliorate some or all symptoms, help manage pain, lengthen lives, etc. Our immune system is perfectly started at birth as breastfeeding is the essential introduction of healthy bacteria (colostrum) into the gut setting you up for the best start in life. Keep in mind the health of the breastmilk is also dependent on the mom's nutritional attention to her own health. Also this is not to suggest that all women must breastfeed or cast judgment on women who simply can't. This is just the biology of the human body and best case scenarios. In the 1950's the Medical Profession and Dairy Industry recommended not breastfeeding and gave out free milk formula in hospitals in N. America to all new moms. This is the post war generation of baby boomers who roughly make up 40% of the entire population of N. America today, the aging generation. This was a propaganda plan to sell formula in an era when convenience and a free gift from a corporation changed an entire generation's healthy start in life.

Your body is designed to heal itself, however only if the correct building blocks are provided for your body to do its job well. I have perhaps repeated myself too often in regard to the farming practices that inject additives, chemicals and toxins into the food you eat and the poor treatment and health of the beef, poultry and dairy industry animals that you may consume daily.

There is science today that says in reality there is no blanket label of breast cancer, colon cancer, etc. It is not one disease; there are hundreds of different types, unique to each person with its own symptoms, methods of diagnosis and treatment. This also supports the importance of each person's immune capabilities and immune reserves to best fight an unforeseen pathogen. And yet still the conventional treatment for all cancers is the same, chemotherapy, radiation and surgery; with all three often applied to each patient. Multi thousands of people have been through some or all of these treatments and it is my absolute hope that you find success and wellness and live a long life. We all do the best we can with what we know and if you have found success that is brilliant. If you find success with conventional and alternative health treatments combined, that is brilliant also. If you find success solely through alternative health treatments, that too is brilliant. Success is the goal and from this chapter I hope you realize the value in looking at all the possibilities, some of which at the very least will benefit a faster recovery during and after conventional treatments.

In 2017 a 9 part documentary-series "The Truth about Cancer: A Global Quest", presents a well-researched and up to date summary of Cancer in our world. (2)

Keep in mind there is a great deal of resistance to alternative points of view other than the conventional medical protocols. This documentary offers the history of present day therapies and the complexities of the human body and how it fights cancers. Specialists in this series are highly educated doctors and pharmacists. No matter what side of the fence you sit on with alternative versus conventional therapies, if you or a loved one has cancer you owe it to yourself, as do all of your doctors to research this documentary. To fear information, which I imagine is at the root of any doctor who doesn't keep up with new research, and patients who fear educating themselves to ask the right questions of those doctors, is shortening lives and reducing quality of life for cancer patients. This is a highly recommended documentary to give you the basics, the facts, and all the options that you may have to consider. There are multiple protocols, far beyond the conventional chemotherapy or surgery options offered by the medical establishment. These few examples are worthy of investigation - Coley's Toxins, Gerson Therapy, Autologous Cell Vaccine, Hyperthermia, Vitamin B-17, IV Vitamin CK3, Hyperbaric Oxygen, Intravenous (IV) Antibiotics with K3, CBD oil (Cannabis), turmeric poultices for breast cancer.   The majority of people are dependent on conventional medicine and protocols suggested by their doctors without question. If you are confronted with the challenge of cancer, you deserve to fully investigate all the modern and scientifically supported options available to you and be able to discuss them with your doctor. Don't forget the importance of having nutritional analysis done to determine any deficiencies you may have.

Yet again the challenge is to research and investigate all the options available rather than default to the conventional cancer treatments prescribed today. Science itself is being questioned regarding the truth of results reported and the financial influences between medicine, science and corporations. Dr. Richard Horton, the current Editor-in-Chief of The Lancet, says, "The case against science is straightforward; much of the scientific literature, perhaps half, may simply be untrue." Dr. Marcia Angell, a physician and longtime Editor in Chief of the New England Medical Journal (NEMJ), which is considered to be another one of the most prestigious peer-reviewed medical journals in the world, makes her view of the subject quite plain: "It is simply no longer possible to believe much of the clinical research that is published, or to rely on the judgment of trusted physicians or authoritative medical guidelines. I take no pleasure in this conclusion, which I reached slowly and reluctantly over my two decades as an editor of the New England Journal of Medicine" A common thread weaving amongst the scandal is the omission of data. It is one thing to publish all the best results, but near criminal to leave out the data that may lead to caution and the need for more research to support a particular drug. Printing this in this chapter alone may anger many young and old scientists, but these are simply the facts printed from the Journal's editors themselves. It doesn't mean that we throw science out the window; it means we must demand the truth, since what good is science if the supporting data and documents are not reported and/or are weighted on the side of success for pharmaceutical companies. It makes no sense other than the fact that we know money to be the motivating force for most corporations.

John Ioannidis, an epidemiologist at the Stanford University School of Medicine, published an article titled "Why Most Published Research Findings Are False," which subsequently became the most widely accessed article in the history of the Public Library of Science. (3)

Keep in mind this is how confusing our present day medical establishment is for people just trying to find the best solution for their particular health problem. Each year, the American Cancer Society estimates the numbers of new cancer cases and deaths that will occur in the United States in the current year and compiles the most recent data on cancer incidence, mortality, and survival. In 2017, 1,688,780 new cancer cases are projected to occur in the

United States. This is the equivalent of more than 4,600 new cancer diagnoses each day. (4)

There is also no doubt that there is brilliant science and success in crisis medicine and organ transplants every day with often profound results.

Back in 2012, The National Cancer Institute (NCI) convened an expert panel to evaluate the problem of cancer's misclassification and subsequent over diagnosis and overtreatment, determining that millions may have been wrongly diagnosed with "cancer" of the breast, prostate, thyroid, and lung, when in fact their conditions should have been termed "indolent or benign growths of epithelial origin." No apology was issued, none was made public and worse yet, no radical change occurred in the conventional practice of cancer diagnosis, prevention, or treatment. The NCI report determined that a commonly diagnosed form of so-called "early breast cancer" known as ductal carcinoma in situ was not inherently malignant and should not have warranted the conventional treatments of lumpectomy, mastectomy, radiation, and chemotherapy. (5) (6) (7)

Breast cancer is the leading cause of cancer deaths in women under the age of 40. Cellphones are two-way microwave radios that should not be kept directly on the body. The fatty tissue of the breast readily absorbs this radiation. Case reports are accumulating of young women with no family history getting a diagnosis of breast cancer. The tumors were unusually located directly underneath the skin where they placed their cell phones in their bra. Some bra manufacturers have a built in pocket for a cell phone, this is not a good idea. (8)

The Susan G. Komen Foundation, promoter of the Pink Campaign has done harm to women by promoting mammography while ignoring the preventive role of a healthy diet rich in organic fruits and vegetables, and good whole food, and self-care. Breast Cancer Awareness Month (BCAM) was launched by Astra Zeneca, a pharmaceutical company that sells cancer treatments on the one hand and carcinogenic pesticides on the other. AstraZeneca was a by-product of one of the world's largest chemical (and carcinogen) producers, Imperial Chemical Industries (ICI). Before being acquired by AkzoNobel in 2008, ICI produced millions of pounds annually of known mammary carcinogens such as vinyl chloride. There are too many examples of the contradictions inherent in these corporations that produce disease causing chemicals and have pharmaceuticals to treat them with. The confusion is they are causing the disease and attempting to cure it from the same source. (9)

This is why at Breast Cancer Action October is called 'Breast Cancer Industry Month,' because it is the month when corporations make money by selling pink ribbon products, of which many contain toxins linked to breast cancer. "Breast cancer is a social justice and public health crisis, and we've seen too little progress for the billions of dollars spent on pink ribbon products," says Karuna Jaggar, executive director of Breast Cancer Action (BCAction), a grassroots organization based in San Francisco. Millions of dollars are raised every October during Breast Cancer Awareness Month with only 20% of the dollars going to research while 80% becomes the profit for corporations that team up with pink ribbon promoters. (10 (11) (12)

The Susan G. Komen Foundation is one of the largest breast cancer organizations in the United States. If these pink ribbons were on products even partly related to breast cancer, or even to women generally, the endless fundraising might be more appropriate. But the Komen branding has gone on everything from Ford Mustangs to baseball bats to buckets of KFC chicken (obesity is a major risk factor for breast cancer). Between the multitude of corporate sponsors they've partnered with and the many personal donations from men and women alike, the foundation raises hundreds of millions of dollars a year with only about 20 percent of which supports research. Of course on top of that is the reality that research is rarely about prevention, but research is mostly about new drugs and medical interventions that benefit pharmaceutical companies. The subject of cancer today is a highly politicized issue.

There are thankfully some new tools that may help in making treatment decisions following a diagnosis of breast cancer. The WISDOM study is led by breast cancer surgeon Dr. Laura J. Esserman who is an outspoken opponent of over diagnosis and overtreatment, and recommends a more cautious approach to breast cancer treatment. There are also many Naturopathic Doctors working with Allopathic Doctors and it is wise for those diagnosed to explore all options in choosing cancer directions and cures. A new, but old, treatment available today for cancer is Cannabis treatments.

Cannabis was one of history's most widely used plants. Tincture of Cannabis was the basis for almost every patent medicine prior to the discovery of aspirin in 1899. On one hand, United States federal government officials have consistently denied that marijuana has any medical benefits, while the very same government actually holds U.S. Patent 6630507 issued in 2003 titled "Cannabinoids as antioxidants and neuroprotectants". *The question must be asked why since that time have medical cannabinoids not been utilized in treating cancers of all types.*

Hemp is a similar plant to Marijuana sharing medicinal properties minus the THC ingredient that gives Marijuana its reputation as a recreational drug. *For 1000 years Hemp was used for rope, twine, medicinals, and cloth.* Sailing ships were loaded with hemp. *The word "canvas" is derived from "cannabis",* because that's what canvas was made from. Sails were made of hemp because salt water deteriorated cotton. Old sails were made into wagon covers and ultimately the original Levi's Jeans. And the pressed oil from hemp seeds was used for paints, food, medicinals and varnishes. Hemp became illegal along with marijuana because they shared the same name and also hemp oil was a direct competitor for diesel, fuel and oil.

The politics that led to the criminalization of hemp were yet again controlled by two powerful rivals, agriculture and industry and the prospect of several multi-billion dollar markets. When Rudolph Diesel produced his engine in 1896, his plan was that it would run off of vegetable and seed oils, *especially hemp, which was superior to petroleum and readily available*. A fuel that was grown by farmers would not be allowed to stand in the way of the petroleum industry. The fall out was the criminalization of hemp to eliminate it as competition in the production of fuel for the motor cars of the future. Along with it marijuana was criminalized in the 1930's in the southwestern United States, and also partly because of racial prejudice against the Mexicans who used it.

Throughout the 1800s, Americans used the word "cannabis" when referring to the plant. Pharmaceutical companies like Bristol-Myers Squib and Eli Lilly used cannabis in medicines — widely sold in U.S. pharmacies — to treat insomnia, migraines and rheumatism. From 1840 to 1900, U.S. scientific journals published hundreds of articles touting the therapeutic benefits of cannabis.

So why does the term "marijuana" dominate the conversation in North America, while most people in Europe and large swaths of Latin America refer to the drug as cannabis, the botanical name for the plant? The answer, in part, is found in the Mexican Revolution, which began in 1910. After the upheaval of the war, scores of Mexican peasants migrated to U.S. Border States, taking with them their popular form of intoxicant, what they termed *"marihuana."* Therefore along with racial prejudice and placing blame on the Mexicans the new word for cannabis became 'marijuana'. The U.S. public already knew cannabis was a healthy and safe medicinal and hemp (from the same family minus the THC) was an extremely useful and practical plant, but *'marijuana'* became bad and was pushed into the consciousness of America to back up the criminalization of the plant. (13)

Along with so many prohibitions of the day, cannabis was included in every anti-narcotics bill, even though marijuana is not a narcotic. Marijuana is pharmacologically distinct from the family of opium derivatives and synthetic narcotics, even though it is commonly called a narcotic, it is not. Facts were not considered because the interest of government was to have it completely removed from society, including medicines, textiles, fuel, etc. Hemp was banned and criminalized at the same time because of the genus name shared with Cannabis sativa, and of course to protect the oil and automobile industry by keeping hemp oil as a fuel source out of the market.

During Hoover's presidency (1921 – 1928), Andrew Mellon became Hoover's Secretary of the Treasury and DuPont's primary investor. He appointed his future nephew-in-law, Harry J. Anslinger, to head the Federal Bureau of Narcotics and Dangerous Drugs. Anslinger's quote in congress, "Marijuana is the most violence-causing drug in the history of mankind. Most marijuana smokers are Negroes, Hispanics, Filipinos and entertainers. Their satanic music, jazz and swing, result from marijuana usage." Secret meetings were held by these financial tycoons. Hemp was declared dangerous and a threat to their billion dollar enterprises. For their dynasties to remain intact, hemp had to go. Hence the Marijuana Tax Act of 1937, which criminalized pot possession throughout the United States and criminalized the growing and using of hemp for fiber, food or clothing.

The politics of lumping hemp in with marijuana demonstrates the extent of the powers of corporations to not just control drugs but to control fiber and all other industrial products. The fiber value of hemp was unrivalled around the world, but because it shared the same genus as marijuana, regardless of the fact that it is nearly 100% THC free, the growing of hemp was criminalized.

In Canada, growing Hemp is a tightly controlled government operation. To grow a simple fibrous plant, that has flourished around the world for thousands of years, is extremely practical and useful, you must have a license and you must buy only certified seed in Canada each year. You are not allowed to save and use your own seed for growing the next year. This is another form of control & corruption that prevents innovation, independence, and prevents easy access to a highly versatile & valuable plant.

The ingestion of Marijuana and Hemp oil as a healing agent is recognized worldwide today as a viable cancer treatment. In raw form, marijuana leaves and buds are actually loaded with an antioxidant, anti-inflammatory, and an anti-cancer nutrient compound known as cannabidiol (CBD) that is proving to be a miracle "superfood" compound capable of treating and reversing a host of chronic illnesses. (14)

The CBD found in the marijuana plant, Cannabis sativa, indica, and ruderalis (three subspecies) is a highly medicinal substance with unique immune-regulating capabilities. Since the human body already contains a built-in endogenous cannabinoid system, complete with cannabinoid receptors, inputting CBD from marijuana or hemp can help normalize the body's functional systems, including cell communication and proper immune function. The way CBDs work is that they bridge the gap of neurotransmission in the central nervous system, including in the brain, by providing a two-way system of communication that completes a positive "feedback loop," according to Dr. William Courtney, a medical marijuana expert and founder of Cannabis International.   As opposed to a one-way transmission, which can promote chronic inflammation of healthy tissue, the unique two-way transmission system engaged by marijuana CBDs mimics the body's own natural two-way communications system. (15)

Though marijuana and hopefully industrial hemp (for its many uses) are to be legalized in various jurisdictions around the world and utilized medically, there will likely be huge delays and conflicts getting it in the hands of doctors and people who need it. Individuals whose systems are compromised by autoimmune disorders, cellular dysfunction, chronic inflammation, cancer cells, and various other illnesses can derive a wide range of health-promoting benefits simply by consuming CBDs. (16)

Anyone who has cancer or a serious illness of any kind needs to be well informed of choices he or she can make in their own wellness plan, and equally important are the choices those you love have to make for themselves.

Mammograms have been recommended for women for decades as a breast cancer screening tool. Because it is considered mainstream, most people wouldn't question the correctness of the choice or the effectiveness the tool actually has on detecting cancer. It is important to know your own body. Never ignore a lump in your breast, however keep in mind that for some women, changes in hormones during normal monthly menstrual cycles can create breast changes. These are known as fibrocystic breast changes. Women with fibrocystic breasts usually get lumps in both breasts that increase in size and tenderness just before they get their period. And after the cycle is complete the tenderness and lumps disappear. High caffeine consumption has been associated with hormonal ups and downs and may influence benign lumps in breast tissue. Make your own choice and do thorough research before choosing a tool that may cause more problems than it discovers.

In 2013 Rolf Hefti, wrote "The Mammogram Myth: The Independent Investigation of Mammography". Ray Peat, PhD, writes in the forward for the book, "Women concerned about the risk of breast cancer will obviously want to read it, and if doctors who regularly advise their patients to have mammograms decide to read it looking for justification of their policy, they will encounter information about cancer in general and health in general that should change their life."

Breast cancer remains the number one cancer-related cause of death in women worldwide. In 2012, there were 1.7 million new breast cancer cases discovered globally.   Also in 2012, the "Top 20" countries for breast cancer rates were all in industrialized regions. Belgium had the highest rate of breast cancer, with Denmark and France not far behind. The highest incidence of breast cancer occurred in North America and Oceania (Australia & nearby islands). The lowest incidence occurred in Asia and Africa. (17) The correlation between industrialization and related chemicals and toxins cannot be overlooked when discussing cancer.

There is a direct correlation between alcohol consumption and breast cancer illustrating the message of self-care and choices that support your healthy immune system. The amount of alcohol consumed is a major determining factor for breast cancer risk for all women globally. Regardless of geography, studies show us that the higher the number of drinks per day, the higher the risk of breast cancer. One example is in Brazil, where in 2012 it was estimated that 22% of breast cancers were directly related to high alcohol consumption. Keep all information you seek in perspective with your personal view of your own health. Some people tolerate alcohol better than others, some drinkers take impeccable care of their health and may have strong constitutions and so none of this information is a blanket statement that applies to everyone.

The reason that breast cancer rates are six times lower in most Asian countries than in the U.S. and Europe is largely attributed to diet and lifestyle. Low breast cancer rates in China and other Asian countries, for example, are connected (in part) to high consumption of green tea. How can we ignore the nutrient deficient and toxic effect that happens to first and second generation Asian-American women? A study conducted by the University of Southern California looked at breast cancer rates between the years 1988-2004. Researchers discovered that Chinese and Filipina women born in the U.S. had invasive breast cancer rates that were roughly 80% and 30% higher respectively than their foreign counterparts. The researchers speculated that this was caused by lifestyle changes in the U.S. that began over 50 years ago.

A western lifestyle and diet is the greatest influence on cancer rates worldwide. By looking specifically at breast cancer statistics between women in Asia and the United States, factors such as environmental pollution, dietary habits, and stress began to be taken seriously by the scientific community as major non-genetic causes for cancer and other disease. While the information is being considered there are few changes that have taken place to inform and protect women.

"Progress" is often thought to be the adoption of 'western' nutritional and lifestyle habits. However statistics show that when people in developing countries adopt Western eating habits and lifestyle, overall health declines and there is an increase in lifestyle-induced diseases such as cancer.

I have pointed out in previous chapters that you are what you eat. Read labels and connect the dots. Many chemicals and preservatives in your food are carcinogenic, so says the science of today.

Ractopamine is banned from food production in at least 160 countries, including countries across Europe, Russia, mainland China, and the Republic of China (Taiwan), due to its suspected health effects. In American animal farming the controversial drug is used in as many as 80 percent of all American pig and cattle operations. It's also used in turkey farming. Ractopamine is a beta agonist drug that increases protein synthesis, thereby making the animal more muscular. This reduces the fat content of the meat and increases the profit per animal. The drug, which is also used in asthma medication, was initially recruited for use in livestock when researchers discovered that it made mice more muscular. Interestingly enough, stubborn weight gain is also a common complaint among asthma patients using Advair (a beta-agonist drug) – so much so that the manufacturer has added weight gain to the post-marketing side effects. Other adverse reactions to beta-agonist drugs include increased heart rate, insomnia, headaches, and tremors. Beta-agonist drugs have been used in U.S. cattle production since 2003. The drug is administered in the days leading up to slaughter, and as much as 20 percent of it can remain in the meat you buy.

In February 2018, Russia issued a ban on U.S. meat imports, warning it would remain in place until the U.S. agreed to certify that their meat is ractopamine-free. As reported by Pravda, Russia is the fourth largest importer of U.S. meats, purchasing about $500 million-worth of beef and pork annually. At present, the U.S. does not even test for the presence of this drug in meats sold, even though animal research has linked ractopamine to birth defects. "The use of highly active beta-agonists as growth promoters is not appropriate because of the potential hazard for human and animal health, as was concluded at the scientific conference on Growth Promotion in Meat Production (Nov. 1995, Brussels)." This report is 23 years old and we still have these drugs in meat that so many people consume every day in America.

Ideally you're already leading a healthy lifestyle, eating good whole foods, exercising and managing stress, but if you're not, it's never too late to start. Each tissue only uses about 10 to 20 percent of its gene complement, and you want to be sure that those genes are the most advantageous ones possible for your health. You can begin to "remind" your cells to express in a healthful way, long before you manifest a disease, by encouraging your genes to express positive, disease-fighting behaviors by leading a healthy lifestyle. (18)

Your health and longevity for the most part is your choice, and you need to know this in order to choose well. Most cancer is caused by lifestyle choices, cardiovascular disease 90% or more, and diabetes type 2 is 100% lifestyle caused. We have been choosing to be victims to our genes and then we give all our power to the pharmaceutical or medical system. We have been largely taught that we have no power over our own health outcome, including prevention, treatment and recovery.

Knowledge is power. It's what you don't know that could kill you.

If you have cancer, reach out to alternative Naturopathic Doctors, open minded Conventional Medical Doctors and gather as much correct and researched information before moving forward with treatment. If necessary seek second and third opinions. Everyone is unique in this situation and knowing yourself, your history and investigating the most recent treatments available, is your job for a full recovery. Most people don't know how their own body works and understanding your immune system and what it requires to do its job is essential for prevention, treatment and recovery.

Independent research links cell phone radiation to a myriad of adverse biological effects, such as DNA chain breaks, blood-brain barrier damage, and disruption of cell metabolism. These biological effects may translate into symptoms such as fatigue, irritability, headaches, and digestive disorders. Worse still these exposures may lead to disease. Thousands of independent studies now link these exposures to a long list of serious diseases, including cancer.

Even the very conservative World Health Organization has classified radiation exposure from cell phones as a "possible Class 2B carcinogen." It would be highly beneficial if there was a way of knowing which phones emit the most (and least) radiation. The U.S. government, via the Federal Communications Commission (FCC), requires all cell phone models sold to be tested for their Specific Absorption Rate, or SAR. Chapter 26, 'Technology' has the information on Specific Absorption Rates (SAR) for cell phones.

Keep in mind the previous discussions on Epigenetics and the powerful influence your environment has on your long term health. *There is evidence to show that suppressed anger can be a precursor to the development of cancer, and also a factor in its progression after diagnosis."* (19) It is important to remember that an attitude of anger has a direct impact on your longevity and health. *The oldest documented person that ever lived was a French woman named Jeanne Calment who made it to 122 years plus 164 days on this earth. She credited her longevity to laughing a lot and not getting stressed out.* She is quoted as saying, "If you can't do anything about it, don't worry about it." Let's contrast this with someone who lived a very healthful lifestyle, ate well, exercised, and could be described as being extremely healthy. He dropped dead of a heart attack at age 61 and people spoke of him as a type "A" personality, who rarely if ever laughed. *Stress can be a silent killer*!

Scientists now have proven that compassion for others not only strengthens happiness within our physiological makeup, but social scientists have discovered it can boost immunity and improve emotional responses to stress. The primary determinant of health for the average person is their attitude. This has been shown over and over again by the scientific fields of psychoneuroimmunology, psychoneurocardiology, and psychoneuroendo-crinology, not to mention cancer research. *Remember, attitude influences success in all areas of your life.*

In 1983, physician Rex Gardner published a study in the British Medical Journal after he studied a number of miraculous healing events. (20) (21) (22) In 1993 Brendan O'Regan and Caryle Hirshberg of the Institute of Noetic Sciences (IONS) surveyed a vast amount of medical literature. *That year they found over 1,200 cases documenting what is called "spontaneous remissions."* These were determined to be unexpected, sudden, and startling cases of complete healings. "Of those cases, 1,051 referred to spontaneous remission of cancer and 334 to other diseases. These were all instances where patients were previously diagnosed via X-rays, biopsies, and extensive tests." *There is so much more to each of us than we have been led to know or understand.*

Let's look at the concern around tattooing today as a cancer risk. Although tattoos have been around for millennia, they are more popular now than ever. In 1960, there were approximately 500 professional tattoo artists operating in the United States. By 1995, that number had risen to over 10,000. Nearly 20 years later 20 percent of Americans have a tattoo and 40 percent of the people in that group are Millennials.

For centuries tattooing had been an art form and cultural expression around the world. Tattooing is an intimate and personal choice, an important part of creating a personal myth around our stories, places and memories. 50% of the inked-up population has between two and five tattoos, and 18 percent have six or more tattoos. There are fascinating sociological studies around tattooing, personal mythology and ritual. Getting a tattoo involves a painful ritual that may take hours and every tattoo is unique. Today tattoos have evolved into works of art that are broadly acceptable in the mainstream.

It is important to know that while the practice of tattooing is regulated, the tattoo ink is not. Health risks associated with tattooing can include infections, allergies, scarring, granulomas (small knots or bumps that can form around particles of tattoo pigment), and MRI (magnetic resonance imaging) complications such as swelling or burning when people with tattoos undergo an MRI. The FDA's National Center for Toxicological Research (NCTR) has begun to investigate tattoo inks to identify their chemical composition and how they break down in the body, however at present there are no federal regulations on tattoo ink.   Research has shown that some pigment migrates from the tattoo site to the body's lymph nodes, which are part of the lymphatic system – a collection of fluid-carrying vessels that drains into the blood and whose job it is to filter out disease-causing organisms.

Here is what you want to investigate about your ink. A study carried out at Copenhagen University Hospital found cancer-causing chemicals in 13 out of 21 commonly used European tattoo inks. The Danish researcher leading this study went on record to say that the millions of Europeans being tattooed using chemical substances of unknown origin should be given detailed information about the inks being used on them, along with the effects on their health. The Tattoo Ink Manufacturers of Europe (TIME) states that up to 5% of tattoo studios use inks containing carcinogenic aromatic amines. They strongly advocate reducing the presence of these carcinogenic components in tattoo inks to zero. Be aware!

Don't forget that your skin is your largest eliminatory organ and when your internal organs are stressed your skin becomes the vehicle for your body to eliminate toxins and is an important part of your overall healing system. This is why rashes and allergic reactions are very visible on the skin, as your body eliminates toxins. This also means that everything you put on your skin is absorbed into your blood stream in varying degrees. Be sure to investigate the safety of the inks you may use for tattoos. A general rule is to not put anything on your body, such as cosmetics, soaps, shampoos, etc. that you wouldn't eat. Though this might sound ridiculous to consider eating your cosmetics, it is a good guide to remind you that your outer skin is as important as your inner organs.   From air fresheners to laundry soap & fabric softeners, deodorants, chemical cleaners, to electromagnetic radiation, it is no small task for youth today to be aware and make choices that matter for optimum health.   When millions of people are choosing toxic soaps, sprays and disinfectants, it takes awareness, common sense, and courage to choose differently for you and your family.

I am hoping by now you have a solid idea of how to be healthy, live long and prosper. The same preventative behaviors apply to all illness you may encounter and hopefully avoid. *Eat well, hydrate well and exercise, have compassion for yourself, read labels, tone up your attitude toward life and those around you, manage your weight sensibly, keep active, quit smoking, drink moderately (or not at all), and choose an attitude of enjoyment and fun throughout your days and your life.*

Chapter 28

Reading

Have you ever thought about how much of your thoughts are truly and authentically your own? We are subject to propaganda, false advertising, and other methods of manipulating our thoughts and perceptions and persuading us to be consumers every day.

Be a free-thinker.   Treasure your ability to form your own opinions, daydream, think critically, and conjure up tales of adventure using your own creative mind.   Reading books is a way to expand your possibilities and understanding of your world. Entertainment, great wisdom, facts and figures, laughter and wonder await you in books that are at your fingertips. Though many still prefer an actual book in their hands to read, eBooks' are an easy and affordable way to search great literature of the past and present. Discuss what you read with friends and encourage them to read books as well.

Reading is incredible. It sparks our imaginations, enhances our critical thinking skills, improves our vocabulary, exercises our brain, and much more. While our love for reading in general will never die, it does seem that these days, its popularity has waned significantly. Many kids and adults alike today can't wrap their heads around sitting and reading for any extended amount of time because they have been conditioned to instead experience new and intense sensory information every few seconds through technology & social media.

Literacy means to have the ability to read and write, along with comprehension – the competence and knowledge to thoroughly understand what you are reading. Reading can enable you to live life more fully. The flow state is described as the experience of being fully immersed in an activity. Psychologists say that the more you are in the flow state the more happy you are, and reading puts you into that place where time seems to stand still. Reading assists you in many ways to add richness to your life, in teaching you about different cultures for example. Reading reduces stress, expands your vocabulary, gives you access to new knowledge and can assist you in becoming a better writer and communicator. It stimulates the mind, and memory, and defers aging.   In some ways reading can introduce you to more people than you could ever meet in your lifetime and therefore offers you up a greater skillset in building relationships and becoming more socially adept.   There are so many genres of literature to explore including all non-fiction which includes informational text such as narrative non-fiction, essays, biographies, history, self-help, etc., and the vast genre of fiction including fantasy, science fiction, drama, poetry, humor, mystery, action & adventure, and the list goes on.

Reading books can literally be a catalyst for change in your life showing you new perspectives and other avenues to pursue.   Whenever you are dealing with a difficult situation in your life, you can reach out to books that share similar experiences that may be insightful, calming, reassuring, and educational for a new perspective of your particular situation.

For young children, no TV or social media device can challenge the mind in the whole sense as reading a book can.   Once the book is in hand the joy of discovery and reading takes over in an instance.   Reading is essential for the developing mind and heart of a child. Reading is always a good idea, and the key is to find something that interests you. The rest is easy. *The world of literature is a magical one*. The lost art of reading is a loss to your adventuresome spirit and you can choose to incorporate reading into your life journey and add brilliance, opportunity and inspiration that you may otherwise not find.

Though public libraries may have lost some of their appeal, the story of the library is one of the most exhilarating in modern culture. To the U.S. historian Matthew Battles, the library was a metaphor for the land of opportunity, a place where new Americans could dream of personal success and support transformation in the lives of all readers.   One book summarizes the 'Great Libraries of the World' edifying spectacular monuments to learning and architecture of the past. Great minds read and great minds respect that the library offers a democracy of learning to all.   Visiting a library in any community will introduce you to the cultural identity of that place as its archive, museum and collective memory. Any travel around the world should include some of the great libraries which include art, museums, book collections, and limitless knowledge all in one place.

Digitization has changed everything and in 2014, eBooks surpassed the sale of paperbacks. There have been obituaries written for hard copy books and libraries over the past few years, however we as a culture will never let that come to pass. Libraries give all those who venture inside a sense of place and it will always be a place where humans congregate.

Reading has a great deal of competition with gaming and technology. Find a book that interests you, one you might read just purely for pleasure, or one that answers questions you have been asking or assists you in resolving a conflict you face.

Atlas of Beauty: Women of the World in 500 Portraits, by photographer Mihaela Noroc, is a spectacular book and journey around the world. Mihaela travelled the world and photographed women in their everyday lives, their jobs, their homes, their cultural clothing and their extraordinary beauty. Buy this book as a gift for your mother if not yourself and prepare to be entranced by the beauty of people in your world. Their stories and the details of their particular culture accompany each beautiful photo of the mothers and daughters and grandmothers of the world.

Read any or all of the books I have listed below or in the list at the end of this book, and seek out topics or genres that interest you and you will change your life for the better as you add other people's wisdom and perspective to your own. *Read at least one of the following books and you will open new pathways and choices for your own success.* Seriously consider balancing your screen time with reading an actual book, and you will notice the benefits immediately.

- *The Four Agreements: A Practical Guide to Personal Freedom*, by Don Miguel Ruiz
- *The Power of Habits*, by Charles Duhigg
- *Thug Kitchen cook book, Eat like you give a F___*, by Michelle Davis and Matt Holloway
- *Love Yourself Like Your Life Depends On It*, by Kamal Ravikant
- *The Code of the Extraordinary Mind: 10 Unconventional Laws to Redefine Your Life and Succeed On Your Own Terms* by Vishen Lakhiani
- *Guide to Lies*, by Daniel Field
- *Long Walk to Freedom*, by Nelson Mandela
- *Blueprint for Revolution by Design*, by Srjdja Popovic

Chapter 29

Politics

Political and social upheaval around the globe suggests that a major paradigm shift is under way. It is important to not despair at the chaos of conflict that surrounds us and the inequities for most of the 7 billion people on the planet. An important choice you can make is to inform yourself of world and community affairs and to infuse your determination with optimism. Democracy is not without flaws, and the task of cooperation and shared decision making has never been easy in any society. While the democratic system determines that 51% are winners and 49% are losers, this often leaves half of the electorate potentially feeling that their voice is not represented. Some call this tyranny of the majority as the losing side takes up the position of opposition to the ruling party. Five of the most common political systems around the world are Democracy, Republic, Monarchy, Communism and Dictatorship. Regardless of the differences, most political systems around our globe are driven and controlled by greed for wealth, resource and power, hence the majority of ongoing armed conflicts on many continents. Britain considers itself as a great democracy and yet is responsible for the colonization of countless lands, and the devastation of indigenous peoples in those places.

Of the 195 countries in the world recognized by the United Nations, according to the Global Peace Index only 11 are not involved in armed conflicts within their own borders. In 2017 Iceland was once again named the world's most peaceful country, followed by New Zealand, Denmark, Portugal, Austria and Denmark on the peaceful country scale. Canada was number 8, while Syria was once again named the least peaceful country. The United States places number 114 out of 195 countries.

Climate change, nuclear contamination, the threat of nuclear war, polluted oceans, proliferation of war and more, confronts all of humanity. Governments are expected to solve problems and manage resources such that citizens can focus on work, family and healthy living. Thomas Hobbe's book 'Leviathan' was written in 1651 and summarizes the structure of society and the function of government. The oldest and simplest justification for government was as protector, providing safety of law and order, and secondly as a provider of goods and services that individuals cannot provide for themselves, such as infrastructure, power, and water systems. The capacity of government to meet current national and global economic, security, demographic and environmental challenges is greatly lacking. We the people can no longer leave our futures up to governments who have become so burdened by conflict, corruption and scandal that basic needs are no longer provided for the young and the old in most societies. Most governments are unsuccessful today largely because their leaders lack vision and parties in power are weak to resist the opposing forces of greed and corruption that surround and often influence and control government.

Youth are rising up and lending their voices to the politics of the day. A perfect example of this is the sorrow around the Feb. 2018 mass shooting in a high school in Florida where 17 people died at the hand of one enraged 19 year old with an assault rifle. Youth are shouting to the world with 'A Call to Action' that laws must change after countless mass shootings in the U.S. over the past many years. They organized a 3 million person march on Washington (simultaneously marches also took place across the U.S. and around the world), their voices are strong and full of truth and I trust this is the beginning of change for a better future. Seniors also must speak to the dysfunction of governments and lawmakers as elders who must defend and support generations to come. When the people rally, governments must respond. Communication is the key to resolution; however the art of communication is not taught or exemplified by present governments and educational institutions. *One solution lies in a dialogue based on mutual respect and the best tool to achieve that is through non-violent communication (NVC) which leads to cooperation*. "NVC has been used for centuries based on consciousness, language, communication skills, and the use of power that enable us to maintain a perspective of empathy for ourselves and others, even under trying conditions," states Marshall B. Rosenberg, PhD.

Globalization favors the freedom of capitalism and consumerism over the needs of people and has caused many voices to be ignored, rewards the rich and elite while leaving the majority of populations around the globe struggling to feed their families. When policies are made by individuals who are disconnected from the people and places they are governing, there will always be social, environmental and political upheaval. Globalization has run its course to the detriment of the planet.

To a large degree, we have come to rely on political systems that are not capable of handling the accelerated times in which we live. Two-party politics and 'yes' or 'no' questions result in simplistic binary decisions unsuited to the complexity of modern day life. In 1907 Winston Churchill said: "Democracy is the worst form of government, except for all the others."

The Democratic or binary approach of winner/loser is perilous and ineffective at meeting the needs of our increasingly technological global society. This winner/loser mentality works for a sporting event, however how can it fully represent all the people? Government must acknowledge a responsibility to make sure that all voices are heard, not just those of the majority and those with the most wealth. Why is it so difficult to collectively care for each other, our natural resources, and the planet at large? Human weakness must be at the root of this problem. As a result, our political systems are simply inadequate and are by default perpetually controlled by individuals in places of power, institutions and corporations. These systems are difficult to change, coupled with an over populated planet and dwindling resources.

Present day politics reminds me of 'The Hunger Games' movie where the lives of ordinary people are a game to the wealthy, narcissistic, ego-driven personalities that seek political office. (1) There is also no doubt that many good meaning people, generous and passionate people, enter the world of politics with intentions of making the world or their communities a better place. In 1884, John Acton, the first Baron Acton historian and moralist, expressed the opinion; "Power tends to corrupt, and absolute power corrupts absolutely. Great men are almost always bad men." Consider the glorified intentions and lies expressed to the public during election campaigns, and the long list of broken 'promises' that follow once the government is elected.

Our indigenous forbearers influenced Ben Franklin and America's Founding Fathers, through the Haudenosaunee (circa 1451 AD), who understood the importance of a council which allowed diverse perspectives to be heard and incorporated into a shared vision of moving forward as a society. Much has been written about The Great Law of Peace of the Haudenosaunee (the "Six Nations," comprising the Mohawk, Onondaga, Oneida, Cayuga, Seneca, and Tuscarora peoples). (2) The Iroquois Confederation is the oldest association of its kind in North America formed during the early part of the 12th century.

Desmond Tutu is a South African Anglican cleric and theologian known for his work as an anti-apartheid and human rights activist. Tutu instructs us that "if you want peace, you don't talk to your friends. You talk to your enemies."

Diversity is celebrated when the majority has food, shelter, their basic needs taken care of. **Conversely racism and crime flourishes** when scarcity, economic inequality and fear are prevalent. The news media, feeding on the black or white, binary, good or bad oversimplification, of the state of our societies perpetuates the divide, the ignorance, and the fear. Most often hatred is the result of needs not being met, fear, or childhood trauma and always influences division instead of cooperation. A great leader must possess compassion, wisdom, and vision for humanity and not have a racist or judgmental bias.

Marianne Williamson, a Spiritual teacher, author and lecturer said; "*We cannot give what we do not have. We cannot bring peace to the world if we ourselves are not peaceful. We cannot bring love to the world if we ourselves are not loving. Our true gift to ourselves and others lies not in what we have but in who we are.*"

Listening is the greatest tool we have for sorting through the conflicts we face every day in life. Educating ourselves and each other and becoming compassionate to our own needs as well as the needs of others is the way to peace in our homes, our neighborhoods and eventually our countries. Cooperation comes with the realization that we are all connected by deep emotional experiences and there is always common ground if we choose to meet there. Everyone we meet was at one time a child, a mother, a father, a sibling, or a friend and with this perspective alone we can see each other more as people than as adversaries.

Social harmony is impossible when individuals are internally conflicted. What does it take to be present, to listen, and to acknowledge the perspective of those who we disagree with? As with many things in the world, our vision is distorted by the cultural and colored lens of our own bias and opinions through which we see things. Only by disassembling your inner conflicts can you change your world view, which allows for all voices to be heard and respected.

Finding a way to make a genuine connection is an essential and powerful way to diffuse conflict. This is where spirituality and self-awareness meets the political process.   This is the first step towards the evolution of cooperation in your life, in your neighborhood and your community at large. *Cooperation is a fundamental law of biological evolution*. We are a species that has developed through biological evolution, and are the result of billions of cells cooperating to optimize life.   We could strive to be in a process biologically, socially, and politically of evolving towards optimizing life for all.

Darwinism, survival of the fittest and its scientific misconceptions pale in comparison to cooperation. Dr. Bruce Lipton speaks of this extensively in his work, stating that compassion is an emotional connection whereas cooperation is the ability to work together towards a common goal and create mutually beneficial results. Sadly most of our political structures are set up for winning or losing with the losing party heavily opposing.   A cooperative political structure could, on the other hand, allow for success on both sides of most situations.

To differentiate between political concepts is important. For example, dictatorship, monarchy and oligarchy are set up for 1% rule over the other 99%. A democracy is described as 51% rule over the other 49%. Through consensus 100% of the people cooperate to create a future that is mutually beneficial for all. There is nothing easy or simple about listening to all sides and determining what is best for all. However, if consensus is considered as a decision-making model for government it requires participants to be open-minded and to consider the opinions of the minority. This also means that individuals must be prepared to compromise and perhaps change their point of view to be more in line with the group. This means that a government must find a balance. If too few people participate in decision making, the consensus would not represent everyone. With too many people involved in consensus, much time and effort is required and it can be very difficult to reach agreement. When you have to make decisions in your own life with family, friends, roommates, or bosses be sure to utilize consensus to assure both parties or entire groups you are involved with come to fair and equitable decisions.

Meritocracy is a political aspiration whereby leadership is determined within a group of people whose progress is based on ability and talent rather than on class privilege or wealth. This is simple common sense as far as I am concerned.   Meritocracy can only exist if the rich have a little less and the poor a little more. Many studies demonstrate that social mobility improves in more equal societies. Social mobility is the movement of individuals, families, households, or other categories of people within or between social strata in a society.   Norway has the greatest level of social mobility, followed by Denmark, Sweden and Finland.   Britain and the U.S. are the most unequal western societies on earth in terms of income distribution and both have much lower rates of social mobility.

Nikola Tesla (1856-1943) was a world renowned Serbian-American inventor, electrical engineer, mechanical engineer, physicist, and futurist best known for his contributions to the design of the modern alternating current (AC) electricity supply system. He sums up his view of politics, science, medicine and greed in the statement, *"Science is but a perversion of itself unless it has as its ultimate goal the betterment of humanity."*

The Law of Cooperation as coined by Scott Malis states that "What cooperates the most, thrives the most." For example; war and slavery are considered the lowest forms of cooperation because they force cooperation, yet there is no refuting the potentially creative (or destructive) power of large groups of people working towards a common purpose. The Cooperatist Movement seeks to develop a community of people promoting consensual cooperation towards goals that benefit all involved parties. Cooperation is a fundamental law of biological evolution. We are a species that has developed through biological evolution, and the result of billions of cells cooperating to optimize life. *It is possible to own less and share more to increase personal wealth and well-being for all*.

Cooperation is an antidote to corporatist ideology which works toward private gain at the expense of the general public or the environment. *Living harmoniously may well be the most beautiful thing that humans can strive towards*. Scot Malis reminds us all of the importance of the next step, *"The next step is a cooperative global society that considers the needs of all species and acts as a steward of this precious planet."*

The most recent example of Youth taking a cooperative stand against the political machine of the U.S. was their march on Washington, on April 20th, 2018. The New York Times analysis of the Gun Violence Archive tallied 239 school shootings since 2014, including those on college campuses, resulting in 138 deaths. In addition, the number of school shootings in the United States between December 2012 and December 2014 totaled 99 shootings: 45 college/university shootings, 29 high school shootings, 12 elementary school shootings, 7 middle school shootings and 1 K-12 school shooting. (3)

After decades of fighting and debate between Politicians, the NRA (National Rifle Association) and citizens at large regarding the accessibility and rights of citizens to own assault rifles, there has been zero change to laws to protect citizens from gun violence. Seventeen students and teachers were shot in a Florida high school on February 14th 2018 (Valentine's Day); students were between the ages of 14 and 17 and 3 were teachers. Survivors of the shooting mobilized to launch the #NeverAgain movement, and the March for Our Lives, a nationwide protest on April 20th 2018 to protest gun violence and to demand legislative changes to the gun laws in America. According to their website, "March For Our Lives is created by, inspired by, and led by students across the country who will no longer risk their lives waiting for someone else to take action to stop the epidemic of mass school shootings that has become all too familiar." (4)

There was also a **National School Walkout** planned to demand Congress pass legislation to keep citizens safe from gun violence at schools, on streets and in homes and places of worship. The National Rifle Association (with over 5 million members) donates millions of dollars every year to Republican lawmakers in Congress. The most recent solution to gun violence in schools is more guns and arming teachers to defend students. Teachers, who have overcrowded classrooms, inadequate supplies, special needs students without additional staff support, and debt ridden school boards, could not possibly be expected to arm themselves and become gun specialists. Countless times over the decades, the NRA has blocked legislation for gun control, better background checks and is considered one of the most powerful political organizations in the U.S. How can anyone defend the rights of a person to legally own an assault rifle with the capacity to shoot many people at once? How can anyone consider that assault rifles are necessary to defend oneself as part of a person's constitutional right to bear arms? Over and over again it has been made clear that legislation will not take guns from people who believe in their right to arm themselves, that proposed legislation is directed only at assault rifles and automatic weapons. Statistics tell us that 89 people in every 100,000 in the U.S. have guns, 31 people in every 100,000 in Norway have guns, 30 people in every 100,000 in Canada have guns, 15 people in every 100,000 in Australia have guns, 6 people in every 100,000 in the U.K. have guns and .6 people in every 100,000 in Japan have guns. In Australia the 'National Agreement on Firearms' prohibited automatic and semiautomatic assault rifles, stiffened licensing and ownership rules, and instituted a temporary gun buyback program that took some 650,000 assault weapons (about one-sixth of the national stock) out of public circulation. Most Norwegian police, much like the majority of British police, do not carry firearms. Japan has highly restrictive firearm regulations and an extraordinarily low gun-homicide rate, which is the lowest in the world at one in 10 million.

Reflecting on the NRA and the politics of the day in the U.S. should cause all sensible people to reconsider their vote in regard to making their country a safer place. But loyalties and political affiliations run deep and are often carried forward from many generations without regard for what America needs now. There is countless research and statistics showing how the NRA influences politics. Find out for yourself and decide if you want them setting the tone for your life in America. There is a great need for common sense, compassion and cooperation to best deal with the challenges ahead.

From the internet to smartphones, the financial crisis to the refugee crisis, Donald Trump to Brexit, author Chris Kutarna believes the forces of politics shaping our world today have been seen before. Five hundred years ago, during the first Renaissance period, big changes occurred in society with the discovery and exploration of new continents, the decline of the feudal system, the growth of commerce, the invention of paper, printing, the mariner's compass, and the invention of gunpowder. To the scholars of the day, it was a time of the revival of Classical learning and wisdom after a long period of cultural decline and stagnation. New maps, new media, and a new human condition helped genius to flourish in Europe. It is a compelling comparison to the present time considering the technological revolution we are immersed in, as well as climate change. The potential catastrophic effects of climate change and other threats to the health of the planet with compromised water and food supply are reminders of history repeating itself.

Kutarna and Ian Goldin in their book, 'Age of Discovery: Navigating the Risks and Rewards of our New Renaissance', argue that we're living in a second Renaissance period and events in history can help us prepare for and even predict the disruptions yet to come.

In the big picture, we have been told that humanity is healthier, wealthier, and more educated than at any time in history. Global average life expectancy has risen by about 20 years over the past 50. And to put that into perspective, it took humanity 1,000 years to achieve the previous 20 year lift in life expectancy. It is important also to differentiate between 'living longer' as a measuring stick for good health. It is possible that living longer is dependent on drugs for the elderly. However, with many young people suffering from obesity, cancer and other diseases I would say our society is not overall healthier.

The greatest challenge Youth have today is to find a new way to exist together peacefully for the betterment of all. *It is far easier to build something new than to fix something that is broken, at least in the world of convoluted politics.*

'World Internship' is an organization that works with partners around the world in twenty countries coordinating customized internship programs for people ages 18-30. Their philosophy is that culture and cultural immersion are key components of personal development with an objective to create leaders who can build a better future for all. If you are searching for purpose or change or adventure to build your skills and gain relevant, global experience this might be an option for you. (5)

The United Nations (UN) has put forth a 17 step plan to save the world. (6) UN sustainable development goals (SDGs) aim to end all poverty, fight inequality and tackle climate change within the next 12 years in order to fulfill their 2030 Agenda for Sustainable Development. These goals were agreed upon at a UN summit in September 2015 by a staggering 193 countries. The UN announced them to the world, declaring: "We resolve, between now and 2030, to end poverty and hunger everywhere, to combat inequalities within and among countries, to build peaceful, just and inclusive societies, to protect human rights and promote gender equality and the empowerment of women." The 169 targets can be found on their website. How can any of these goals be met without individual countries taking care of their own people?

In crafting the Sustainable Development Goals, the UN launched an "unprecedented outreach effort", in which 5 million people from all over the world were consulted on their visions for the future. Nearly 10 million votes were cast in a survey of people's priorities. According to the UN, the key to success will be creating multi-stakeholder partnerships that bring together local and regional governments, the private sector and civil society. *Perhaps this will be the politics of the future.* Sustainable Development Goals are engaging youth today through Facebook and twitter. There are some exciting conversations taking place between generations of people all working toward the common goals of a healthy future.

There are many opportunities that await your participation. We have to become the change we want to see in the world. In Webster's dictionary the world 'Politic' is defined as "(of an action) seeming sensible and judicious under the circumstances". The definition of 'Politics' is the art or science of government. Apply common sense and determination in all areas of your life and become an advocate for political and social change in your neighborhood, community and country.

You aren't just the leaders of tomorrow; you are making huge changes to the world around you, right now. Through social media or 'hashtag' activism, writing online or taking part in a protest, or signing a petition you become the change the world needs. Find ways to influence the politics of the day, change your life and the world around you. Volunteer, write to politicians, and help motivate each other to take a step toward positive change. In order to know the world better there are organizations that can get you exploring and working and contributing to a better world. *Workaway and WOOF (Workers on Organic Farms)* are organizations that connect individuals, businesses and societies from 170 countries where anyone can share honest work and travel the world or work locally. In exchange for work you receive accommodation and meals and become immersed in different cultures, skills and languages.

The website 'www.workaway.info' offers all people of all ages fair exchange, volunteer and work opportunities. SumOfUs is a global advocacy organization and online community that campaigns to hold big corporations accountable on issues such as climate change, worker's rights, discrimination, human rights, animal rights, corruption, and corporate power grab. (7) Avaaz is a U.S.-based online site launched in January 2007 that promotes global activism on issues such as climate change, human rights, animal rights, corruption, poverty, and conflict. (8) Collective Evolution is an on line organization that is creating change through transforming consciousness. (9) Free The Children believes in a world where all young people are free to achieve their fullest potential as agents of change. Free The Children is an international charity and educational partner, with more than 1.7 million youth involved in their innovative education and development programs in 45 countries. (10)

You have inherited a political world that came from darker events in recent history like 9/11, the Afghanistan War, the Iraq War, and many more wars plus the global consciousness of our collective impact on climate change. Along with the technological revolution that informed your younger years you are far more liberal, highly optimistic, and exceedingly patient when it comes to major life decisions, than previous generations. Your demographic diversity and increased exposure to different lifestyles, ethnicities and cultures has made you far more tolerant with social issues than any generation before you. *Let your optimism remind you that the political world you have inherited comes from generations of wealthy, elitist, and conservative thinkers.* And with that, your challenge is to make effective use of the wisdom and experience of politicians who care and respect you and your society and incorporate your greater view into the discussion of what is possible for your country.

Millennials (born between 1980 and 2000) will begin taking over government leadership positions around the year 2020. *When you start holding and using real power over governments around the world, consider the sheer size of your collective generation of 100 million in the US and 1.7 billion globally.* This means when the younger of you reach voting age, which may be right now, you will become a voting block too large to ignore.

As the number of democratic nation's increases, there is a greater likelihood that world peace can be achieved. There are currently 123 democracies in the world out of 193 countries. It took more than two centuries for the opportunity for most people in democratic countries to have a role in shaping their government and the rule of law. In 1796 when the Constitution of the U.S. was written, only white males over the age of 21 had the right to vote. New Jersey's constitution of the same year was a bit different whereby all adult inhabitants who owned a specified amount of property, which included women as property, could vote. For the next 113 years women would not be able to vote in any U.S. state. (11)

By 1870 the 15th Amendment passed stating the right to vote could not be denied based on race. However, many states enacted restrictions and intimidation to prevent other races to register to vote. In 1876 the Supreme Court ruled that Indigenous People are not citizens therefore could not vote. In 1882 people of Chinese ancestry were prevented by law to become citizens and hence could not vote. In 1890 Wyoming was the first state to allow women the vote. It would be another 40 years in 1920 before the 19th Amendment was passed, giving women throughout the U.S. the right to vote. Miguel Trujillo, a Native American and former Marine, sued New Mexico for not allowing him to vote in 1947. He won and New Mexico and Arizona were required to give the vote to all Native Americans. 1964 would be the first time that African Americans would have the right to vote. All those years and all that bigotry, while considering themselves a democracy.

History matters. 43% of young people today don't bother to vote and ignore the efforts and enormous suffering and struggle of generations before them to obtain that right to vote for them. Your vote matters, it should be you that decides your own future. If you don't vote, you are giving some of the ultimate power to others to make decisions about the leaders and laws that will shape your future, most likely based on outdated perspectives incongruent with your youthful views. (12)

If you don't vote you can't complain later. If you embrace your right to vote you will also have an opportunity to keep up with current events, the politics of the day and what you want for your future and the future of your community. Most likely Youth don't vote because they have not been encouraged or taught the value of voting throughout all those years in school or being bored with old ideas and ancient history. Frustration and shock at the state of the world, the idea of 'How did this happen to our planet and our societies?' may be enough of a reason to not bother voting. The truth is that nothing will change if you don't participate and become a part of that change. I also do not intend to disavow the education system that you were raised in. No doubt teachers did their best and taught what they could in underfunded, crowded circumstances. However, there is no doubt that had youth been encouraged and told the truth regarding the politics of the past and present, the majority would be more involved and interested in the politics of today.

You are the future and education must change to promote interest and responsibility in your participation in the institutions that govern your country. The truth of history must be taught. It is time to view youth as a positive force for transformative social change, and all societies should aim to enhance youth participation in politics. Youth have the power now as evidenced by your influence on corporate America via social media. With the size of your demographic, you have the power to change everything about how we govern, cooperate, and have compassion for each other. You can strive to find common ground within your own circles and can insist and teach tolerance and inclusion to generations before you and to future generations as well.

Starting right now, you can change the world. You each have an opportunity to make something extraordinary with your short time in this world. If enough people begin to embrace the principles of cooperation while developing the capacity to communicate and listen compassionately perhaps the world and her people can heal. *As Gandhi stated, "Be the change you want to see in the world."*

Insist on peace in your household, your community, your school, your neighborhood, and your city. Promote kindness and be generous in all that you do. Consider joining one of the promoter groups for social change on line or in person in your own neighborhood. I can't remind you enough how important your participation is, and how valuable your opinions, ideas and passion are to making the world a better place. Explore other cultures and evaluate your tolerance and compassion for other races and cultural differences.

Youth has the potential to be all powerful and influential on the world stage of politics and social change. *Stand up for Peace in the world. All that you have to offer your communities and countries in innovation, creativity, and new thinking can open up the politics of the world to a better way, a way towards peace.*

Summary

Honestly, the best advice possible for you to live a fulfilled and happy life is to 'know yourself'. If you live in circumstances that are conflicting with your life goals, and you don't truly know yourself well, how can you change your circumstances for the better? For example if you have subliminal internal anxiety and aren't aware of it you will not be able to manage your reactions to events in your life, or see clearly how a situation impacts you at the core of your being.

Mikhail Litvak, Russian psychologist, psychiatrist, and author, has an influential theory called 'Psychological Aikido'. Aikido is a modern form of Japanese self-defense created by Morihei Ueshiba. Most physical attacks come in a linear form, and what aikido teaches is how to move in a circular movement. This requires a calm, relaxed mind and body and a great deal of self-control.

Psychological aikido works in many of the same ways. Psychological Aikido is a high-level approach to self-defense using the core principles of aikido to turn and lead, deflect and redirect critical, negative, manipulative or emotionally aggressive behavior away from you. His teachings can be used to create insights into your life, your relationships, and your choices. (1)

Remember that the road to success is never achieved through the desire to be liked by everyone. Spend time looking in the mirror; and give up the biases you may hold against your body and your own image, the person you see is your best ally and advocate. **Love yourself first and foremost;** once this is truly achieved, doors to success open and the next step you need to take will appear. If the job you have prevents you from achieving personal growth in your given circumstances, reassess and plan for a change.

Don't chase happiness yet know that it is within you. If you feel you need to prove something to someone, then you are in a constant state of unworthiness and their opinion of you matters more than your own. Have compassion and kindness for yourself and it will come easily that you offer this to those around you. Judgment of yourself implies your life is in a fixed-state, however, the truth is, life is constantly changing.

Most people have bought into the idea that circumstances have to be just right in order to change. Don't allow lack of motivation to be an excuse for not taking positive action in your own life. If you postpone making a change and think that at some point in the future you will have the courage, confidence and motivation to make that change you may never get there. **Lack of motivation has been misunderstood for decades.** In order to make your dreams come true you are going to have to do things that are challenging. Because your brain is wired to keep you alive, motivation only works for the things that are easy. Your brain is designed to stop you at all cost from doing anything that might hurt you. For generations before you, if there was hesitation the brain detected a threat and would prevent any follow-through of actions that might increase the risk of the situation. In today's stressful society, the brain continues to resist taking actions that may increase risk, however subtle, and therefore it is a big challenge to take corrective action when you face risk. The hesitation is most often surrounding immediate concerns about the difficulty or success of an idea you may have. During that micro moment when you hesitate, it sends a stress signal to the brain. **This is a known phenomenon called the spotlight effect when the brain magnifies the risk. You are one decision away from a totally different job, income, life, or relationship.** Learn to take control of that micro moment of hesitation and make a decision that makes your life better. If you change your decisions you change everything.

Tom Belyeu's company **'The Impact Theory'** is about the acquisition of skills and putting those skills to the test in service of something bigger than oneself. **His mission is to free people from The Matrix and he wants to end the poverty of poor mindset.** Here are a few of his thoughts on how to achieve that. "1. Human potential is nearly limitless. 2. Personal growth is the highest priority of dedicated achievers. 3. You can acquire new skills in any area at any time through focus and disciplined practice. 4. See beyond your current self to the opportunity of becoming the best version of yourself. 5. Mistakes are a great teacher to those who are willing to admit that they've made one. 6. Everyone has something to teach you. Learn from whomever you can. 7. Do not make excuses. 8. Have VERY clear goals." (2)

Admit the truth of your reality; though at times harsh and difficult, this awareness will help you to be competent and capable of handling your life.

Place high value on the care, health, and welfare of the people, animals, and plants in your immediate and outward environments. Reject institutionalized racism, resource destruction, and greed. Humanity must recognize the rights of the animals that sustain us and the reality that we are all part of the whole of the earth and depend on each other for survival.

Milan Kundera wrote "Dogs are our link to paradise. They don't know evil or jealousy or discontent. To sit with a dog on a hillside on a glorious afternoon is to be back in Eden, where doing nothing was not boring-it was peace." Be absolutely resolute in your goal to befriend animals, to assist animals and allow them to be your friend and support. The rewards are limitless in this endeavor.

The majority of memorable moments of 2017 started with a question and more than ever before in history humanity asked the question HOW? Based on research and social media in 2017 here is a partial list of the questions that humans asked: how do wildfires start, how far can North Korean missiles go, how much will the Trump wall cost, how many refugees are in the world, how do hurricanes form, how to board up a window in a storm, how to calm a dog in a storm, how to help flood victims, how to help refugees, how to help Puerto Rico, how to help Mexico, how to help Las Vegas, Rohinga, etc. , how to make a protest sign, how to run for office, how to watch the eclipse, how to make a difference, how to be a strong woman (#metoo), how to be a good parent, how to be a superhero (wonder woman, firefighters), how to be fearless, and how to move forward. *This is brilliant and encouraging to know that people are asking themselves and each other, ways to be better in the world.*

Science now recognizes the 'no-cebo' effect while researching the placebo effect. No-cebo effect is the consequence of a negative thought. Remember that a negative thought is equally as powerful as a positive thought in controlling your health. A chronic negative thought pattern can cause illness and disease and reminds us that health is more controlled by our mind than genetics. Activities like yoga and meditation teach positive thinking and reinforce peace of mind, which in turn creates positive brain chemistry which also is a protective measure against disease. Misplaced and disproportionate anger is destructive and it negatively affects innocent people and animals around you. *Stop it, understand it, control it and solve it.*

Do not be a member of the new strain of fact resistant humans. *Be a conscientious evaluator of information*. All people have the capacity to understand and make better choices, take your time with decisions and move forward with confidence no matter how small or great your decision is.

Know that there are organizations and forces in the world who truly want to invest in Youth, in you and your potential. Since 1981 The NY Times annually offers 12 genius awards of $625,000 each. This year in the U.S. 23 genius awards were given out. *Never underestimate your potential*.

Of the 965 genius awards to date, 209 (or 21.7%) of the recipients were born outside the United States, according to Cecilia Conrad, who leads the fellowship program.   Her research found that immigrants were overrepresented among the winners of the Pulitzer Prize for music, of the National Humanities Medal and especially of the John Bates Clark Medal, which recognizes brilliant American economists under the age of 40. Over the past three and a half decades, thirty-five percent of these economists were foreign-born, including people from India, Turkey and Ukraine.

"Many of a country's finest minds and brightest ideas are forged when dreamers from elsewhere encounter an unfamiliar place with unimagined possibilities," writes Frank Bruni of the New York Times. There's a creative spark in that convergence that powers greatness. That's the moral of the Nobel Prize. The U.S. alone has had more than 350 Nobel winners. More than 100 of these have been immigrants and individuals born outside of the United States. Immigrants are often reminders that gratitude breeds greatness after finding abundance in a new country, often after leaving loss and despair behind.

An article about immigrants in The Atlantic points out that "immigrants or the children of immigrants have founded or co-founded nearly every legendary American technology company, including Google, Intel, Facebook, and of course Apple (Steve Jobs' father was Abdulfattah Jandali)."

Throughout this book I have attempted to point out your limitless potential, possibilities, and the opportunities that are in front of you; helping you to determine what you are really here to do.   With personal introspection you will open up your world to realize your greater purpose.

It has been said that the purpose of life is to actually live it and being fully alive is part of remembering ourselves, what matters to us and the fact that we are component parts of an entire universe.

Know the Truth and the Truth shall set you free. Knowing the possibilities within you is a huge game changer. Trust yourself, your intellect and learn to weigh the facts, the pros and cons, and many of your decisions will be made clear to you. *Resist the bait that society dangles before your eyes enticing your ego and consumerism.*

It is always in your best interest to be reflective and choose wisely over and over again in your life. *Let go of the need to be right.*

Meaningful human existence is founded on choice, free will and compassion for self and others. Gratitude isn't something that happens to you, it is a choice and a skill set that needs to be exercised daily.

Feed and hydrate your body well for your best health and performance and know that a great deal of your long term health is dependent on the choices you make every day. Prioritize organic food and good water, get to know your local growers and avoid processed foods when you can. When you feed yourself well you will have energy, a clear mind and creativity at your disposal to do what you love.

Cooking from scratch is the single most powerful thing you can do for yourself and your family to improve your mind, body and heart. Cooking can be simple, delicious and fun. Purchase healthy ingredients and cook your own meals.

Uncover the blind spots in your mind and free your life. Blind spots in your mind may be unexamined spaces where dogma has locked a door, distracting you from thinking for yourself. Blind spots can keep you bound to someone else's story, and close you off from the truth.

Peace of mind comes with thinking for yourself and having confidence in the voice of your own intuition. Apply curiosity to every rule and condition that you face and with that, your opportunities will expand, your choices become clear and you will take your next step with confidence.

In the blink of an eye everything can change, so forgive often, love from your heart and appreciate all you have daily. *The Hawaiian practice of Ho'oponopono* is a timeless technique of forgiveness. The Indigenous Peoples of Hawaii understood on a gut level that to harbor resentment against others hurts the person who refuses to forgive. How can anyone feel good about themselves and their own life when they spend their days feeling they have been wronged? The Hawaiian word ho'oponopono comes from ho'o which means "to make" and pono which means "right". The repetition of the word pono means "doubly right" or being right with both self and others. Ho'oponopono is a process by which we can forgive others and ourselves.

Rather than the simple thought of forgiving someone for something they did to you, it is more about forgiving yourself for the thoughts and feelings you hold toward that particular situation. *There are four simple steps to this method — love, forgiveness, gratitude, and repentance — and it doesn't matter in what order you do the steps.* This can all be done in your mind at any time with the awesome power of your intentional will to make it happen. It can but doesn't have to include the person who may have offended you. These intentions are the only forces at work, and these forces have incredible power. (3)

You have a one to five second window between taking action and losing the opportunity. This is previously described as the hesitation that you mistakenly might consider lack of motivation or incentive. Take action within that short window and you will make things happen in your life you would otherwise not. There is an old saying that *'Ambition is neutered by self-doubt'* therefore be confident in your choices and actions, and you will learn by each and every step you take.

Keep informed about the reality around you, both in your community and globally. *Reading can seriously damage your ignorance.* There are solutions to most problems. Saving 4 billion trees a year from unsustainable deforestation by using hemp for paper instead of timber and a myriad of alternative energy solutions are two of the many that the world needs to implement.

Know the difference between helping others and being of service to them. Often the perspective of wanting to help someone may suggest you are seeing them as having a problem or even worse that they are a problem needing to be fixed. Service is a relationship between equals whereas helping can incur debt. This is not to judge who you help or how you help or when you help. Rachel Naomi Remen wrote 'In the Service of Life' and offers us all an opportunity to examine what service means in our lives. Helping, or fixing can incur debt making that someone you help feel they owe you. However, when serving someone in need, the exchange is mutual and there is no debt. She describes the difference between helping which gives a feeling of satisfaction whereas when serving, the feeling of gratitude is experienced. There is collaboration with serving someone and Mother Teresa told us long ago that "We serve life not because it is broken, but because it is holy." Therefore when we serve others, we are serving the wholeness and mystery of life. Rachel reminds us that over time, fixing and helping are draining and depleting and can lead to burn out. Service is renewing. "Fundamentally, helping, fixing, and service are ways of seeing life. When you help, you see life as weak; when you fix, you see life as broken. When you serve, you see life as whole. "

Mark Twain said 'travel is fatal, fatal to bigotry, racism, and prejudice". Be well adjusted members of your global society, neighborhood, city and country. Remind yourself the world is full of good and generous people. Travel within your neighborhood and your community has equal value to global travel.

NASA launched the Voyager spacecraft in 1977 with the scientific objective of photographing the planets of the outer solar system, which furnished the very first portrait of our cosmic neighborhood.

But the Voyager also had another, more romantic mission. Aboard it was the Golden Record — a time-capsule of the human spirit encrypted in binary code on a twelve-inch gold-plated copper disc, containing greetings in the fifty-four most popular human languages plus one from the humpback whales, 117 images of life on Earth, and a representative selection of our planet's sounds, from an erupting volcano to a kiss to Bach to a Bulgarian folk song.

Carl Sagan, an American astronomer, cosmologist, astrophysicist, astrobiologist, author, science popularizer, and science communicator envisioned the Golden Record, and he thought the music selection would say something about our species that no words or figures could ever say. The purpose of the Golden Record was to convey our essence as a civilization to some other civilization.

The true objective of the Golden Record was to mirror what is best of humanity back to itself in the midst of global instability, for it seemed as global citizens we have forgotten who we are to each other and what it means to share this small, fragile, and harmonious planet.

When the Voyager completed its exploratory mission and took the last photograph — of Neptune — NASA commanded that the cameras be shut off to conserve energy. It was Carl Sagan who insisted the spacecraft be turned around to take one final photograph of Earth. And so, on Valentine's Day of 1990, the Voyager took the now-iconic image of Earth known as the "Pale Blue Dot". A timeless reminder as stated by Carl Sagan, that "everyone you love, everyone you know, everyone you ever heard of, every human being who ever was... every hero and coward, every creator and destroyer of civilization, every king and peasant, every young couple in love, every mother and father, hopeful child, inventor and explorer, every teacher of morals, every corrupt politician lived out their lives on this pale blue dot".

In the chaos of our cultural moment, think about how small a proportion of the news this year was devoted to truth, integrity and compassion for the human race, the earth and all her inhabitants.

It is impossible to fully contribute to the present moment in any meaningful way if you are engulfed by it. Too much of the news is fake news, soap opera politics and melodrama around the world. Take a different view, step back and assess the moment with an open mind and only then can you live your life and do the work this era and time asks of you.

Common sense can come at any age. Make a commitment to put your phone or device down when face to face with friends or family. Sharing a meal together is one of the most intimate, fun and delicious ways to spend time, be mature enough and respect your friends enough to put your phone down and be face to face enjoying each other's company. If no one else is putting their phone down, you be the one to stand up for quality time together and you be the one to educate your friends or family and begin better ways of doing things. Youth today experience more images in one day than a youth in the 14th century saw in their entire lifetime. One day! *The unexamined consequences in your life of addiction to technology are enormous. Manage your time now to prevent health risks to mind, body and relationships in the future regarding your use of technology.*

Every choice you make every day influences the world and your future. Make choices not based on how this is good for you now, but how your choice will affect the whole of your life and future generations. It is your absolute responsibility to pass the world on in a better and safer state to the children of the future.

Here is Dr. Jane Goodall's message for 2018 to the world. "Let us send up our prayers for greater understanding and make a commitment to do what we can, however little, to promote peace and harmony around us. To actually take action and to take action every day, not make a promise that is just words."

Remember your moral compass and the direction you intend to go in your life. Question outdated beliefs that may be counterproductive and use your intuition to let go of parts or all of what you have been taught in this regard if necessary for your best good. Pay attention to what you see and hear without any form of judgement, because judgement will color the truth of what you need to know and understand in any given situation. Be curious and seek out the information that gives you all the facts you need and do not continue or allow yourself to be part of the problem you are trying to resolve. As you grow and change, be sure to monitor yourself to make sure your values equal your behavior and thinking. It is very helpful to clarify what you value, write them down and live up to them. This exercise can be solitary or a collective exercise with family or friends.

Most important is to stay true to yourself, protect your integrity and your values and don't sell them for anything. Imagine how limiting your journey might be if you set your compass to guide you only a few miles. Expand your horizons and continually expand your compass setting to your neighborhood, community and the greater world. Remember to be patient, there will be set backs; you have to take all the steps it requires to go on a journey of self-discovery. *Remember that people will never do more for you than they do for themselves.* Be mindful and choose wisely who you spend time with, who influences you, and who you admire.

Albert Einstein said "The fate of humanity is entirely dependent upon its moral development."

Michelle Roya Rad writes; "Defeat irrationality, the enemy within. Some of your worst enemies are not outside of you, but within you. To be rational means to be able to respond with care, to not over react, to be patient, to look for the depth of truth before making a judgment, to be a critical thinker, to focus on the solution, and to not be an emotionally impulsive human being. In addition, it means to build a curious mind. Bring that scientist mind out and evaluate before acting or judging. This will minimize your damage and maximize your productivity."

Never forget your sense of humor, you can't be angry and laugh at the same time. Stop taking things personally or too seriously and make every moment count. This doesn't at all rule out spending time doing nothing, chilling, reading comics, staring at the ceiling or playing video games. We all need down time and time to rest. Be flexible with your journey, the destination will always be waiting for you.

Just a few words can hold the weight of a story untold. An example might be; "Next year for sure bro....." Make time for friends and occasions to celebrate life, do what you love, because time might run out for that particular opportunity and you can't beg, borrow or steal another week gone by.

Lao Tzu teaches us, *"If you want to awaken all of humanity, then awaken all of yourself; if you want to eliminate the suffering of the world, then eliminate all that is dark and negative inside of yourself; truly the greatest gift you have to give is that of your own self-transformation."*

Get out there and make your life the best life ever! This means that you must continue to learn and grow every day for your entire life. Seriously consider the interconnectedness you have with all life. *If humans had more reverence for 'life' in all forms, a way from war to peace would become a priority. You are a wonderful human being, you truly are.* Learn for a lifetime.

Most obstacles in life will succumb to consistent, sustained, intelligent, and positive action. If you don't believe in yourself, don't ask anyone else to.

"We are what we repeatedly do. Excellence, then, is not an act, but a habit." (Aristotle, 384 – 322 BC) So don't waste your precious time comparing yourself to others.

"Until you value yourself, you will not value your time." ~ M. Scott Peck

Book Ideas

Please keep in mind there are endless choices for fantastic reading. Discuss with your friends and mentors books that have changed their lives and expand all the possibilities for your own great reading.

- *Way of the Peaceful Warrior*, Dan Millman
- *Shaman, Healer, Sage; A Guide to Healing*, Alberto Villoldo
- *Awaken the Giant Within: How to Take Immediate Control of Your Mental, Emotional, Physical and Financial Destiny*, Tony Robbins
- *The Power of Now: A Guide to Spiritual Enlightenment*, Eckhardt Tolle
- *How to Win Friends & Influence People*, Dale Carnegie
- *Conversations with God: An Uncommon Dialogue*, Neil Donald Walsch
- *After the Long Silence*, Sheri S. Tepper
- *The Gate to Women's Country*, Sheri S. Tepper
- *The Road Less Traveled: A New Psychology of Love, Traditional Values, and Spiritual Growth*, M. Scott Peck
- *Think and Grow Rich*, Napoleon Hill
- *A New Earth: Awakening to Your Life's Purpose*, Eckhardt Tolle
- *Living in the Light: Follow Your Inner Guidance to Create a New Life and a New World*, Shakti Gawain
- *Altered Genes, Twisted Truth: How the Venture to Genetically Engineer Our Food Has Subverted Science, Corrupted Government, and Systematically Deceived the Public*, Steven M Druker
- Wired to Eat, Robb Wolf
- *Perennial Seller*, Ryan Holiday
- *The Mind-Gut Connection*, Emeran Mayer
- *The Human Superorganism*, Rodney Dietert, PhD.
- *The Disease Delusion*, Jeffrey S. Bland
- *Barking Up The Wrong Tree*, Eric Barker
- *Captivate*, Vanessa Van Edwards
- *The Moral Landscape*, y Sam Harris
- *Homo Deus*, Yuval Noah Harari
- *Norse Mythology*, Neil Gaiman
- *The Power of the Other*, Henry Butt
- *Walt Disney*, Neal Gabler
- *Hit Makers*, Derek Thompson
- *Sum*, David Eagleman
- *Stealing Fire*, Jamie Wheal and Steven Kotler

- *Pre-Suasion*, Robert Cialdini
- *The Honest Truth About Dishonesty*, Dan Ariely
- *Evolving Ourselves*, Steve Gullans and Juan Enriquez
- *The Mindful Athlete*, George Mumford
- *Born Standing Up*, Steve Martin
- *Give and Take*, PhD Adam Grant
- *Grit*, Angela Duckworth
- *Wake Up Happy*, Michael Strahan
- *Tools of Titans*, Tim Ferriss
- *Pitch Anything*, Oren Klaff
- *The Subtle Art of Not Giving a Fuck*, Mark Manson
- *The Coaching Habit*, Michael Bungay Stanier
- *Deep Work*, Cal Newport
- *Strangers to Ourselves*, Timothy D. Wilson
- *Peak*, Robert Pool and Anders Ericsson
- *The Five Dysfunctions of a Team*, Patrick Lencioni
- *Tripping Over the Truth*, Travis Christofferson
- *The Emperor of All Maladies*, Siddhartha Mukherjee
- *Keto Clarity*, Jimmy Moore and Eric C. Westman
- *Einstein's Intuition*, Thad Roberts
- *The Rise of Theodore Roosevelt*, Edmund Morris
- *The Motivation Manifesto*, Brendon Burchard
- *How to Fail at Almost Everything and Still Win Big*, Scott Adams
- *Sapiens*, Yuval Noah Harari
- *Under New Management*, David Burkus
- *Switch*, Chip Heath and Dan Heath
- *The Unbearable Lightness of Being*, Milan Kundera
- *#AskGaryVee*, Gary Vaynerchuk
- *Managing Oneself*, Peter F. Drucker
- *The Heart and The Fist*, Eric Greitens
- *Originals*, Adam Grant
- *The Brain's Way of Healing*, Norman Doidge
- *Tomorrowland*, Steven Kotler
- *Misbehaving*, Richard Thaler
- *The Practicing Mind*, Thomas M. Sterner
- *If Aristotle Ran General Motors*, Tom Morris
- *Unbeatable Mind*, Mark Divine
- *The Truth*, Neil Strauss
- *Giant Steps*, Tony Robbins

- *Money Master the Game*, Tony Robbins
- *Unlimited Power*, Tony Robbins
- *So Good They Can't Ignore You*, Cal Newport
- *Hooked*, Nir Eyal
- *Psycho-Cybernetics*, Maxwell Maltz and Dan Kennedy
- *The Art of Learning*, Josh Waitzkin
- *Abundance*, Peter H. Diamandis and Steven Kotler
- *Who's Got Your Back*, Keith Ferrazzi
- *Mating in Captivity*, Esther Perel
- *Elon Musk*, Ashlee Vance
- *The Hard Thing About Hard Things*, Ben Horowitz
- *Waking Up*, Sam Harris
- *Why Beautiful People Have More Daughters*, Alan S. Miller and Satoshi Kanazawa
- *Sex on the Brain*, Daniel G. Amen
- *Growth Hacker Marketing*, Ryan Holiday
- *Trust Me I'm Lying*, Ryan Holiday
- *The Marshmallow Test*, Walter Mischel
- *The Myth of Mirror Neurons*, Gregory Hickok
- *Talk like TED*, Carmine Gallo
- *Total Recall*, Arnold Schwarzenegger
- *Creativity Inc*, Amy Wallace and Ed Catmull
- *The Rational Animal*, Vladas Griskevicius and Douglas T. Kenrick
- *The Innovators*, Walter Isaacson
- *Essentialism*, Greg McKeown
- *Never Eat Alone*, Keith Ferrazzi
- *The Rise of Superman*, Steven Kotler
- *Top Brain Bottom Brain*, G. Wayne Miller and Stephen Kosslyn
- *Brain Changer*, David DiSalvo
- *Take Yourself to the Top*, Laura Berman Fortgang,
- *Unlimited Power*, Anthony Robbins, '
- Feel the Fear and Do It Anyway, Susan Jeffers,
- *Be Your Own Life Coach*, Fiona Harrold
- *Dejunk Your Life*, Helen Foster.
- *A Mind of Your Own*, Kelly Brogan
- *The Whistleblower, Confessions of a Healthcare Hitman*, Dr. Peter Rost, MD
- *All books* by Walt Whitman

- *The Power of Music: Pioneering Discoveries in the New Science of Song Book*, Elena Mannes
- *Testosterone Rex: Myths of Sex, Science, and Society*, Cordelia Fine
- *The School of Greatness and The Mask of Masculinity*, Lewis Howes
- *A Fearless Heart*, Thupten Jinpa
- *Hidden Messages in Water*, Dr. Masaru Emoto
- *One Spirit Medicine: Ancient Ways to Ultimate Wellness*, Alberto Villoldo
- *The Brains Way of Healing*, Norman Dodge, MD
- *The Global Brain*, Peter Russell
- *Dissolving Illusions: Disease, Vaccines and the Forgotten History*, Dr. Suzanne Humphries
- *The Female Immigrants Guide*, Susan Moody
- *Block Chain Revolution, How the Technology Behind Bitcoin is Changing Money, Business, and the World*, Alex and Dan Tapscott
- *12 Rules for Life: An Antidote to Chaos*, Jordan B. Peterson
- *Peace and Power: Building Communities for the Future*, Peggy L. Chinn
- *The Brain That Changes Itself*, Norman Doidge
- This Changes Everything, Naomi Klein
- No is Not Enough, Naomi Klein
- The Inconvenient Indian, Thomas King

References

Introduction

(1) http://www.shiftingbaselines.org/op_ed/

Chapter 1 - A Call to Action

(1) https://phys.org/news/2017-02-earth-size-worlds-orbiting-star-life.html
(2) https://www.psychologytoday.com/blog/theory-knowledge/201201/finding-our-moral-compass

Chapter 2 – Who do you think you are?

(1) http://www.pewinternet.org/2011/11/09/part-1-teens-and-social-networks/
(2) pss.sagepub.com/content/early/2015/01/14/0956797614562862.abstract
(3) www.tandfonline.com/eprint/eknqdpMRxPUWscxXJzxk/ful
(4) https://www.livescience.com/1827-bad-memories-stick-good.html

Chapter 3 – Health & Performance

(1) 4-Hydroxynonenal (HNE), a Toxic Aldehyde in French Fries from Fast Food Restaurants: A. Saari Csallany1; · I. Han1 · D. W. Shoeman1 · C. Chen1 · Jieyao Yuan1
(2) http://www.gracelinks.org/260/animal-feed
(3) http://www.foodmatters.com/article/whats-really-in-a-big-mac
(4) http://www.nutritionmyths.com/does-frying-in-oil-produce-trans-fats/
(5) Sausenthaler et al 2006, Mente et al 2009, Weston A. Price Foundation 2009, Dalainas & Ioannou 2008, Franklin Institute
(6) Puligundla P, Variyar PS, Ko S and VSR Obulam. 2012. Emerging Trends in Modification of Dietary Oils and Fats, and Health Implications – A Review. Sains Malaysiana 41(7)(2012): 871–877.
(7) https://www.independentsciencenews.org/health/the-great-dna-data-deficit/
(8) https://articles.mercola.com/sites/articles/archive/2013/05/29/codex-front-groups.aspx

(9) https://www.fda.gov/ForConsumers/ByAudience/ForWomen/FreePub
    lications/ucm313215.htm
(10) https://wellnessmama.com/25415/problem-with-pads-tampons/
(11) http://www.ehaontario.ca/help-with.html
(12) http://pharmadeathclock.com/
(13) http://www.pimatisiwin.com/online/wp-
    content/uploads/2011/08/07Shroff.pdf
(14) Barzansky and Gevitz, 1992; Edlin and Golanty, 2009
(15) Ullman, 2007, p. 42
(16) http://www.telegraph.co.uk/news/uknews/prince-
    charles/10433939/Prince-Charles-and-homeopathy-crank-or-
    revolutionary.html
(17) http://www.healthy-holistic-living.com/cancer-causing-
    products.html?t=HHL
(18) Brown et al. The role of skin absorption as a route of exposure for
    volatile organic compounds (VOCs) in drinking water. Am J Public
    Health. 1984 May; 74(5): 479–484.
(19) Kasting and Kretsos.Skin Pharmacol Physiol 2005;18:55-74
(20) https://raindancecosmetics.ca/?p=1268
(21) https://www.ncbi.nlm.nih.gov/pubmed/18704106
(22) http://www.safecosmetics.org/get-the-facts/chemicals-of-
    concern/talc/
(23) https://www.cancer.org/cancer/cancer-causes/talcum-powder-and-
    cancer.html
(24) http://www.crueltyfreekitty.com/ultimate-guide-to-cruelty-free-
    makeup/
(25) https://draxe.com/propylene-glycol/
(26) Hepatology 2005;42:1364-72).
(27) JAMA 2006;296:87-93
(28) JAMA Pediatr 2016;doi: 10.1001/jamapediatrics.2016.1775
(29) JAMA Pediatr 2014;168:313-20
(30) Lancet 2014;doi:10.1016/S0140-6736(14)60805-
(31) Am J Epidemiol 2016;doi: 10.1093/aje/kww154
(32) Am J Med 2010 Mar;123(3):231-7
(33) https://www.ncbi.nlm.nih.gov/pubmed/25655639
(34) http://file.scirp.org/Html/3-1980073_34065.htm
(35) https://www.sciencedaily.com/releases/2009/08/090827202513.htm
(36) https://scialert.net/fulltext/?doi=ijds.2007.104.115
(37) Gh. R. Jahed Khaniki , 2007. Chemical Contaminants in Milk and Public
    Health Concerns: A Review. International Journal of Dairy Science, 2:
    104-115.

(38) https://www.naturalnews.com/010443_cows_milk_asthma.html
(39) https://www.citizen.org/sites/default/files/public-hospitals-infant-formula-marketing-report-april-2016.pdf
(40) https://nccih.nih.gov/about/staff/bushnell
(41) https://www.ncbi.nlm.nih.gov/books/NBK19956/
(42) http://hub.jhu.edu/2017/02/02/sleep-brain-memories-mice-study/
(43) http://greatergood.berkeley.edu/topic/mindfulness/definition

Chapter 4 – Your Extraordinary Brain

(1) https://www.rndsystems.com/research-area/blood--brain-barrier-permeability
(2) https://www.webmd.com/drugs/2/drug-9475/ritalin-oral/details
(3) https://www.npr.org/2011/03/12/134456594/study-diet-may-help-adhd-kids-more-than-drugs
(4) https://www.theguardian.com/society/2011/feb/04/adhd-diet-food-children-behaviour
(5) https://www.focusforhealth.org/autism-rates-across-the-developed-world/
(6) http://people.csail.mit.edu/seneff/glyphosate/Groton_Seneff.pdf

Chapter 5 – Depression and Mental Health

(1) https://www.ncbi.nlm.nih.gov/pmc/articles/PMC4172306/; https://www.scientificamerican.com/article/is-depression-just-bad-chemistry/
(2) http://www.recover-from-grief.com/7-stages-of-grief.html
(3)) https://www.psychiatry.org/patients-families/depression/what-is-depression
(4) https://www.scientificamerican.com/article/is-depression-just-bad-chemistry/
(5) Eby, G.A., & Eby, K.L. (2006). Rapid recovery from major depression using magnesium treatment. Medical Hypotheses, 67(2), 362-370.
(6) http://www.voanews.com/a/more-people-die-from-suicide-than-from-wars-natural-disasters-combined/2438749.html
(7) https://www.ncbi.nlm.nih.gov/pmc/articles/PMC1414751/
(8) https://www.heartmath.org
(9) https://www.statnews.com/2016/07/21/depression-suicide-physicians/
(10) https://www.camh.ca/cundillcentre/Pages/default.aspx

(11) https://www.helpguide.org/articles/depression/teenagers-guide-to-depression.htm

Chapter 6 - The Politics of Food

(1) https://www.acsh.org/news/2018/01/17/fake-honey-problem-and-science-can-solve-it-if-government-gets-out-way-12429
(2) https://www.ucalgary.ca/utoday/issue/2015-12-02/vet-med-researchers-use-lentils-combat-water-poisoning-bangladesh
(3) http://www.globalhealingcenter.com/natural-health/3-ways-sugar-and-artificial-sweeteners-affect-gut-health/
(4) https://www.acsh.org/news/2016/11/21/glyphosate-os-most-important-meal-day-10455
(5) https://www.huffingtonpost.com/carey-gillam/iarc-scientists-defend-gl_b_12720306.html
(6) https://www.scientificamerican.com/article/widely-used-herbicide-linked-to-cancer/
(7) https://www.centerforfoodsafety.org/files/glyphosate-faq_64013.pdf
(8) https://www.naturalnews.com/055363_glyphosate_Roundup_honey.html
(9) https://www.baumhedlundlaw.com/toxic-tort-law/monsanto-roundup-lawsuit/where-is-glyphosate-banned/
(10) http://www.globalresearch.ca/new-risks-of-gmo-food-glyphosate-uncovered-scientists-ground-breaking-research/5574264?print=1
(11) http://www.ewg.org/foodscores/content/bpa_bombshell_industry_database?x=1
(12) https://www.labroots.com/trending/chemistry-and-physics/4912/gmo-corn-non-gmo?
(13) https://en.wikipedia.org/wiki/Hygiene_hypothesis
(14) http://www.mensjournal.com/health-fitness/nutrition/the-truth-about-tilapia-20150624
(15) http://news.agropages.com/News/NewsDetail---21069.htm
(16) https://www.chinadialogue.net/.../5153-The-damaging-truth-about-Chinese-fertiliser-a
(17) https://www.fooddemocracynow.org/

Chapter 7 – Water; Essential for all Life

(1) https://www.chrisbeatcancer.com/fluoride-is-poison/

(2) http://thelancet.com/journals/lanneurol/article/PIIS1474-4422%2813%2970278-3/abstract

(3) https://www.ncbi.nlm.nih.gov/pmc/articles/PMC4418502/

(4) http://thelancet.com/journals/lanneurol/article/PIIS1474-4422%2813%2970278-3/abstract

(5) http://www.quality-drinking-water.com/chlorine.html

(6) A Guide to Healthy Drinking Water: All You Need to Know about the Water You Drink, Book by Patrick J. Udeh

(7) https://www.pri.org/stories/2016-01-13/5-countries-dump-more-plastic-oceans-rest-world-combined

(8) https://www.unicef.org/media/media_92690.htm

Chapter 8 – Life Goals

(1) http://www.wpp.com/wpp/marketing/digital/the-future-of-technology/

(2) https://www.jeffsanders.com/life-planning-strategies-that-really-work/

(3) http://projectlifemastery.com/my-life-plan-how-to-manage-your-life-be-productive-balanced-and-create-lasting-fulfillment/

(4) http://www.mindofwinner.com/create-personal-development-plan/

Chapter 9 – Education

(1) https://www.research2.uky.edu/events/your-role-changing-hearts-and-minds-science

(2) https://www.rawstory.com/2018/01/81-percent-of-americans-cant-name-a-single-living-scientist/

(3) https://news.nationalgeographic.com/news/2006/05/0502_060502_geography_2.html

(4) https://www.edcan.ca/wp-content/uploads/EdCan-2008-v48-n4-Ghosh.pdf

(5) http://www.collective-evolution.com/2015/05/16/editor-in-chief-of-worlds-best-known-medical-journal-half-of-all-the-literature-is-false/

(6) http://www.thelancet.com/pdfs/journals/lancet/PIIS0140-6736%2815%2960696-1.pdf

Chapter 10 – Truth is the New Frontier

(1) https://philosophynow.org/issues/86/What_Is_Truth

(2) https://www.goodreads.com/book/show/22107280-blueprint-for-revolution

Chapter 11 – Family

(1) https://www.cnvc.org/

Chapter 12 – Emotions

(1) https://psychcentral.com/lib/the-upward-spiral-using-neuroscience-to-reverse-the-course-of-depression/
(2) https://www.psychologytoday.com/blog/somatic-psychology/201004/the-connections-between-emotional-stress-trauma-and-physical-pain

Chapter 13 – Spirituality/Religion

(1) https://www.theguardian.com/world/2018/mar/21/christianity-non-christian-europe-young-people-survey-religion
(2) https://www.childtrends.org/wp-content/uploads/01/Spirituality-and-Religiosity-Among-Youth.pdf
(3) https://www.allaboutreligion.org/what-is-true-religion.htm
(4) https://en.wikipedia.org/wiki/Quran
(5) https://en.wikipedia.org/wiki/Hebrew_Bible
(6) http://www.patheos.com/library/christianity#u3pMqwErlcyyk5pS.99
(7) http://www.dawahskills.com/comparative-religion/islam-man-made-religions/
(8) https://www.allaboutspirituality.org/paganism.htm
(9) http://www.dawahskills.com/comparative-religion/world-religions-classification-history/
(10) https://en.wikipedia.org/wiki/Christian_right
(11) https://en.wikipedia.org/wiki/Christian_right

Chapter 14 – Society & History

(1) https://www.northernsun.com/Build-Community-Poster-(4193)
(2) http://fortune.com/2014/10/31/inequality-wealth-income-us/
(3) https://www.ted.com/talks/michael_kimmel_why_gender_equality_is_good_for_everyone_men_included/discussion?awesm=on.ted.com_dJUU&utm_medium=on.ted.com-

twitter&utm_campaign=&utm_source=direct-on.ted.com&utm_content=ted-iphone#t-88

(4) https://www.psychologytoday.com/us/blog/head-games/201308/what-women-want-in-men
(5) http://dark-mountain.net/about/manifesto/
(6) http://powertochange-film.com/
(7) https://www.oxfam.org/sites/www.oxfam.org/files/file_attachments/bp-youth-inequality-global-120816-en_0.pdf
(8) http://www.cbc.ca/radio/thecurrent/the-current-for-march-28-2017-1.4042750/yale-historian-shares-lessons-of-20th-century-tyranny-relevant-today-1.4042768

Chapter 15 – Decisions

Chapter 16 – Relationships

(1) https://en.wikipedia.org/wiki/Forgiveness

Chapter 17 – The Inevitability of Change

Chapter 18 – Dating &Sex & Birth Control

(1) https://www.liebertpub.com/doi/full/10.1089/vio.2014.0022#utm_campaign=vio&utm_medium=email&utm_source=pr
(2) https://jamanetwork.com/journals/jamapsychiatry/fullarticle/2552796
(3) http://www.bbc.com/earth/story/20161221-the-real-reasons-why-childbirth-is-so-painful-and-dangerous
(4) http://uk.clearblue.com/planning-for-a-baby/fertility-myths-and-facts
(5) http://blog.paleohacks.com/chemicals-condoms/
(6) http://www.glydeamerica.com/chemical-free-condoms/
(7) http://www.ext.colostate.edu/pubs/foodnut/09323.htm
(8) http://www.iaac.ca/en/752-89-nutrients-affected-by-the-pill-by-dr-judith-fiore-nd-summer-2012
(9) http://www.who.int/reproductivehealth/topics/ageing/cocs_hrt_statement.pdf
(10) http://gerardnadal.com/2012/02/15/world-health-organization-data-on-birth-control-pill-and-estrogen- replacement-carcinogenicity/
(11) http://news.bbc.co.uk/2/hi/uk_news/england/humber/3446403.stm
(12) https://www.cnn.com/2017/09/26/health/std-highest-ever-reported-cdc/index.html
(13) https://kidshealth.org/en/teens/std.html

(14) http://onlinelibrary.wiley.com/doi/10.3109/00016346809156845/abstract

(15) http://www.collective-evolution.com/2016/06/27/why-this-man-stopped-watching-porn-gives-us-all-something-to-consider/

(16) http://www.teachingtransgender.org/authors/

(17) https://www.theatlantic.com/international/archive/2012/02/gloria-steinem-on-rape-in-war-its-causes-and-how-to-stop-it/252470/

(18) http://www.womensmediacenter.com/women-under-siege/

(19) http://www.nationalgeographic.com/magazine/2017/01/

(20) http://www.cracked.com/blog/how-men-are-trained-to-think-sexual-assault-no-big-deal/

(21) www.partnersforyouth.ca/wp-content/uploads/.../Consent-and-Boundaries-2017.docx

Chapter 19 – Happiness

Chapter 20 – NOW is the only place your life exists.

(1) https://www.bustle.com/articles/156224-11-ways-to-avoid-multitasking-focus-more-each-day

Chapter 21 – Stress

(1) https://draxe.com/cortisol-levels/

(2) https://www.scienceofpeople.com/science-perfect-nap/

(3) https://www.nature.com/news/2010/101128/full/news.2010.635.html

(4) http://news.ncbs.res.in/research/late-effects-stress-new-insights-how-brain-responds-trauma

(5) https://www.heartmath.org/

(6) https://www.ncbi.nlm.nih.gov/pubmed/12024758

Chapter 22 – Nutrition

(1) http://www.rense.com/general33/legal.htm

(2) http://geneticroulettemovie.com/

(3) http://www.globalresearch.ca/new-risks-of-gmo-food-glyphosate-uncovered-scientists-ground-breaking-research/5574264?print=1

(4) http://non-gmoreport.com/articles/scientists-ground-breaking-research-uncovers-new-risks-gmos-glyphosate/

(5) http://discovermagazine.com/2015/march/19-life-in-the-fast-lane

(6) https://www.ncbi.nlm.nih.gov/pubmed/23609067

(7) https://newresearchfindingstwo.blogspot.ca/2015/02/powerful-reasons-to-eliminate-aluminum.html

(8) http://livingtraditionally.com/powerful-reasons-eliminate-aluminum-life/

(9) https://www.ncbi.nlm.nih.gov/pmc/articles/PMC4421777/

(10) http://www.ewg.org/research/healthy-home-tips/tip-6-skip-non-stick-avoid-dangers-teflon

(11) http://www.superjuiceme.com/

(12) https://twitter.com/RachelsNews

(13) http://www.joannablythmanwriting.com/books.html Book: Swallow This

(14) https://www.ncbi.nlm.nih.gov/pmc/articles/PMC3261946/

(15) https://www.sciencedaily.com/releases/2017/03/170315094550.htm

(16) http://www.smh.com.au/national/health/peter-gotzsche-founder-of-the-cochrane-collaboration-visits-australia-to-talk-about-dangers-of-prescription-drugs-20150204-136nqc.html

(17) http://www.consumerreports.org/cro/magazine/2012/01/arsenic-in-your-juice/index.htm

(18) https://www.cancer.org/cancer/cancer-causes/arsenic.html

(19) https://www.atsdr.cdc.gov/csem/csem.asp?csem=1&po=8

Chapter 23 – Music & Dance

(1) http://www.healthfreedoms.org/more-evidence-that-musical-training-protects-the-brain/

(2) https://hwaairfan.wordpress.com/.../singing-together-brings-heartbeats-into-harmony/

(3) http://www.music2spark.com/2011/11/28/the-elderly-how-music-benefits-their-health/

Chapter 24 – Dare We Discuss Vaccinations?

(1) http://www.collective-evolution.com/2016/10/27/didnt-vaccines-eradicate-diseases-an-untold-truth-about-vaccines/

(2) https://worldmercuryproject.org/

(3) http://www.geoengineeringwatch.org/vaccine-mandates-adults-are-next-dr-sherri-tenpenny-sounds-the-alarm/

(4) https://www.law.cornell.edu/uscode/text/42/300aa-22

(5) http://www.globalresearch.ca/the-toxic-science-of-flu-vaccines/5554257

(6) http://www.nbcnews.com/health/health-news/flumist-nose-spray-vaccine-doesn-t-work-experts-say-n597411

(7) https://vaccinechoicecanada.com/media/letter_toronto_star_flu_vaccine_claims_not_supported_by_evidence/

(8) https://list.uvm.edu/cgi-bin/wa?A2=SCIENCE-FOR-THE-PEOPLE;5dcbb2f9.1608

(9) https://www.countable.us/bills/hr897-114/positions/51f02bc0-58d6-47fe-9131-db95dbb40e35

(10) https://www.cdc.gov/zika/vector/aerial-spraying.html

(11) https://www.cdc.gov/vaccines/schedules/downloads/child/0-18yrs-child-combined-schedule.pdf

(12) https://www.cdc.gov/flu/protect/vaccine/thimerosal.htm

(13) https://anhinternational.org/hpv-vaccination/

(14) https://www.ecowatch.com/kennedy-mercury-cdc-autism-2147157503.html?page=5

(15) https://www.jnj.com/media-center/press-releases/johnson-johnson-and-partners-announce-first-efficacy-study-for-investigational-mosaic-hiv-1-preventive-vaccine

(16) https://www.cdc.gov/flu/professionals/vaccination/effectiveness-studies.htm

(17) http://www.thalidomide.ca/the-canadian-tragedy/

(18) https://www.supremecourt.gov/opinions/10pdf/09-152.pdf

(19) https://articles.mercola.com/sites/articles/archive/2011/03/22/betrayal-of-consumers-by-us-supreme-court-gives-total-liability-shield-to-big-pharma.aspx

(20) Langmuir, A.D. (1962), Medical Importance of Measles. Am J Dis Child 103(3):224-226

(21) https://jamanetwork.com/journals/jamapediatrics/article-abstract/500100?redirect=true

(22) http://vk.ovg.ox.ac.uk/disease-vaccinated-populations

(23) http://www.sciencemag.org/news/2014/04/measles-outbreak-traced-fully-vaccinated-patient-first-time

(24) https://www.mercatornet.com/features/view/the-hpv-vaccine-and-cancer-prevention-expert-evidence/20464

(25) https://economictimes.indiatimes.com/industry/healthcare/biotech/healthcare/controversial-vaccine-studies-why-is-bill-melinda-gates-foundation-under-fire-from-critics-in-india/articleshow/41280050.cms

(26) https://www.cancer.org/latest-news/who-should-get-the-hpv-vaccination-and-why.html

(27) https://www.naturalnews.com/045418_flu_shots_influenza_vaccines_mercury.html

(28) https://en.wikipedia.org/wiki/Thiomersal_controversy

(29) https://www.thoughtco.com/list-of-poisons-609279

(30) http://www.vaccinationcouncil.org/2012/02/18/the-deadly-impossibility-of-herd-immunity-through-vaccination-by-dr-russell-blaylock/

(31) http://www.thevaccinereaction.org/2015/06/the-misunderstood-theory-of-herd-immunity/

Chapter 25 – Addiction and Recovery

(1) http://www.quitsmokingsupport.com/whatsinit.htm

(2) https://www.news-medical.net/health/Could-E-Cigarettes-Cause-Cancer.aspx

(3) http://www.abc.net.au/triplej/programs/hack/iceland-teen-substance-abuse/8208214

(4) http://www.huffingtonpost.com/johann-hari/the-real-cause-of-addicti_b_6506936.html

(5) http://upliftconnect.com/opposite-addiction-connection/

(6) https://www.sciencedirect.com/science/article/pii/S0376871601001181

(7) https://www.psychologytoday.com/us/blog/ending-addiction-good/201405/the-dangers-combining-alcohol-and-marijuana

(8) http://pubmedcentralcanada.ca/pmcc/articles/PMC3477605/

(9) http://neuroscience.onair.cc/addiction-overview/

(10) https://www.linkedin.com/pulse/6-scientific-reasons-why-you-should-consider-smoking-ingle-bigfix-

(11) https://www.addictionsandrecovery.org/recovery-skills.htm

(12) http://www.MindBodyRelaxationGuide.org

(13) https://www.addictioncenter.com/community/letting-go-of-bad-influences/

(14) http://www.CognitiveTherapyGuide.org

Chapter 26 – Technology

(1) http://www.newphilosopher.com/articles/can-technology-save-us/

(2) https://inthemoment.io/

(3) https://www.sciencedirect.com/science/article/pii/S0013935118300367

(4) https://www.cdph.ca.gov/Programs/OPA/Pages/NR17-086.aspx

(5) http://www.who.int/mediacentre/factsheets/fs193/en/

(6) https://thetruthaboutcancer.com/sar-value-cell-phone-radiation/?gl=5a135280595c97c02ef6dfd1
(7) https://www.pcsteps.com/9891-what-is-sar-value-cell-phone-is-it-dangerous/
(8) https://cancerresearchideas.cancer.gov/a/idea-v2/185373
(9) http://www.pnas.org/content/111/24/8788.full
(10) http://emwatch.com/house-wiring-radiation/
(11) http://www.science20.com/florilegium/what_are_symptoms_electromagnetic_hypersensitivity
(12) https://emf-doc.weebly.com/health-effects.html
(13) http://www.createhealthyhomes.com/emf_research.php
(14) http://www.emraustralia.com.au/emr-safety-health/emr-safety-and-health
(15) www.wehlinfo@wehliving.org.

Chapter 27 – How Not to get Cancer

(1) http://www.cancer.ca/en/cancer-information/cancer-101/childhood-cancer-statistics/?region=on#ixzz4fTwGEIJO
(2) https://www.cancertutor.com/global-cancer-documentary/
(3) http://www.globalresearch.ca/editor-in-chief-of-worlds-best-known-medical-journal-half-of-all-the-literature-is-false/5451305
(4) https://onlinelibrary.wiley.com/doi/full/10.3322/caac.21387
(5) https://breast-cancer-research.biomedcentral.com/articles/10.1186/bcr842
(6) https://breast-cancer-research.biomedcentral.com/articles/10.1186/bcr842
(7) https://jamanetwork.com/journals/jama/article-abstract/1722196?redirect=true
(8) https://pocketbra.com/
(9) https://www.bcaction.org/
(10) https://bcaction.org/the-cancer-industry/
(11) https://thinkbeforeyoupink.org/resources/history-of-the-pink-ribbon/
(12) https://www.marieclaire.com/politics/news/a6506/breast-cancer-business-scams/
(13) https://www.leafly.com/news/cannabis-101/where-did-the-word-marijuana-come-from-anyway-01fb
(14) https://patients4medicalmarijuana.wordpress.com/medical-use-of-cannabis-video/the-government-holds-a-patent-for-medical-marijuana/
(15) http://norml.org/library/item/introduction-to-the-endocannabinoid-system
(16) https://drcarolyndean.com/

(17) https://www.wcrf.org/int/cancer-facts-figures/data-specific-cancers/breast-cancer-statistics

(18) http://articles.mercola.com/sites/articles/archive/2014/09/30/genetics-research.aspx

(19) https://www.psychologytoday.com/us/blog/the-forgiving-life/201709/anger-and-cancer-is-there-relationship

(20) https://thetruthaboutcancer.com/sar-value-cell-phone-radiation/?gl=5a135280595c97c02ef6dfd1

(21) https://cancerresearchideas.cancer.gov/a/idea-v2/185373

(22) https://www.ncbi.nlm.nih.gov/pmc/articles/PMC1550198/

Chapter 28 – Reading

Chapter 29 – Politics

(1) http://upliftconnect.com/the-evolution-of-cooperation/

(2) https://en.wikipedia.org/wiki/Great_Law_of_Peace

(3) https://www.statista.com/statistics/407979/us-school-shootings-by-type-of-school/

(4) https://www.marchforourlives.com/

(5) https://www.worldinternships.org/why-world-internships/

(6) https://www.weforum.org/agenda/2017/08/the-un-has-a-17-step-plan-to-save-the-world/

(7) https://www.sumofus.org/

(8) https://secure.avaaz.org/page/en/

(9) http://www.collective-evolution.com/

(10) http://therevolutionmovie.com/index.php/change-the-world/become-an-activist/youth-activism/

(11) https://interactive.aljazeera.com/aje/2016/us-elections-2016-who-can-vote/index.html

(12) https://www.huffingtonpost.com/grace-masback-/8-reasons-why-youth-shoul_b_8693178.html

Summary

(1) https://www.scribd.com/document/368173101/Mental-Alchemy

(2) http://impacttheory.com/about/

(3) https://www.psychologytoday.com/us/blog/focus-forgiveness/201106/hawaiian-forgiveness-and-the-three-transgressions